WAR AND PEACE IN THE CAUCASUS

To the memory of my Father

VICKEN CHETERIAN

War and Peace in the Caucasus

Russia's Troubled Frontier

HURST & COMPANY, LONDON

First published in the United Kingdom by
HURST Publishers Ltd,
41 Great Russell Street, London, WC1B 3PL
© Vicken Cheterian, 2008
All rights reserved.
Reprinted 2011
Printed in India

A catalogue data record for this volume is available from
the British Library.

ISBNs
978-1-85065-929-7 *casebound*
978-1-85065-987-7 *paperback*

www.hurstpub.co.uk

CONTENTS

ACKNOWLEDGEMENTS

This book is the outcome of continuous work in the Caucasus region since 1992. First, I visited the region as a journalist in March and April 1992, and since then I have returned to it every year, several times. I have also spent a total of five years living or working in the region, based in Yerevan. I reported on the wars of the early 1990's, mainly writing for the Swiss daily the *Neue Zürcher Zeitung* and the French monthly *Le Monde diplomatique*. Later, in 1996, I initiated a project entitled "Caucasus Media Support Project" where I aimed to bring together journalists from various sides of the conflicts in the Caucasus so that through dialogue they get a more realistic grasp of the perspective of their "neighbouring-enemy". This project was possible thanks to financial support from the Swiss Federal Department of Foreign Affairs. More recently, in 2002, I received another grant from the Swiss Agency for Development and Cooperation, to set up a media training and research centre in Yerevan, called the "Caucasus Media Institute" (since renamed as "Caucasus Institute"). While this book has been influenced by all of the above-mentioned experiences, it remains the direct result of a doctoral work that I completed at the Graduate Institute of International Studies in Geneva.

Over the years I received so much generous support and encouragement that it will be difficult to name everyone here. I would like especially to thank Andreas Oplatka and Ulrich Schmidt from the *Neue Zürcher Zeitung* and Alain Gresh and Dominique Vidal from *Le Monde diplomatique* for their trust and support which enabled me to return again and again to the various corners of the Caucasus, and discover what is new and unravelling. Many thanks to Claude Wild from the Swiss Foreign Ministry for his support of a risky project, as well as to Ilaria Dali-Berlasconi and Philippe Zahner from SDC. And especial thanks to Mohammad-Reza Djalili and Andre Liebich my professors at the Graduate Institute. Lastly, the detailed remarks of my examiner Ronald Grigor Suny to my thesis have been extremely helpful, and his books on the history of the Caucasus were an inspiration throughout the years.

The secret of returning to the region time and again is probably the charm of the Caucasus, with its peoples stubbornly hospitable, and its mountains that hide the view of the valleys behind only to surprise you with its natural beauty and diversity of its identities. I have profited enormously from long discussions with colleagues and friends. I would especially like to thank Hakob Asatryan, Vahan Ishkhanian, and Aris Ghazinian for long conversations and travels to various parts of the Caucasus, Shahin Rzayev for his friendship and engagement, Kemal Ali for organizing a wonderful visit to Baku. Many thanks to Ghia Nodia for sharing his insight to the complex developments and multilayered history of modern Georgia, to Marina Muskhelishvili, and Ivlian Khaindrava. My work in Yerevan at the Caucasus Media Institute delayed this book by three years, only to enrich it by layers of new perspectives. I am very thankful to Mark Grigorian and Alexandr Iskandarian for sharing with me such an adventure, to Haik Demoyan for providing me with many elements from his archives, to Niculin Jäger for his hospitality, and to Otto Simonett for his remarks on an earlier version of the current book.

I would not have been able to carry out this project without the love and support of Carine, Varoujan, Jivan, and Noé.

I dedicate this book to the memory of my father, who was never able to see the country he loved so much.

INTRODUCTION

When I started the current work, two preoccupations prompted me to study the causes of the conflicts in the Caucasus. The first was the feeling of the extraordinary historical moment that I had witnessed as a correspondent while covering the conflicts in the early 1990s. In most books and articles analyzing the sources and developments of the conflicts I had a feeling that this was lacking; that conflicts were taken as the "normality" and not the "exception". At the moment, when I was reporting on the conflicts erupting one after the other, I could not find words to describe this feeling, nor to discover patterns to analyze their deeper secrets. Years later I still share the belief that those events were unique and extraordinary, and therefore need a distinct treatment when analyzed.

The second problem I faced was the linking between the conflicts and nationalism, so common in the period following the collapse of the USSR—in mass media, academia and political circles. Two ideas were associated with this interpretation of nationalism as the main source of conflict. One was that the peoples of the Caucasus had some "historic antagonism" going back to medieval times. The continuation of this notion was to isolate the conflicts from their immediate historical context—again this very unique Soviet Union, and its unique way of collapsing under its own weight—and looking for context in pre-Soviet, if not medieval periods. Again, instinctively I could not subscribe to such interpretations.

As a child I was in Soviet Armenia in 1980, invited to spend summer holidays in a Pioneer camp, at the height of Brezhnev period. I was surprised by the nationalist attitudes, the antagonism towards the Azeris expressed during football matches, the belief in "uniqueness" of the Armenians, etc. Moreover, I was well acquainted with Soviet Armenian literature from my schooling in Beirut, where we read the poems of

1

Hovannes Shiraz and Silva Gabudikian, singing of the beauty, the pain and hopes of the nation. What led to the Armenian nationalism commonly shared in the Soviet Armenia of the 60s and the 70s, to which I was exposed to a certain extent, with expressions in literature, sports, sculpture, etc., finding expression in 1988 in the form of mass mobilization on the Opera Square of Yerevan?[1]

The second major problem when faced with the growing and increasingly interesting literature on the contemporary Caucasus is the interpretations given for the outcome of the conflicts. Admittedly, it is difficult to explain such complex outcomes as those of the Karabakh, Abkhazia and Chechnya wars. Against all expectations, Karabakh Armenians were able to mobilize a military force and organize efficient self-defence in the villages of Karabakh and around the town of Stepanakert, which saved them from suffering the same fate as other Armenian communities in Baku or Kirovabad. Moreover, the Karabakh Armenians went on the offensive outside the administrative boundaries of Mountainous Karabakh and occupied large sectors of Azerbaijan proper to the west, south and east of their territories, causing a wave of internally displaced people several times the total population of Karabakh itself. Similarly, the outcome of the military conflict in Abkhazia goes against traditional wisdom. The heavily outnumbered Abkhaz were not only able to organize resistance against the Georgian troops; they went on the counter-offensive, marking an unexpected victory that not only pushed back the Georgian governmental troops, but also the ethnic Georgian (mainly Mingrelian) population that had been living for generations in Abkhazia, numbering more than double the entire ethnic Abkhaz population itself.

One of the most popular explanations of the Karabakh and Abkhaz victories was the key role attributed to outside forces, or to put it bluntly to the Russian factor. This interpretation became very fashionable in the summer of 1993, when the Georgian forces were pushed out of Sukhumi and the Karabakh units went down their mountains to attack Azerbaijani towns in lower Karabakh, one after the other. Western journalists, often relying on interviews given by experts and politicians in the Caucasus, attributed those outcomes to Russian manipulation,

---

1   The Opera Square was the initial sight of mass demonstrations in Yerevan.

and thought there was a new strategy by Moscow to reshape a new empire. In the imagination of many at the time the parallel was made with the period of 1918-21, and the expectation was high to see how Russia was going to reformulate its hegemony over the South Caucasus and the other territories of the former empire.

Yet, this interpretation disregards political and military developments in the Caucasus itself. At the time when Armenian forces were entering the Azerbaijani towns of Agdam, Fizuli and Jebrayil there was a power vacuum in the Azerbaijani capital as a result of the power struggle in Baku. When Karabakh forces entered those towns, the Azerbaijani front had all but collapsed as a result of a bitter power struggle that characterized post-Soviet Azerbaijan and had divided the political elite in the capital and left the front-line without the necessity support. It was this fact that gave the Armenian forces their military superiority, and not a sudden resurgence in Russian support. The same is also true for the Abkhazia war, although there Russian interference in support of Abkhaz fighters was more visible, nevertheless remaining a secondary factor. The Russian intervention was not the major cause of the Georgian defeat—or the Abkhaz victory! It was the incredible disorganization on the Georgian side which contrasted with a much more disciplined and determined fighting force on the Abkhaz side. The "Russian intervention" line of interpretation could not hold, especially after the war in Chechnya, the huge difficulties the Russian troops faced in entering Groznyy, and their final, humiliating defeat and withdrawal in August 1996. If Russia could not pacify one of its supposed provinces to the north of the Caucasus Mountain chain, how could one attribute to Russia the role of manipulating the conflicts in the South Caucasus? Moreover, the much awaited Russian "come-back" to the South Caucasus, as well as to the other regions of the former USSR, did not occur, and we need a new interpretation that places the Russian role in post-Soviet conflicts in this perspective.

What I propose in this research is not to exclude what was suggested before, the role of nationalism or Russian intervention in the conflicts, but to develop a new narrative that includes those elements but puts them into a new perspective. Both nationalism and Russian intervention, political, logistic and military, did play a role in the beginning, development and outcome of the conflicts. I also bring new elements to

3

interpret the conflicts, to reconstruct a new narrative, proposing a different way of looking at the same events, giving more weight to some interpretations and facts and less to others. I start by looking at the conditions of the Soviet collapse, trying to make my point: if the Soviet Union had survived longer than 1991, if the health of Andropov had permitted him to rule longer, if Gorbachev had chosen a different path to reform the Soviet state… We can still imagine many different cases like this, and my aim here is not to venture into virtual history, but to show how strongly the way in which the USSR collapsed conditioned the emergence of forces to occupy the vacant space, and therefore created the background, the immediate vacuum leading to the violent clash.

This work aims to study the interrelation between the collapse of the Soviet Union and the clash of rising national projects that emerged to occupy the empty terrain. To do this I had to take a broad look: to study the conditions of the Soviet collapse, the visions of past and future as they were shaped in the Caucasus in Soviet times, and the detailed historic developments that led to the conflicts. This is a large subject matter, helped by the latest studies based on archival material, the biographies of key historical figures, and a new attempt to study the Soviet collapse,[2] both on the level of theoretical orientation and on that of detailed factual precision. This said, while progressing in the research, I came across several topics which need further research and theoretical scrutiny. These are beyond the scope of the study, but they would have brought additional precision: what were the real policy debates in the Kremlin about the rising national movements in Armenian and Georgia, and was there any attempt to repress those movements? At what level were those decisions taken? Finding answers to those questions would bring additional clarification about the circumstances leading to the tragic events of Sumgait in 1988 and the Tbilisi tragedy of April 1989. What is the real story behind the putsch in Moscow in 1991? Was it, as Gorbachev and his close collaborators describe,, a last, desperate attempt by most high-level Soviet officials, excluding the President

---

2   The conditions of the Soviet collapse were the subject of heated debate among
     Sovietologists in 1992-93, who basically expressed their astonishment at the
     event, and the fact that no one foresaw this coming collapse. After a long si-
     lence, there was a second wave of publications on the Soviet collapse starting
     from the late 1990s.

himself, to stop the disintegration of the Soviet state? Or, as some other sources suggest, was it a machination that went out of control? Further research might bring additional precision to those questions, and on the final pages Soviet history, but would not bring much change to the direction of the current analysis. Whether Sumgait and Tbilisi were planned at the highest level of the Soviet hierarchy, or at an intermediary, military or republican level, or whether it was the explosion of an angry nationalist mob, or not, the result was that after those acts of violence the Soviet state lost its control over Armenia and Georgia, and after the failed, bizarre putsch attempt, the Soviet Union ceased to exist. The analytical framework and the narration proposed here attempt to understand the causes of the conflict, yet they reflect clearly my experience, the ideas I brought with me to the Caucasus while covering the conflicts as early as 1992, and the continuous contacts and work with actors in the region since then. In the words of Waltz, "our estimates of the causes of war are determined by our presuppositions as much as by the events of the world about us."[3]

In providing an interpretation of the causes of the conflicts away from the nationalist antagonism paradigm, and framing it within the historic upheaval caused by the Soviet collapse, we come to interesting results—not only in the field of political and historic knowledge—and reach a better understanding of the nature and extent of the conflicts in the Caucasus. By doing so, we limit the causes of the wars to the uncertainties linked to the Soviet collapse, and the emergence of new state units in this region. Such an analysis opens new perspectives to address the current problems and find solutions to the conflicts in the Caucasus.

---

3   Kenneth N. Waltz, *Man, the State and War*, New York: Columbia University Press, 2001 (first published in 1954), pp. 224-5.

1

THE END OF THE SOVIET UNION AND
THE RISE OF NATIONALISM

The disruption of expectations

The Caucasian wars of the early 1990s were essentially the result of a double process: state collapse and state building. It was the collapse of the USSR that opened the field to the emergence of competing forces to propose new institutional settings, building new states on the debris of the Soviet Union. The collapse of the Soviet Union was a complex process, much more complex than the post-colonial independence of African or Asian states, since it simultaneously marked the end of an imperial setting and a profound change in the socio-economic structure. The state, its essence, its role, and its ownership were at the centre of those changes. Therefore, it will be necessary to look at the processes of state transformation to narrate the history of the Caucasian wars.

An important route to understanding the wars of the Caucasus is through the study of the conditions of the Soviet collapse. Without looking at the specificities of the Soviet state, and the way it collapsed, one would take the conflicts in the Caucasus of the late 1980s and early 1990s out of their historical environment, and misinterpret their causes, their nature, trajectory, and results. By putting the conflicts in the context of Soviet collapse, these conflicts, but also overused concepts such as "nationalism", "separatism", "territorial integrity", "independent state", and so on, take a different connotation.

The disintegration of the Soviet Union came as a surprise, and was surprisingly peaceful. For a state seen by much of the rest of the world as a menace to global stability, with a self-proclaimed messianic, inter-nationalist project that devoted much of its industrial output to military purposes, and a highly structured internal police system, its collapse with virtually no internal struggle caused much stupefaction among experts who had spent decades observing the Soviet might and deciphering its mystery. The disintegration of the USSR, unlike the collapse of Nazism at the end of the Second World War, or the fall of the Ottoman and the Austrio-Hungarian Empires at the end of the Great War, happened without any outside military pressure. Nor did it happen under internal revolutionary threat, or mass mobilization opposed to the existing sys-tem, as was the case with the collapse of Tsardom in February 1917.

If the collapse of the USSR in a relatively short few years is surpris-ing, so also are the historic events of the summer of 1991, which pre-cipitated the collapse. It is rare in history that in a country nearly all of the leading persons in power including the prime minister, the defence minister, the head of the intelligence services, and the presidential chief of staff plot to take power in a coup. Usually, such leaders do not need to organize a coup to take power, since they are the power. Yet, that is exactly what happened in Moscow in August 1991. In the words of the then President of Armenia, Levon Ter-Petrossian, "the centre commit-ted suicide".[1]

In a few short months following the failed August coup of 1991, the Soviet system stopped functioning. A power struggle in the capi-tal between reactionaries, symbolized by the leaders of the coup, and liberals, gathered around the head of the Russian Federation Boris Yeltsin, squeezed the remaining legitimacy out of the last president of the USSR, Mikhail Gorbachev. Popular, nationalist movements mobi-lized thousands in demonstrations and strikes, disrupting the already suffering Soviet economic machine. The once mighty Red Army was being withdrawn from all quarters, from Afghanistan, from the former satellites in Eastern Europe, and its strength sharply reduced. The in-volvement of the armed forces in repressing popular movements in Tbilisi and Vilnius was yet another blow to the image and prestige of the Soviet armed forces. Most important, the competition between the Soviet leader Mikhail Gorbachev and the newly elected president of

---

1   Quoted in Michael Mandelbaum, "Coup de Grace: The End of the Soviet Un-ion", *Foreign Affairs*, Winter 1991/1992, p. 165.

the Russian Federation Boris Yeltsin paralyzed the state institutions, and created a situation of dual power. Whatever the long-term causes of the crisis of the Soviet Union, in the short term the August coup attempt made it impossible to govern. In a short instance of time, "the idea of the disintegration of the Soviet state moved from the wholly unimaginable to the completely inevitable within the popular mind – both within the USSR and outside."[2] The state that was created by the greatest revolution in the 20th century was undone without much glory. On 25 December 1991 Gorbachev left his office in the Kremlin, making place for the new ruler of the palace, Boris Yeltsin. The only outside appearance of this change was the bringing down of the red flag and its replacement with the Russian tricolour. But with it a whole world had come to a change.

The nationalities question had a major role in destabilizing Soviet institutions. The political reforms initiated by Gorbachev, aiming at democratizing the Soviet state, had created powerful contradictions. Archie Brown has argued that the Gorbachev reforms aiming at democratization created tensions between the Soviet system and the demands of the nationalities, which had to be solved at the expense of one or the other.[3] It was highly destabilizing to change the political system from authoritarian to democratic rule while simultaneously questioning the boundaries of the state: *perestroika* and *glasnost* increasingly unleashed demands of nationalities in the union republics for self-rule and even outright independence from Moscow. As the shock-wave of democratization initiated from the top of the Soviet state reached the bottom of society, the legitimacy of the Soviet system was increasingly questioned. In a twist of dialectics, it was the national question that destabilized the Soviet state and led to its collapse, and the collapse of the state transformed the nationalities question into political forces that tried to occupy the terrain and led to violent clashes. The contradiction between democratic reforms and insecurity about state boundaries was to be a poisoned inheritance for the newly independent republics, and be one of the factors of destabilization in the Caucasus.

---

2   Mark R. Beissinger, *Nationalist Mobilization and the Collapse of the Soviet State*, Cambridge University Press, 2002, p. 5.

3   Archie Brown, *The Gorbachev Factor*, Oxford University Press, 1997, pp. 252-4.

Very few Western scholars had imagined the possibility of the collapse of the Soviet system.[4] One of them was Hélène Carrère d'Encausse, who in her classical work on the development of nations and nationalism within the Soviet Union focuses her study on the demographic changes and the migratory movements within the Union. She noticed that titular nations were reinforcing their political control over the union republics. As a result, there was an increasing resistance of the various peripheral nations to Russification, through defence of the status of their own national language. More than most other experts, Carrère d'Encausse predicted the possibility of the Soviet "explosion", because of resistance to official policies in the Caucasus and Central Asia. Her work was influenced by numerous events at the time, notably demonstrations in various regions of Georgia, including the capital Tbilisi in mid-April 1978. This mobilization took place to oppose a constitutional reform project that removed the place of the Georgian language as official language in the republic.[5] The work of Carrère d'Encausse became popular thanks to her analysis of the developments within Central Asia, and to the passive resistance to Soviet rule among its Muslim populations. The Soviet intervention in Afghanistan pushed this marginal region into the forefront of superpower confrontation, and increased international interest in possible political changes inside Soviet Central Asia.

Although Carrère d'Encausse noticed the affirmation of national identity in the Soviet south, and the incapacity of the Moscow ideologues to solidify the identity of the "Soviet nation", she saw the future explosion of the empire not through actions taken in the centre of the pyramid itself, but through the rebellion of the nationalities. Moreover, she focused on the specificity of Islam, and the development of Sufi *tariqat* in Central Asia, a region which proved to be the most conservative in the USSR, remaining relatively unchanged even at the height of *perestroika*. Central Asian nations claimed sovereignty very late by com-

---

4   Many authors have argued about the instability of the Soviet system, at their head the architect of the October Revolution Leon Trotsky, who in his criticism of Stalinism argued that the Soviet "bureaucracy" would trade for political power with economic advantage, that is, support a change from the state monopoly over property to a system of private ownership. See Leon Trotsky, *Revolution Betrayed, What is the Soviet Union and Where is it Going?* first published 1936.

5   Hélène Carrère d'Encausse, *L'Empire éclaté, la révolte des nations En U.R.S.S.*, Paris: Flammarion, 1978, p. 218.

parison with the European or Caucasian republics of the Soviet Union, following the failed putsch in Moscow in the summer of 1991, and did so more out of lack of options than out of a political project of detaching from the USSR. In spite of much merit that Carrère d'Encausse's study had in revealing the political tendencies among the Soviet nationalities, it failed to bring the analysis of the Soviet malaise to the centre of the system itself, to the leadership of the Communist Party from where the attempts to reform the system were to start a decade later.

It was the reforms initiated in the centre that destabilized the previously existing and highly rigid system, and unleashed popular forces outside the control of the party-state structures. It was the centre that initiated the reforms, yet it was the periphery and the popular movements developing there that made *perestroika* impossible to achieve. This grass-roots movement brought the Caucasus into the centre of political developments. This region had played a leading role in Soviet history, with key leaders such as Stalin, Beria and Mikoyan coming from there, and yet the Caucasus played a marginal role in politics, economics, or the Soviet military under Brezhnev. It was the popular movements that developed there—the first being the Karabakh movement that demanded unification of the Nagorno Karabakh Autonomous Region with neighbouring Soviet Armenia—that set free popular mobilization from below, which immediately spread to neighbouring regions of the Caucasus, reaching the far-away Baltic states.

Following the collapse, bewilderment reigned in the circles of researchers specializing in Soviet studies. "It was inconceivable," wrote Jerry Hough, that the Soviet military would let its state collapse "without even being seriously bloodied. Simply inconceivable. I still don't believe it."[6] In some cases experts could explain why the coming Islamic revolution was not foreseen in the West in 1979, but the same cannot be said about the Soviet Union; few Westerners studied Iran, unlike the USSR. "No one, it seems, foresaw the collapse with any clarity; no one predicted it, despite the vast efforts and expenditures that had been devoted to Sovietology," argues W.R. Connor.[7] Connor goes on to ex-

---

6   Jerry Hough, "The Fall of Gorbachev", *Politics of Soviet Economic Reforms*, 2,1 (1992), p. 2, quoted in Brian D. Taylor, *Politics and the Russian Army, Civil-Military Relations, 1689-2000*, Cambridge University Press, 2003, p. 206.

7   W.R. Connor, "Why Were We Surprised?" *The American Scholar*, Winter 1991,

plain that mainstream Sovietology was too dedicated to the study of the Soviet Union as a competitor of the West, concentrating on studying its military forces, its economic performance, its agricultural productivity, and closely following the relations among its political elite, but leaving out "the changes and attitudes that were taking place in other parts of the Soviet society".[8] Another author defends Sovietology as a body of studies that "was useful in advancing shared knowledge of how the system operated. Some theories that were wrong were more useful than some that proved right because they forced ideas to confront empirical data."[9] Theory could forecast what could be described as the ordinary and everyday, while historic events such as revolutions are outside that scope: they involve the breakdown not only of the power structure, but also of the underlying logic that supports it; forecasting under such conditions becomes simply impossible. "Most social scientists," writes Michael Cox, "were—and presumably remain— much better equipped at dealing at stable political patterns rather than with radical shifts in structure. (…) [S]ocial science has always been better at predicting continuity than discontinuity."[10]

In the direct aftermath of the Soviet collapse, in the years 1992-93, a timid debate started among historians and political scientists specializing in Soviet studies. There was not so much a study of the root cases of this singular historical event, but more soul-searching by Sovietologists wondering why the coming collapse was largely undetected. Few could argue that the experts studying the Soviet Union were successful in predicting the coming collapse. "We were all wrong," writes one observer of Soviet affairs.[11] Another goes further in his criticism, suspecting the knowledge on which most Sovietologists based their much elaborated views: "Pundits, politicians, and undergraduates who could not locate

---

p. 175.

8   Ibid., p. 176.

9   Thomas F. Remington, "Sovietology and System Stability", *Post-Soviet Affairs*, July-September 1992, p. 258.

10   Michael Cox, "Whatever Happened to the USSR? Critical Reflections on Soviet Studies", in Michael Cox (ed.), *Rethinking the Soviet Collapse, Sovietology, the Death of Communism and the New Russia*, London and New York: Pinter, 1998, p. 17.

11   Charles H. Fairbanks, Jr., in "Introduction", *The National Interest*, Spring 1993, p. 7.

the Volga river on a map would happily write essays or deliver speeches about Gorbachev's real intentions."[12] The crisis was so fundamental that some experts went so far as re-examining the meaning of International Relations studies, and the way the discipline had functioned throughout the Cold War era.[13]

Collapse of a system or of an empire?

The debate about the reasons of the collapse of the Soviet Union rotate around the question, was it a collapse of a system or a collapse of an empire? Was it the economic organization of the USSR that witnessed a long term fall in productivity which led to the Gorbachev phenomenon, or was it its national-territorial division with its failure to integrate the various nations into a new Soviet citizenship, while succeeding in creating proto-nation-states?

Before entering into the details of this debate, it is worth mentioning that not all specialists analysed the failure of the Soviet Union as "collapse". Some looked at the events through the prism of "reform". This view is especially prominent among those experts studying Soviet-Russian economic changes. "The reforms have not arisen out of the daily interests of any particular group of people, let alone social groups, but rather from society's awareness of being in an impasse," writes a key Russian economic decision-maker.[14] The Soviet elite was by now completely disarmed, and had to borrow concepts and a world-view from its former antagonist, from "Western capitalism", and go as far as to pretend that it was the choice of the society as a whole.

To go back to the question of why the Soviet Union collapsed: several interpretations are possible. One focuses on the failure of the socialist economic model, leading into a crisis. This systemic crisis was due to the heavy cost of Soviet productivity, because production was badly adapted to consumers' needs and tastes, and because of chronic

---

12   Peter Ruthland, "Sovietology: Notes for a Post-Mortem", *National Interest*, no. 31 (Spring 1993), p. 109.

13   John Lewis Gaddis, "International Relations Theories and the End of the Cold War", *International Security*, Vol. 17, No. 3, Winter 1992-93, pp. 10 and 17.

14   Sergei Vasiliev, "Economic Reform in Russia: Social, Political, and Institutional Aspects", in Anders Aslund, Anders Aslund (ed.), *Russia's Economic Transformation in the 1990s*, Pinter, 1997, p. 33.

shortages. For Victor Zaslavsky it was the model of planned economy structured around the militaro-industrial complex which was decaying to a degree that was taking the whole society into "counter-modernization": "As the strength of the central state was eroded by declining productivity and depletion of resources, the state-engineered system of social stratification began to unravel."[15] Katherine Verdery argues that the attempted economic reforms in socialist countries aimed at creating a "dual" economy, a centrally administered section dominating heavy industries and a privatised section to produce consumer goods. Yet this attempt to mix two systems did not succeed in Eastern Europe and the USSR, because the part of the bureaucracy depending on the second won the upper hand, owing to developments in Western capitalism. "...it is not simply socialism's embrace with capitalism that brought its fall but the fact that it happened to embrace a capitalism of a new 'flexible' sort."[16] A second interpretation is that economic modernization led to the creation of a new social reality, with educated masses, specialized workers, etc., which formed a new civil society. This new society could no more be ruled by "totalitarian" methods developed under conditions of mass industrialization and urbanization, as applied in the Soviet Union in the 1930s.[17]

Another line of explanation considers that in spite of its economic difficulties, the Soviet system could survive, and even reform its institutions. This theory suggests that considering the Soviet state in the 1980s as a "totalitarian" regime is a mistake, and that the Soviet state had greatly evolved since the Stalinist years. For this school the Soviet collapse was due to ill-conceived reforms, mixed with bad leadership, without which the system could have recreated itself—in other words, the collapse was the result of an "accident". For the early versions of this school, the responsibility has to go to Gorbachev.[18] Later versions

---

15   Victor Zaslavsky, "The Soviet Union", in Karen Barkey and Mark von Hagen (eds), *After Empire, Multiethnic Society and Nation-Building*, Boulder, CO: Westview, 1997, p. 89.

16   Katherine Verdery, *What was Socialism, And What Comes Next?* Princeton University Press, 1996, p. 34.

17   Francis Fukuyama, "The Modernization Imperative, the USSR as an Ordinary Country", *The National Interest*, Spring 1993.

18   Myron Rush, "Fortune and Fate", *The National Interest*, spring 1993. The same position is expressed by Victor Kuznetsov, "The Economic Factors of USSR's

of the same theory focus on the role of Boris Yeltsin and the Russian democrats in undermining the Soviet state.[19] Another distinct trend of thought looks at the military spending and economic capabilities of the USSR, and attributes the collapse to imperial overstretch. *Perestroika* was conditioned by the Communist Party leadership's realization of the need to reduce military spending to revitalize the economy; but in spite of the new directives, the military kept spending at the previous pace, which necessitated deeper reforms within the party and the state.[20] Last but not least, the collapse is attributed to Soviet nationalities policies and ethnic mobilization against the Soviet centre power.[21]

For the purposes of the current work, it is important to emphasize not only the diversity of the proposed causes of the Soviet collapse, but the depth of the crisis. The Soviet collapse, unlike that of other imperial powers, cannot be reduced to a central theme, to one aspect such as "decolonization", or to military defeat. The Soviet collapse was the fall of an ideology, an empire and a system simultaneously, which means that all the various interpretations have their merits and are useful as analytical instruments.

The attempt to conceptualize the Soviet collapse was abandoned during most of the 1990s, for several reasons. First, most specialists working on the Soviet Union had their personal interpretation of what the Soviet Union was in its essence, and its future course. Those specialists found their personal narrations shattered, and preferred moving away from Soviet to "post-Soviet" studies, leaving to a future generation of

---

Disintegration", in Anne de Tinguy (ed.), *The Fall of the Soviet Empire*, New York: Columbia University Press, 1997, pp. 264-78.

19   Roman Laba, "How Yeltsin's Exploitation of Ethnic Nationalism Brought Down an Empire", *Transition*, Prague, 12 January 1996, pp. 5-13.

20   Geir Lundestad, "'Imperial Overstretch', Mikhail Gorbachev and the End of the Cold War", *Cold War History*, Vol. 1, No. 1, August 2000, pp. 1-20, and William Odom, *The Collapse of the Soviet Military*, New Haven and London: Yale University Press, 1998.

21   Ronald Suny, "Incomplete Revolution: National Movements and the Collapse of the Soviet Empire", *New Left Review*, London, September-October 1991, pp. 111-25. Another interpretation is that Yeltsin's manipulation of ethno-nationalism to grab power from Gorbachev led to the collapse of the USSR on the lines of constituent republics; see Roman Laba, "How Yeltsin's Exploitation of Ethnic Nationalism Brought Down an Empire", *Transition*, Prague, 12 January 1996, pp. 4-13.

researchers the hard work of revisiting the theories that had constructed our conception of what the Soviet Union was. Whether friend or foe, individuals had developed a psychological accommodation with the existence of the Soviet Union, which was taken to be a source of stability in an otherwise rapidly changing world. Its unexpected removal created an element of uncertainty difficult to overcome for those who had scrutinized the Soviet Union over decades.

A second reason was that the demand was high from various quarters, such as international organizations, different diplomatic agencies, the mass media, and the emerging third sector, to study the immediate, unfolding events for which practical policy formulations were urgently needed, and leave the more theoretical questions to be answered at a later stage. The collapse of the Soviet Union continued to pose a series of new questions that needed to be addressed from a practical point of view. It led to the formation of fifteen newly independent states, whose policies in the domains of security, foreign orientation, economic restructuring, and approach to privatization needed to be studied. Many experts converted into consultants working with the new governments, or back home with the public or private sector. Moreover, new regional concerns and interests emerged, creating new fields of studies in the domain of policy making, and among post-Soviet studies, which were hidden or even non-existent in the previous decade. The most popular topics in the post-Soviet area were Russian economic transformation, privatization, newly emerging nationalism, conflicts in the Caucasus, Russian military reform, Caspian oil and its geopolitical dimension, Islamism in North Caucasus and Central Asia, democratic reforms and the emergence of the "third sector", etc. This huge demand exhausted human and financial resources, and diverted them from more historic, but also theoretical research.

And the third reason is that to propose interpretations about the Soviet collapse, a larger revision of the theories about the nature of the USSR was necessary—in other words, to revise the theories that had failed to foresee the possibility of the collapse itself. From the perspective of the collapse, the Soviet Union deserved an entirely new biography. This, in turn, needed a certain distance from the events, a certain historic depth. The enormous effort of writing the history of the USSR and revisiting the debates about the nature of the Soviet state still remains to be undertaken.

Filling the void with imported rhetoric

There are many consequences of the collapse of the USSR; one of them is the end of the global vision it sponsored. The collapse of Soviet ideology, its polarized vision of human history, and its class analysis of contemporary politics left behind a vast intellectual vacuum. The policies of *perestroika* and *glasnost* had launched a deep debate within Soviet society, which, after decades of official control of the media, publication sector and the universities, opened a dynamic period of challenging taboos and looking for new horizons. But with the collapse of Soviet certainties this enterprise of critical thinking was left without a general structure, lost its context. Artists, writers, journalists, the whole *intelligentsia* who were used to dealing with the Soviet system, its immobility, its contradictions, its authoritarianism, were suddenly left in loneliness, they were orphaned. The Soviet authorities had imposed on their societies a dualist vision of the world, between a positive image of "socialism" and a negative one of the capitalist enemy. With the collapse of the positive image, what was presented in the past as negative was adopted and changed into a positive one, and any discourse resembling that of the *ancien régime* was faced with ridicule, scepticism and rejection.

This vacuum opened the way to the importing (and imposing) of ideas coming from the West, and mainly from the United States.[22] The migration of ideas, concepts, and visions from the Western context to a post-Soviet one, although it had a certain functional use in the early 1990s, brought with it several negative consequences as well. First, post-Soviet societies were defenceless against ideas, theories and policies imported from the outside, which lacked a larger semantic sense for their own culture. Second, the Soviet past was considered to be irrelevant, and a break was created between the "before" and the "after". To develop any policy only the new, often volatile context was studied, with the assumption that Western concepts and theories were the

---

22   Andrei P. Tsygankov, "The Irony of Western Ideas in a Multicultural World: Russians' Intellectual Engagement with the "End of History" and "Clash of Civilizations"", *International Studies Review*, Malden MA, 2003, Vol. 5, pp. 53-76.

only relevant ones, which implied removing the subject of study from (Soviet) history and the political context (the consequences of Soviet collapse). Yet, the Western vision was not always the most objective and best suited one when it came to understanding events in the Soviet/ post-Soviet context: "[T]he objectives of the West in the former Soviet South (...) is identity-driven and involves principally Western-dominated international organizations, states and non-governmental civil society organizations. They reflect a desire to make the region 'more like us', both because Western actors believe their principles and norms to be better and because they believe that their spread serves the interests of the West in the world politics," writes Neil MacFarlane.[23]

In an incredible irony of history, Western Sovietology, which had failed to read the coming Soviet collapse was now invited to advise the new republics, headed by the Russian Federation on what to do next! There is a strong link between the failure of Sovietology and the failure of the Western-inspired reforms in Russia under Yeltsin. The West had a direct self-interest in the countries emerging from the Soviet experience, independent of Western sponsored values. Certain of these values were articulated around such ideas as "privatization", "market economy", "shock-therapy" in the economic realm, and "democratization", "civil society", "pluralism", "parliamentary elections" in the political one. They were considered to be positive developments, regardless of the concrete socio-political underpinnings in which those reforms were pushed.

These concepts imported or borrowed from the West, which were not value-free, soon led to confusion and misunderstanding. For Stephen F. Cohen the major fallacy is the idea strongly entrenched in major governmental agencies in the US, as well as within leading international organizations, that following the collapse of the Soviet system the countries emerging from it were ready to accept liberal democracy and a market economy based on Western conceptions.[24] The critique could be taken a step further. Concepts like "privatisation", "property rights", "democracy" and "civil society", in a word the whole armament of transition

---

23   See: *Western Engagement in the Caucasus and Central Asia*, London: Royal Institute of International Affairs, 1999, pp. 9–10.

24   Stephen F. Cohen, "Russia: Transition or Tragedy?", in Michael Cox (ed.), *Rethinking the Soviet Collapse: Sovietology, the Death of Communism and the New Russia*, London and New York: Pinter, 1998, p. 242.

studies, can be seen as inappropriate for the study of societies emerging from Soviet rule. "One begins to see that these terms do not label useful concepts: they are elements in a massive political and ideological upheaval that is by no means restricted to the 'East.'"[25] The discrepancy between real socio-political change and balance of power on the one hand, and on the other the desire to be part of the Western club of states with attributes such as a pluralist political system with elections, political parties, opposition, civil society, etc., led to the emergence of what some call "imitation democracy", "guided democracy", and eventually "virtual politics".[26] Another assumption that was largely shared by transition studies has come under heavy criticism lately, the projection that mass privatization will trigger political change from authoritarianism directly into the democratic model.[27] Reality is always much more complex and mass privatization took many states away from the Soviet model into the bosom of new shades of the twilight zone.

From nationalism paradigm to geopolitics

Early studies on the political developments in the Caucasus analyzed them through the primordial nationalism paradigm. The new political movements were seen as echoing past, pre-Soviet tensions and antagonism suppressed under the Soviet period, but not resolved. Later interpretations focused on great power politics, Russian neo-imperial designs, or power struggle between the former declining power of Moscow and the growing global ambitions of the US under the shadow of struggle for the control of Caspian hydrocarbon resources.

To understand the dominance and shifts in focus of analysis of the studies, one has to go back to the unfolding events of the late 1980s and early 1990s. Starting from February 1988, mass mobilization independent from the ruling party first started in Stepanakert, a provincial town in Western Azerbaijan and the capital of the Mountainous Ka-

---

25   Katherine Verdery, *What was Socialism, And What Comes Next?* p. 38.

26   See Andrew Wilson, *Virtual Politics, Faking Democracy in the Post-Soviet World*, New Haven: Yale University Press, 2005; Dimitri Fourman "De Gorbachev à Poutine: les illusions perdues", *Politique Internationale*, Paris, No 109, 3/2005, pp. 253-73.

27   Thomas Carothers, "The End of the Transition Paradigm", *Journal of Democracy*, Vol. 13, No. 1, January 2002, pp. 6 and 7.

rabakh Autonomous Region. In a few days it spread to the Armenian capital Yerevan, taking the form of huge demonstrations and strikes unparalleled before. Soon, bloody events overshadowed the rising popular mobilization in the Caucasus, with pogroms introducing violence to the newly evolving independent political expression. While the demonstrations in Armenia continued throughout the year and the next, new demonstrations erupted in Sukhumi and Tbilisi, with conflicting claims between Georgians and Abkhaz. In 1989, armed clashes erupted in South Ossetia, between Georgian and Osset bands fighting for the control of Tskhinvali, the regional centre of South Ossetia. By 1991, political fever hit the north of the Caucasus mountain chain, with Chechens, Ingushes, Ossets, Kabardin, Balkars, Karachais, Cherkess, and the numerous peoples of Daghestan mobilizing, expressing past grievances, and formulating often contradictory political demands.

To analyze this variety of new, largely unknown, and complex situations, scholars were unprepared and unable to understand and grasp the extent of change while events precipitated it. Outside the narrow circle of a few linguists and historians, few knew much about the contemporary conditions of the peoples of the Caucasus. Literature was lacking as well as scholars. Therefore, initial interpretations about the spring of nationalities, Caucasus style, could only draw references from limited sources. The most convenient sources were history books, looking at the region in the 19th and the early 20th century, inevitably suggesting similarities between current and past conflicts and concluding about the continuous nature of the events. The mobilizations of today seemed to echo conflicts in 1905 or 1918. As a result, the conflicts of the late 1980s were seen as the reactivation of old woes, the continuity of ancient confrontations that were interrupted by the artificial intervention of the Bolsheviks: "The situation of Nagorno-Karabakh provides the most extreme example of the inherent dangers when the conflicts contained during the Soviet period become active once again."[28]

The second wave of interpretations, looking at the conflicts from a great power angle, started to gain in importance starting from 1993, and continues to dominate in the available literature until today. This can be explained, once again, by the changing circumstances in the

---

28   Suzanne Goldenberg, *Pride of Small Nations*, p. 8.

Caucasus, as well as in Moscow. In December 1991 the Soviet Union was no more, and the conflicts in the Caucasus entered a new stage. On the military level the withdrawal of the Soviet factor left the local antagonists face to face, leading to full-scale military operations in Karabakh and Abkhazia. On the political level, the conflicts were no more internal tensions of a single state (the Soviet Union) but conflicts across international borders (Armenia and Azerbaijan), or conflicts where a great power intervened (Russian intervention in the conflict between Georgia and Abkhazia). The evident Russian military intervention in the conflicts across the newly established international borders of Russia, and the unexpected outcome of the conflicts—in which the military forces of Azerbaijan and Georgia were defeated by smaller territorial entities such as Mountainous Karabakh, South Ossetia, and Abkhazia, which had fewer human and material resources—led to a new set of interpretations focusing on Russian geopolitical designs.[29]

In the meantime, there was a more general shift of attention following the end of the Cold War, whereby the formerly marginal conflicts in the Third World came to the centre of attention. "Ethnic conflicts" was the lens through which conflicts were seen from the Great Lakes and the Horn of Africa to the Balkans, the Caucasus, and Central Asia. An impressive proportion of the political literature of the 1990s left in oblivion the great chain of events of the preceding decade—the end of the East-West confrontation and the collapse of the Soviet Union—and looked at the new context of the 1990s as events in themselves and not as shock-waves resulting from that gigantic earthquake that reshaped world politics. Some authors go as far as finding a link between over-emphasizing the horrors of the ethnic wars and the oblivion that covered the madness of the Cold War.[30] Most studies of post-Soviet nationalism paid too little attention to the context of the collapse of a highly centralized, authoritarian regime, which left a vast vacuum behind, and propose nationalism as a primary *cause* of this collapse, to conclude that the conflicts are the logical results of the clashes between different rising nationalisms.

---

29   Thomas Goltz, "Letter From Eurasia: The Hidden Russian Hand", *Foreign Policy*, No. 92, Fall 1993.

30   See Tom Nairn, "Breakwaters of 2000: From Ethnic to Civic Nationalism", *New Left Review*, London, November/December, 1995.

It was not only Western analysts who lacked references and analytical tools; so did local experts on whom many foreign analysts depended for their information and understanding of the unfolding developments. For many, not only did the conflicts echo the inter-ethnic clashes of 1905-7 and those of 1918-20; in addition the collapse of the USSR recalled the fall of the Tsar in 1917, and consequently many expected a return of the Russian power to the Transcaucasus (since renamed as the "South Caucasus") once the power struggle in the imperial capital had been settled. Throughout the years when I worked in the Caucasus, I was surprised to see how bewildered local professors, journalists and politicians were concerning the gigantic changes taking place around them. Once in the late 1990s I was complaining to a university professor in Yerevan that for many local journalists it was difficult to provide interesting political analysis since they lacked understanding about major developments such as the collapse of the Soviet Union. The professor picked up the conversation and said, "Yes, the collapse of the USSR was a great tragedy, it was all because Gorbachev was an agent of the West…"

The changing political circumstances led to re-evaluation of our understanding of "nationalism". In the mid-1980s, when Gorbachev's *perestroika* was still at its height and the new popular mobilizations emerged, these new political movements carried numerous slogans and demands, varying from environmental demands to national, even democratic ones. "Perhaps not surprisingly, the most serious national uprisings were liberative, rising in particular from first-order titular national movements," wrote Ian Bremmer in 1993.[31] In the absence of political parties, national groups were the best positioned to mobilize masses, to "become political parties" themselves by marginalizing liberal, dissident, environmentalist groups that were also emerging in the late 1980s. As long as the national movements positioned themselves in opposition to the Soviet authorities—in which people were by then already disappointed—and were subjected to repression and persecution, Western analysts, politicians, and the media perceived them as "democratic", as "like us". It did not take long to transform the "liberative" image of the

---

31   Ian Bremmer, "Reassessing Soviet Nationalities Theory", in Ian Bremmer and Ray Taras (eds), *Nations and Politics in the Soviet Successive States,* Cambridge University Press, 1993, p. 20.

national movements into a reactionary, archaic one; in fact, the change happened in a few months, enough time for the sudden disappearance of the Soviet state to open the space for the clash of various national movements, by now described as "ethnic conflicts".

War, state-building and globalization

The wars in the Caucasus erupted at a moment when the larger context was one of hope and optimism. At the end of the Cold War there was once again a short moment of hope when many experts and leaders thought that international relations could enter a new age, in which new rules and regulations could be applied to global politics. The Soviet experience showed that military might was futile, and by itself it was not a source of power. In the 1990s many believed that in the future the military would be relegated to a secondary position in world affairs, and much of the global hierarchy of power and authority would be defined in the field of economic competition. This "age of hope" had different intellectual expressions, from Fukuyama's idea of the victory of liberal democracy, to the idea of global civil society. With the end of the nuclear nightmare, and the former enemies across the Iron Curtain expressing the best will of collaboration, the idea that new principles could be developed for the management of world affairs sounded real. In this new age international conflicts could be managed differently, the international community being more sensitive towards the repression of minority groups and violations of individual human rights.

Some even advanced the idea that war as a mechanism for regulating conflicts within and between societies had outlived itself, and would soon be considered to belong to the past, including the leading British military historian Paul Keegan:

> As we contemplate this end-of-the-century world, in which the rich states that imposed remilitarization from above have made peace their watchword and the poor states that suffered remilitarization from below spurn or traduce the gift, may war at last be recognised as having lost its usefulness and deep attractiveness?[32]

Simultaneously, and as a result of the collapse of the Soviet power and the end of East-West confrontation, there was a radical change in

---

32   Paul Keegan, *History of Warfare*, London: Pimlico, 1994, p.56.

global conflict patterns. Certain wars looked like reaching their conclusion, although retrospectively we can describe some of them as being in a process of transformation rather than reaching an end of the cycle. Among those were the conflicts in the Middle East, stretching from Lebanon to Afghanistan, with the war in Lebanon coming to an end; later, the Madrid conference gave hopes for a conclusion of the Israelo-Palestinian conflict; and the international actors abandoned Afghanistan, letting it become a localized war-zone to be divided and destroyed by the former Mujahideen fighters, while the country seemed irrelevant to world affairs. Similarly, the end of the East-West confrontation either put an end to local conflicts like those of Central America and Africa or transformed them from a global competition with local roots to local wars without any international resonance.

While the old wounds continued to bleed, the collapse of the Eastern bloc, symbolised by the fall of the Berlin Wall, led to new conflicts: the wars for the succession of Yugoslavia and the USSR. For most of those who were looking forward to a new world order, the new conflicts felt like an act of betrayal, and sounded like the voices of an archaic animal accidentally reawakened from the dark ages. In Western Europe, but also in North America, the Yugoslav wars were much more immediate, studied and reflected upon, owing to the direct intervention of those states and international organizations in the Balkans, while for a long period the war zones of the former Soviet Union were left primarily to Moscow to manage. In the wars of the Caucasus, until the Russian military invasion of Chechnya in December 1994, there were few Western journalists on the ground, while most of those who covered the events were Moscow based correspondents of major agencies or papers who covered the Karabakh or the Abkhazia conflict by short trips of three to four days. As a result, very often the conflicts of the Caucasus were studied with the debate around the causes of the Balkan wars in the background. Some even saw in those conflicts in Karabakh, and in Croatia and Bosnia, as well as in the "new" wars in Africa, a new pattern of conflicts linked with the end of the Cold War and the beginning of a new era: that of globalization. "Indeed," wrote Mary Kaldor referring to a visit to the Karabakh war zone in 1992, "the experience of wars in other places [such as Africa and South Asia] shed new light on my understanding of what was happening in the Balkans and the former Soviet Union."[33] Therefore, while referring to texts written in the early 1990s, one should be careful with terms such as "ethnic conflicts", "secession", "break-up", etc. since those terms refer not only to the conflicts in Karabakh or Abkhazia, but also to those in Croatia and Bosnia, and later in the Great Lakes region of Africa, with all the potential confusion resulting.

While some scholars saw at the source of the new wars the resurgence of archaic antagonisms, others looked at the new forces of globalization, and the pressure they created to redefine group identity, as the source of the post-Cold War conflicts. Globalization was seen as a technology-driven economic trend which was influencing social structures and in some cases dislodging the state and marginalizing national identity. According to Ignatieff, "vast sections of the world – central Africa, parts of Latin America, central Asia – are simply drifting out of the global economy altogether into a subrational zone of semipermanent violence."[34] For Kaldor, "the processes known as globalization are breaking up the cultural and socio-economic divisions that defined the patterns of politics which characterized the modern period. The new type of warfare has to be understood in terms of this global dislocation."[35]

How far can we fit the causes of the conflicts in the Caucasus into this analysis? Could we say that the forces of globalization led to destabilizing of the existing socio-economic tissue of the Caucasus in the 1980s, and thence to the violent conflicts of the 1990s? Was it the penetration of global economic patterns that destabilized the Soviet order in the Caucasus, leading to the chaos of ethnic wars there?

Again, I would argue that it was the other way around in the causal hierarchy, if we are to explain the causes of the conflicts in the Caucasus. It was rather the destabilization of the Soviet order in the Caucasus and its rapid collapse that opened up the space for ethnic mobilization and the emergence of multiple national movements, the clash of which led to the cycle of violence in the Caucasus. The global actors, whether in the economic or the political domain, penetrated the region in the

---

33 Mary Kaldor, *New and Old Wars, Organized Violence in a Global Era*, Stanford, CA: Stanford University Press, 2001, p. 1.

34 Michael Ignatieff, *The Warrior's Honor, Ethnic War and the Modern Conscience*, London: Chatto and Windus, 1998, p. 98.

35 Mary Kaldor, *New and Old Wars*, p. 70.

last stage of this process. The major oil deal between Azerbaijan and a consortium of Western companies, known as the "Deal of the Century", which could be considered as the opening note of the globalization processes in the Caucasus, was signed in September 1994, a few months after a cease-fire agreement was reached in the Karabakh war. In other words, the wars in the Caucasus cannot be attributed to globalization, where the lines between politics, organized crime and standing armies get confused. The Caucasian conflicts did not develop as a result of state structures weakening under the influence of multinationals and international financial institutions. Again, what is specific to the conflicts in the Caucasus in the early 1990s is the sudden collapse of the existing state structures, and the security dilemma this event created. Here, the region of the Caucasus differed substantially from that of Yugoslavia, since it was a largely isolated frontline region of the Soviet Union, and did not have the kind of exchanges that Yugoslavia enjoyed with the West.

Nevertheless, characteristics of globalization have enveloped the Caucasus probably at a faster rhythm than many other post-Soviet regions, since the collapse of the USSR eventually led to acceleration of globalization processes. As I will argue later, the wars of the new era, the era of globalization, are characterized by the weakening and the shrinking of the state and the spread of private actors. This phenomenon took on a highly specific shape in the USSR as a result of accelerated weakening of Soviet institutions and the final collapse of the Soviet state, making the wars in the Caucasus erupt in historically unique circumstances, absent in the case of other conflicts such as those in Africa, Latin America and South Asia.

State, separatism, ethnic conflicts

At the end of the Cold War, two federative states collapsed and a new framework of legitimacy was necessary to define the conditions of succession. The difficult questions were how to define the rules of succession, and who was eligible to define them. On what principles could new legitimacy be attributed? And how optimal could any given choice be from the perspective of stability and preservation of security, and the viability of the new entities? There was no easy solution to these questions. The international community gave a clear, albeit problematic answer: the republican units that composed the Yugoslav federation or the Soviet Socialist Union were recognized as new members of the international club of recognized states, through membership of such organizations as the UN or the OSCE. This solution had its advantages: the succeeding republics had more or less well defined borders as well as some institutional framework that could take over state functions. Moreover, most of those republics represented ethnic groups and therefore could recreate a base for a new national legitimacy.

In most cases this accommodation worked well: from the former Soviet satellite states in Eastern Europe to Siberia and the Chinese border, from the Czech Repubic to Kazakhstan we have new states that enjoy a certain degree of legitimacy and have revealed a high degree of stability. Yet, the formula adopted by the international community could not accommodate all cases: we did not have in the early 1990s—we do not have yet until now—an international instrument to regulate the inherited problems in cases where the republican framework of USSR or Yugoslavia did not enjoy legitimacy for an important fraction of its population. The eruption of conflicts—and the weak state institutions that have emerged since—continue to plague the political landscape of the east of the European Union, as the direct result of this legitimacy problem.

The conflicts erupted where two references of legitimacy clashed: on the one hand there were the new union republics acceding to international recognition as independent states, and at the same time there were ethnic movements mobilizing around the idea of their rejection of this new legitimacy, which they saw as the reinforcing of one ethnic rule over them minus the imperial centre. In Yugoslavia or the Soviet Union not all frontiers reflected the ethnic map, nor did all minorities agree to be ruled by the titular nations. The old equilibrium that was conditioned by the leading role of Moscow (or Belgrade) was now shattered and the definition of the new political hierarchy took place in a context of unfolding uncertainty. For the local actors the context in which the dramatic changes were happening differed radically from that of their colleagues in the West: they stood on the side of the losers of the Cold War, whether they adhered to the Communists' ideology or not. They were entering not a new world with fulfilled promises, but a world of an open door to a dark tunnel. Their reference was not the possible future, but the fearful past. It was this contradiction between the effort to redefine the new cadre of the nation-state, and the rebellion of parts of the local populations often belonging to ethnic minorities, that led to the eruption of the conflicts in the Caucasus as well as in the Balkans.

For many, self-determination of nations is seen as a destabilizing factor. "Statehood has become the ultimate prize of nationalists; their banner is self-determination and their demands are territorial. There are no halfway houses between subordination and equality, between independence and autonomy," writes Gidon Gottlieb.[36] Although the author identifies the importance of statehood in a modern international system that marginalizes other forms of self-determination, he fails to explain why nations turn to nationalism, under what conditions "extremist" demands of separatism are put forward, or when nationalism erupts into violence and wars. Common sense and memory tell us that demands for separatism often lead to political conflict, with a high chance that it can turn violent. So why do people take the risk of posing such demands, and in what conditions, is a legitimate question that needs to be asked to understand why certain groups are radicalized. Yet, many analysts have failed to study the context that led to radical movements. "Ethnic" conflicts and calls for "self-determination" were seen as challenges to the status quo, the most immediate sign of disturbing a global peace hoped for and promised after a long century of instability, World Wars and a Cold War.

Certain concepts, definitions and analytic tools were hastily used while studying the Caucasian events. As a result, certain confusion has been created, a mask that makes the understanding of the historic developments difficult to grasp. For example, numerous studies analyse the conflicts in the Caucasus using the term "state" to describe the Georgian side in early 1992, and the Abkhaz and Osset popular mobilizations as "separatist" movements. Although the term reflected the legal status of Georgia after 1991, when it was recognized as an independent state by the world community, it did not reflect with precision the reality on the ground: to anyone acquainted with the real Georgia in the months following the collapse of USSR, it is an enormous exaggeration, if not

---

36   Gidon Gottlieb, "Nations Without States", *Foreign Affairs*, May/June 1994, p. 102. For another critical paper on self-determination, see Charles Tilly, "National Self-Determination as a Problem for All of Us", *Daedalus*, Summer 1993, pp. 29-36.

a gross mistake. The authority of the legal Georgian "state" in 1991-94 did not go far beyond the centre of Tbilisi. Even as late as 2003 Georgia was characterized as a "weak" or "failing" state, with practically no army, a corrupt police corps, and an inefficient administration. Much of the significance of the Rose Revolution of November 2003 should be seen in the reaction of part of the ruling Georgian elite against the failures of Shevardnadze, and as a fresh attempt at state-building, rather than political democratization.

Was statehood the prize of nationalists, or was it a necessary project to fill the void left behind by the collapse of Soviet state institutions? How to explain that, from a total of over 30 territorial conflicts in the Caucasus, we had only five major inter-ethnic clashes in the aftermath of Soviet collapse? How do we explain that most of the conflicts were between titular nations and former autonomous entities?[37] Last but not least, how can we explain that in the three major conflicts (Karabakh, Abkhazia, and Chechnya in the 1994-96 war), the smaller entities were victorious in their struggle against the titular nations? Revising our understanding of what we mean by concepts such as "states" in the immediate aftermath of the Soviet demise is a necessity for a deeper understanding of the overall political movements and changes in the Caucasus.

The conflicts

Many of the analysts and researchers studying the causes of the conflicts in the Caucasus have ignored the centrality of the Soviet collapse. I will try to bring this basic historic event to the core of my analysis—not abandoning other useful interpretations, such as the role of nationalism, neo-imperial policies, etc., but constructing a hierarchy of interpretations and narrate the conflicts under a new light. The central question could be therefore formulated in the following way: how, in the years of the weakening of Soviet institutions, a new political space was created; and how was the emergence of the new political movements in the Caucasus transformed into conflicts under the conditions of the collapse of the Soviet Union?

---

37 Nagorno-Karabakh, South Ossetia, Abkhazia and Chechnya, in the form of the Checheno-Ingush Republic, had various degrees of autonomous status under the Soviet rule. The conflict between North Ossetia and Ingushetia is of a slightly different form, but does not contradict this observation.

I will argue that it was the weakening of Soviet control, the collapse of its ideological grip and lack of police repression, which triggered mass mobilizations in search of an alternative political system. The nature of those movements was shaped by the political culture of the Soviet Union, and the conditions in which the Soviet system was being undone.

Moshe Lewin underlines the necessity to learn Russian pre-revolutionary institutions and traditions so as to understand the making of the Soviet Union, and to study the Soviet experience for an explanation of the political developments of Russia in the past decade.[38] Similarly, it is necessary to understand the Soviet past, the institutions it created, its political culture, and the conditions in which the Soviet institutions were collapsing, to assess the origins of the conflicts in the Caucasus. Studying this period is like a delicate play between selective elements of continuity and the sudden, disruptive, revolutionary change often hidden under layers and layers of events and documents, facts and names of people and places.

While there are a number of good studies of the individual conflicts in the Caucasus, I suggest that in order to understand even one, it is necessary to look at the Caucasus region as a whole to look for patterns of its conflicts in the last days of the Soviet Union, and as the new independent republics emerged. The conflicts concerned are those of Nagorno Karabakh, South Ossetia, Abkhazia and the Pregorodniy Rayon of North Ossetia, and the two Chechen wars.

Studying state collapse in the African context, William Zartman gives the following definition:

It [state collapse] refers to a situation where the structure, authority (legitimate power), law, and political order have fallen apart and must be reconstituted in some form, old or new. On the other hand, it is not necessarily anarchy. Nor is it simply a by-product of the rise of ethnic nationalism: it is the collapse of old orders, notably the state that brings about the retreat to ethnic nationalism as the residual, viable identity.[39]

---

38   Moshe Lewin, " La Russie face à son passé soviétique ", *Le Monde diplomatique*, Paris, December 2001. http://www.monde-diplomatique.fr/2001/12/LEWIN/15967

39   William Zartman, "Introduction: Posing the Problem of State Collapse", in William Zartman (ed.), *Collapsed States, The Disintegration and the Restoration of Legitimate Authority*, London: Lynne Rienner, 1995, p. 1.

When applying this description of state collapse to the post-Soviet context, one should add two characteristics that were lacking in the African context: first, there had been seven decades of highly centralized state-rule in the Soviet Union; and second, this state got weaker and disappeared in a very short time, in a matter of few years. In the republics of the Caucasus, the legitimacy, authority, and power of Soviet institutions such as the Communist Party, the police, the army, the judiciary, the Soviet rouble, collapsed—simultaneously. The retreat of the former authority stimulated different things in different contexts, leading sometimes to the formation of a new order based on new institutions and new legitimacy, and at other times to conditions resembling anarchy more than a new statehood, resembling the description of state collapse or "failed states".

In this context nationalism, although an important factor in explaining the conflicts, is seen as insufficient by itself. To explain the conflicts, the eruption of mass nationalist movements can be seen as an effect of the initial cause—that is, the collapse of the Soviet state. But to explain why certain popular mobilizations were more important, longer lasting and more intense and even violent, the particular history of each given nation will play the key role. In considering the three major regional conflicts, Karabakh, Abkhazia and Chechnya, we find that each nation has a traumatic moment in its near past: the Karabakh Armenians with the First World War Genocide, which led to the wiping out of Armenian presence from much of historic Armenia where their people had had a continuous presence for more than twenty-six centuries; the Abkhazians with their demographic decline in their own historic territory since the 1860s, after their defeat by the Tsarist armies and the following mass exodus to the Ottoman empire, a trend accentuated by Soviet policies under Beria; and the Chechens with the 1944 mass deportations that had genocidal consequences for the Chechen nation, and is strongly imprinted in the memory of the entire Chechen people. The mobilization of Karabakh Armenians, the Abkhaz, and the Chechens could be attributed to the collective trauma they shared as a group, and this sentiment led them to take to the streets in a moment of wide uncertainty, an act that simultaneously rebelled against the injustice of history and tried to mobilize to shield the community from new dangers. Lastly, the newly independent national elites in the new capitals, the Azerbaijani elite in Baku, the Georgian elite in Tbilisi, and the Russian leadership around Yeltsin, decided for various political reasons, but mainly because of the political culture as it was developed within Soviet institutions, to answer the challenge of nationalist mobilization with military force. This initiative—the attempt to repress popular nationalism by military force—was the direct cause of the conflicts. In many cases nationalism expressed its will, yet was not confronted by repression. There were nationalism mobilizations in various degrees in several regions in the Caucasus such as Samtskhe-Javakheti, the Armenian inhabited regions of southern Georgia, Kabarda, and Daghestan, in northern Azerbaijan areas inhabited by the Lezgins, or elsewhere in post-Soviet space, the most prominent example being Tatarstan. But the lack of military repression against political nationalism was the main factor why in those cases there were no violent conflicts, and as political trends changed, those nationalist movements had less relevance and less mobilizing capacity.

Although the intention of the work is to emphasize the central role played by the Soviet collapse and thus shed a new light on the conflicts of the Caucasus and propose a somewhat new narration, it is not my intention to impose a deterministic dimension on the analysis. Neither is such an approach necessary, nor helpful to illustrate the thesis of this work. Nationalism, elite struggle, foreign interventions are necessary support to give the subject matter full appreciation. As E.H. Carr suggests, the "historian's approach to the problem of cause is that he will commonly assign several causes to the same event." He adds, "The true historian, confronted with this list of causes of his own compiling, would feel a professional compulsion to reduce it to order, to establish some hierarchy of causes which would fix their relation to one another, perhaps to decide which cause, or which category of causes, should be regarded in the last resort' (…) as the ultimate cause, the cause of all causes."[40]

The geographical, ethnic and political similarities are additional difficulties for those who would wish to study the root causes of the conflicts by looking at an individual conflict. Often, one conflict had a direct impact on another through a spill-over effect. Or else, on the contrary, a conflict in a neighbouring land served as a safety valve: by

---

40   E.H. Carr, *What is History?* London: Macmillan & Co., 1961, pp. 83 and 84.

attracting the most militant part of the political scene it diverted their efforts, and shaped the internal political discourse of a group or a republic. For example, the conflict between the Abkhaz and the Georgians attracted thousands of volunteers from the northern Caucasus, thus defusing much tension in regions like Kabardino-Balkaria or Karachayevo-Cherkessia. If it is suggested that the central explanation for the Karabakh Armenians' revolt is Armenian nationalism, and that Armenians in the late 1980s were strongly driven by the myth of Greater Armenia, then one has to give a valid explanation of why Javakheti Armenians or Krasnodar Armenians did not follow the same path, why in their case the desire to create a state from "sea to sea" did not have a mobilizing effect. In the case of the Chechen conflict, if historical antagonism against the Russian empire and fierce resistance that goes back to the late 18th century are suggested as the explanation, it is necessary to explain why similar political mobilization did not rouse the Avars of Daghestan, who in the 19th century played a central role in anti-Russian rebellion. If an interpretation is based on the weight of Russia's role in the conflicts in the South Caucasus, it should consider Russian policy in the northern part of the mountain chain and, in particular, in Chechnya in 1994-96. The historic context, the lines of mobilization and conflict, and the outcome of the conflicts have numerous similarities, which justify a regional approach and a comparative study of the conflicts.

In conclusion, in order to develop the central argument of the current study, which is the centrality of the Soviet collapse as the root cause of the Caucasian conflicts, various interpretations provided so far will be studied. After analysing the interesting suggestions, but also the shortcomings from this "list of causes", the research will proceed to develop a hierarchy of explanation that will consider theories of state collapse and their consequences, and use theories of post-empire state-building to analyse the New Independent States of the Caucasus in the past decade: Does a given interpretation explain why the conflicts erupted at a certain moment? Does it explain why one conflict erupted into war, while others did not? Does it explain the kind of mobilization and military operations? Does it explain the military outcome of the conflict? Does it explain why the violent stage of the conflict ended, and in what circumstances? Does it explain the emergence of political forces that succeeded the conflict stage?

In order to unravel this bunch of complex questions, I will try to find assistance in psychohistory. Saul Friedländer defines psychohistory as "the comparative study of past psychological phenomenon".[41] Historic trauma is a strong political instrument in mass mobilization, even more so in moments of radical transformation. Tirza Hechter, writing of the "function of mythologizing a perceived traumatic experience in which ideologies come to play a central role in the political agenda," suggests that "the collective as a whole accepts certain myths as though these were the accurate representations of the group's history."[42] Looking at the role of trauma in mass consciousness could help us reassess the political mobilization of Karabakh Armenians, the Abkhaz, the Chechens, etc.

Lastly, one should reflect upon the policies adopted by the titular nations confronting the ethnic mobilization of their own minorities. To address the radical questions raised by Karabakh Armenians, by Abkhazians and Ossetians, and by the Chechens, the ruling circles in Baku, Tbilisi, and Moscow decided to use military force to suppress dissent. This choice of means to address problems which are in their nature political reflects both the nature of the governments in power in most post-Soviet republics in the early 1990s and the desire of the new rulers to use "external" wars to impose "internal" political unity at a time of power struggle back in the capitals.

This leaves us with the last question: why did certain tensions lead to violent conflicts? Why did certain ethnic groups mobilize around political slogans considered radical by their neighbouring ethnic groups, while in other cases post-Soviet political agitation did not radicalize so far? In other words, out of the multitude of territorial conflicts in the vast Soviet space, and some dozen territorial claims in the region of the Caucasus, why did we have those five wars? Can we learn lessons from other tense situations, which did not mobilize into explosion?

The root causes of the conflicts as suggested above are not enough alone to answer these questions. The Soviet collapse provides the necessary condition, the background of the drama of the individual conflicts. In this analysis it is the necessary condition to "explain", but it

---

41   Saul Friedländer, *Histoire et psychanalyse*, Paris: Seuil, 1975, p. 211.

42   Tirza Hechter, "Traumas, Conflicts, and Mythology", *International Journal of Middle East Studies*, Cambridge University Press, 35 (2003), p. 440.

is not sufficient. Each conflict is a story in itself, has a biography of its own. Each popular mobilization is marked with the past trauma of its own people, who, in a moment of historic uncertainty, in a moment of mass fear, reflected upon their own past and through it drew their own proper conclusions and political expression.

2

HISTORY, INTELLECTUALS AND CONFLICTS
IN THE CAUCASUS

History, historic debates, and conflict about interpretation of history
mutated to become ideologies of mobilization and antagonism during
the last decades of the Soviet Union. Debates that were initially articulated among a handful of specialists—historians, linguists, archaeologists—took on a life of their own and were catapulted towards the
political arena, to take a new form and a new social role. True, history
was always politicised in the Soviet Union, it was never permitted to
evolve too far away from political dogma. Under the shadow of political
control historians developed a more subtle discourse distinct from the
Soviet official line, often for the defence of the nation and against either
the Russian central power or a rival neighbouring nationality. It was
this marginal discourse that succeeded in mobilizing the imagination of
the masses and emerging new elites, the intelligentsia and the working
class, as the legitimacy of the Soviet ideology weakened. As this chapter
will describe, in the case of conflicts those historic debates evolved into
ideologies of confrontation, and historians became political activists for
the defence of the nation.

Many who have been interested in studying the roots of the contemporary conflicts in the Caucasus have looked to the past and found continuity between the 19th century Great Caucasian Wars, the "Armeno-
Tatar Wars" of 1905-7, or the clashes between the central authorities
of the Georgian Republic and Abkhaz and Osset formations, and the
conflicts that erupted in late 1980s. Others looked at the roots of the
conflicts in the Soviet period and within the system that the Soviets set

up in the Caucasus and elsewhere through the ethno-territorial system, the official histories, and the group identities this system reflected, with all the hierarchy and power relations resulting. Although the system imposed by the Soviet authorities gave a semblance of stability, it also encouraged competition between the various groups over status, territory, resources, and power. While the official ideology repressed political nationalism, this competition found other routes to self-expression. This half-hidden articulation of nationalism found various forms—literature, opera, historic writings, archaeology, etc.—and grew in volume and importance in the Brezhnev era. As the crisis of the Soviet state and its dominant ideology deepened, the nationalist discourse claimed the role of alternative ideology and framed the newly developing political space, eventually achieving dominance over rival political currents critical of Soviet ideology such as environmentalism and pro-democratic movements.

The new ideas that mobilized the masses in the Caucasus in the late 1980s had been brewing over a certain period of time. What did those ideas evolve from? How did they find expression in the Soviet system? What was their role in mobilizing the masses and creating antagonistic propaganda and ideologies that led to the wars in the Caucasus? These are some of the questions this chapter will try to address, by studying how the officially sanctioned vision of history in Soviet times, which was supposed to provide legitimacy to the Soviet system and its components such as union republics, autonomous republics, and autonomous regions, was—because it was based on ethnic identification of individuals and territories—a double-edged sword. At a moment of weakness, it became an instrument that was used to destabilize the Soviet system itself and create clashes from within.

The "nation", "nationalism", and "national territory" in the late Soviet period

The conflicts in the Caucasus, before turning violent in streets and villages, and before separating former neighbours by front lines, were fought on the level of ideas, among the chosen few. The Soviet system had on the one hand encouraged the creation of national histories and national cultures, and on the other hand limited the free discussion of those ideas; the result was a distorted vision of the past and therefore of the group, reinforced by repetition, and frustrated by the official Russian cultural superiority and domination. The visions of historians, poets, journalists, and professional intellectuals about the past of the Caucasus, and therefore about the situation of their own nation-states throughout the centuries, clashed on the pages of books and specialized publications. This created a dominant vision in which one's own nation was the legitimate heir of long and rich civilizations, developing an autochthonous status for itself, its language and its ethnic groups, "proving" physical presence in the slopes and valleys of the Caucasus since the dawn of history. On the other hand, neighbouring ethnic groups did not enjoy a similar status, their history was often negated and their status downgraded to that of "newcomers", whether this newcomer arrived in its current territories a century or three or ten centuries ago. In an age of nation-building affected by contradictory political fashions, restrained conditions, and often limited historical or archaeological references, debate about the past and the study of "ethnogenesis" had the role of creating the ideological basis of the union republics and their borders established in the first decade of the Soviet state; in this process methodological persistence and factual precision were not often respected, even less so by non-professionals who needed historic, linguistic, and archaeological references for political reasons. "Differences in approaches to early history were by no means insignificant to the creation of the ideology of confrontation, which played a major role in the Karabakh, Abkhazian and South Ossetian tragedies."[1]

The Soviet Union was founded to be the state of the working class, where other differences including those based on national particularism were supposed to vanish as the society developed towards higher stages of socialism and eventually reached mature communism. With the legitimacy of the Soviet socialism starting to fade in the post-Khrushchev era, the "form" took over the "content": the national idea became stronger and looked more real than before. With the decline of the socialist dream coupled with the relaxation of the Stalinist repression, the imagined nation became legitimate in the eyes of the Soviet-made intel-

---

1   Victor A. Shnirelman, *The Value of the Past: Myths, Identity and Politics in Transcaucasia*, Osaka: National Museum of Ethnology, 2001, p. 15.

ligentsia, and eventually in the eyes of the wider public.[2] As the Soviet Union declared its weakness in the form of *perestroika*, and entered its phase of decline with a self-deceptive "restructuring" programme, the national idea was ready as an alternative political system, with its widespread values as an alternative narrative that could explain and justify the existing reality, and an institutional framework that could be mobilized for action. In the last decades of the USSR, while the official ideology remained that of Marxism-Leninism, the intelligentsia—a group nurtured by the Soviet system and dominating much of its institutions in the republics—were developing a rival and challenging national ideology. The spread of the nationalist ideology was in itself a reflection of the growing control of the ethnic elites over the political mechanisms and economic resources of the Soviet periphery (the ethnic territories including the union republics and autonomous regions) and the weakening of the central authority, and consequently of its ideology. During the entire phase when the Soviet Union was stable, those contradictory visions of the nation and its legitimate rights could coexist, as long as they were preserved in limited areas; the discourse "migrated"[3] from the public, from the area of history books, journals, and TV screens to literature, poetry, archaeology, ethnology, and popular folklore. But once the Soviet capacity to contain weakened, the idea of the nation not only challenged the power of the Moscow authorities, but also clashed with rival visions of neighbouring nations over such resources as territories and populations. Those clashing visions very soon invaded the streets, flooding into demonstrations, leading to transfers of population and eventually to full-scale wars with all the attributes of modern wars.

Most of the leaders of the national movements in the South Caucasus were intellectuals, who for long years in the Brezhnev era were fighting for the defence of national language, history, and memory. The leader of the Armenian Karabakh Movement and the first President of independent Armenia, Levon Ter-Petrossian, was a philologist and a specialist in medieval manuscripts; Zviad Gamsakhurdia, one of the

---

2   Ronald Grigor Suny looks at this in much detail in *The Revenge of the Past, Nationalism, Revolution, and the Collapse of the Soviet Union,* Stanford, CA: Stanford University Press, 1993, pp. 84-125.

3   "…déplacement des discours" in the words of Marc Ferro, in *L'Histoire sous surveillance,* Paris: Calmann-Lévy, 1985, p. 79.

leading Georgian dissidents in the 1980s and the first elected President of Georgia, was a professor of literature, a translator of Shakespeare, and the son of a famous Georgian poet, Alexander Gamsakhurdia; Abulfaz Elchibey, the leader of the Azerbaijani Popular Movement, who became the first freely elected President of Azerbaijan, was an Arabist. The leading Azerbaijani historian Ziya Buniatov entered the political field, becoming one of the founders of the Yeni Azerbaijan (New Azerbaijan) party which was the party of power under Heydar Aliev, and a member of the Milli Majlis (parliament) after 1995. Buniatov was assassinated in Baku in 1997, in circumstances which remain unclear.[4] Ardzinba, the self-proclaimed President of Abkhazia, is a historian of the medieval Caucasus, and Stanislav Lakoba, the former Deputy Speaker of Abkhazia, is also a historian. This pattern repeats itself partially in the North Caucasus: Yuri Shanibov (Musa Shanibov), the head of the Kabardin National Movement and one of the leaders of the Confederation of Peoples of the Caucasus (KNK), was a professor of sociology at Nalchik university;[5] although the first President of Chechnya, Djokhar Dudayev, was a general, there were several intellectuals in its leadership as well, such as the Vice-President under Dudayev, Zelimkhan Yandarbiev, a poet who after the assassination of Dudayev became the acting President of Chechnya. Military leaders have had their share of the leadership of the emergent national movements, alongside poets and professors, in the North Caucasus: apart from the example of Dudayev, there was the election of the former Soviet Army artillery officer Aslan Maskhadov to the presidency of Chechnya in 1997, and there was Ruslan Aushev, President of Ingushetia from 1993 until he was pushed by the Kremlin to resign in 2002.

There is no doubt that intellectuals and their perception of the nation played a key role in the emergence of the conflicts in the Caucasus. It was their capacity to articulate a vision of the nation, its glorious

---

4   While officials accused Vilayati al Fakih Hezbullah, the Iranian linked radical group, of being behind the assassination, certain figures of the opposition including Ali Kerimli, head of the National Front Party (Reformist), have openly accused the ruling elite of being behind the assassination as a result of an internal power struggle. I am grateful to Shahin Rzaev for providing me information about the political activities of Ziya Buniatov.

5   For more on Yuri Shanibov see Georgi M. Derluguian, *Bourdieu's Secret Admirer in the Caucasus, A World-System Biography*, Chicago University of Press, 2005.

past and current grievances, relevant to the political upheaval of the late 1980s, that was able to mobilize the emerging political forces. The nationalist intellectuals had two things necessary to exercise political leadership and become the absolute political force in such a short time frame: on the one hand, a radical rejection of Soviet, socialist, egalitarian ideology, by referring to the idea of the nation; and at the same time the capacity to claim long tradition, a body of thought, past political struggles, and an institutional framework, all necessary to be seen as credible and legitimate leaders in the eyes of the masses, by referring not only to the idea of the nation in the pre-1917 period but also to an intellectual tradition and numerous institutions that existed and developed in the Soviet era. No other movement could do this as effectively as the intellectuals expressing a nationalist project, because the ground for their political work was already there, existing in the late Soviet reality. Neither the emerging environmentalists nor the pro-Western democrats could challenge the hegemony of the nationalists for long, because although they could claim a radical break with the Soviet Union, they had only a shallow presence in the societies among which they were trying to recruit.

History, and the way history is imagined, have continued to play a central role in the shaping of the conflicts, even an increased role. Many years after the open confrontation ended, the conflict around history is as present as ever, showing that the smouldering sources of conflict are still with us. As we will see in the last chapter, the destruction of an ancient Armenian cemetery by 200 or so Azerbaijani soldiers in December 2005 led to an uproar in Armenia and international condemnations, while official reaction in Azerbaijan can be put as: the ancient cemetery was not Armenian, but Caucasian Albanian and therefore Azeri, and therefore we cannot destroy our own culture...[6]

Since the late 19th century, scholars studying nations and nationalism have been confronted with a major problem: concepts such as origin, ethnicity, language, territory and state did not always overlap, and not at all times in the past. As a result, many scholars made an effort to

---

6   Ganira Pashayeva: "Ancient Christian Monuments in Azerbaijan are Albanian", *Azerbaijan Today*, 24 January 2008: http://www.today.az/news/politics/42581. html; Azeri Press Agency, "Armenians Create website named Djulfa,", 18 January 2008: http://en.apa.az/news.php?id=42476.

reconcile the "errors" of history that did not correspond to the contemporary imperative of the national vision. In the late 19th century Russian historians, archaeologists and anthropologists, faced by the discoveries of mainly German scholars charting the Russian empire, tried to force the formula "name equals language equals territory equals state".[7] The classical problem is that history is often too complicated for this equation to be valid; this means selective claims and counter-claims, in turn resulting in clashes of visions of the nation. Such debates evolve into political clashes in times of systemic change, when societies move away from multi-ethnic empires and enter the age of the nation-state. The difficulty in such transformations is how to find justification for the birth of the new state and development of its institutions that can be seen as legitimate in the eyes of its constituency.

Although the Soviet Union was set to eliminate national differences, it nevertheless created national-territorial entities, becoming "the first modern state to place the national principle at the basis of its federal structure", in the much quoted phrase of Richard Pipes.[8] For the Bolsheviks, concessions to the national aspirations of the former colonized peoples of the Russian empire were a necessary step towards the goal of eliminating the national differences in the future classless society. They were also an honest attempt to put an end to a long history of expansion, conquest, colonization, and repression practiced by the regime of the Tsars against the conquered nations of Europe and Asia, and a future model of fraternity between the workers of various nations.

As a result of the institutional framework established by the Bolsheviks in the aftermath of the revolution and the Sovietization of the former Russian colonies, the titular nations in the union republics, as well as in the autonomous republics and the autonomous regions, received large sets of institutions which became the framework for the activities and development of the vision of the nation, unavailable in the conditions of the *ancien régime*. Those institutions included an ethnically defined territory, and cultural autonomy expressed through educational institu-

7   Yuri Slezkine, "N. Ia. Marr and the National Origins of Soviet Ethnogenesis", in Ronald Grigor Suny and Michael D. Kennedy, *Intellectuals and the Articulation of the Nation*, Ann Arbor: University of Michigan Press, 2001, p. 212.

8   Richard Pipes, *The Formation of the Soviet Union: Communism and Nationalism, 1917-23*, Cambridge, MA: Harvard University Press, 1954, p. 112.

tions and mass media in which the national language was dominant, but also structures such as writers' and artists' unions with subsidized national literature, national symbols such as flags and hymns, museums commemorating the national past and its cultural achievements, and the production of national histories. Moreover, the ethnically defined territory also enjoyed a local administrative structure dominated by a titular nation, with relative independence from the central authorities in running local affairs, gifted with a national *nomenklatura*. Therefore, the ruling elites of the national entities could refer to those numerous institutions to legitimize their political, nationalist project, and mobilize the masses around it. Those national groups that were not recognized by the Soviet system did not enjoy those privileges.

For many nationalist writers, the few years of national independence between the fall of Tsarism and the Sovietization that followed are presented as the reference for their aspirations, contrasted with long decades of Soviet rule in which these aspirations were trampled underfoot. The Bolsheviks are largely seen as enemies of nationalism, as having aimed to construct a post-national political and social structure. But as the Bolsheviks took power in Russia and expanded their power over most of the former imperial realm, their policies towards the national minorities took an unexpected form; as Ronald Suny has argued, the project of the Soviet state contained a certain tension between socialist internationalism and nationalism (or the national liberation programme). The concessions made in the early years of the Soviet formation to the national aspirations of the various peoples of the former Tsarist Empire were understood by the Bolshevik leadership as temporary steps on the road of their social engineering project in which the idea of the nation would become less pronounced. The nature of Soviet policies towards the non-Russian ethnic groups was often pragmatic, and politically conditioned—in other words, it contained numerous contradictions. Studying the language policies of the Soviet Union at the height of Stalinism, one author concludes: "The very nature of the Soviet multinational state remained ambiguous to its rulers."[9] It was thought that if the national ambitions

---

9   Peter A. Blietstein, "Nation-Building or Russification? Obligatory Russian Instruction in the Soviet Non-Russian School, 1938-1953", in Ronald Grigor Suny and Terry Martin (eds), *A State of Nations, Empire and Nation-Making in the Age of Lenin and Stalin*, Oxford University Press, 2001, p. 253. The level of Russian language education also varied widely in this period. In 1938-39, "In

of the peoples colonized by the former empire were satisfied, the political drive for the national groups towards separatism would decrease, if not disappear completely. But very soon, as the state institutions took a rigid form, the "Soviet Thermidor" led to the development of a ruling "caste" of bureaucrats, according to Trotsky's criticism of the Stalinist regime. The Soviet adventure developed into something different from the initial utopian project imagined by the Bolshevik revolutionaries when they were still dispersed between exile and the underground. Among other aspects the policy towards national minorities took a specific turn, evolved into a new experiment. "Rather than a melting pot, the Soviet Union became the incubator of new nations."[10]

The territorial divisions imposed by Moscow that often echoed Tsarist administrative divisions, the brief independent republics following the revolution, the forced collectivisation under Stalin, the mass repression of the intelligentsia and the national cadres, the deportation of entire populations, left an imprint on the national consciousness in unique ways. The diffused identities that formed the basis of national-territorial divisions in the 1920s turned into developed nations under the long-term impact of Soviet-made institutions. In the words of Rogers Brubaker, "The Soviet Union was neither conceived in theory nor organized in practice as a nation-state. Yet while it did not define the state or citizenry as a *whole* in national terms, it did define component *parts* of the state and the citizenry in national terms."[11] The Soviet Union developed nationhood, while it repressed nationalism as a political expression, as it repressed any other independent political thought and action.

The initial temporary policy of promoting an ethno-political hierarchy became permanent, it made ethnic politics a factor of growing importance in the internal institutional life, in division of territory and resources. The ethnic hierarchy had numerous levels, with the Russian nation represented as the model and reference of the new Soviet citizen, followed by the titular nations of the republics occupying dominant positions within

---

Azerbaijan, for example, Russian was taught in only 40-50 per cent of all rural primary schools in that school year; in Armenia the figure was 70-80 per cent": Blietstein, p. 260.

10   Ronald Suny, *The Revenge of the Past*, p. 87.

11   Rogers Brubaker, *Nationalism Reframed, Nationhood and the National Question in the New Europe*, Cambridge University Press, 1996, p. 29.

their structures, while in a third position came the various autonomous structures within the Union republics, and ethnic minorities without any administrative structure were left at the bottom.[12] This hierarchy of ethnic groups was best expressed in the political structures such as the positions distributed within the Communist Party leadership, the central state bureaucracy, and the military establishment. As we will see later, the Soviet military policies of ethnic preference were to have important consequences in the later wars in the Caucasus. Consider the ethnic structure of the Soviet armed forces, and nationality policies within this institution: while Caucasians, as well as Central Asians, were numerous in the armed forces, they were hardly represented in the higher echelons of the Red Army. For example, in 1990, 97 per cent of the officer corps was Russian, Byelorussian, Ukrainian, and Tatar.[13] Moreover, the Soviet army followed a policy of imposing military service outside one's own national republic. While low fluency in Russian could be one reason to explain this low representation of Caucasians in the military, one should not exclude political motivations as well.

The "nationalizing state" of Brubaker, which came about in the conditions of independent nation-states in central-eastern Europe, took a particular form for the fifteen union republics that made up the USSR and the many more autonomous structures, where the nation-building process was structured, imposed, led, encouraged, financed—but also on occasions repressed, when it found political expression—by the Soviet state.

Within the Soviet hierarchy of nations, the representation of the history of a given nation played an important role in legitimising the importance, and therefore the political relevance, of a given ethnic group. For ethnic minorities, access to certain privileges within the system could only be granted to what the Soviet authorities considered as an authentic indigenous ethnic group. According to Victor Shnirelman:

---

12   This "ethnic hierarchy" was practiced in different ways in different Soviet institutions. If one takes the most important melting pot, the Red Army, the following hierarchy could be noticed: the Russian and generally Slav element in the higher echelons of the army, the Baltic and the other Christian nations (Armenians and Georgians) occupying a second position, with the Muslim peoples at the base of the pyramid, where their role within the Red Army was limited to construction battalions and kitchen work; very few specialized officers of the army had a Central Asian background.

13   William E. Odom, *The Collapse of the Soviet Military*, New Haven: Yale University Press, 1998, p. 45.

[T]he concept of authenticity was of crucial political importance, to the extent that it made them artificially conserve and retain those folk traditions, which, under different conditions, would have failed to survive in the industrial and post-industrial environment. For the same reason, the primordialist approach enjoyed great respect within Soviet ideology. Thus, a prestigious past was unanimously valued as a highly desirable support for arguments, which might facilitate a successful struggle for desirable privileges.[14]

In a highly ideological context, national historians had to create new national histories of Abkhazia, Armenia, Azerbaijan, Chechnya, Georgia, Ossetia and many others, which at the same time could be compatible with the directives arriving from Moscow, and reflected the political needs in the power struggle for recognition within the context of the Caucasus. For the Soviet authorities, after creating new ethno-territorial entities at different levels (union republics, autonomous republics, autonomous regions, etc.) it was important to provide the new entities with distinct attributes of a "nation": history, literature, language, alphabet and culture. During this process of "nation-building", coherent methodology, factual precision, and simple scientific integrity were not always respected, to say the least. While professional historians tried to follow a certain degree of methodological coherence in specialised publications, they felt freer to express their mind, if not their feelings, in popular publications. What Shnirelman calls "amateur authors", such as journalists, writers, and various intellectual celebrities, were less restricted by a scientific methodology or a professional ethic.

The attempts to legitimise the national-territorial entities created by the Soviet rule led to rewriting of history not only in the Soviet centre, but also in the periphery republics. As Valery Tishkov puts it, certain professionals such as ethnologists and archaeologies have a heavy share of responsibility in this enterprise. "Political and heavily ideological archaeology and ethnography have flourished for decades in the academies – central and peripheral – of the former Soviet Union."[15] Soviet sponsored intellectuals were thus the gravediggers of the Soviet multinational state.

---

14   Victor A. Shnirelman, *The Value of the Past: Myths, Identity and Politics in Transcaucasia*, Osaka: National Museum of Ethnology, 2001, p. 4.

15   Velery Tishkov, *Ethnicity, Nationalism and Conflict in and After the Soviet Union*, London: SAGE Publications, 1997, p. 13.

The situation got only worse in the late *perestroika* years, when the idea of the nation became the banner of struggle against the embattled Soviet regime. In the case of Georgia, a French historian remarked after attending a history conference in Tbilisi that history was increasingly "escaping" professional historians in the name of fighting against "Bolshevik nihilism".[16] To claim a new system of legitimacy, history had to be called as witness, and history was transformed from an academic domain into an instrument of ideology building.

In this race to achieve the status of the oldest, autochthonous ethnic group in the Caucasus, not all nations had the same departing point, not all national histories provided the same resources. While Armenians and Georgians could refer to a long past of national-state formation, an individual literature, language, and a unique alphabet going back centuries, the same was not available for others, for example Azerbaijani historians and intellectuals. "It was territory rather than history that until recently was of importance for the Azeries, who identified their homeland with their native habitat (vatan)," writes Shnirelman.[17] As a result, many intellectuals representing nations that did not have historic references to reflect the contemporary needs of legitimating their Soviet institutions through the optic of long-surviving national traditions had the choice of either losing the battle or simply creating a national tradition. An example was the great writer of Azerbaijan Mirza Fath Ali Akhunzade, who wrote in the vernacular that he called "*turki*" and not "*azeri*", and most often called himself Persian.[18]

I mentioned above that in the first generation of leadership of the national movements, the proportion of intellectuals was very high; this was followed by a prominent presence of military people, especially in Chechnya and Ingushetia. I also argued that visions of the national history, and the history of neighbouring nations, played a significant role in preparing initially intellectual clashes about one's own place, about the glorious national past, and about the loss of national prestige and

---

16   Charles Urgewicz, "La Transcaucasie face aux fantômes de son passé: le cas géorgien", in Mohammad–Reza Djalili (ed.), *Le Caucase postsoviétique: La transition dans le conflit*, Brussels: Bruylant, 1995, p. 39.

17   Ibid., p. 21.

18   Olivier Roy, *La nouvelle Asie centrale, ou la fabrication des nations*, Paris: Seuil, 1997, p. 122.

authority mainly due to neighbouring national groups. This competition was influenced by Soviet policies of creating ethnic hierarchies, where autochthonous ethnic groups had more prestige, respect, and eventually political power, compared with "newcomers".

The work of historians, therefore, came under double pressure. On the one hand they had to work within the institutional and ideological frame of the Soviet policies of a given time. On the other hand, they had to bear in mind the public opinion and the social pressure of their own culture, and to promote the interest of their own ethnic group and defend it against pressure coming from the centre or neighbouring competitors. These working conditions of Soviet historians led to two shortcomings. Scientific methodology had to be sacrificed to bend history and serve either party directives or the interest of the nation. On the other hand, the politicisation of history led to a high level consensus within the profession, tolerating little diversity, discussion or debate that could challenge the official version of the past or the present needs of history in the ongoing political battles.

In the following section, I will summarize the dominant interpretations of the history of individual nations that came into conflict with other visions present among neighbouring ethnic groups, or even with those promoted by a neighbouring Soviet Socialist Republic.

The Karabakh conflict in Armenian historiography

For Soviet Armenian historians, the Karabakh question was one of the most burning issues. In contrast with Diaspora Armenian historians who were haunted by the Armenian Genocide by Ottoman Turkey during the First World War, and the First Armenian Republic under the Tashnaktsutyun (1918-20), Soviet Armenian historians were engaged in a struggle to defend or reclaim the Armenian character of Mountainous Karabakh, in an ongoing and hardly veiled political struggle between Yerevan and Baku. This struggle shaped much of Armenian (as well as Azerbaijani) historiography in the post-Stalin Soviet era. The debate among historians, in its turn, had a direct impact in shaping public opinion and the creation of national stereotypes and "historical myths".

Armenian historians worked to address the questions of the Armenians' presence in the eastern parts of Asia Minor since antiquity; the linguistic relationship between Armenians and other peoples that lived in the same lands, with a special focus on the kingdom of Urartu and its ethnic and cultural composition; the Armenian presence in Artsakh and Utik, medieval provinces on the eastern borders of the Armenian kingdom which compose the contemporary Karabakh region, in both its mountainous and its lower parts; the nature of the Caucasian Albanian people; and the ethnic composition of Karabakh and Nakhichevan, as well as Yerevan province, in the Tsarist period.

Armenian historiography and archaeology tried to find continuity between the earlier Nairi civilization (13th century BC) and Urartian civilization (around Lake Van, 9th to 7th centuries BC) and the Armenian kingdom that developed around the 6th century BC.[19] According to René Grousset, the Armenian tribes entered the kingdom of Urartu around the 7th century BC; that kingdom was much weakened by long wars against the Assyrian Empire to the south, and resisted Scythian invasions coming from the north. But many Armenian historians in the last two decades of the Soviet era tried to push back the Armenian presence in the eastern parts of Asia Minor to centuries earlier than the 7th century BC, without sufficient compelling evidence to support their arguments. In this period, a young generation of Armenian historians tried to identify the Hayasa polity[20] with later Armenian ethnic and linguistic characteristics, projecting an Armenian presence in what is now eastern Turkey and the southern Caucasus back to the second millennium BC.[21] The short-lived empire of Tigran the Great (or Tigran II, 95-55 BC) that stretched from the Caspian Sea to the Mediterranean, but was later defeated by the Roman legions of Pompey, is a landmark of Armenian military achievements and the strength of its statehood, two elements that are scarce in the Armenian history of the Middle Ages, and especially after the 11th

---

19   René Grousset, *Histoire de l'Arménie*, Paris: Payot, first published in 1947, 1984 edition, pp. 45-7. Grousset calls the Urartian kingdom "Arménie préarméninenne".

20   In the Armenian language, *Hay* means Armenian, and *Hayasdan* means Armenia.

21   Graham Smith, Vivien Law, Andrew Wilson, Annette Bohr and Edward Allworth, *Nation-building in the Post-Soviet Borderlands, The Politics of National Identities*, Cambridge University Press, 1998, p. 51. See the detailed discussion of Armenian historiography concerning the questions of "migrants" versus "indigenous people" in Shnirelman, *The Value of the Past*, chapters three and four, pp. 33-55.

century. On the other hand, the adoption of Christianity circa 301 AD (Armenia was the first nation to elevate Christianity to be the state religion) was not emphasized, because of its religious nature and its clash with official Soviet atheism—religion in general being reduced to its cultural dimension and its role in the formation of national identity. Religious symbols such as churches and monasteries were used as landmarks to identify the territorial expansion of the Armenians in past centuries.[22] Similarly, the creation of the Armenian alphabet in the 5th century by the priest Mesrob Mashdots was celebrated as a landmark in Armenian history, but void of its religious dimension.

Those discussions were taking place in a period when the Armenian presence in Asia Minor was challenged by Turkish and Azerbaijani historians, who had "Turkified" the early Hittite civilization in Anatolia and the Caucasian Albanian one to the east on the shores of the Caspian Sea. As a response to such arguments, Soviet Armenian historians tried to push theories that ethnic Armenians were "natives" to the region, and therefore had to negate the thesis that Armenians were "migrants", even if such a migration could have taken place twenty-six centuries earlier! In the context of the Soviet era competition for "indigenous" status was important to acquire legitimacy and political status within the Soviet hierarchy of nations. Old manuscripts, archaeological evidence, ruins of monasteries, cemeteries, references in Hellenistic, Roman and Byzantine sources were all important components to prove a long Armenian presence in the eastern part of Asia Minor, the result being the politicising of history, archaeology and philology.

The battles between Armenian and Azerbaijani historians had a special focus on the origins, nature, and evolution of the Caucasian Albanians. There are few references to this people, or tribal alliance, which lived in regions lying between the eastern borders of Armenia and Georgia and the Caspian Sea, and between the Caucasus mountains in the north and the Kura and Arax rivers in the south.[23] They were called *Aghvank* in

---

22   The reduction of religion to its cultural dimension was not only a problem in historic perspective, but also affected Armenian historiography; most of the major classical Armenian historical works such as the *History* of Agathangeghos, the *History* of Movses Khorenatsi, and the *History of Vardan and the Armenian War* of Eghishe evolve around religion and its role in Armenian history.

23   Enayetullah Reza, *Azerpayjan yev Aran (Govgasyan Albania)* [in Armenian, translated from Persian, "Azerbaijan and Aran (Caucasian Albania)"], Yerevan:

Armenian, *Arran* in Persian and Arabic writings, *Albania* in Greek and Byzantine records. An ancient Caucasian people now long extinct, the Caucasian Albanians have left little traces, and much of their history remains to be explored and narrated; therefore a great deal of exploration and research is needed to recompose their history. Nevertheless, their history is currently being exploited for political purposes in the ongoing struggle over the Karabakh region, and is used to legitimate one claim or the other.

To face Azerbaijani claims about the Caucasian Albanians, Armenian historians have concentrated their efforts on emphasizing the link between the Armenian statehood of past centuries and the contemporary territories of Karabakh. The Armenian argument is based on demonstrating that the frontier between Armenia and Caucasian Albania was the Kura river, that Karabakh (both the lowlands and the mountainous region) was until the fifth century the two easternmost provinces of Armenia Artsakh and Utik, that even after it was occupied by the Caucasian Albanians Armenian was spoken in those territories; and demonstrating the close link between Armenians and Caucasian Albanians, whereby those later came under Armenian religious, linguistic, and cultural influence by being converted to Christianity under Armenian influence and becoming part of the Armenian church.[24]

Another issue of controversy was the demographic composition of Mountainous Karabakh (as well as Zangezur and Nakhichevan). While Azerbaijani sources insisted that Armenians were newcomers to the Karabakh territories, mainly because of Russian imperial policies at the beginnings of the Tsarist domination over the Transcaucasus, Armenian sources provide different figures concerning those population movements in the early 19th century.[25] Moreover, Armenian historians felt

---

Piunik, 1994, p. 26.

24   On the history of Artsakh and Utik provinces of Armenia, and their relations with Caucasian Albania see: Patrick Donabedian and Claude Mutafian, *Artsakh, Histoire du Karabagh*, Paris: Sevig Press, 1989, pp. 10-16.

25   One historian writes that of the 40-45,000 Armenians who migrated from Persia to the newly conquered Russian territories "only a small fraction stayed in the region of Karabakh, from which some were later dispersed into other cities. Some of them even reached Tiflis [Tbilisi] and laid down permanent residence there." From T.Kh. Hagopian, *Hayasdani Badmagan Ashkharakroutyun* [in Armenian: Armenian Historical Geography], Yerevan: Midk, 1968, p. 444.

obliged to refute these charges and prove long-term Armenian presence in Mountainous Karabakh, and referred to the numerous Armenian monasteries in Karabakh (whether within the administrative borders of the Nagorno Karabakh or in neighbouring regions), such as Tsitsernavank (V-VI centuries), Dadivank (XII-XIII centuries), or Gandzasar (XIII century), and numerous *khachkars,*[26] and the absence of similar Azerbaijani monuments over the same territory dating from before the 18th and 19th centuries. Armenian historians also refer to the presence of Armenian noble rulers in Karabakh in the late Middle Ages, the Armenian *meliks* (nobles) who retained semi-independent rule within the Persian Empire in the 16th century.

Armenian sources insist that in the upper part of Karabakh a predominant ethnic Armenian population continued to live there all through Persian rule and until the arrival of the Russian empire in the region. They regarded Azerbaijanis as the descendents of Turkic tribes who migrated to the Transcaucasus from the 11th century. Karabakh was seen as the last bastion of resistance of an Armenian political system which came under Turkic rule very late in history, that is, around the 17th century. More than anywhere else, Armenians in Karabakh have preserved a drive for autonomy, and tried to exploit any chance to revive their self-rule. In this perspective, the Karabakh Armenian struggle is articulated as a fight for self-determination and decolonization (not from Russian and Soviet, but from Azerbaijani rule). From the early 20th century, protests and struggle continued during the Soviet era through a series of petitions signed by Karabakh Armenian intellectuals and sent to Moscow. As early as 1962, a petition signed by 2,500 Karabakh Armenians was sent to Khrushchev to denounce anti-Armenian policies applied by Baku, reminding the Soviet leader of the initial promise to attach Mountainous Karabakh to Armenia. The culmination of this struggle was the start of the movement for *miyatsoum* (unification) in 1988, when the leadership and the Armenian population of Mountainous Karabakh clearly expressed their will through the unanimous vote of the Supreme Soviet of the Mountainous Karabakh Autonomous Oblast in February 1988 and the popular demonstrations in Stepanakert,

---

26   *Khachkars* (in Armenian it literally means cross-stones) are tombstones in the centre of which there is traditionally the form of the cross, with various motifs decorating its sides, sometimes referring to Biblical stories.

calling for Karabakh to be brought under Soviet Armenian jurisdiction. From the Armenian perspective, the annexation of Karabakh (as well as that of Nakhichevan) to Azerbaijan was the result of Soviet foreign policy aiming to please nationalist Turkey under Mustafa Kemal, and was explained by the personal intervention of Stalin himself to reverse a previous ruling by local Communists to include Karabakh (as well as Nakhichevan) within the newly created Soviet Armenia.[27]

Azerbaijani historians and the Karabakh question

Soviet Azerbaijani historians had a difficult task in adapting historical writing to the political requirements of the Soviet state. The concept of Azerbaijan itself was recent when the Soviet Union was formed, being a contemporary phenomenon, linked to the Musavat-led independence of Azerbaijan in 1918-20. Nevertheless, Azerbaijani historians had to lay claim to deep historic roots to legitimize the Soviet Azerbaijani republic, to bring a multi-ethnic and multi-lingual unit under homogeneous rule. Moreover, under the pressure of Soviet policies of territorial pressure on Persia at the end of the Second World War, Azerbaijani history had to play a role to justify and legitimize Stalin's ambitions. To solve this riddle Azerbaijani historians had to insist on the territorial unity of Azerbaijan and to disregard ethnic, linguistic and religious inconsistencies, with all the problems such an approach could create.

By the 1980s, Azerbaijani historians were leading battles on three fronts: to reassess the relationship of Azerbaijan with Soviet and Russian influence (which had for many decades presented the Muslim nations of the USSR as profiting from the civilizing mission of Russian conquerors); to lay claim to southern Azerbaijan (following a long tradition of historical works claiming that Azerbaijan was "divided" as a result of imperial plots between Russians and Persians); and to struggle to find legitimation and historical justification for Azerbaijani rule over Karabakh.

---

27 Nakhichevan received the status of an Autonomous Republic, and Karabakh the lower status of an Autonomous Region, and were both placed within the Azerbaijani SSR. Tishkov, op. cit., p. 232; Christopher J. Walker, "The Armenian Presence in Mountainous Karabakh", in John Wright, Suzanne Goldenberg and Richard Schoefield (eds), *Transcaucasian Boundaries*. London: UCL Press, 1996, p. 100.

While reference to the major themes of Soviet history continued, subtle differences aimed to revise the basic tenets of Soviet historiography and its claim of Russia bringing a more advanced civilization to Azerbaijan. As we have seen at the beginning of this chapter, Soviet dogma needed "national histories" to justify and legitimate the Soviet administrative system, in which union republics had to claim legitimacy for their ethno-territorial existence while remaining clearly subordinated to the leading role of the Russian culture and civilizing mission.[28] The main themes of Azerbaijani historiographic "revisionism" focused much on the relationship between Russians and Azerbaijanis, whether in the Tsarist or the Soviet period, on the ethnogenesis of the Azerbaijanis and the cultural past of Turkic and Muslim peoples, and on the conditions in which Azerbaijan "joined" the Soviet Union. Various studies reflected questions intellectuals had already posed in the early 20th century, and were typically challenged the intellectual argumentations of Tsarist and later Soviet hegemony. Again, as in the debates in the early 20th century, those new histories looked at the broader history of the Turkic peoples of the USSR in its entirety, and the role that Azerbaijani intellectuals played in this context.

This "reclaiming of history", as Audrey A. Altstadt called it, nevertheless oscillated between opposition to Soviet official historiography, around which the various Turkic histories could have been seen under a unified shade, and another tendency whereby the main aim became to justify and legitimize the individual character of the Union Republics.

In the late 1980s and early 90s numerous historians, whether from the USSR or Westerners, over-emphasized Russian and Soviet policies of creating distinctions among Turkic and Muslim nations of the Soviet Republics:

This confused usage in Russian [of Turk, Turkic, and Turkish, which in Russian would be Turek, Turkskii, and Turetski] was not, however, merely an error. The use of "Turkic", like the so-called "national" names (Uzbek, Kazakh, Azerbaid-

---

28   On the leading role of the Russian language in the Soviet system, see Paul R. Brass, "Language and National Identity in the Soviet Union and India", in Alexander J. Motyl (ed.), *Thinking Theoretically About Soviet Nationalities*, New York: Columbia University Press, 1992, pp. 110-11. See also the chapter by Simon Dixon, "The Russians: the Dominant Nationality", in Graham Smith (ed.), *The Nationalities Question in the Soviet Union,* London: Longman, 1990, pp. 21-39.

zhani) applied in the 1930s, constituted an attempt to portray a greater ethnic and linguistic distance between groups and subgroups than actually exists. (...) [T]he Soviet regime strove to divide the Central Asians geographically by drawing borders, as well as culturally and politically. (...) "Separate" histories were created which ignored or denied common origin".[29]

While it is difficult to argue against the fact that the Soviets did try to challenge pan-Islamic, North Caucasus Mountain Peoples', and pan-Turkic identities, one should not presume that within these categories major divisions did not exist, and that without Soviet policies such cross-continent solidarity would have led to political formations embracing such diverse regions, peoples, and societies such as those living in Azerbaijan and in the North Caucasus, the Middle Volga, and Central Asia. Nor did such a unity of Turkic or Muslim peoples exist in any political sense prior to Tsarist colonialism or Soviet rule, to make it possible to see Soviet policies as responsible for dividing previously existing peoples. The contrary claim is nearer to historic reality: both Russian and Soviet rule brought political unity over societies and territories that were divided by local clans and tribes, imbued with regional identities and ruled by khanates suffering from internal divisions, competitions, and violent struggles. The weakening of the localist identities and the khanate system opened the way to the formation of nation-state structures. According to Tadeusz Swietochowski, Tsarist dismantling of the khanates in reforms in the early 19th century "weakened deeply local particularisms" and led to the formation of "territorial blocks" which did not exist in the region before the arrival of the Russians.[30]

Azerbaijani historians had a difficult time challenging the Armenian perspective, and proving as legitimate Azerbaijan's rule over the land attributed to it by the Soviet state, through references in ancient history (the "name equals language equals territory equals state" perspective). This was because, in the past, the people of Azerbaijan had identified themselves through a multitude of categories other than that of the "nation"—or to be more precise, categories that in the modern age could be converted to that of the modern nation. Those categories were

---

29   Audrey L. Altstadt, "Rewriting Turkic History in the Gorbachev Era", *Journal of Soviet Nationalities*, Summer 1991, Vol. II, Number 2, p. 82.

30   Tadeusz Swietochowski, *Russia and Azerbaijan, A Borderland in Transition*, New York: Columbia University Press, 1995, p. 17.

on the macro level linked to the empire in which they lived at a given moment, for example the Safavids or the Qajars, who were originally Turkic speaking dynasties of Iran and who dominated much of the Transcaucasus, and with Shiism, the official religion and ideology of the Persian empire.[31] On the micro level, they identified themselves with the geographical region in which they lived, and in the context of which their social tissue and regional particularism was developed.

Therefore, the "resources" at the disposal of Armenian and Azerbaijani historians working on the ethnogenesis of their peoples were uneven. One book summarizes the differences in the following manner:

Ethnogenetic studies began in both republics in the 1940s, but their starting points, goals and basic historical resources were quite different. First, the relative rich Armenian historiographical tradition can be traced back to the first millennium AD, whereas the Azerbaijani historiographical tradition was really established only in the twentieth century. Secondly, the Armenians can plausibly refer to the Kingdom of Tigran the Great (95-56 BC) as the cradle of their statehood, whereas Azerbaijanis have no real past polity to celebrate before the establishment of the Azerbaijani SSR. Finally, the Armenians have been known as a distinct ethnic group with their own proper name since the first millennium BC, whereas the consolidation of the Azerbaijanis as a coherent ethnic group took place only after the 1920s.[32]

It is difficult to find a consensus on the designation of the present-day Azerbaijanis before the twentieth century. Swietochowski says that they were called "Shirvanis and sometimes even by the medieval name Arranis".[33] The Russians called them "Tartars", or Caucasian Muslims, which were also terms used in European sources. At the moment of the creation of the first Azerbaijani state (1918-20), its elite had difficulties deciding whether to have a pan-Turkish, pro-Persian, pro-Ottoman, Great Azerbaijani, or independent Azerbaijani stand, and the choice was dictated by the political winds blowing at any given moment of

---

31   Although the ethnic roots of Shah Isma'il Khan, the founder of the Safavid dynasty in Tabriz in 1501, are debated, he was a native of Ardebil and a Turkic-speaker. See Brenda Shaffer, *Borders and Brethren, Iran and the Challenge of Azerbaijani Identity*, Cambridge, MA: MIT Press, 2002, p. 19. On the roots of the Qajar dynasty, see: Cyrus Ghani, *Iran and the Rise of Reza Shah, From Qajar Collapse to Pahlavi Power*, London: I.B. Tauris, 2000, p. 1.

32   Graham Smith et al., op. cit., p. 50.

33   Tadeusz Swietochowski, op. cit, p. 10.

this troubled period. Until then Azerbaijanis identified themselves with their Sunni-Shi'a divide, with regional belonging, or with the greater Iranian cultural domain. It was only in the early 20th century that ideas of pan-Turkism, and later Azerbaijani nationalism, started developing among the Azerbaijanis in Baku, Elizavetpol (now Ganja) and Tabriz, under the influence of the rise of a new intelligentsia and European influence.

A major issue in the historic debate about the Azerbaijani ethnogenesis is the relationship between northern (Azerbaijani republic) and southern Azerbaijan (Iranian Azerbaijan). Are they one people? Or are they two distinct ethnic groups who started speaking a similar Turkic dialect and therefore created an outer appearance of similarity? In the 4th century AD two state structures were identifiable in the area called Azerbaijan today: Caucasian Albania, situated to the north of Arax (or Aras) river, and Aturpatakan in the south, around today's northern Iranian city of Tabriz.[34] Contemporary Azerbaijani historians as well as some Western writers claim that Azerbaijanis in the Republic of Azerbaijan and in Iran are one people, divided by the Russo-Iranian partition of 1828 with the Turkmanchai treaty.[35] Other historians, especially Iranian authors, consider that the two peoples had distinct origins, and no confusion must be made between the two. For example, Enayetullah Riza emphasizes the distinctness of Caucasian Albanians from the population of Aturpatakan by saying that between these two peoples other tribes and ethnic groups lived, such as the Talish.[36] Shireen Hunter has written to show how Soviet policies of expansion towards Iranian territory have been behind the "Myth of Greater Azerbaijan", and how this myth has been adopted by Azerbaijani nationalist intellectuals since the Soviet collapse. For example, Hunter shows how Azerbaijanis claim

---

34   See Audrey L. Altstadt, *The Azerbaijani Turks, Power and Identity under Russian Rule*, Stanford, CA: Hoover Press, 1992, p. 2.

35   Swietochowski, *Russia and Azerbaijan,* op. cit., p. 6-7; Brenda Shaffer, *Borders and Brethren, Iran and the Challenge of Azerbaijani Identity*, Cambridge, MA: MIT Press, 2002, p. 4.

36   Enayetullah Riza, *Azerbaijan yev Aran*, Yerevan: Pyunik, 1994, p. 15. On the separate histories of Caucasian Albania (northern Azerbaijan) and Arran (southern Azerbaijan), see Shireen Hunter, "Greater Azerbaijan: Myth or Reality?" in M.-R. Djalili (ed.), *Le Caucase postsoviétique: La transition dans le conflit*, Brussels: Bruylant, 1995, pp. 115-42; and Atabaki Touraj, *Azerbaijan, Ethnicity and the Struggle for power in Iran*, London: I.B. Tauris, 2000, pp. 7-13.

that their country was "divided" in the conspiracy of the Turkmanchai agreement of 1828 between Russia and Persia, while in fact Turkmanchai was a capitulation for the Persian Qajars, concluded to avoid losing Tabriz—a former capital—and what is now Iranian Azerbaijan to the Russians.[37] Without going into too much detail on this historical controversy, it is interesting to emphasize that the initial Armenian mobilization around the Karabakh question diverted Azerbaijani nationalism away from the question of Southern Azerbaijan and the creation of Greater Azerbaijan, and thus kept Azerbaijan away from a potential and much more dangerous clash with its huge neighbour to the south, the Islamic Republic of Iran.

In the 1960s, Azerbaijani histories tried to develop theories that were politically expedient at that moment. Two leading figures in this enterprise were Igrar Aliev and Ziya Buniatov, specialists in ancient history. Aliev defended his thesis entitled "History of Media" in 1960, in which he focused on the early stages of Iranian history and developed a concept of the role of Media in the formation of the Azeri ethnogenesis. He wrote of the influence of various peoples and tribes who had left their mark in history on the territory of today's Azerbaijan, including the Medes and Albanians, who in fact spoke very different languages belonging to two distinct linguistic groups: the first Iranian and the second Caucasian. This was an intellectual answer "to the call of the Azerbaijan authorities to provide arguments in favour of the autochthonous formation of the Azeri people."[38] Later, in a book published in Baku Buniatov focused exclusively on the "Albanian" line, dropping the inclusion of Medes as proposed by Aliev. For Buniatov, the modern Azerbaijanis were direct descendents of the Caucasian Albanians.[39]

---

37   Shireen T. Hunter, *The Transcaucasus in Transition, Nation-Building in Conflict*, Washington: The Center for Strategic and International Studies, 1994, p. 60; and Swietichowski, op. cit, p. 6.

38   Shnirelman, op. cit., p. 118.

39   The original work in Azerbaijani was titled *Azarabaijan Vii-ix asrlarda* (Baku: Dovlat Nashiyati, 1965). See Michael P. Croissant, *The Armenia-Azerbaijan Conflict, Causes and Implications*, London: Praeger, 1998, p. 22, footnote 56. See also Shnirelman, ibid., pp. 120-2. Buniatov's book was initially published in 5,000 copies, but was reprinted in 1989, at the time of the start of the Karabakh conflict, in 35,000 copies—yet another indication of the role played by historical debates in the nationalist mobilizations taking place in the late Soviet period.

In order to resolve the contradiction between the Turkic identity of contemporary Azerbaijanis and the Caucasian culture of the ancient Albanians, Azerbaijani historians started looking for references to Turkic presence on the western shores of the Caspian starting from the pre-Christian era.[40] In other words, the Caucasian Albanians of the pre-Christian era and until the 7th century were brought closer to the contemporary Turkic identity of the Azerbaijanis. The question of authenticity of such claims was secondary, as was the fact that such manipulations of history confused the characteristics of the little known Caucasian Albanians. In later writings Professor Buniatov claimed that Karabakh Armenians were not really Armenians, but "Armenized Albanians". By virtue of such an intellectual spin Armenians, in the mind of Professor Buniatov and his students, had no right to claim to the churches, *khachkar*s, and monasteries of the Middle Ages that litter the landscape of contemporary Karabakh, and this cultural heritage belongs to the Azerbaijanis, since it is the descendants of Caucasian Albanians (the ancestors of contemporary Azerbaijani people) who can lay claim on the cultural heritage of Mountainous Karabakh.

An Azerbaijani scholar, a teacher of history in the Azerbaijani Academy of Sciences, in order to stress Azerbaijan's legitimate right over Mountainous Karabakh, after quoting Buniatov and his student Farida Mammedova concludes: "Thus, over a period of 1600 years, Karabakh as a whole and its upper section (Nagorno) in particular formed part of Azerbaijani state formations or represented of themselves an administrative unit of the Azerbaijani provinces."[41]

Other historians went back to a period twenty-four centuries before and created maps of historic Azerbaijan including the present-day Karabakh but also "southern Azerbaijan", which is the Turkic-speaking region of contemporary north-western Iran.[42] For Azerbaijani authors, therefore, Armenians of Karabakh, as well as Armenians of contempo-

---

40   Audrey L. Altstadt, "Azerbaijanis Reassess Their History", *Report on the USSR*, Munich, 18 August 1989, p. 18.

41   Sulejman Alijarly, "The Republic of Azerbaijan: Notes on the State Borders in the Past and the Present", in John F.R. Wright, Suzanne Goldenberg and Richard Schofield (eds), *Transcaucasian Boundaries*, London: UCL Press, 1996, p. 124.

42   Altstadt, op. cit., p. 19.

rary Armenia, were migrants moving to Tsarist controlled lands from Iran or from the Ottoman Empire in the early 19th century.[43]

In other words, for official Azerbaijani historiography, Karabakh is an ancient land of the Caucasian Albanian civilization, which strangely enough left behind Armenian churches and *khachkars*[44] but since these Armenian churches and *khachkars* are the creations of Caucasian Albanians who are the ancestors of contemporary Azerbaijanis they should belong to Azerbaijan. On the other hand, the contemporary Armenian population is considered to be descended from migrants who were encouraged to move to Karabakh by the invading Russian armies, and consequently have no legitimate right to claim Karabakh as Armenian. For Armenian historiography, on the other hand, Azerbaijanis are descendents of Turkic tribes who were introduced to the Caucasus with the invasions starting with the Seljuk waves of the 11th century,[45] and consequently "newcomers" to the long history of the region. Clearly, between the Armenian interpretation of history and the Azerbaijani recreation of it there is an obvious clash and little possibility of dialogue, at least under the circumstances of competition as it was conditioned by the Soviets. Armenian and Azerbaijani historians, who were under pressure from the Soviet bureaucracy on the one hand and from their societies on the other, had little choice but to present themselves as indigenous peoples to preserve their titular nation status, and to present their neighbours as migrants, regardless of the historical evidence. Such a reading of the past has contemporary consequences: both neighbours look at each other as newcomers, as inherently not belonging to the region but an outside element to the region, and consequently not rep-

---

43 Alijarly talks about Armenian population of Karabakh increasing from 8.4 per cent in 1823 to 34.8 per cent in 1832, op. cit., p. 127.

44 Although the writings on those churches are in Armenian, Azerbaijani authors argue that the Caucasian Albanians borrowed the Armenian language but yet kept their distinct ethnic characteristics.

45 Grousset considers that the Seljuk invasions of Asia Minor had a permanent effect whereby the "Turkoman herdsman replaced the Byzantine peasant", and gave "the country not only its Turkic but also its steppelike character", but considers that the same conversion did not happen elsewhere in Iran: "In Persia, despite the founding of Turkic nuclei (in Khurasan, Azerbaijan, and near Hamadan), the population remained basically Iranian." See René Grousset, *The Empire of the Steppes, a History of Central Asia*, translated from French by Naomi Walford, New Jersey: Rutgers, 1999, pp. 155-7.

resenting its interests in any legitimate sense but reflecting the interests of outside forces. For Baku intellectuals Armenians are mere agents of the Russian imperial project, while for Armenians Azerbaijan is a simple instrument in the great Pan-Turkic conspiracy. Interestingly, this image of "newcomer" or temporary guest does not encourage dialogue or negotiation, since a "guest" is both temporary and not qualified for a negotiation between equals.

This debate among historians was to become the background ideology to mobilize Armenians and Azerbaijanis, and lead the conflict of Karabakh to a war between the two neighbours, as we will see in the next chapter.

Georgian historical narration and Abkhazia

In the late *perestroika* period, Georgian historians started revising the principles on which Soviet Georgian historiography was woven. Two areas of their work in the late 1980s had great impact on later political developments. The first was the revision of Georgian-Russian and Georgian-Soviet relations; and the second was the presentation of the place of the Abkhaz and the Ossets in past centuries, and their relations with Georgia. Politically, the issue of revising Georgian-Russian relations, and that of marginalization of the roles of the Abkhaz and the Ossets, ethnic minorities in Georgia who enjoyed territorial autonomy under the Soviet regime, overlapped to create a situation of instability. For example, the 9 April 1989 mass demonstrations in Tbilisi, in which thousands descended on the Georgian capital to express their wrath about events in Abkhazia, were heavily repressed by the Soviet army, with nineteen killed. The two dimensions, the two difficult problems of Georgian historians' revision and Georgian political mobilization, were simultaneously present.

Historians broke several taboos of the Soviet period. The annexation of Georgia by a decree of Alexander I in 1801, and the conditions in which Georgia was incorporated into the Soviet state in 1921, were central topics.[46] The character and the historical role of Noe Zhordania,

---

46   The integration of Georgia into the Russian Empire proceeded over several stages. In 1783 a first treaty of alliance was signed between Catherine II and Erakli II, the King of Kartli and Kakheti, placing Georgia, which was under Persian threat, under Russian protection. But this alliance was not enough to protect

who was Prime Minister of Georgia before its Sovietization, and the political struggles of this period, as well as a reassessment of Joseph Stalin, Sergo Ordzhonikidze and Lavrenti Beria, three ethnic Georgians who played a leading role in Soviet history in the first half of the twentieth century, were subjects of debate.[47] The reassessment of Stalin within Georgian society remains an interesting subject that could reveal how much his figure overshadows Georgian political tradition, but we still need to wait for an in-depth study on the subject before reaching any useful conclusions. It is clear that from the mid-1950s Stalin was for the Georgian public more a national figure than a Soviet symbol, and de-Stalinization in the late 1950s led to popular opposition in Georgia. Revising the "internationalist" policies of Soviet Russia in 1921 brought the whole legitimacy of Soviet power in Georgia into question, opening the way to Tbilisi's separation from Moscow's orbit.

From the early works of Soviet Georgian historians, the place of Abkhazia in history was controversial. A particular sharp debate separated Georgian and Abkhaz historians on the origins and the ethnic elements of the population in the Abkhazian kingdom of the Middle Ages (8th-10th centuries). The Abkhazian kingdom emerged in the west while Tbilisi and most of eastern Georgia remained under Arab rule.[48] The ethnic composition of Abkhazia in the 19th and 20th centuries, Stalin era policies and especially the personal role of Beria, a Mingrelian born in Abkhazia, and Moscow's motives in its Abkhazian policies continue to be subjects of controversy.[49]

The major historians who laid the ground for historical teaching in Soviet Georgia minimized the historic individuality and the political

---

Georgia, and Tiflis (Tbilisi) was taken by Persian troops in 1795 and burnt. Russian troops entered the Georgian capital for the first time in 1796. Following the annexation of Tbilisi and the eastern regions in 1801 to the Russian empire, from 1804 to 1810 the rest of the Georgian provinces were annexed to the Tsarist domains. Abkhazia was absorbed into Russia in 1810.

47   Elizabeth Fuller, "Filling in the 'Blank Spots' in Georgian History: Noe Zhordania and Joseph Stalin", *Report on the USSR*, Munich, 31 March 1989, pp. 19-22.

48   Ronald Grigor Suny, *The Making of the Georgian Nation,* Bloomington: Indiana University Press, 1988, p. 30.

49   On Beria's role in shaping Abkhaz policies, see Stanislav Lak'oba, "History: 1917-1989", in George Hewitt (ed.), *The Abkhazians: A Handbook*, New York: St Martin's Press, 1998, pp. 94-6.

and cultural specificities of the Abkhazians, and assimilated them into Georgian history. In the 1930s, in Georgia as in other republics, historians were ordered to prepare an official history.[50] In this work, the Abkhazian Kingdom of the Middle Ages was presented as a "west Georgian state", its population described as composed of various Georgian tribes, and its role in the emergence of a unified Georgian Kingdom in the 10th century shifted to other, Georgian, actors. Although a distinct Abkhaz people and culture were recognized, their political identity was integrated in the larger Georgian history, and reduced to it. The Kingdom of Abkhazia was considered to be no more than a title for Georgian kings. "[T]he textbook aimed at painting a picture of a uniform Georgian nation, and ethnic minorities should not play obstacles in the way of developing that picture." In the meanwhile, a book by Pavle Ingoroqva identified the ancestors of the Abkhaz as a "Georgian tribe with a Georgian dialect".[51] He considered the Abkhaz to be newcomers to their current territory, as a result of migrations in the 17th century, their "real" homeland being relocated to the North Caucasus. Some predicted that the book was a prelude for the deportation of the Abkhaz people. Initially, this book received much praise in the Soviet media, but later it was withdrawn from circulation under protests from Abkhazians, as the Stalin-Beria era was nearing its end. The works of Ingoroqva became taboo for several years, but his ideas and the intention of proving a unified and dominant Georgian past did not lose their appeal, and gained popularity by the late 1980s.[52]

---

50 The work was prepared by Academician Ivane Javakhishvili (1876-1940) and his students Simon Janashia and N. Berjenishvili. The book was first published in 1941, and is essentially an account of teleological development from tribes to the consolidation of the Georgian nation, and "expansionism" towards the past; it lays claim to "Hittite-Iberian" ancestry (although leading scholars by that time had revealed the Indo-European features of the Hittite civilization), the Urartian state was declared a Georgian state; the book suggested a Georgian substratum was found in the Hellenistic Pontus kingdom, and claimed the existence of early Georgian writing dating from pre-Christian times, etc. For a detailed account, see Shnirelman, op. cit., pp. 236-7.

51 Ibid., p. 242.

52 For example, in the works of Giorgi Melikishvili, 1959, the Abkhazian Kingdom was once again referred to as "Kingdom of Georgia". On Ingoroqva see Ghia Nodia, "The Conflict in Abkhazia: National Projects and Political Circumstances", in B. Coppieters, G. Nodia and Y. Anchabadze (eds), *Georgians and Abkhazians, The Search for a Peace Settlement*, Cologne: Bundesinstitut für

The historical constructions first developed in the times of Stalin and Beria continued to be mainstream in Georgian historic writings of the past two decades. One Georgian historian refers to the Middle Ages to use the terms "Georgian state" and "Abkhazia" as synonyms. Abkhazia and Abkhaz meant Georgia and Georgians: "From the early 10th century, the advantage in the struggle for the unification of Georgia – and hence Inner Kartli – gradually shifted into the West-Georgian state or Abkhazian Kingdom."[53] The author considers that the development of Ajar identity, as well as that of Meskhets or Turk Meskhets, was the result of forced Islamization under Ottoman occupation in the 16th century. For that historian Georgian history is a continuous progress towards national unification, as a result of a "conscious" struggle of the Georgian people, unification being the expression of the interest of the "main social classes".[54] Other expressions of identities are seen as diversions, the result of foreign influence or failures of the Georgians, and not analysed for what they are independently of the idea of a unified and homogeneous Georgian national identity.

The development of a particular Abkhaz identity was considered to be a result of recent invasions from the north: "The foundations of Christianity in Abkhazia were further weakened by the penetration of compact masses of Abkhaz-Adyghe migrants from the Northern Caucasus, this process becoming especially active in the 17th century."[55] Two leading historians at Tbilisi university add to this idea, by saying that as a result of the migrations from the north, the ethnic character of Abkhazia changed: "The incursions of Caucasian mountaineers and civil wars caused severe losses to the Christian population, a large part of which was massacred, and another kidnapped and sold in Ottoman markets."[56] Once again, the indigenous status of the Abkhaz was questioned. Similarly, the Ossets had settled on the southern slopes of the Caucasus in similar migration waves in the 15th-16th centuries, and

---

ostwissenschaftliche und internationale Studien, 1998, p. 26.

53   Mariam Lordkipanidze, *Essays on Georgian History*, Tbilisi: Metsniereba, 1994, p. 32. The same idea is repeated on pp. 10 and 49.

54   Ibid., p. 34.

55   Ibid., p. 11.

56   Nodar Assatiani and Alexandre Bendianachvili, *Histoire de la Géorgie*, Paris: L'Harmattan, 1997, p. 198.

therefore, according to the values of the time, were to be considered as "guests" in Georgia.[57] Georgian authors also point to the continued predominance of Georgian population of Abkhazia from the Middle Ages to the 19th century, when the Georgian (in this case Mingrelian) population of Abkhazia was superior in numbers to its Abkhaz population.[58] What is missing in this account is the fact that following the end of the Caucasian Wars and the defeat of the North Caucasian tribal alliance in its war against the Russian armies (1864), the Abkhaz as well as numerous other North Caucasians were massively deported to the Ottoman Empire, an event which altered the ethnic composition of Abkhazia as well as the entire North Caucasus, making the Abkhaz a minority in the land called after their name.

Without entering into a detailed account of the formation of the Georgian and Abkhaz nations in the past centuries, one can see the implications of this historic debate on the formation of conflicting visions between the two narratives, and its role in the Georgian-Abkhaz conflict. According to Georgian historiography as developed in the Soviet times, the great Abkhaz state that existed from the 11th to the 13th century was Abkhaz by name, but belonged to the Georgian civilization by its substance. A more cautious analyst articulates this idea in the following manner: "...the medieval Abkhaz kingdom was part of the Georgian cultural and political realm. (...) Whenever Georgia, or Western Georgia, represented a unified political structure, Abkhazia was part of it. (...) This history has led the Georgians to believe that Abkhazia is a legitimate part of Georgia, despite the fact that, ethnically speaking, the Abkhaz are not related to the Georgians."[59]

To conclude: by the late 1980s, contemporary Abkhaz were presented in Georgian historiography as recent migrants (in some cases as arriving in the early 17th century) from the north, who had changed the ethnic composition of the land. Therefore they were "guests", and not natives who could claim a high degree of political rights to the land

---

57   Ibid., p. 196.

58   Lordkipanidze writes that according to the "1886 Household Census in Abkhazia (Sukhumi district, by the administrative division of the period) the total of inhabitants was 68,773. Of these 34,806 were Georgians and 28,320 Abkhazians." Op. cit., p. 202.

59   Ghia Nodia, "The Conflict in Abkhazia: National Projects and Political Circumstances", op. cit., pp. 16-17.

they occupied. Similarly, the Ossets are presented as recent migrants, while the Ajars and the Meskhets are ethnic Georgians converted to Islam under the Ottoman occupation. The conclusion is that the autonomous entities of Abkhazia, Ajaria and South Ossetia are illegal, simply Bolshevik creations to weaken Georgian statehood: "the Act of 4 March [1921, the creation of Abkhaz Soviet Socialist Republic] was illegal, for it had no historical or [j]uridical basis..."[60] On the basis of those arguments, the post-Communist Georgian leadership made clear distinctions in its policies "on the distinction between 'indigenous' and 'settlers'."[61] And this historical reading had political translations with tragic consequences.

Abkhaz claims to history

The Abkhaz historians, in their turn, propose a version of Abkhaz history that is autonomous from the Georgian narrative, and contradicts it both in its narration and in its conclusions. According to Abkhaz historiography, most of northeastern Asia Minor was occupied by ancient tribes who were the ancestors of today's Abkhazians, and it was the arrival of the Kartvelians that pushed them to the highlands.[62] Oleg Bgazhba writes that Abkhaz tribes dwelt in what is now Abkhazia starting from "the first centuries of our era."[63] The author underlines the leading role played by Abkhazia in the 10th and 11th centuries in expanding eastward, and thus founding the "Kingdom of the Abkhazians and the Kartvelians".[64] Abkhazian authors also underline the fact that in the golden age of Georgian power, from the 11th to the 13th century, the Georgian Bagratid dynasty were first styled kings of "Abkhazians and Kartvelians" thanks to the leading role played by the Abkhaz in Georgian statehood, and that the most venerated of the Georgian monarchs,

---

60   Lordkipanidze, op. cit., p. 206.

61   Stephen Jones, "Georgia : a failed democratic transition", in Ian Bremmer and Ray Taras (eds), *Nations and Politics in the Soviet Successor States,* New York: Cambridge University Press, 1993, p. 295.

62   Graham Smith et al., p. 55.

63   Oleg Bgazhba, "History: first-18th centuries", in George Hewitt (ed.), *The Abkhazians: A Handbook,* New York: St. Martin's Press, 1998, p. 59.

64   Kartvelians are the main component of the Georgian nations, and the self-designation of Georgians.

Queen Tamar (1184-1213) gave her son Giorgi as a second name La-sha, which is translated from Abkhaz as "enlightener of the universe".[65] Following several wars with Mingrelians, the Abkhaz, with the support of north-Caucasian tribes, restored in the 17th century their border up to the Inguri River, which is the current border separating Abkhaz from Georgia. The author draws the following conclusion:

We have demonstrated that Abkhazia together with its autochtonous popula-tion enjoyed a history quite independent from any Kartvelian entity up to the time when, by right of dynastic succession, the united kingdom of the Abkhaz-ians and Kartvelians came to subsume the 200-year-old Abkhazian Kingdom in 978.[66]

Following the Mongol invasion, Abkhazia and Georgia emerged once again as two separate entities, according to Bgazhba. Another au-thor puts it more bluntly: "Contrary to the claim that Abkhazia has always been a part of Georgia, the real historical situation was quite different, because from the 13th century until 1918 Georgia as a single state simply did not exist."[67]

The Abkhaz in their turn argue that Abkhazia was incorporated into the Tsarist Russia as an independent entity in 1810, and not when the Georgian kingdom was annexed to Russia in 1801. This fact is presented to prove the autonomy of the Abkhaz political system from Georgian statehood in the early 19th century. The ethnic composition of Abkhazia is also a subject of much debate; Abkhaz sources insist that it is the Geor-gians, and more particularly the Mingrelians, who are the newcomers to the land of Abkhazia, mainly as a result of the catastrophic results of the Caucasus Wars of the 19th century. According to Stanislav Lak'oba, following the defeat of the North Caucasian resistance against the Rus-sian Tsarist armies in 1864, "entire swathes of Abkhazian territory were stripped of their ancestral inhabitants as much of the native population was expelled in various waves to Ottoman lands," and their villages were colonized by Mingrelian migrants who were attracted by the fertile soil of

---

65   Bgazhba, op. cit.. p. 63.

66   Ibid., p. 65.

67   Viacheslav A. Chrikba, "The Georgian-Abkhazian Conflict: In Search for Ways out", in Bruno Coppieters, Ghia Nodia and Yuri Anchabadze (eds) *Georgians and Abkhazians, The Search for a Peace Settlement*, Cologne: Bundesinstitut für ostwissenschaftliche und internationale Studien, 1998, p. 53.

Abkhazia.[68] As a result of those massive deportations, there is an important ethnic Abkhaz minority today in Turkey, as well as in other Middle Eastern countries which were once parts of the Ottoman Empire, known as Caucasian *muhajirs* (migrants).[69] The colonization of Abkhazia by Mingrelian settlers, and the decline of the ethnic Abkhaz population of Abkhazia in the following decades, are attributed to conscious Georgian policies in the late 19th century, in the years of the republic, and in Soviet Georgia. But even taking the period after the Caucasian Wars, one can see the reason for Abkhaz alarm and complaint about a policy of colonization: the ethnic Abkhaz constitute 32 per cent of the overall population of the province in 1921, 27.8 per cent in 1926, and 18 per cent in 1939.[70] In the latest Soviet census of 1989 their numbers were about 97,000, 17 per cent of the total population of Abkhazia.

The Abkhaz account of the role of the Bolsheviks and Soviet policies also differs dramatically from the Georgian one. Following the February Revolution, the Abkhaz formed their own "Abkhaz People's Council" (*Abkhazskiy Narodniy Sovet,* ANS) and became part of the North Caucasian Republic, or Mountain Republic.[71] When Georgia declared its independence on 26 May 1917, "Abkhazia was outside the borders of its territory and formed a constituent part of the Mountain Republic."[72] The relationship between the two sides in the years of the Menshevik Republic was conflictual, with the Georgian army invading Abkhazia and disbanding the ANS, and facing strong political as well as armed resistance from the Abkhaz side.

---

68   Stanislav Lak'oba, "History: 18th century-1917", in George Hewitt (ed.), *The Abkhazians: A Handbook*, New York: St. Martin's Press, 1998, p. 88.

69   The numbers of the Abkhaz Diaspora in Turkey is not exactly known, and different estimates put the number of Abkhaz and the closely linked Abaza in Turkey to be between 100,000 and half a million. See Viacheslav A. Chrikba, "The Georgian-Abkhazian Conflict: In Search for Ways out" in G.N. Bruno Coppieters and Yuri Anchabadze (eds), *Georgians and Abkhazians, The Search for a Peace Settlement*, p. 53, footnote number 6.

70   See Urjewicz, op. cit., p. 229, and Shnirelman, op. cit., p. 209.

71   The Mountain Republic "was composed of Daghestan, Checheno-Ingushetia, Ossetia, Karachay-Balkaria, Abkhazia, Kabardia, and Adyghea", according to Stanislav Lak'oba, "History: 1917-1989", in George Hewitt (ed.), *The Abkhazians: A Handbook*, New York: St. Martin's Press, 1998, p. 90.

72   Ibid., p. 90.

With the invasion of the Red Army, the balance of forces between Georgia and Abkhazia changed. On 31 March 1921, Abkhazia was declared an independent SSR, but under the pressure of Sergo Ordzhonikidze, Abkhazia and Georgia were linked together by a "special union treaty". According to the Abkhaz sources, Stalin's henchman in the Caucasus Lavrenti Beria had a special responsibility in the suffering of their people under Soviet rule, and for the application of a policy of imposing Georgian domination over the province. He is also seen as the person playing a major role in downgrading the status of Abkhazia from that of a Soviet Socialist Republic to that of an autonomous republic within the Georgian SSR in 1931.[73]

To conclude, the Abkhaz historians have developed a version of their history, which contradicts the Georgian one. First, they insist on their rightful place in early history, by underlying their presence in the Caucasus region even before the arrival of Kartvelian tribes. They also present the leading role of the Abkhaz in the unification of Georgia, and underline the independent ethnic and cultural identity of the Abkhaz in the Middle Ages; they attribute the decline in the Abkhaz population to the Caucasian Wars, and later to the policy of colonization. To develop a foundation for their right to separate political entity, they note that Abkhazia joined the Russian empire independently from Georgia; that during Georgia's independence Abkhazia sought to be an independent political entity directed towards membership in the Mountain Republic, and that it joined the Soviet Union as a Union Republic, although this status was later downgraded because of Stalin-Beria policies.

The conflict background of the North Caucasus

The question "who is the first settler on this territory?", which has played a key role in the debates around the historical identity of Karabakh and Abkhazia, played no role in the conflicts among the peoples of the North Caucasus and Russia. The Chechens, as well as Kabardin, the Adyghes and the peoples of Daghestan, were the uncontested native populations before the Russians appeared on the horizon of the steppes.[74] Two his-

---

73   S. Lak'oba, op. cit., pp. 94-5.

74   This said, Chechen historiography nevertheless did work on proving its ancient roots and centuries-old presence in the North Caucasus. Like Armenians and Georgians, Chechen historians traced back their past to the Hurrians, and the

torical events played a key role in the imagination and interpretation of the war in Chechnya. The first is the reference to the Great Caucasian War of the 19th century, and the second is the deportations ordered by Stalin of the entire Chechen and some other peoples to Central Asia during the Second World War, under the pretext of their alleged collaboration with the invading German armies. Behind those events there is a certain aspect of the Russian-Chechen relationship, and a broader Russian-Mountaineers relationship, which needs to be presented.

For the Russian empire, the justification for occupying the steppe and the mountains of the Caucasus had several dimensions including the geopolitical, ideological and legalistic. The invasion of the Caucasus brought Russia closer to its aim of reaching "warm waters", a precondition, according to Russian political figures of the 19th century, for the future development of their state and for becoming a great power. In the 18th century, the Russian emperors took on themselves to liberate the Christian nations living in the southern Caucasus, the Armenians and the Georgians,[75] as part of what became known in the diplomatic circles of the time as the Eastern Question, as the rationale behind their southern expansion towards regions controlled by the Ottoman and Qajar dynasties. The Russian victories on the battlefields were later transferred into permanent gains through peace treaties. Of the thirteen Turkish-Russian wars, the one in 1774 that ended in Turkish defeat and the treaty of Kuchuk Kainardji gave Russia control over the Black Sea coast and the Tatar steppes, influence over Moldavia and Wallachia, and the legal right of protection of the Christians of the Caucasus.[76] The treaty opened the way for the Russian occupation of Georgia and Armenia. Russia considered that it had received the legal right to rule over the peoples of the Caucasus as a result of its victories over the Ottomans

---

kingdom of Urartu. See Moshe Gammer, "Nationalism and History: Rewriting the Chechen National Past", in Bruno Coppieters and Michel Huysseune (eds), *Secession, History, and the Social Sciences*, Brussels: VUB University Press, 2002, p. 120.

75   Matei Cazacu, *Au Caucase, Russes et Tchétchène, récits d'une guerre sans fin*, Geneva : Georg, 1998, pp. 32-3.

76   Alan Palmer, *The Decline and Fall of the Ottoman Empire*, London: John Murray, 1995, p. 45.

and the Qajars, and peace treaties signed in the aftermath of its military victories.[77]

The peoples of the North Caucasus and especially the Cherkess (Circassians) in the west and the Chechens and the peoples of Daghestan in the east, strongly objected to passing from Ottoman to Russian rule. The initial Russian contact with the peoples of the North Caucasus, and especially with the Cherkess, was based on expressions of allegiance to the Tsar. But once this was transformed into direct rule, with Cossack colonies, chains of fortresses, heavy taxes and population displacements, the peoples of the North Caucasus started a series of rebellions against Russian rule. On the other hand, the Russian rationale of liberating Christian peoples of the Caucasus could not impress the non-Christian peoples of the region. By the time of the Russian arrival, Islam was strongly developing among certain ethnic groups of the western part of the north Caucasus, such as the Abkhaz and the Cherkess, as well as among the Chechens and the Ingushes.[78] The Russian invasion, and the role of Islam as a unifying ideology in the face of the invaders, accelerated the spread of Islam among the Cherkess, and even more so among the Chechens and the Ingushes.

From a Russian perspective, the Chechens have been presented often as villains and robbers, as dangerous fighters and ruthless enemies, in both Russian popular culture and high literature. Pushkin, Lermontov and Tolstoy in their distinguished ways have written about the mythic beauty of the Caucasus, and about the ferocity of the Chechen and Cherkess fighters. Pushkin's poem *Prisoner of the Caucasus* continues to inspire writers, journalists, and film makers.[79]

The official Soviet discourse towards the Mountain Peoples of the Caucasus has varied widely. In the 1920s, in a spirit of anti-imperialistic policies, the Bolsheviks accepted wide internal autonomy for the mountain dwellers, and recognized their past anti-colonial struggle. In this period, "portraits of Shamil and his *naibs* [replaced] those of Lenin"

---

77   The treaties of Gulistan in 1813 and Turkmanchai in 1828 transferred the Persian possessions of Daghestan and in the south Caucasus, as far as the river Arax, to the Russians.

78   Galina M. Yemelianova, "Sufism and Politics in the North Caucasus", *Nationalities Papers*, Vol. 29, No. 4, 2001, p. 662.

79   See for example the film entitled *Prisoner of the Caucasus*, 2002, by the Bielorussian documentalist Yuri Chasctschewatski.

and the Soviet historiography of this period stressed the anti-Tsarist and national-liberation character of the resistance in Chechnya and the North Caucasus.[80] Then came the forced collectivisation, in which the North Caucasus territory was the first where collectivisation was introduced in a complete way, with the kulaks as a class "liquidated". This aggressive policy sparked new rebellions in the North Caucasus, most violent and widespread in Chechnya, but also spreading to Daghestan, Ossetia, Kabardin, Balkaria and Karachay territories. The official Soviet interpretation was that these revolts were of a counter-revolutionary character, led by "mullah-nationalist ideologists".[81]

Many Soviet historians concerned with the First Caucasian War "even today under *glasnost*, continue to pretend that the Caucasian wars, the expulsion of the Cherkess and the Stalin deportations were all due to the misdeeds of the Caucasians themselves."[82] In the run-up to the "Second Caucasian War", that is the Russian invasion of Chechnya in 1994, the old stereotypes on the Caucasian mountain peoples re-emerged.

The post-Soviet Russian discourse to justify the war (or wars) in the North Caucasus follows a similar line: the war in Chechnya in 1994 was for the defence of the Federal State, and "to restore the constitutional order". The old view that the situation in the North Caucasus is unstable because of "banditism" among the Chechens became once again prominent among Russian leaders and writers. Even a highly analytic mind such as Valery Tishkov, in his book on ethnic conflicts in post-Soviet space, starts narrating the war in Chechnya with his entire first page and a half talking about criminality in Chechnya, to conclude: "Being rather sceptical about the 'criminal version', I cannot ignore some very recent journalistic investigations in this direction."[83]

---

80   Abdurahman Avtorkhanov, "The Chechen and the Ingush during the Soviet Period and its Antecedents", in Marie Benningsen Broxup (ed.), *The North Caucasus Barrier, The Russian Advance Towards the Muslim World*, London: Hurst, 1996, p. 154.

81   Avturkhanov, ibid., p. 160.

82   Marie Benningsen Broxup, "Introduction: Russia and the North Caucasus", in Marie Benningsen Broxup (ed.), *The North Caucasus Barrier, The Russian Advance Towards the Muslim World*, London: Hurst, 1996, p. 15.

83   Valery Tishkov, *Ethnicity, Nationalism and Conflict in and After the Soviet Union,* p. 184.

The recent wars are interpreted as the defence of Russia against the fate of the Soviet Union. Following the collapse of the USSR, the fear of disintegration of Russia on a similar scenario was very much present in the minds of policy makers and observers alike.[84] If the Russian authorities did not defend the territorial integrity of the Russian Federation, and Chechnya got its independence, other ethnic-territories could follow the same road, and even destroy Russian statehood. Another predominant reason for the war, which is linked with the first, is Russia's defence against Islamic fundamentalism and its multiple threats. Differing from the self-interpretation of the 19th century wars, the explanations given for the post-Soviet conflicts invoke defence and self-preservation against an "external" threat. For both the Yeltsin and Putin administrations, "the imminent disintegration of the Russian Federation" was a reason or a pretext for going to war in Chechnya.[85]

The religious interpretation was dominant in the 18th and the 19th century Caucasian authors, who saw the conflict as one between Islam and *giaours* (unbelievers, from the Arabic *kafer*).[86] The wars of Sheikh Mansour and Imam Shamil were led under the banner of Islam, and were fought not only against the Russian invaders but also against Chechens, Ingushes, Daghestanis and other Caucasian peoples who applied *a'dat* (traditional law) instead of the *shari'at* (Islamic law).

Later interpretations by Chechen or Western authors sympathizing with the Chechen perspective narrate the conflict as a struggle for liberation from colonial oppression. A leading example of this perspective is Benningsen Broxup. Commenting on a declaration of the Chechen pro-independent president Djokhar Dudayev, proposing a peace treaty to Russia, she writes:

This statement refers to the fact that the North Caucasus had been at war against Russia, in an effort to preserve its independence, almost uninterruptedly since the end of the eighteenth century. This epic struggle, in comparison

---

84   Charles Urjewicz, "De l'URSS à la CEI: le début ou la fin de la Russie?" *Hérodote*, Paris, January-March 1992.

85   Matthew Evangelista, *The Chechen Wars, Will Russia Go the Way of the Soviet Union?* Washington: Brookings Institution Press, 2002, p. 123.

86   See for example the notes of Ibragim-Bek Sarakaev, *Po Trushchobam Chechni*, Vladikavkaz, 1913, reprinted in 1991, pp. 5-6 ; B.G. Gabisov, *Chechentsi I Ingushi, Problema Proiskhazhdenie*, Groznyy: Kniga, 1991.

to which even Abdel Qadir's resistance to the French conquest of Algeria pales, is little known in the West and in most of the Muslim world.[87]

Authors who adopt this perspective of a colonial and national liberation struggle often make a direct link between the events starting from 1785, with the first battle between Russian armies and Chechen rebels led by Sheikh Mansour, and the Russo-Chechen conflict of the post-Soviet period. In describing the rebellion of Mansour Ushurma, one writer makes the following conclusion: "Following a first encounter, the insurgents abandoned Aldy which was later destroyed by a Russian detachment, an action which is going to be repeated in this war until 1996.[88]

In another example, published a couple of months before the humiliating defeat of the Russian forces in Groznyy and before their withdrawal from Chechnya, one author writes: "All the history of Chechnya after the Russian conquest is one of a permanent struggle for independence which was hardly eased during the Soviet period."[89] This view of a historic continuity has been much present in the discourse of Chechen leaders, such as the first president of post-Soviet Chechnya, Djokhar Dudayev, to justify a radical political position and a demand for Chechen sovereignty.

Naturally, historians should take a more careful approach before declaring that they see events as a single process over a period of two or three centuries. While emphasizing the Chechens' determination in resisting Russian rule, and the instrumentalization of the past by various politicians to justify and mobilize around contemporary themes, a historian should be capable of assessing differences in appreciating the nuances and changes in historical context. While keeping in mind the possibility of recurrence of sentiments such as fear and antagonism, historians should explain why certain phenomena do continue over a large period of time and not take this continuity for granted; they should try to strike the right balance between continuity and change, especially when covering events of historic significance. In the early 90s of the past century, in spite of the Russian horrors during the era of colonialism, in spite of the repressions under Stalin and the forced exile of an entire nation, the change brought

---

87   Marie Benningsen Broxup, in Preface to *The North Caucasus Barrier,* p. ix.

88   Matei Cazacu, op. cit., p. 34.

89   Mairbek Vatchagaev, "La Tchétchénie et la guerre de Caucase au XIX siècle", *Hérodote,* Paris, No. 81, April-June 1996, p. 105.

under Gorbachev was an occasion to reformulate Chechen-Russian relations anew while excluding violence and repression. Yet this did not
happen, and it is not enough to refer to the past to explain the contemporary wars. While admitting that human beings do have the capacity to
repeat past mistakes, one cannot deny that they also have the capacity to
learn positive lessons from past horrors, and make peace and avoid future
wars. After looking at three centuries of Russo-Chechen relations, Moshe
Gammer writes: "And yet the answer to the question whether the first
Russo-Chechen war was inevitable is necessarily a negative one."[90]

One major difficulty a historian faces in making a teleological link between the Great Caucasian Wars of the 19th century and the post-Soviet
conflicts in the North Caucasus is that the first involved tribal alliances
guided by Sufi Muslim ideology, while the second involved secular nationalism based on the political vision based on Chechen interests that
was the leading force of the Chechen rebellion. The series of wars between 1785 and 1865, when the Cherkess were finally defeated, was not
a Chechen war against the Russians but a more general resistance, in
which one should admit the Chechens played an important role. There
has not been a similar pan-Caucasian rebellion against the post-Soviet
Russian rule in the region of the North Caucasus, neither in 1994, nor
in 1999.[91]

The first great rebellion was led by a man called Ushurma, a key figure in Chechen history, who later adopted the name Mansour (Arabic,
meaning victorious). He was a Chechen peasant who, after a revelation,
started preaching Islam among the peoples of the North Caucasus, and
became the first to call for religious war, or *ghazawat*, against the infidels.
He led the first Caucasian rebellion against the Russians in 1785, which
lasted for six years. Among the three leaders of the Caucasian rebellion
that succeeded Sheikh Mansour, none was Chechen; they were Ghazi
Mouhammad, Hamza Bek, and the most famous figure of the Caucasian
resistance, Imam Shamil, all from Daghestan.[92] Imam Shamil led a longer
and bloodier war against the Russians, which terminated with his sur-

---

90   Moshe Gammer, *The Lone Wolf and the Bear, Three Centuries of Chechen Defiance of Russian Rule*, London: Hurst, 2006, p. 206.

91   Vicken Cheterian, "Caucasian Solidarity: a Myth?" in *Labour Focus on Eastern
Europe*, Oxford, Number 50, Spring 1995, pp. 73-8.

92   M. Vatchagaev, op. cit. pp. 99-102; M. Cazacu, op. cit. p. 39.

render in Gunib, in the mountains of central Daghestan, to the Russian general Alexander Bariatinskii in 1859. It is worth mentioning that in the Soviet period it was often tolerated to present Imam Shamil as a "progressive", anti-colonial leader, while Sheikh Mansur was either censored or presented under a negative light until the late *perestroika* period.[93]

The 19th-century Caucasian Wars did not take place only in the Chechnya-Daghestan part of the North Caucasus. With contemporary events unfolding in Chechnya, and references repeatedly made to history from this angle only, the history of the Circassians (the Cherkess, or the Adyghes) is all but forgotten. Yet they continued their war five more years after the Gunib capitulation of Imam Shamil.

In the centre of Nalchik, the capital of the Kabardino-Balkaria Autonomous Republic, which is part of the Russian Federation, there is a stone monument under which one can see engravings commemorating the first contacts between Russian nobility and Kabardin princes. This monument constructed in the Soviet era aims to commemorate the friendly relationship, and the "voluntary incorporation" of the Kabardin within the Russian Empire. The theme of voluntary incorporation of the Caucasian peoples into the Tsarist realms is a repetitive archetype, which the post-revolutionary Soviet historiography wanted to stress, rather than submerging in the long and bloody history of conquest and resistance. In the case of the Kabardin, and other peoples constituting part of the larger Cherkess family of Caucasian peoples,[94] the consequences were dramatic. Once they were the largest of North Caucasian peoples, and now they are reduced to a small minority following the exodus and forced deportations after the defeat of their over two-decade-long rebellion, which was crushed in 1864. The entire Ubykh population was deported to the Ottoman Empire, where they were largely assimilated.[95] The Cherkess, who were estimated to have

---

93   Moshe Gammer, "A Preliminary to Decolonizing the Historiography of Shaykh Mansur", *Middle Eastern Studies*, January 1996, 32/1, pp. 191-202, and by the same author, "Nationalism and History: Rewriting the Chechen National Past", op. cit, pp. 124-7.

94   Known as Cherkess or Circassian in Russian and Western sources, this people uses itself the term Adyghe, which includes the Cherkess, Adyghes, and Kabardin. They belong to the north-west Caucasian family of languages, which also includes the Abkhaz and Ubykh languages.

95   The North Caucasus peoples who were massively deported, besides the Ubykhs,

been several hundred thousand in the early 19th century, include today around 350,000 Kabardin and 120,000 Adyghes in the North Caucasus.[96] Although in reference to North Caucasian resistance against Russian advances the name of Imam Shamil is the most famous, and the battles of Daghestan and Chechnya come to mind, the war in the 19th century was the hardest in the west, in the lands of the Kabardin, as Paul Henze mentions:

But Shamil is only part of the history of North Caucasian resistance. His successes were all in eastern Caucasus. The resistance of the Circassians in the western Caucasus is at least as significant, for it began earlier, lasted longer and ended more disastrously for those who were fighting to defend their freedom.[97]

Yet, in the moment of Soviet collapse, we did not see any mass disturbances among the Cherkess, nor an anti-Russian rebellion in Daghestan inspired by the legendary Shamil. If we leave aside the short conflict between the Ossets and the Ingushes over a dispute for the control of a suburb of Vladikavkaz and its surrounding villages, the only conflict in the North Caucasus, and the bloodiest of all the post-Soviet conflicts, remains that of Chechnya.

Therefore, in spite of the long and historical resistance in the North Caucasus against Russian imperial advances, one should be careful and introduce the necessary nuances to accommodate changes that have taken place between the 18th century, the Soviet era, and the underpinnings of the current conflict. As one analysis suggests, "decisions to fight against the Russians in the Caucasian Wars of the nineteenth century were made not by Caucasian national groups, but rather, by tribal federations."[98] Moreover, the separation of the Chechens from the Ingushes as distinct ethnic groupings was conditioned by their par-

---

were the Abkhaz, the Abazas, and the Cherkess (Adygeis). The most massive deportations took place in 1864, with 400-600,000 people deported. See Alexandre Toumarkine, "La diaspora 'tcherkesse' en Turquie", *Hérodote*, Paris, No. 81, April-June 1996, p. 154.

96   According to the 1989 census. See Roger Caratini, *Dictionnaire des Nationalités et des Minorités de l'ex-U.R.S.S.*, Paris : Larousse, 1992, pp. 183-4.

97   Paul B. Henze, "Circassian Resistance to Russia", in Marie Benningsen Broxup (ed.), *The North Caucasus Barrier, The Russian Advance Towards the Muslim World*, London: Hurst, 1996, p. 62.

98   Jane Ormord, "North Caucasus: Fragmentation or Federation?" in Ian Bremmer and Ray Taras (eds), *Nations and Politics in the Soviet Successor States*, Cambridge University Press, 1993, p. 448.

ticipation, or non-participation, in the anti-Russian struggle. The populations of the North Caucasus region underwent profound change in their self-definition in the modern period, and the most important part of this was the formation of national identities.

The event that has left the deepest scar in contemporary Chechen memory, and has the most relevance to understanding the on-going conflict in the Caucasus, is the mass deportations ordered by Stalin in 1944. Four ethnic groups from the North Caucasus were entirely rounded up, put into trains and exiled to Siberia or Central Asia. These peoples were the Chechens, the Ingushes, the Karachays and the Balkars, who were deported to join other "punished peoples" in exile such as the Volga Germans, the Crimean Tatars, and the Kalmyks. Later, the Meskhets of Georgia were equally deported, on the same accusations of having "collaborated" with the Nazi enemy, even though neither Georgia nor Chechnya was occupied by the German armies. It was this selective deportation ordered by Stalin, based on an official identification of an individual as belonging to a national group, which laid the ground for strengthening of national identities in the North Caucasus. "If it was possible to speak of the North Caucasian nationalities as groups without distinct national histories in the earlier decades of the twentieth century, this was no longer true after 1944."[99]

The 1944 deportations directly shaped the "lesser" conflict of the North Caucasus: the Osset-Ingush conflict over the Prigorodnyi Rayon of Vladikavkaz, the capital of the North Ossetia Autonomous Republic. As mentioned above, the Ingush people were deported, mainly to Kazakhstan, with the rest of the "punished" peoples. As a result, the Checheno-Ingush Autonomous Republic was dissolved, and its territory, villages, and homes were distributed to its neighbours. When the Ingushes started returning to their homes from 1956 onwards, and the Checheno-Ingush ASSR was restored, Prigorodnyi Rayon, which is actually a suburb of Vladikavkaz, was not included in it.[100] It was the struggle to retake this region that erupted into mass violence in 1992, leading to several hundred casualties and tens of thousands of displaced people.

---

99   Ibid., p. 452.

100   On the background of the Osset-Ingush conflict, see *The Ingush-Ossetian Conflict in the Prigorodnyi Region*, New York: Human Rights Watch/Helsinki, 1996, pp. 9-11.

The deportations of 1944 were the event that led to the success of the Stalinist policy of creating entities in the North Caucasus based on national identities. After the deportations, the national consciousness of the Chechens was radically different from that of the Avars or Laks or the other neighbouring peoples of Daghestan. Moreover, Chechen national psychology was deeply traumatized by the deportations and therefore political preoccupations of the Chechens have been of an entirely different nature since, while the neighbouring Daghestani peoples were increasingly accommodating themselves with Soviet rule. One should look at the events of 1944, and not the war led by Shamil, to understand the unfolding of events in the North Caucasus following the collapse of the Soviet power.

History, historians, and the articulation of conflicting positions

The role of historians was not limited to developing a version of history in which the role of the nations they represented had a dominant role and that of neighbouring nations was diminished. Nor was it limited to preparing politicised and clashing visions of the past in the work context created by Soviet policies. In the early years of mass politics, at the height of *perestroika* and *glasnost*, they played a direct role in articulating political positions and demands, addressed initially to the Soviet leadership in Moscow, based on the specific vision of history their profession had developed in the previous years. Those demands rotated around the idea of territorial exchanges and the upgrading or downgrading of the political status of certain regions, and in particular that of autonomous republics and regions. The politicized work of historians fitted well with the Soviet tradition whereby historians prepared studies that directly reflected official ideology, or tried to justify it. Thus the role historians played in the period of Soviet collapse can be seen as a continuation of, and not a break with, the Soviet legacy. In the late 1980s many historians ceased to be historians and entered the arena of political struggle, by providing the ideology of mass mobilization.

In the struggle around Karabakh, both Armenian and Azerbaijani historians worked on texts, in some cases in *samizdat* form, sometimes even printed and distributed through official channels, to develop and propagate their visions of the Karabakh problem, which became the background on which political forces articulated their demands.

A first example of such a document was prepared by two professors at the Institute of History at the Academy of Sciences of the Armenian SSR.[101] The document represents a historical summary of the Karabakh region relying on sources varying from the Greek geographer Strabo and the medieval Armenian historian Movses Khorenatsi,[102] to explain the conditions in which in 1921 it was decided to place the region within Azerbaijan, while having an autonomous structure with ethnic (Armenian) character; there is a chapter discussing "The Problem of Mountainous Karabakh in the light of Leninist Concept of National Self-Determination".[103] The book arrives finally at the contemporary problems of the demographic changes in Karabakh and economic under-development, two issues around which much of the argumentation of the Armenian side was articulated to debate the right of Karabakh to be unified with Armenia.

More significant than its content is the way this document was used. It was sent to political leaders in Moscow, as well as being distributed over various Soviet delegations visiting Yerevan to study the emerging Armenian mass movement, or to mediate between Yerevan, Baku and Moscow. Therefore, this document prepared by historians became an instrument for political action, with significant impact in articulating a political discourse, which was to become dominant in Armenia during the rise of the Karabakh movement.

Azerbaijani historians played an identical role. The leading text was written by Igrar Aliev, the top Azerbaijani expert on ancient languages, and the chairman of the department of Early History at the Institute of History in Baku. The document, entitled *Mountainous Karabakh: History. Facts. Events* (in Russian), was written between February and November 1988, at the height of Armenian mass mobilization around the Karabakh question, and published in the next year.[104] This document

101   G.A. Galoyan, and K.S. Khudaverdyan (eds), *Nagorni Karabakh, Istoricheskaya Spravka ('Mountainous Karabakh, Historical Documentation' in Russian)*, Yerevan: Akademiya Nauk Armianskoi SSR, 1988.

102   Ibid., pp. 7 and 8.

103   Ibid., pp. 37-44.

104   Igrar Aliev, *Nagorni Karabakh: Istoria. Fakti. Sobitia.* ("Mountainous Karabakh:

was a direct response to the work of the Armenian historians Galoyan and Khudaverdyan referred above. Aliev sets out to prove the historic right of Azerbaijan over the contested territory, by dedicating three quarters of the work to discussion of past ages, starting from prehistory. The document starts by emphasizing the idea that the mountainous and lower parts of Karabakh have always depended on each other in history, and that the economy of the Autonomous Region of Mountainous Karabakh has been an "organic part" of the economy of Azerbaijan SSR.[105] The next idea Aliev develops is that Armenians are not autochthonous to the region of Transcaucasus, but moved to the region from their historic homeland, located in the upper valley of the Euphrates river. The author takes much pains to present his view that before the arrival of the Armenians, the inhabitants of the region of Karabakh were the Albanians, and part of the Albanian political system until the creation of the Karabakh (or Ganja) "Beglargeg" rule, while later in the 18th-19th century it was ruled by the Karabakh Khanate, until its incorporation within the Russian state. Therefore, concludes Aliev, the decision to integrate Mountainous Karabakh within the Azerbaijan SSR "constitutes realization of Leninist national policy of the CPS, and corresponds to the Leninist principles of national-state building."[106] The author dismisses criticism concerning the situation of Karabakh at the time, stating, "The question of the development of popular economy and culture of Mountainous Karabakh has always been in the centre of attention of the party and Soviet organs of Azerbaijani SSR".[107]

Another leading Azerbaijani historian, Ziya Buniatov, was one of the most active Azerbaijani scholars to protest against Armenian demands for the unification of Karabakh with Armenia. Following the mass demonstrations in Stepanakert and Yerevan, and after the pogroms in Sumgait, Buniatov published an article in Baku whereby he repeated the idea that Armenians are newcomers to Karabakh, by saying that:

History. Facts. Events", in Russian), Baku: Elm, 1989.

105   Igrar Aliev, *Nagorno Karabakh*, pp. 3 and 4. This argument about economic dependency was a reflection of the rationale put forward by the Soviet authorities to link Mountainous Karabakh with its ethnic Armenian population within Azerbaijan.

106   Igrar Aliev, *Nagorno Karabakh*, p. 28.

107   Igrar Aliev, *Nagorno Karabakh*, p. 90.

[T]he oldest Armenian cemetery stone in Maraghashen [a village in Karabakh] is no more than 160 years old. How can they say that Karabagh belongs to Armenia? (...) The Sumgait tragedy was carefully prepared by the Armenian nationalists. Several hours before it began, Armenian photographers and TV journalists secretly entered the city where they waited in readiness. The first crime was committed by a certain Grigorian who pretended to be Azerbaijani, and who killed five Armenians in Sumgait. As for what follows, it is no more than a technical question because there was no way to stop the enormous crowd...[108]

Ziya Buniatov's article was written at a time when, in response to Armenians' mass mobilization and pressing demands, the Azerbaijani street was mobilizing in its turn. The leading Azerbaijani historian was giving an interpretation of the growing conflict, and a very unfortunate justification to the anti-Armenian massacres in Sumgait. For the leading Azerbaijani historian, the conflict, including the unjustifiable massacres of ethnic Armenians living in Sumgait, were part of a larger "Armenian plot", prepared by the Tashnak party from abroad, to occupy Azerbaijani territories, starting with the claims for unification of Karabakh.

Another example of the direct participation of historians in articulating political demands comes from Abkhazia. The "Abkhazian Letter", composed in 1988 was drafted by I.R. Markholia, head of the Department of Pre-Revolutionary History of the Abkhazian State Museum, and G.N. Trapeznikov, a researcher at the Institute of History of the USSR in the USSR Academy of Sciences, and was signed by 60 leading Abkhaz scholars and cultural figures. This letter became a founding document for the struggle for the Abkhaz sovereignty from Georgia.[109] The letter was drafted for, and sent to, the Nineteenth All-Union Communist Party conference held in June 1988. It criticized Tbilisi's policy of marginalizing the Abkhaz and assimilating them, and demanded a return to the pre-1931 status for Abkhazia, which was equivalent to a Union Republic of the USSR and independent from political hegemony of Tbilisi. The "Letter", as it was known, received public support

---

108   Ziya Buniatov, "Why Sumgait", *Elm*, Baku, 13 May 1989, p. 175. An English translation of excerpts of the article can be found in Appendix III of Levon Chorbajian, Patrick Donabedian and Claude Mutafian, *The Caucasian Knot: the History and Geo-Politics of Nagorno-Karabagh*, London: Zed Books, 1994, pp. 188-9.

109   Lak'oba, "History: 1917-1989", p. 101.

on 18 March 1989 at a mass meeting in the village of Lykhny, a former capital of the Abkhaz, and was signed by 32,000 inhabitants of Abkhazia, including five thousand who were not ethnically Abkhaz. After the meeting in Lykhny, the document was sent to the Soviet leadership including the General Secretary, M.S. Gorbachev, and the Chairman of the Council of Ministers of the USSR, N.I. Ryzhkov, as well as to leading academic and research institutes.

By order of the Soviet Georgian leadership, a group of Georgian scholars from the Academy of Sciences prepared an "answer" to the "Abkhazian Letter".[110] The Georgian answer started by an excursion in which the historic Colchis Kingdom was presented as a Georgian kingdom, and the Abkhaz were said to be late colonizers of the region; Abkhazia, it was asserted, had a continuous ethnic Georgian character even after the collapse of the united Georgian kingdom in the 13th century, and the Abkhaz had migrated from the North Caucasus in the 17th century. The authors also denied any repression or assimilation of the Abkhaz and their culture, with the exception of the period 1937-53, at the height of Stalinist repression, when all the Soviet nationalities including the Georgian nation suffered from a similar repression—another way of saying that the Abkhaz were never discriminated against within Georgia.

Viktor Shnirelman explains how ideological as well as political pressures conditioned the historic-academic debates in the decades preceding the collapse of the Soviet Union.[111] To have a higher status in the hierarchy of Soviet nationalities, it was necessary to "prove" a long, desirably indigenous, historic presence, to justify the contemporary administrative and state borders by references in history, and to "prove" a linguistic as well as demographic continuity of the titular nation in its newly created Soviet homeland. Shnirelman also emphasizes that in this struggle the balance of forces was not equal. While Soviet Socialist Republics such as Armenia, Azerbaijan and Georgia had their institutional means such as mass media, school textbooks, universities, etc. to develop and distribute their versions of history, sub-units such as

---

110   Po povodu iskazheniia gruzino-abkhazkikh vzaimootnoshenii (otvet avtoram "Abkhazkogo pis'ma"). *Zaria Vostoka*, Tbilisi. 28-30 July, 1989.

111   V. A. Silverman, *The Value of the Past: Myths, Identity and Politics in Transcaucasia*, Osaka: National Museum of Ethnology, 2001.

the autonomous republics of Abkhazia or Chechnya, or autonomous regions such as Mountainous Karabakh or South Ossetia, had very limited means, and sometimes only oral narration for the spread of alternative versions of their history and culture.

After decades of writing history to defend the nation within the narrow constraints of Soviet rules, the historians were free to express themselves unrestrained at last. But their new freedom came into effect in a new context. The weakening of Soviet dictatorship went hand in hand with the free fall of Soviet ideology and legitimacy. The new social movements in formation in the urban centres of the Caucasus and the historic centres of the contested autonomies needed a new source for legitimacy, and if the last seven decades of Soviet rule were written off, the new movements and their leaders needed to look back in history for guidance, to look back to help guess the future. The search for a new source of legitimacy revisited history, and this wave brought historians to the forefront of political debates. And the role historians played in the context of the Soviet collapse was to find a glorious and everlasting past to justify territorial claims, or present counterclaims, arming the masses for the clashes to come. In this exercise, they borrowed much from the works they had previously produced on the orders (*zakaz*) of the Soviet authorities.

This "new history" differed from the more complex version that was debated during the Soviet period in several ways. The "new history" was extremely reductionist, heavily politicized; centuries were reduced to single ideas, "details" contradicting the vision of the eternal nation and the newcomer neighbour-enemy were excluded. The new history was necessary for slogans, for mass mobilization, or for outright propaganda, and in those years history was equated to slogans and propaganda.

3

THE KARABAKH CONFLICT

After spending a week in Warsaw and Moscow, in March 1992 I arrived in the Armenian capital Yerevan. This was literally a few weeks after the collapse of the Soviet Union, and people at the time could not grasp what was happening to them. Armenia was technically an independent nation, but people failed to understand what that meant. They talked about "*angakhutyun*", which means "independence", when they referred to post-Soviet Armenia, an expression which at the time meant a combination of uncertainty, chaos, lack of reference, and loneliness for Armenia. When people used the expression "*bedutyun*", meaning "state", they referred to the Soviet Union, the state in which they were born and had lived all their lives, which had suddenly and inexplicably disappeared.

In April 1992 I spent a week in Mountainous Karabakh. At the time, Karabakh was cut off from Armenia proper, and the only way to go there was by air. With two other journalists—photographers from the French Armenian Diaspora—I was lucky to be in a Yakovlev-40, a 32 seated passenger plane from which all seats had been taken off, and which had instead been filled with sacks of flour. I was lucky because we were sitting on top of flour and not in a plane transporting diesel or ammunition. There were a dozen or so fighters and government officials flying with us, returning from Yerevan back to their land in Karabakh. The plane took off from Erebuni airport in Yerevan and took height, to avoid Azeri anti-aircraft fire. When it was above Khojali airport, it went down in circles until it landed. Outside the airport you could see burnt-down houses, the result of the February 1992 fighting during which the Karabakh Armenian forces took over the airport. There were hundreds of people walking in all directions: soldiers, peasants, children, and women. There was no fuel in Karabakh, no public transport, no taxis. In the regional capital Stepanakert there were no shops, no restaurants, and more generally no economy. Money had no function in this war economy. We were given rooms in the Hotel Karabakh, which had neither electricity nor running water, and which was partially destroyed by Grad missiles fired from Shushi, the impressive town to the west of Stepanakert, visible from my hotel window. After a week and numerous interviews in the Stepanakert, Marduni, and Hadrut regions, and after the last days spending under fire, I travelled with two (different) journalists and five wounded civilians in the back of a truck to reach the capital and from there fly back to Yerevan.

In those days it was difficult to be an optimist. Armenia was landlocked, had no access to its traditional partner Russia, had no energy sources; its borders with Azerbaijan in the east and Turkey in the west were closed, and it was at war with its neighbour Azerbaijan over Mountainous Karabakh. Following the 1988 earthquake in which over 25,000 people perished, a third of Armenian industry was in ruins, and the collapse of the USSR had made the rest redundant. The situation in Karabakh seemed even more bleak. The region was completely encircled by Azerbaijani forces, and was facing an enemy force superior in arms, ammunition and numbers. In the year 1992 many in Armenia, but also in neighbouring Azerbaijan and Georgia, thought that the newly achieved independence of their countries was a temporary phenomenon. Many compared the situation with the three short years of 1917-20, when after the fall of the Tsarist Empire the Transcaucasus became independent from Russia and the republics of Armenia, Azerbaijan and Georgia emerged, until the Bolsheviks eventually took over the former Tsarist provinces and integrated them in a new state to be known as Union of Soviet Socialist Republics. Similarly, in 1992, many thought that the independence of Armenia would last as long as the political turmoil in Moscow, and would end once the Russians redefined their system and regained their power. In the meanwhile, the Caucasus had to go through chaos, wars, population exchanges and much suffering.

The making of the Karabakh conflict

The conflict in Mountainous Karabakh casts a long shadow over the modern history of the Caucasus. The interplay between historic events and their role in shaping contemporary ones is a delicate issue: what element of current political developments may be the reflection of historic ills left "uncorrected", and what is genuinely the result of more recent changes and events? Although many specialists writing about the Karabakh conflict have talked about deep rooted antagonism between Armenians and Azerbaijanis, clashes between the two groups in mountainous Karabakh first erupted during the upheavals of 1905-7, with the emergence of nationalist parties on both sides, during what was known as the "Armeno-Tatar Wars". Later, between 1918 and 1920, several wars, massacres and deportations pitted the two sides, as the Tsarist Empire collapsed and independent Armenia and Azerbaijan fought each other for the control of three disputed regions: Nakhichevan, Zangezur, and Mountainous Karabakh. In the weeks following the entry of the Red Army to Armenia, Karabakh was recognized by the Communist leadership of Azerbaijan as part of Soviet Armenia. But in 1921 this decision was reversed by the Caucasian Bureau of the CP as a result of the intervention of Stalin himself, and it was decided to place Mountainous Karabakh within Soviet Azerbaijan, with the status of an autonomous region.

The conflict in mountainous Karabakh was the first major political mobilization in the late Soviet period, which was later transformed into inter-state war as the Soviet Union collapsed and Armenia and Azerbaijan fought an undeclared war over control of Karabakh. The territorial boundaries of the present Mountainous Karabakh go back to the formation of the USSR in the early 1920s. Mountainous Karabakh Autonomous Oblast had an area of 4,400 sq. km. and a total population of 162,000 (1979) of whom 123,000 were Armenian.[1] Although the region does not have important geopolitical significance, nor important natural wealth other than forests and water resources, Karabakh has huge symbolic importance for both Armenian and Azerbaijani modern national identity.[2]

1   *Nagornii Karabakh, Istoricheskaya Spravka*, Yerevan: Akademiya Naouk Armianskoi SSR, 1988, p. 7 (in Russian).

2   For a historic background on Mountainous Karabakh conflict, see: Patrick Donabédian and Claude Mutafian, *Artsakh, Histoire du Karabagh*, Paris: Sevig Press, 1989; Christopher Walker (ed.), *Armenia and Karabagh, Struggle for Unity*, London: Minority Rights Publications, 1991; Levon Chorbajian, Patrick Donabedian and Claude Mutafian, *The Caucasian Knot, The History*

Armenian grievances

Throughout the Soviet period Armenians remained dissatisfied with the 1921 arrangement that left Karabakh within Azerbaijan. Armenian activists, and several authors after them, mention economic and cultural grievances to explain or justify the Karabakh Movement: Karabakh Armenians did not receive the amount of public investment compared to other parts of Azerbaijan; Karabakh ethnic Armenians did not have enough educational material in Armenian, were not allowed to receive books from neighbouring Soviet Armenia, could not follow television programmes broadcast from Yerevan. In 1964 Armenians sent a petition to Moscow demanding a change in the administrative borders in the south Caucasus to include Karabakh within the Armenian SSR, as a solution to the continuous dissatisfaction in Karabakh. The Soviet authorities refused to contemplate any change of boundaries, while the situation of Karabakh Armenians did not witness any improvement. The coming of Heydar Aliev, a former KGB officer, to power in Baku only accentuated this repressive policy.[3]

While reading or listening such arguments, it is easy to understand that the real issue is not the economic "backwardness" of Karabakh, nor the level of culture its citizens enjoyed regardless, whether this culture was "Armenian", "Azerbaijani" or "Soviet". Probably the economic level of Karabakh was not qualitatively different from other Azerbaijani mountainous regions—although Karabakh Armenians probably compared their lot with neighbouring Armenia, and not with provincial Azerbaijan. Essentially, Armenians were dissatisfied with Azerbaijani identity politics, which saw in ethnic Armenians an alien or even dangerous element and repressed any expression by them, whether in political or even cultural terms. We may add another argument that is often quoted to explain the Karabakh movement of 1988, the demographic shift within Karabakh: the percentage of ethnic Ar-

and Geopolitics of Nagorno-Karabagh, London: Zed Books, 1994; Azerbaijan, Seven Years of Conflict in Nagorno-Karabakh, New York: Human Rights Watch/ Helsinki, 1994; Thomas Goltz, Azerbaijan Diary, Armonk: M.E. Sharp, 1998; Michael Croissant, The Armenian-Azerbaijani Conflict, Causes and Implications, Westport, CT: Praeger, 1998.

3   Anton Kochinian, "Gharapaghi Hartse 60-agan Tvaganner" [in Armenian: "The Question of Karabakh in the 60's"] Karoun, Yerevan, July 1989, pp. 92-4.

menians was constantly decreasing, while that of ethnic Azeris was on the rise (see Table 1). For Armenians, this represented a deliberate policy of Baku to impose an ethnic Azeri character over Karabakh. Armenians feared that the fate of Karabakh would follow that of Nakhichevan, where the percentage of ethnic Armenian inhabitants was reduced from a substantial 40 per cent of the total population at the time of the Sovietization of the region to a mere 2 per cent in 1988.[4]

The heart of the matter was not a struggle over resources, or the fight for the recognition of a specific culture. The source of the problem was that after seven decades of Soviet rule Armenians did not consider Azerbaijani rule over them as legitimate, and they feared its long-term consequences, which they imagined would be loss of their identity. Simultaneously, Karabakh Armenians were in a difficult position. Theoretically they were supposed to enjoy a certain degree of autonomy, but practically, in the Soviet system of vertical command, even the most insignificant matter had to be referred to Baku. Boris Kevorkov, the ethnic Armenian ruler of Mountainous Karabakh Autonomous Region under Aliev, was seen by the Armenian population as a puppet loyal to Baku, and not a legitimate leader.

Year:	1926	1939	1959	1970	1979	1989
Total	125.3	150.8	130.4	150.3	162.2	189.1
Armenians	111.7	132.8	110.1	121.1	123.1	145.5
Percentage	89.1	88.1	84.4	80.6	75.9	76.9
Azeris	12.6	14.1	18	27.2	37.3	40.6
Percentage	10.1	9.3	13.8	18.1	22.9	21.5
Russians 0.6	3.2	1.8	1.3	1.9	1.9	
Percentage	0.5	2.1	1.4	0.9	0.8	1

Table 1: Ethnic composition of Mountainous Karabakh Autonomous Region, in thousands and in percentage of the total.

Armenian inhabitants of Karabakh, and the intelligentsia of Yerevan, did not stay indifferent towards the situation of Mountainous Karabakh and its political status subordinated to Baku. As early as the 1920s Armenians in Karabakh and the regions around formed an

---

4   Akam Ayvazian, *Nakhichevan*, Yerevan: Hushartsan, 1995, p. 7; Mikhail Gorbachev, *Memoirs*, London: Bantam Books, 1995. Chernyaev quotes Gorbachev saying that "the Armnian population there [Nakhichevan] dropped from 40 to 1.5 per cent." Anatoly Chernyaev, *My Six Years With Gorbachev*, University Park: Penn State University Press, 2000, pp. 182-3.

underground organization aiming at the unification of Karabakh with neighbouring Soviet Armenia. Even under Stalin there were protests against keeping Karabakh—as well as Nakhichevan—under Azerbaijani rule. Aghasi Khanjian, the First Secretary of the Armenian CP, is reported to have worked towards the restoration of those two provinces to Armenia. His efforts led to clashes with Beria, who shot him dead in his Tbilisi office in 1936.[5] This did not restrain his successor at the head of the Armenian CP, Harutunian, from continuing efforts to call Moscow to revise the frontiers between Armenia and Azerbaijan and attach Karabakh to Armenia. In 1962, 2,500 signatures were collected by Karabakh Armenians and sent to Khrushchev denouncing Azerbaijan's discriminatory policies. This started a series of petitions from the region addressed to Moscow, and supported by thousands of signatures.[6] Another petition sent to Nikita Khrushchev in 1964 complained of the "repopulating the Armenian villages of Martuni and Mars with Azerbaijanis" and added twelve points of specific grievances; it concluded: "We request a prompt decision so as to reincorporate Mountainous Karabagh and all adjacent Armenian regions into the Armenian SSR, or to make them part of RSFSR [Russian Soviet Federal Socialist Republic]."[7]

There was unanimity between Soviet Armenian officials and the political dissidents around the Karabakh question. With the formation of the Yerevan branch of the "Helsinki Group" to oversee the application of the Helsinki Final Act signed in 1975, the issue of the rights of Karabakh Armenians was one among others related to violations of human rights in Soviet Armenia.

---

5   Christopher Walker, "The Armenian Presence in Mountainous Karabagh", in John F.R. Wright, Suzanne Goldenberg and Richard Schofield (eds), *Transcaucasus Boundaries*, London: UCL Press, 1996, p. 103.

6   Claire Mouradian, *Arménie, de Staline à Gorbachev, histoire d'une république soviétique*, Paris: Ramsay, 1990, pp. 254-5.

7   This letter was written on 19 May 1964, and first published in the Diaspora publication *The Armenian Review*, Boston, Autumn 1968. See Gerard Libaridian, *The Karabagh File, Documents and Facts on the Question of Mountainous Karabagh 1918-1988*, Cambridge: The Zoryan Institute, March 1988, pp. 44-6.

Karabakh in the age of reforms

In the age of *glasnost*, Armenian mobilization around the Karabakh cause could only intensify. Armenian intellectuals living and working in Yerevan, such as Zori Balaian, or those working in Russia, such as Gorbachev's economic consultant Abel Aganbekian or the historian Sergei Mikoyan, increased their declarations in all-Union publications, as well as foreign ones, about the Karabakh issue. Delegations from Stepanakert or Yerevan took turns to go to Moscow to express their dissatisfaction, and their complaints received a certain attention. One report mentions a Karabakh Armenian delegation led by the filmmaker Edmond Keoseyan carrying a "petition signed by close to 100,000" persons, meeting high ranking officials in Moscow who later put "forward their case to the Committee of Nationalities for their evaluation."[8] On 12 February 1988 a delegation of Karabakh intelligentsia flew to Moscow and presented to the Kremlin sixty thousand signatures demanding the unification of their Autonomous Region with Soviet Armenia.[9] A *New York Times* article talked of three separate delegations carrying petitions to Moscow. The first delegation composed of 12 people went to Moscow in November 1987, while the second met a non-voting member of the Politburo, Pyotr Demichev, in the Kremlin; he later considered the demands of the delegation "neither anti-Soviet nor nationalistic."[10] The third delegation made its pilgrimage to Moscow in "early" February, and found an even warmer reception. "When they came back, they were celebrating their victory," said Mofses Gargisyan, editor of a dissident magazine in Yerevan. "They really thought they had won."[11]

As the tension in Stepanakert rose, demonstrations in Yerevan became more frequent, and delegations from Armenia and Karabakh regularly visited the centre of Soviet power demanding the application of "Leninist"

largest city in NK

---

8 "Report of a Karabagh delegation Meeting with Soviet official in Moscow", *Asbarez*, Los Angeles, 21 January 1988.

9 Pakur, *Yev Nra Shurch*, Yerevan: Arevik, 1990, p. 6 (in Armenian). It is not clear whether the January and February petitions are one and the same, or two separate ones.

10 Felicity Barringer and Bill Keller, "A test of change explodes in Soviet", *New York Times*, 11 March 1988. The quote comes from Igor Muradyan, a member of the delegation and an early leader of the Karabakh Movement in Yerevan.

11 *New York Times*, 11 March 1988.

principles of nationalities policy in the case of Karabakh. Armenian activists and intellectuals had the perception that Moscow was at last listening to them, that they could solve this problem through constitutional ways, and within the limits of Soviet legality. They naively thought that their national demands coincided with the official policies articulated around *perestroika* and *glasnost*. In the meantime, a new event took place that became a milestone in the mobilization of the Armenians of Karabakh. On 20 February 1988 the Soviet of the Mountainous Karabakh Autonomous Region met in a special session to discuss the increasing tension within the region. After heated debates, the Karabakh Soviet adopted a resolution by the vote of 110 out of a total of 140 deputies demanding "to transfer the Autonomous Region of Mountainous Karabagh from the Azerbaijani S. S. R. to the Armenian S. S. R."[12] For Levon Ter-Petrossian, this was a unique event where a "state structure could adopt an independent decision"[13] without previous orders from above, from Moscow. When the news reached Yerevan, small environmentalist activists who were demonstrating against the construction of a new chemical plant in one of the suburbs of Yerevan swelled immediately and in a couple of days attracted hundreds of thousands. They gathered at the Opera Square in support of the Karabakh Soviet demand for *miyatsoum,* or unification in Armenian.[14] Thus an autonomous political movement came into being, independent from the official party-state-KGB structures of the Soviet Union, and in the following few years had not only a deep impact on the politics of the Transcaucasus, but also a transformative effect throughout the Soviet Union.

Karabakh, Southern Azerbaijan and the Baku intelligentsia

While for Armenian intellectuals and dissidents the issue of Karabakh was a topic of mobilization, for Azerbaijani intellectuals it did not have

---

12   The text of the resolution was published in *Sovetakan Gharabagh*, Stepanakert, 21 February 1998. An English translation can be found in Libaridian, *The Karabagh File,* op. cit., p. 90. See also Chorbajian *et al., The Caucasian Knot,* op. cit., p. 149. 17 deputies voted against and 13 abstained. The English translation of the text of the resolution can be found in the same book, on p. 180.

13   Author interview with Levon Ter-Petrossian, Yerevan, 18 December 2004.

14   According to press reports, up to 1 million demonstrated in Yerevan by the last week of February 1988. See William Eaton, "1 Million Reportedly Take Part as Protests Continue in Armenia", *Los Angeles Times*, 26 February 1988.

the same significance in Soviet times. Until the start of mass mobilization in Stepanakert and Yerevan in 1988, the question of Karabakh did not constitute part of the Azerbaijani national agenda. Karabakh was part of Azerbaijan, and the official policies of Baku were enough to counter Armenian actions; there was no need for independent mobilization within the Azerbaijani intelligentsia and broader social circles. Outside a handful of historians, who were engaged in debates with their Armenian colleagues about the ethnic, linguistic and cultural identity of lost tribes of the Caucasus in early history and the Middle Ages, or the ethnic composition of Karabakh and Zangezur in the 19th century and population movements in those regions, the larger public—even the greater part of the Azerbaijani intelligentsia—did not take notice of the existence of such a debate. In mainstream Azerbaijani art and literature the Russo-Persian wars of the early 19th century, and the "division" of Azerbaijan as a result of the Treaty of Turkmanchai (1828), was the dominant theme, and the cornerstone of Azerbaijani national identity. Such expressions of nationalism, directed against Iran and not against Russia, were not only tolerated but actively encouraged by Moscow, as a Soviet foreign policy instrument to influence Iran and formulate territorial claims towards it. "Soviet Azerbaijani intellectual publications indicated that the subject of the connection between Azerbaijanis in the north and the south was of constant interest throughout the post-World War II period. These writings, produced primarily for readers in the republic of Soviet Azerbaijan, were published almost exclusively in Azerbaijani and rarely in Russian."[15] The official institutions in Azerbaijan encouraged raising of the "South Azerbaijan" problem, and a main centre for publicizing this issue was the Azerbaijan Writers Union, since many of its members had been active in Iran under Soviet occupation.[16] For example, during a congress of the Azerbaijani Writers' Union in 1986, Ismayil Shikhli argued for incorporating themes from

---

15   Brenda Shaffer, *Borders and Brethren, Iran and the Challenge of Azerbaijani Identity*, Cambridge, MA: MIT Press, 2002, p. 72.

16   David Nissman, *The Soviet Union and Iranian Azerbaijan, The Use of Nationalism for Political Penetration*, Boulder, CO: Westview, 1987, pp. 46-7. Shaffer mentions that an outspoken champion of unification between the two Azerbaijans in Baku was none other than Mirza Ibrahimov, a long term head of the official Writer's Union. In *Brother and Brethren*, p. 72.

Southern (Iranian) Azerbaijan into Soviet Azerbaijani literature.[17] The debate about the separation of Azerbaijan between "north" and "south" and between two foreign empires, Russian and Persian, was the dominant debate among Azerbaijani intellectuals until February 1988, while the problem of Karabakh and the rivalry with Armenia was a marginal one.[18] In December 1989 thousands of Azerbaijani demonstrators, led by the Popular Front of Azerbaijan, gathered in several spots near the Soviet-Iranian border in the Nakhichevan Autonomous Republic, attacked border posts and burned them down, and crossed the Arax river to the other side, to Iran. Many chanted slogans for the unity between "north and south Azerbaijan". With the emergence of the Karabakh problem the political context changed dramatically, and the question of "southern Azerbaijan" was pushed to the background under the pressure of developing events. It is difficult to imagine what the consequences would have been had the Azerbaijani national movement developed in the absence of the Karabakh factor, pouring its energies and mobilized masses to the other side of the Arax river, and clashing with the guardians of the Islamic Republic of Iran.

The question of "southern" Azerbaijan remains on the political agenda for many Azerbaijani political activists. Nizami Guliev, a member of the Milli Majlis (Azerbaijani parliament) and an activist of the Popular Front of Azerbaijan, stressed the importance of unifying the two parts of Azerbaijan. For Guliev, this unification should be seen in the context of "collapse of empires", like the unification of the two parts of Germany. "The Popular Front is just in its struggle for the unification of the two parts of the Azeri people. The thirteen million Azeris have the right to their language and to practice their culture."[19] He added that this could happen as a result of democratic developments within Iran.

Not only did the Armenian and Azerbaijani intelligentsias have different perceptions about their national problems under the Soviet re-

---

17   Mark Saroyan, *Minorities, Mullahs and Modernity: Reshaping Community in the Former Soviet Union,* University of California International and Area Studies Digital Collection, Research Series #95, 1997, p. 220. Internet address: http://repositories.cdlib.org/uciaspubs/research/95/

18   Shireen Hunter, "Azerbaijan: Search for Identity" in Ian Bremmer and Ray Taras (eds), *Nations and Politics in the Soviet Successor States,* Cambridge University Press, 1993, pp. 229-30.

19   Author interview with Nizami Guliev, Baku, 2 July 1999.

96

[handwritten marginalia: role of mediation had been played by Moscow during USSR. now? what?]

gime, and different perceptions of the situation of Karabakh; they did not have instruments and channels for negotiations to regulate existing problems, nor any means for restraint once the conflict erupted. This role of mediation had been fulfilled for seven decades by the Moscow authorities. The Azerbaijani leadership was ill-equipped to articulate a position in response to the Armenian demands. In a characteristic manner Ayaz Mutalibov, a high-level Azerbaijani party official, said in answer to the questions of a TASS correspondent: "In many areas of national economy, Nagorno-Karabagh, in which Armenians make up the majority, is noticeably ahead of the average indicators of the entire republic."[20] He added: "There are more kindergartens, hospital beds and libraries per capita of its population compared to an average in Azerbaijan."[21] In other words, for the Baku authorities discussions and negotiations were not on the agenda.

Sumgait: the birth of the Karabakh conflict

There are individual events that come to trigger decade long conflicts. The operation of the Colombian Army in May 1964 in Marquetalia not only led to the birth of FARC (the Colombian Armed Revolutionary Forces) but also set into motion a conflict which is now over four decades old. The attack in Ain al-Remmane, a suburb of Beirut, against a bus full of pro-Palestinian activists on 13 April 1975 led to the fifteen-year-long "little wars" of Lebanon. Describing those events is a difficult task for a historian, because time has transformed them into potent political symbols. According to a Colombian researcher, even the name of the operation launched by the Colombian army in Marquetalia is the subject of one of the most passionate debates in Colombian historiography.[22] The reason is that it has become the founding myth not only of the conflict, but also of the political traditions that emerged out of the armed confrontation and developed as institutions under the legitimacy of this founding myth. Any interpretation given by the historian could follow the positions defended by one side of the conflict or the other,

---

20   TASS, 23 February 1988, reprinted in Libaridian, op. cit., p. 99.

21   Ibid., p. 100.

22   Eduardo Pizarro Leongomez, "Le mythe fondateur des FARC", translated into French in *Courrier International*, Paris, No. 711, 17-23 June 2004, p. 12.

and can potentially be seen as defending the new political system that took power after the events, or criticizing it.

The bloody events in Sumgait in the last three days of February 1988 have played a similar role in the Karabakh conflict. The first blood was spilled in Sumgait, turning a political confrontation which was just taking form into a violent one. Before Sumgait, it was possible to imagine a *deus ex machina* intervening and calming the passions, proposing compromises, or imposing a new order. After Sumgait, such an eventuality became hardly possible. Sumgait opened the doors of Caucasus history into the unknown, launching an adventure that broke the old rules of the political games, without defining new ones. While trying to describe the events of Sumgait, one is confronted with two sets of questions. First, was Sumgait an "explosion" of passions, a spontaneous action by uncontrolled and uncontrollable masses, or was it planned and organized? And, if it was a planned event, who bears the responsibility—who could possibly organize such an action, and what political forces had an interest in it?

According to Garry Wills, any analysis of war has to consider three stages in its development: "the causes of war, the conduct of war, and the consequences of war."[23] What Wills considers as the causes of war in itself could be divided into two distinct parts; the first is the background of war, various historic, cultural, economic factors that lead to the building up of antagonistic sides and a rise in tension, which create general conditions for violence to take place; the second is a conscious effort by a group of people who profit from changing political circumstances to advance a programme, or try to preserve the existing political arrangements, through the use of violence. This use of violence, initially intended as precise and limited in time and space, bears the risk of changing the rules of the existing political order established this far, and creating an atmosphere of fear and uncertainty, thus sparking a long and bloody conflict. While a large part of conflict studies has focused on the second stage, the conduct of war after it starts, it is highly important to study the causes of war. For Wills, to study a just war, one has to embark on its causes, since once a war erupts it is extremely difficult, if not impossible, to keep it under control and not to reach extreme prac-

---

23   Garry Wills, "What Is a Just War?" *New York Review of Books*, Volume 51, Number 18, 18 November 2004.

tices and hurt innocents or destroy their property, thus questioning the moral high ground of the warring sides.

Now, what exactly happened in Sumgait is naturally controversial. There are "facts" that are contested by some, while others propose a different set of alternative facts, or different interpretations for the same facts. Eventually, each side of the conflict has a different version of the events, to defend its own position in the conflict. Moreover, researchers and commentators, whether from the region or from outside, consciously or not, have defended one version or another of the events in Sumgait, and by doing so have revealed their sympathies towards one of the conflict sides.

As we have seen, the peaceful campaign to transfer Karabakh to the Armenian SSR led to mass mobilization in Armenia in February 1988, starting with the vote of the Karabakh Soviet on 20 February that led to demonstrations in the next days in Stepanakert and Yerevan. In a short time, several isolated clashes led to a chain reaction and a major explosion of violence. Even before Sumgait, several dispersed acts of violence were reported. Two days after the resolution of the Karabakh Soviet, anti-Armenian disturbances broke out in the town of Hadrut in Nagorno-Karabakh, injuring sixteen and killing two. On the same day, 22 February 1988, the head of the Azerbaijani Communist Party, Kyamran Bagirov, arrived at Aghdam. On the same day also a group of Azerbaijanis moved to the neighbouring Armenian town of Askeran, on their way to Stepanakert, burning down property and overturning cars. The Soviet press reports that the "first outburst occurred in Azerbaidzhan's Agdam District (...) Nationalistically inclined elements managed to assemble a crowd and lead it to Askeran District in Nagorno-Karabakh 'to establish order.' As a result of the clash two people were killed and many were hospitalized with injuries."[24] The two killed were young Azerbaijanis from Aghdam, probably killed by police officers. For many Azerbaijani authors this was "the first blood" and therefore the responsibility of the initiation of the bloody conflict should go to the Armenian side.[25]

24   The article is signed by Yu. Arakelyan, Z. Kadymbekov and G. Ovcharenko: "Emotion and Reason", *Pravda*, 21 March 1988. English text in: *The Current Digest of the Soviet Press* (hereafter *CDSP*), XL, No. 12, 1988, p. 9.

25   Taleh Ziyadov, "Eine Vergessene Tragödie Im Kaukasus", *friZ*, Zurich, No. 3, 2005, pp. 14-16; Adil Baguirov, "Top 5 Myths Circulating about the Nagorno-Katabakh Conflict", *Azerbaijan International Magazine*, Baku, Spring 1998.

In the same days, high level officials from Moscow arrived in Baku, Stepanakert, and Yerevan. Among them were Georgi Razumkovsky and Pyotr Demichev (who met an Armenian delegation earlier in February 1988 in Moscow), both Politburo candidate members, arriving in Stepanakert on 22 February; Alexander Katusev, the deputy Attorney General of the USSR, in Baku; and the Moscow envoys Vladimir Dolgikh and Anatoly Lukyanov who arrived at the same time in Yerevan. Katusev in Baku and Dolgikh in Yerevan made somewhat strange but quite similar statements to the local media. On 27 February Katusev said on Baku radio that "as a consequence of those disorders, two inhabitants of Aghdam district ... fell victim to murder."[26] Katusev gave two names, both Azerbaijani.[27] It is difficult to attribute this to human error, since the text of the declaration was seen by the First Secretary of the Karabakh Regional Party Committee, Henrik Poghosian, "who insisted that the mention of the victim's nationality be removed from the announcement. Poghosyan explained to Katusev that isolated from other relevant facts the announcement would cause grave consequences".[28] Dolgikh made a similar declaration in Yerevan, telling Armenian TV that there were "clashes in Karabakh between Armenians and Azeris; there are casualties."[29] As we shall see later, the declarations played a fatal role in the eruption of violence.

Sumgait, an industrial city situated on the Caspian coast to the north of Baku, was inhabited by 223,000 people of a mix of ethnicities, including a substantial Armenian minority (15-20,000). Built in the 1940s, it was then populated by Azerbaijanis who were deported there from Armenia as Stalin was making space for Armenian repatriates after World War II. Other Azerbaijani families had moved there only recently, in

---

26   *New York Times*, 11 March 1988.

27   Robin Lodge, "Moscow Reports New Violence in Troubled Transcaucasia", Reuters, Moscow, February 29, 1988. According to this report, the two victims are: "two youths aged 16 and 23 (...) It was clear from the names of the victims, Bakhtiar Uliyev and Ali Gadzhiyev, that they were Azerbaijanis."

28   Samuel Shahmuratian (ed.), *The Sumgait Tragedy, Pogroms against Armenians in Soviet Azerbaijan*, Volume I, Zoryan Institute, MA, 1990, p. 4. This volume, based on interviews with Sumgait survivors a few months after the events, gives a graphic description of the pogrom.

29   From *Kommunist*, Yerevan, 25 February 1988, quoted in: Igor Nolyain, "Moscow's initiation of the Azeri-Armenian conflict", *Central Asian Survey*, 13 (4), pp. 541-63, 1994 (p. 541).

the 1980s.[30] A creation of rapid Soviet industrialization efforts, the city suffered from a deep social crisis, including unemployment and housing problems. According to the Azerbaijani official paper of 1 March, "On February 28 a group of hooligan elements provoked disturbances in Sumgait. There were instances of outrages and violence." Under the title "Communique" the paper did not give any details about who were the "hooligans", nor about the identity or the number of the victims, but concluded: "Measures have been taken to normalize life in the city…"[31] On 3 March, the same newspaper added some information: "Unstable and immature people who fell under the influence of provocative rumours and inflammatory talk about the events in Nagorno-Karabakh and Armenia were drawn into illegal actions." And: "Tragic events occurred, and there were fatalities."[32] Two days later *Pravda* added that the number of those killed was 31, "among them people of various nationalities."[33] The number rose to 32 dead, 197 injured (among them "about" 100 policemen), and 47 arrested.[34]

A long article in *Pravda* on 21 March studied extensively, for the first time the background of the conflict in Karabakh.[35] It mentioned the complex history of the province, and emphasized that the status of the province was only decided in 1923, taking into "consideration first and foremost which republic will enable the region to develop more rapidly in economic and social respects"; this decision, it went on, did not put an end to controversy over the issue, which erupted "again and again" each time "Armenian leaders stood to benefit by distracting public attention from the numerous unsolved economic and social problems…" After criticizing the Communist old guard of Armenia,

---

30 Audrey L. Altstadt, *The Azerbaijani Turks, Power and Identity Under Russian Rule*, Stanford, CA: Hoover Institution Press, 1992, p. 197.

31 *Bakinsky Rabochi*, "Communique", 1 March 1988. English translation in *CDSP*, XL, No. 9, 1988, p. 7.

32 *Bakinsky Rabochi*, "On the Situation in Sumgait", 3 March 1988. English translation in *CDSP*, XL, No. 9, 1988, p. 9.

33 *Pravda*, 5 March 1988; in *CDSP*, XL, No. 9, 1988, p. 9.

34 "In the USSR Prosecutor's Office", *Pravda*, 22 March 1988, in *CDSP*, XL, No. 12, 1988, p. 11.

35 The article is signed by Yu. Arakelyan, Z. Kadymbekov and G. Ovcharenko, "Emotion and Reason", *Pravda*, 21 March, 1988, in *CDSP*, XL, No. 12, 1988, pp. 7-9.

and the egoistic nationalism of the demonstrators, the article admitted that real "problems exist" and listed some: "We were told that even now (...) Azerbaidzhan's executive agencies still stifle local initiative, that capital investments in Nagorno-Karabakh are lower per capita than in other parts of the republic, that arbitrary orders 'from above' in Baku eliminated the study of the history of the Armenian people in Armenian language schools, and even the program of cultural ties with Armenia has to be approved by republican departments." Eventually focusing on current events, the newspaper reported that violence first erupted when a crowd from Aghdam moved towards Askeran (a town in Karabakh, half-way between Stepanakert and Aghdam) igniting clashes. As a result "two people were killed" and many more injured. And: "The events of Sumgait were more awful." A certain "General V. Krayev" was quoted as saying, "There would have been more casualties if the residents hadn't helped us." This strange information about a Soviet general present in Sumgait during the tragic events, according to *Pravda*, while the Soviet army failed to stop a pogrom carried out by a mob armed with knives and chains creates ground for suspicion.

The declaration of "General V. Krayev" about Sumgait civilians helping the army to put down the violence is equally bizarre. But as we saw earlier, the reports in the Soviet media were often political essays rather than journalistic reporting, written in political organs in offices far away from the actual events, and full of contradiction. This long article in *Pravda* seems to have been written by shadow authors: one of its "authors", Yuri Arakelyan, later disavowed any knowledge of or involvement in this article, protesting to the *Pravda* editors: "By putting my signature beneath the dishonest materials of the Communist Party, you have insulted me before the whole country."[36]

But who were those "hooligans" who perpetrated the crimes, and why did the police or the army not intervene earlier? In his paper, Igor Nolyain refers to several sources to show that the criminals in Sumgait came from all over Azerbaijan. He quotes a Russian dissident, Andrei Shelkov, who went to Sumgait just after the events, as saying "the violence was the work of Azeris who came to Sumgait from throughout

---

36   Felicity Barringer, "Pravda writer disavows article on Armenia," *New York Times*, 23 March 1988.

102

Handwritten margin notes:
2 Azeri kids killed in Aghdam
NK. announcement that those killed in Hadrut were Azeri sparked Sumgait
(32 dead 150 injured)
ALL MOSCOW's FAULT

Azerbaijan."[37] The army seems to have arrived only "three to five days" after the pogrom started, although even a small force was enough to stop a criminal group of fifty people from continuing the rampage for several days. Strangely enough, while the local police stood still, and troops from other garrisons took several days to arrive to a town in turmoil, the Deputy Interior Minister of the USSR, Nikolai Demidov, was quoted saying that he himself "went to Sumgait during the clashes," adding that the local militia "proved to be not up to the job".[38] Was the Deputy Minister in Sumgait during the clashes to evaluate the functioning of the local police force? Why could he not manage to bring in forces from Baku or even from Russia for three days? Was Katusev's declaration of Azerbaijanis' deaths an attempt to stir up trouble? At least this is what foreign journalists thought a few days later: "It is considered highly likely that the disclosure of the two Azerbaijani deaths led to the violence in Sumgait and Kirovabad."[39] For Nolyain, it is clear that the events in Sumgait were organized and monitored by the centre, with the knowledge of the head of the state, and Katusev's declarations to Baku Radio were the clear signal: "It divulges Moscow's double ulterior aim: to calm the Armenians while bloodying them, and to leak that Azeris are moved by 'ethnic hatred' and not by the KGB provocateurs."[40] He fitted this into a more general policy of Russia towards its colonies:

Many reporters and Sovietologists apparently don't know that 'a history of conflict predating' the USSR includes the same method to instigate the Caucasian peoples against each other. In the 18th and 19th centuries, tsars used the same technique to subjugate the Caucasus.[41]

But the KGB's acts—whether with the knowledge of the Soviet Politburo or without—cannot on their own write the history of the Caucasus. If the Armenian and Azerbaijani intelligentsias had rejected the logic of inter-ethnic conflict and had a different vision of how to solve the real and difficult political questions that the transformation of the

---

37   Igor Nolyain, "Moscow's Initiation of the Azeri-Armenian Conflict", *Central Asian Survey*, 13 (4), pp. 541-63, 1994, p. 542.

38   *Reuters*, 18 April 1988.

39   Felcity Barringer, "Soviet Armenians mourn their dead", *New York Times*, 9 March 1998.

40   Igor Nolyain, "Moscow's initiation of the Azeri-Armenian conflict", p. 558.

41   Nolyain, p. 559.

USSR was posing, they could have tried a different political development other than ethnic violence.

What was lacking in Baku in those crucial days was an outright mobilization to condemn those acts of massacre, and thus dissociate Azerbaijan from the crime just committed. Instead, Ziya Buniyatov accused the victims[42], reflecting the opinions of a leading historian and the intellectual mood in Baku. In face of the immensity of the developments, the only explanation was to think in categories of plots. A more powerful argument, which has found resonance until today, is the one put forward by another historian, Igrar Aliev. He considers that the pogroms in Sumgait were a reaction to Armenian actions:

> Days-long meetings in Yerevan, eyewitness stories about persecutions and violence against Azerbaijanis living in Armenia, led to a group of rootless elements, who had no relation to the Azerbaijani people, succeeding in provocation of a part of the youth to commit public disturbances…[43]

What Igrar Aliev recounts here later took the shape of another narrative, which with time took on a life of its own, by being quoted and re-quoted without any checking back to the original source. According to this, the fifty or so "hooligans" who committed the crimes in Sumgait were themselves victims, ethnic Azeri refugees from the Armenian town of Ghapan. The position of Azerbaijani intellectuals and public figures is highly important; instead of condemning the acts of violence in Sumgait and thus making it an isolated event, they justified the pogroms, or even accused the victims of being responsible for the acts of violence. Such a position was instrumental in having Sumgait events repeated elsewhere in the coming months, in Kirovabad (Ganja), Baku, and many other localities.

Western authors, wishing to take a "neutral" position in this interethnic conflict, have found it appropriate to present the initial act of violence as if it came from both sides. For one author looking at ways to resolve the conflict, "Violence was unleashed, with each side claiming that the other initiated the hostilities. Hundreds of thousands of refugees were created as both Armenians and Azeris fled to avoid the fight-

---

42   Ziya Buniatov, "Pochimou Sumgait?", op. cit.

43   Igrar Aliev, *Nagorni Karabakh: Istoria, Fakti, Sobiti* (in Russian: "Mountainous Karabakh, History, Facts, Events"), Baku: Elm, 1989, p. 96.

ing or were expelled or forced out."[44] The description is neutral—and lacks precision—in an attempt by the author not to take sides. We are unable to know who started the violence or where. Did violence start in Sumgait with the pogroms of February 1988, or was it the result of a furious Azerbaijani mob composed of refugees freshly arrived from Armenia? Was Sumgait action or reaction? An author, who has written extensively on the Caucasus, is more precise and proposes the theme of the refugees:

major question

> In January, large numbers of Azeris had fled their homes in Armenia due to harassment; (…). In Azerbaijan, Baku radio reported that two Azeris had been killed in Karabakh, and as a result counter-violence erupted and the ethnic conflict (…) followed its own logic. This led to the pogrom of Sumgait, where Azeri thugs, with the help of frustrated refugees from Armenia, attacked Armenians in the dark industrial town of Sumgait....[45]

all Azerbaijan's fault?

For this narrative, the Sumgait pogrom was a reaction not to political demands, but to violence from the Armenian side. The author claims that there were massive deportations of Azeris from Armenia in January 1988, that is even before the resolution of the Karabakh Soviet (20 February) and the start of demonstrations in Stepanakert and Yerevan. Yet, although Cornell's narrative incorporates the Azerbaijani version of events, he does not provide us with facts, and it is difficult to know his sources. It is also very unlikely that "harassment" could cause the fleeing of "large numbers" of people from their place of origin to a neighbouring country. In a later writing, the author mentions the possibility of Azerbaijani refugees from Armenia, but diminishes its significance, and influenced by Nolyain's analysis tends to lean towards the possibility of outside manipulation of this conflict: "The discussion on Sumgait is difficult to conclude; the event remains a mystery and makes no sense.

---

44   Patricia Carley, *Nagorno-Karabakh Searching for a Solution*, Washington: United States Institute for Peace, at: http://www.usip.org/pubs/peaceworks/pwks25/pwks25.html

45   Svante E. Cornell, "Turkey and the Conflict in Nagorno Karabakh: A Delicate Balance," *Middle Eastern Studies* Vol. 34, No. 1 (January 1998), pp. 51-72. The author expressed a similar position a year later: "During 1988, ethnic cleansing first in Armenia and later in Azerbaijan developed unhindered…" without presenting any facts about how, when, where, and how many people were displaced. Svante Cornell, "The Devaluation of the Concept of Autonomy: National Minorities in the Former Soviet Union", *Central Asian Survey*, Vol. 18, No. 2, 1999, p. 190.

There was no mobilized Azeri ethnic nationalism to speak of on 26 February 1988."[46]

It is true that Azerbaijanis suffered discrimination in Armenia as Armenians did in Azerbaijan all through the Soviet period, and there was regular migration of Azerbaijanis from Armenia to Azerbaijan to seek better living conditions. But one cannot find traces of mass ethnic violence either in Armenia or in Azerbaijan until late February 1988, that is until the Sumgait pogroms.

Similar positions are defended by Azerbaijani authors: these commentators consider that Sumgait was not the main event, that the trigger to the conflict should be seen as the killing of the two Azerbaijanis in Askeran, four days earlier: "…even before these murders, there was the fact of expulsion of Azerbaijani population from Armenia, particularly from the Megri and Kafan districts, by February 1988 numbering in thousands, even according to official statistics."[47] Sometimes in the imagination of some authors roles are reversed. Adil Baguirov writes that "Armenian nationals actively participated in the mob" and adds to this KGB involvement, while "Azerbaijan and its people" were meanwhile in Baku and elsewhere "involved in saving the lives of many of their Armenian neighbours."[48] It is well documented that Azerbaijanis in Sumgait, as well as later in the Baku pogroms, did save their Armenian friends and neighbours, by hiding them in their own apartments or providing them protection in various forms. Baguirov is not mentioning this to underline the numerous cases of solidarity Azeris expressed towards their Armenian neighbours, but is trying to make victims into criminals, which has nothing to do with any attempt to understand past events and is not any special expression of political wisdom; it is simply a propaganda effort that unfortunately continues as the historic distance between the present and those dark days widens.

One should add that in February 1988 there was no violence committed in Armenia to generate Azerbaijani refugees. The demonstrations in Armenia in early 1988, and until the pogroms in Sumgait,

---

46   Svante Cornell, *Small Nations and Great Powers, A Study of Ethnopolitical Conflict in the Caucasus*, London: Curzon, 2001, p. 83.

47   Adil Baguirov, "Top 5 Myths Circulating about the Nagorno-Katabakh Conflict", *Azerbaijan International Magazine*, Baku, Spring 1998.

48   Ibid.

remained peaceful and within the limits of civil disobedience. As the demonstrations were gaining volume in Yerevan's Opera Square, and days before the pogrom in Azerbaijan, Gorbachev received the poetess Silva Kaputikian and the journalist Zori Balaian, to discuss the Karabakh situation. Gorbachev himself acknowledged the peaceful nature of the demonstrations, "noting with approval that the crowds marching through the streets hushed when they passed a hospital, to avoid disturbing patients."[49]

Three Armenian politicians who played key role in the late 1980s as leaders of the Karabakh Movement had different interpretations of "why Sumgait?" For Levon Ter-Petrossian, the leader of the Karabakh Committee and later the first President of independent Armenia, the Sumgait events "turned the constitutional process to physical clashes. (...) Until then, we believed that if the Soviet Union was going towards democratization those questions had to be opened."[50] Although Sumgait dramatically changed the context of the Karabakh problem, Ter-Petrossian believes that it was organized "neither by Moscow, nor by Baku". What about the passivity of police and armed forces for several days? "There could have been provocations by GRU,[51] or others. The local police and authorities collaborated in the events. (...) And as for Moscow being late by three days in intervening, I do not find in this any organized element, we know that the state was badly organized. Look at Beslan and Nord Ost."[52] He added that in those dramatic days the Politburo in Moscow "had difficulties to take decision" due to the unforeseen developments in the Caucasus.

Vazgen Manukian, the former mathematics professor who became the "ideologue" of the Karabakh Movement, was one of the most influential leaders of contemporary Armenian politics. He said, "[Sum-

---

49   *New York Times*, 11 March 1988.

50   Author interview with Levon Ter-Petrossian, Yerevan, 18 December 2004.

51   GRU: military intelligence.

52   Beslan and Nord Ost were terrorist operations launched by Chechen fighters on the territories of the Russian Federation, the first in a school in the town of Beslan in North Ossetia in September 2004, and the second in a Moscow theatre in October 2002. In both cases the reaction of the Russian Special Forces was heavy handed and badly organized, and medical intervention to help the victims was nearly non-existent. As a result, there were 344 civilian victims in Beslan and the official death toll of civilian victims in Nord Ost was 129.

gait] was organized. Armenians and Azeris lived in the Soviet Union as neighbours, the existing contradictions did not go out of the limits of daily life, and there was no hatred between the two peoples. (...) I cannot say on what level the events were organized, whether it had reached up to Gorbachev, or whether it was organized on the level of Azerbaijani Central Committee First Secretary level, I do not have such information, but it is clear that the events were organized."[53] For Manukian, the problem of the Soviet leadership in those days was to reform the countries' economy, to restructure its political system, while at the same time trying not to lose its control over the Communist Party. In the Brezhnev era the party had turned into "khanates" in the various republics. In Central Asia, "cotton affairs" were a way to gain control over the local party apparatus. In the Caucasus the way to break the local clan structure was through inter-ethnic conflicts. "What concerns the issue of refugees from Ghapan, there is a mistake in chronology: it was first the events in Sumgait, and only later Azeris from Ghapan were expelled."[54]

Similarly, *The Washington Post* reported at the time that "incidents of violence in Gafan [Ghapan] could not be confirmed by Soviet officials. Armenians have flatly denied that any violence took place in connection with their protests, and the official Soviet media also reported none."[55]

Ashot Manucharian, another member of the Karabakh Committee, the fiery orator of the demonstrations in Opera Square—the Trotsky of the Armenian demonstrations—also says Sumgait was organized, but his analysis differs from previous ones. For Manucharian, the conflict was organized by the Soviet secret services "as a work[56] against Gorbachev's political project. Without the KGB it was impossible to organize such an event. In Azerbaijan there were no organizations, not even mobilization yet on the Karabakh issue."[57] He added that there

---

53   Author interview with Vazgen Manukian, Yerevan, 18 December 2004.

54   Ibid.

55   Gary Lee, "Tensions Build as Ruling on Soviet Region Nears", *The Washington Post*, 21 March 1988.

56   Manucharian used the Armenian expression "*gordz*", which is the translation from the Russian "*delo*", which meant in the Soviet context a KGB organized plot to persecute a suspicious person. Here Manucharian meant by "work" a KGB organized plot.

57   Interview with Ashot Manucharian, Yerevan, 18 December 2004.

were people both in Armenia and in Azerbaijan who had an interest in the Karabakh issue, and the "KGB encouraged those people to mobilize a larger movement. But very soon they lost the control over the movement."[58] Manucharian also said that the first forced migration of ethnic Azerbaijanis from Armenia started as late as November 1988, after the anti-Armenian pogrom in Kirovabad (now Ganja, the second major urban centre in Azerbaijan). In the early weeks of the Karabakh Movement, Armenian intellectuals and activists were very conscious that they were treading a fine line between posing Armenian particularist demands thanks to *glasnost* and hurting the reform movement by their mass mobilization. According to Zori Balayan, a journalist and writer and one of the early leaders of the Karabakh movement: "We understand that all the demonstrations were a result of glasnost and perestroika (...) Now, if we believe in glasnost and perestroika, we must take care not to harm them by our actions."[59]

Among a number of Azerbaijani leaders, the idea that Sumgait was organized as a result of a KGB plot is equally popular. For the leader of the Azerbaijani Musavat Party, Isa Gambar, Sumgait was initiated so that Moscow could keep its leverage on both Armenians and Azeris. "That pogrom was organized to drive a wedge into future relations between Azeris and Armenians (...) unfortunately, when a secret organization conducts an operation on such a scale, there is no record of proofs of their guilt -- these services know how to cover up their wrongdoing."[60]

Looking back at past events, one's memory will necessarily be shrouded with interpretations and explanations that are relevant to one's understanding of the order of things, corresponding to one's worldview. In the absence of hard documentary evidence, KGB reports or Central Committee documents, it is impossible to completely dmystify this event so charged with emotions. In the meanwhile, we can do one thing: to study how Sumgait changed the course of the events, how different sides reacted to it, used it, as we will see in the next part.

---

58   Ibid.

59   Bill Keller, "Armenians and Glasnost, Soviet press debate on regional discord underlines party split on democratization", *New York Times*, 28 March 1988.

60   Jolyon Naegele, "Azerbaijan: Armenians and Azerbaijanis remember suffering", *Radio Free Europe/Radio Liberty*, 2 March 1998.

Looking at the larger picture of political manipulation in the last years of the USSR, one can see that a KGB-prepared "provocation" could suit the trend of events. The Soviet secret services intervened in the political domain to bend, blackmail, or discredit individuals and organizations, and even provoke events, known as "active measures" or "special tasks". Those methods were also used by the KGB in this period, under the orders of the Soviet leadership. Andrew Wilson has looked at Soviet leadership efforts through KGB agents to manipulate dissident groups, create fake "opposition" parties controlled by agents, and thus weaken any independent political initiative and narrow the possibilities of their political action. As the USSR cancelled Article 6 of its constitution, which guaranteed the leading position of the CP, and adopted a pluralistic political system, the KGB initiated a number of "opposition" parties including the nationalist Pamyat (Memory), or The Liberal Democratic Party of the Soviet Union—later of Russia— led by the notorious Vladimir Zhirinovskii. That party was second only to the CP to be registered as an official party by the Soviet administration. Its "first role was a fake liberal, not a fake nationalist, initially designed to steal democratic votes".[61] Other such operations, as suggested by Wilson, included the launching of the hard-line Union (Soyuz) fraction within the Soviet parliament, the Interfronts in the Baltic republics, Moldova and Ukraine, and Intersoiuz in Uzbekistan, supporting the preservation of the Soviet Union (December 1990), and possibly the "Virtual Coup" of August 1991.[62] In this context, organizing a pogrom in Sumgait to stifle the growing independent Armenian political activism does not seem out of context. "In the eyes of the Kremlin, what happened in Sumgait was 'hooliganism', but what was going on in Armenia – mass mobilization, nationwide strikes and political demands – was much more dangerous."[63]

The effect of Sumgait on the Armenian psyche was devastating. "Sumgait influenced us very strongly. It was like putting salt on our wounds. We had already complexes linked with the 1915 Genocide,

---

61   Andrew Wilson, *Virtual Politics, Faking Democracy in the Post-Soviet World*, New Haven, CT: Yale University Press, 2005, p. 23.

62   Ibid., p. 27.

63   Alexie Zverev, "Ethnic Conflict in the Caucasus 1988-1994" in Bruno Coppieters (ed.), *Contested Borders in the Caucasus*, VUB Press, 1996, pp. 21-2.

with our former history, and Sumgait made us understand that Soviet Union was no guarantee against new massacres."[64] The overlap between the 1915 Genocide and the Sumgait pogrom was strongly emphasized in the imagination of the Armenians. A number of the Sumgait victims, and later the dead of the early clashes on the various fronts of Karabakh or near the border with Nakhichevan, are buried in the park surrounding the memorial of the Genocide victims in Dzidzernakapert, in the Armenian capital. And what power can mobilize people to go to war as much as fear and victimization?

As the conflict unfolded, Azerbaijan acquired its own myth of victimhood. During the entry of the Soviet army to Baku in January 1990 dozens of activists were killed, turning the whole population of Azerbaijan against Moscow and weakening the grasp of the Communist Party over the republic. But even more, it is the massacre in Khojali, a small town near the main airport in Mountainous Karabakh, that remains a wound until today.

Moscow loses control

Whatever Moscow's role was in the Armenian mobilization for the unification of Karabakh with Armenia, and whatever its role in the Sumgait pogroms, in the following months its role in the Transcaucasus was limited to desperate attempts at conflict management, while progressively the Kremlin lost control over the events and over the political processes in both Armenia and Azerbaijan. Whatever it tried to achieve, whatever step it took, it backfired and weakened even more its hold over the Transcaucasus.

Moscow failed to punish those who initiated violence, whether in Sumgait or elsewhere. Soviet official papers initially reported up to 80 arrested for "hooliganism" in Sumgait, but the trials were a pathetic show that did not satisfy the Armenian demands for justice, and mobilized Azerbaijani nationalism for the defence of the Sumgait "heroes". The failure of the Soviet authorities to punish severely the culprits later led to similar events elsewhere in the Caucasus and Central Asia. In 1989-90 inter-ethnic clashes took place in Abkhazia and South Ossetia (as we will see later), as well as in Osh and Uzgen in southern

---

64   Author interview with Vazgen Manukian, Yerevan, 18 December 2004.

Kyrgyzstan between ethnic Uzbeks and Kyrgyz, and pogroms against Meskhetian Turks in the Uzbek part of the Ferghana Valley.[65] Although those inter-ethnic clashes gave the central authorities room for some short-term manoeuvring, in the medium term they were catastrophic for the image, prestige and power of the Soviet authorities, and undermined dramatically the legitimacy of the Soviet state.

According to Vazgen Manukian, in the first few days of the mass demonstrations in Yerevan the Soviet Army was brought in there. "If the army had the order to repress us, they could have put an end to the movement right away, just like China did in Tiananmen. But either Gorbachev did not want or did not dare to use force."[66] Massive bloodshed by the Red Army needed direct and clear orders from the master of the Kremlin. Such an eventuality would have put a final stop to the logic of Gorbachevite reforms, of restructuring, transparency, democratization, and better relations with Western democracies. Squeezed between the prerogatives of reform and the pressure of popular mobilization in Yerevan, and later in other capitals of the Baltic States and the rest of the Caucasus, Gorbachev's policies were half-hearted measures of political crisis management and the threat of repression.

The first decision the Kremlin took was to study Armenian demands. On 23 March 1988, the Presidium of the Supreme Soviet met to study the situation in Mountainous Karabakh, and came to a decision rejecting the "recarving of national-state and national-administrative borders, which can lead to unpredictable consequences..."[67] In an earlier article published two days earlier, the official *Pravda* had already given the tone. It said that the Soviet leadership was not likely to accept any change of borders, since this would open the door for more demands of border adjustments elsewhere in the Soviet Union. It would also disturb the existing administrative mechanisms, and have serious repercussions

---

65   On the inter-ethnic clashes in Osh, see Valery Tishkov, *Ethnicity, Nationalism and Conflict in and After the Soviet Union*, London: Sage, 1997, chapter 7, pp. 135-54; on the clashes in the Ferghana Valley between Uzbeks and Meskhets, see Kenneth Weisbrode, *Central Eurasia: Prize or Quicksand?, Contending Views of Instability in Karabakh, Ferghana and Afghanistan*, London: International Institute for Strategic Studies, Adelphi Paper 338, 2001, pp. 47-8.

66   Author interview with Vazgen Manukian, Yerevan, 18 December 2004.

67   Gary Lee, "Kremlin rebuffs demands of Armenian Nationalists", *The Washington Post*, 23 March 1988.

on the economy. The article harshly criticized the Armenian leaders, accusing them of diverting the attention of the public from "unresolved social problems",[68] and recalled that in the 1918-20 war between Armenians and Azerbaijanis over Karabakh "a fifth of the population" was killed.[69] To conclude, the Karabakh campaign was "anti-socialist".[70]

The article in the organ of the CP was like a cold shower to the Armenians. Troops were sent to Yerevan to stop street demonstrations, which had reached to up to one million in late February and early March. Moscow's position did not calm the mobilization in Yerevan, but rather changed its nature. The self-image of the Karabakh movement shifted from being part of the new policies of reform to becoming an anti-Soviet movement seeking national independence.

Meanwhile, as a reaction to demonstrations and events in Armenia and Karabakh, a parallel popular mobilization started in Baku. In mid-May tens of thousands demonstrated in the Azerbaijani capital to support one of the defendants charged over the Sumgait pogrom, 20-year-old Talekh Ismailov, and also to protest against the burning of houses belonging to Azerbaijanis in villages near Yerevan. A population exchange, or as it was later termed "ethnic cleansing", accelerated between the two republics. In most cases Armenian families in Azerbaijan and Azerbaijani families in Armenia exchanged each others' houses, fearing an escalation of the situation.[71] In other cases, population exchange took rather the form of ethnic cleansing, where people left under threat, or following a new wave of pogroms, as we will see later.

In the meantime, Moscow tried to use the opportunity of unrest in Armenia and Azerbaijan to introduce a change in leadership of the local communist parties. The first change was the sacking of Boris Kevorkov, the ethnic Armenian ruler of Karabakh who was extremely loyal to Baku, who lost his position on 24 February 1988. In Azerbaijan, Bagi-

---

68   *Izvestia* and *Pravda* on 24 March 1988. Excerpts in English can be found in *The Current Digest of the Soviet Press*, XL, No. 12, 1988, pp. 11-12.

69   Charles Powers, "Unrest won't change borders, Pravda indicates", *Los Angeles Times*, 22 March 1988.

70   "Pravda criticizes Armenian demands", *Chicago Tribune*, 22 March 1988.

71   Author's notes based on interviews in April 1992 with two Armenian families in Vardenis (Armenia), who had exchanged their apartments in Ganja and Baku with the ethnic Azeri inhabitants of the houses where they lived at that moment.

rov was replaced by Abdul-Rahman Vezirov, a career diplomat, and in Armenia Karen Demirchian was replaced by Suren Harutunian, a party functionary, both in May 1988. Earlier, in the autumn of 1987, Heydar Aliev, the former boss of the Azerbaijani CP, was excluded from the CPSU Politburo. But these changes did not create preconditions for the local Communist Parties to tackle the Karabakh problem. On the contrary, each new party leader took positions reflecting the power balance between Moscow on the one hand and, on the other, the rising tide of mass mobilization and public opinion back home. Poghosian— who became the new party chief in Karabakh—energetically defended the Armenian cause, while Harutunian declared to demonstrators in Yerevan that Armenian deputies would "vote in favour of unification" in the republic's Supreme Soviet. In Azerbaijan Vezirov declared to a rally in Baku that the Azerbaijani party leadership "had voted to reject the idea of giving up Nagorno-Karabakh."[72] The reshuffling of old party leaders did not lead to solving of the deep rooted problems, but to the destabilization of the Communist Party structures in Armenia and Azerbaijan, and further weakening of the pillars of the Soviet state.

In July 1988 the Presidium of the USSR Supreme Soviet appointed Arkadi Volsky, a member of the CPSU Central Committee, as its delegate to Mountainous Karabakh, with sweeping powers. This move was a compromise measure by Moscow; while taking the political and economic management away from Baku, it did not satisfy Armenian demands for unification. The Volsky Committee was the most elaborate effort Moscow would ever try to find a compromise in this conflict. Nevertheless, this measure did not ease the tension, and the developments in Karabakh and bordering regions of Armenia and Azerbaijan progressively developed into a civil war. Volsky introduced a state of emergency in Karabakh and the neighbouring Aghdam district.[73] Moscow's choice of its envoy was revealing of the kind of policies the centre imagined for Karabakh and the Caucasus: he had been an adviser to Andropov and Chernenko on industrial issues, and the Soviet leadership wanted to bring change through massive investment in Karabakh

---

72   The two quotes are from: Paul Quinn-Judge, "Armenian protests gather momentum", *Christian Science Monitor*, 14 June 1988.

73   See the "Address" signed by A. Volsky in *Kommunist*, Baku, 25 September 1988; English translation in *CDSP*, Vol. XL, No. 38 (1988), p. 9.

and neighbouring areas, with a 400-million rouble development pro-gramme, as its answer to the brewing inter-ethnic clashes. Later, Gor-bachev confessed that this economic emergency programme was inef-fective, as the Baku authorities "were distributing the monies from the centre according to their own wishes, with only a small part reaching the intended recipients."[74] He was also supported by a large military force composed of 5,400 Interior Ministry troops, a military force which would make sure in the following three years that the localized clashes would not grow into a larger war. But this attempt failed to do more than freeze the situation. Most of the funds allocated for the revival of Karabakh did not go further than Baku. After more than a year of crisis management, the USSR Supreme Soviet abolished Volsky's Commit-tee in November 1989. Azerbaijani rule over Mountainous Karabakh was re-established, restoring the *status quo ante*. This step taken by the Kremlin was explained as a punishment for Armenians, among whom the rule of the CP was peacefully overthrown and progressively disman-tled, and the pro-independent leaders of the Karabakh Committee had taken over the republican leadership. Yet this step too did not help, since both Karabakh and Armenia took more radical measures to end Baku's influence over the mountainous region, and create conditions for Armenian self-rule in Karabakh.

Mobilization in Azerbaijan

Azerbaijan's independent political movement came into being un-der outside pressure, and had to take a reactive form. The Azerbaijani intelligentsia was unprepared for *perestroika*. Not only was the party leadership hostile to the new line in Moscow, but also the Azerbaijani intellectuals did not have the independent activism of underground organizations, such as existed in neighbouring Armenia and Georgia. While in Armenia there was mobilization around cultural rights, or environmental causes, issues that mobilized people in the mid-1980s and even took the form of street demonstrations in 1987, before being swept away by the wave of nationalist mobilization, in Azerbaijan the process was the other way round. It was nationalist mobilization around the idea of defence of Azerbaijani territorial integrity which opened the

---

74   Mikhail Gorbachev, *Memoirs*, London: Bantam Books, 1997, p. 433.

way for discussion of other problems of the Soviet system, including the enormous ecological disasters in this oil producing nation. The result was the emergence of an opposition movement which was rapidly radicalized under the pressure of events, but also fragmented, lacking coherent leadership and a strategic vision, and unable to control its own supporters, simultaneously coming under heavy pressure from republican and central authorities. "The fact that the first and most persistent bearers of a glasnost'-style political activism in Azerbaijan emerged not among the majority Azerbaijanis but from within the Armenian population of the NKAO [Nagorni Karabakh Autonomous Oblast] would set the process of political change in the republic along a troubled, contradictory path."[75]

The demand of the Karabakh Soviet for border change, and mass demonstrations in Stepanakert and Yerevan, surprised public opinion in Baku. Later came the shock and the stigma of the Sumgait pogroms, the sense of insecurity and population exchanges. For the Azerbaijani public, the understanding was that those events were orchestrated by Yerevan because of Armenian territorial ambitions towards Azerbaijan.

Throughout 1988-89 Vezirov tried to reform the Azerbaijani Communist Party (AzCP) structures, while trying to keep Karabakh under Azerbaijani rule. Vezirov introduced a massive purge within the party, and in two months alone (December 1988 and January 1989) "2,532 cadres, including 612 in position of leadership, were censored by the party and 22 officials were removed from their posts" within the KGB and Ministry of Internal Affairs alone.[76] Simultaneously, he tried to keep the newly emerging Azerbaijani opposition formations away from the political scene, to ensure that politics remained the monopoly of the AzCP.

In spite of the AzCP's policies, in November 1988 the first mass demonstrations broke out in Baku and in other cities of Azerbaijan. They were triggered by rumours that the Karabakh Armenian authorities were cutting down trees at the Topkhana nature reserve near Shushi (Shusha), in collaboration with an Armenian aluminium enterprise and without the authorization of Baku. It is interesting to note the symbolic

---

75   Mark Saroyan, "The 'Karabakh Syndrome' and Azerbaijani Politics", *Problems of Communism*, September-October 1990, p. 16.

76   Ibid., p. 21.

[handwritten: AZERBAIJANI POPULAR FRONT]

[handwritten: APF]

importance of nature preservation, one of the initial foci of mobilization in a number of Soviet cities during *perestroika*, overlapping with the inter-ethnic rivalry in the Topkhana affair. Thousands demonstrated in Baku, to demand a stop to felling of the forest, but also to assert Azerbaijani authority over Karabakh.[77] The event led to the initiation of the first informal groups in the country. Among them were Birlik (Unity), the Azerbaijan Resurgence Party, the Kizilbash People's Front and the Social Democratic Organization of Azerbaijan. But the most important organization that later played a historic role was the Azerbaijani Popular Front (Azerbaychan Khalq Chebhesi, APF). Started by a group of writers and intellectuals led by the author Babak Adalati, it was initially concerned with development of relations with Southern Azerbaijan, the old cause of the Azerbaijani intelligentsia. In March 1989 an "initiative group" was formed to lead the APF, composed of writers such as Ismayil Shikhli, Yusif Samadoghlu, and Sabir Rustamkhanli. *[handwritten: Goals of APF]* The goals of the Front were the democratization of Azerbaijani society; the sovereignty of Azerbaijan within the USSR; relations with Southern Azerbaijan; and environmental protection.[78] Created on the model of popular fronts in the Baltic countries, the APF initially included leaders coming from different political horizons, varying from the populist Nemet Pankhov to the Social Democrat Zardusht Alizade.[79]

It was the Karabakh conflict that gave the APF mass appeal. During 1989 the APF mobilized several strikes, and imposed a blockade of transport of goods and fuel from the territory of Azerbaijan to Armenia. Although initially the AzCP tried to ignore the Popular Front, the influence of the Front grew in proportion to the incapacity of the authorities to find a way out of the crisis. The APF came under the control of younger intellectuals such as the physicist Tofik Gasimov, the Arabist Abulfaz Aliev (Elchibey), and the historian Ekhtibar Mamedov,[80] who

---

77   Since then 17 November is celebrated as "National Revival Day". See Azar Panahli, "When a Tree isn't a Tree, The Topkhana Demonstrations of 1988", *Azerbaijan International*, Baku, Autumn 1994.

78   Audrey Altstadt, *The Azerbaijani Turks, Power and Identity under Russian Rule*, Stanford, CA: Hoover Institution Press, 1992, p. 205.

79   Ariel Kyrou and Maxime Mardoukhaiev, "Le Haut-Karabakh, vue du côté Azerbaïdjan", *Hérodote*, Paris, No. 54-55, 1989, p. 268.

80   Later, in 1991, Mamedov broke with the Popular Front. Now he is the head of the National Independence Party.

117

led the more radical fraction of the movement. The APF's influence became so great that the Communist Party ruler Vezirov had to negotiate with its leadership and sign a "protocol" of ten points, so that the Front would end its strikes that were paralyzing the economy of the republic. The most important points of the protocol were the legalization of APF, the lifting of a military curfew, and enactment of a sovereignty law.[81] In return, APF promised to end the strikes and to ease the blockade of railway communications.

This success in such a short time had a price. As the APF radicalized its positions on the Karabakh issue, its ranks swelled with "the lowest strata of society – the urban poor, the unemployed, the several hundred thousand Azerbaijani refugees",[82] and simultaneously its leadership lost the support of urban intelligentsia which could not identify itself with the aims and the militant faction of the Front. The population exchange between Armenia and Azerbaijan had by then displaced around 200,000 ethnic Azerbaijanis from Armenia, and from villages of Mountainous Karabakh, to urban centres in Azerbaijan, polarizing public opinion and radicalizing the opposition movement.

Ideologically, the APF adopted secular, pan-Turkist positions, and rejected Islamic orientation. This ideological position was in harmony with the world-vision of the APF, that is antagonism towards Iran—which, according to the APF, by its occupation of Southern Azerbaijan had divided the Azeri homeland into two—and was a pro-Western position by its opposition to Russian (and Soviet) domination over Azerbaijan. In early 1989 the APF developed its first political programme; in this document, it defined how it imagined the identity of its people: "the platform stated the name of the people of Azerbaijan as the 'Azerbaijani Turks'".[83]

The political developments within Azerbaijan continued the violence against the Armenian minority there. A new tragedy took place in Kirovabad (now Ganja), the second largest city of Azerbaijan. There, in

---

81   Bill Keller, "Nationalists in Azerbaijan win big concessions from Party chief", *New York Times*, 13 October 1989.

82   Elizabeth Fuller, *Azerbaijan at the Crossroads*, London: Royal Institute of International Affairs, 1994, p. 3.

83   Brenda Shaffer, *Borders and Brethren, Iran and the Challenge of Azerbaijani Identity*, Cambridge, MA: MIT Press, 2002, p. 132.

compact neighbourhoods within the old town, an Armenian community of 40,000 lived. On 21 November 1989, events similar to those in Sumgait took place there, causing the departure of the Armenians from Kirovabad.[84]

In January the situation in Azerbaijan escalated further. In spite of the existing agreement between the Communist authorities and the Front leadership, uncontrolled regional groups, under the banner of the APF, destroyed fortifications and crossed the border into Iran, demanding free movement between Azerbaijan and Iran. The demonstrations, which first started in the Nakhichevan Autonomous Republic, soon spread to other southern regions such as Lenkoran. For the radical wing of the Popular Front, the spontaneous poplar uprising was a step in the right direction, for the unification of the two parts of Azerbaijan. On the other hand, moderate and secular factions of the opposition were suspicious towards those border events, and towards Islamic and pro-Islamic Republic slogans chanted in those uprisings, and they feared that such events could be used against the opposition movement in Azerbaijan.[85]

Events soon took yet another dramatic turn. In the west of the country, to the north of the administrative border of Mountainous Karabakh, Armenians were expelled from Khanlar and Geranboy in Shahumian district.[86] In Baku, the opposition organized demonstrations against the government's handling of the Karabakh crisis on 11 January 1990, which lasted for several days. On 14 January a radical group on the margins of a demonstration moved to the Armenian neighbourhood of Baku, organizing yet another pogrom against the elderly of Armenian origin who still had not found refuge outside Azerbaijan. Several dozens were killed, and the last Armenian population within Azerbaijan (excluding Karabakh) was wiped out. Later, the survivors were transported by the Soviet authorities to Turkmenistan across the Caspian Sea, or through an airlift to the southern Russian region of Stavropol.

---

84   Christopher Walker (ed.), *Armenia and Karabakh, the Struggle for Unity*, London: Minority Rights Publications, 1991, p. 128.

85   Tadeusz Swietochowski, *Russia and Azerbaijan, A Borderland in Transition*, p. 203.

86   Svante Cornell, *Small Nations and Great Powers*, p. 89.

A large army formation estimated around 26,000 troops was sent to Baku on the night of the 19-20 January. The main reason for sending the troops was to establish law and order, after the Soviet regime in Azerbaijan had come near collapse and the supporters of the Popular Front had virtually taken power in Baku and most of the regions of Azerbaijan. The Soviet troops met resistance, and clashes led to scores of victims. According to the memoirs of Alexander Lebed, who was heading the Tula Regiment, the air bases in the west of the country at Yevlakh and Gyanja, where the Soviet airborne troops were deployed, were surrounded by demonstrations. The roads between Ganja and Baku were blocked with barricades, and once the Soviet troops reached Kala airfield near Baku, they discovered that the base was surrounded by several dozen lightly armed Azeri volunteers, and even within the perimeter of the airfield there was gunfire.[87] In the following hours, the Soviet troops destroyed the resistance of the Azerbaijani Popular Front and took over control of the Azerbaijani capital. "Black January", as it was later known in Azerbaijani sources, became the (first) reference to victimhood in Azerbaijani mass consciousness,[88] playing the same role as the pogroms in Sumgait in the Armenian consciousness. According to Azerbaijani sources, over 170 people died in the clashes of 19-20 January, although the official website dedicated to the commemoration of the Black January victims counts 132 names.[89] It is interesting to note that Azerbaijanis felt victims not of Armenians, but of acts committed by the Soviet troops, under orders from the Kremlin.

After the Baku events, Moscow replaced the Communist chief in Baku, Vezirov, with Ayaz Mutalibov, the former chairman of the Council of Ministers. A state of emergency was declared and an armed force of 11,600 troops was stationed in Baku to safeguard the authority of Mutalibov and prolong Soviet rule in Azerbaijan by an additional two years. But policy towards the Karabakh conflict did not change under Mutalibov. On the contrary, repression increased to new levels.

---

87   Harold Elletson, *The General Against the Kremlin, Alexander Lebed: Power and Illusion*, London: Warner Books, 1998, p. 107.

88   See the Azerbaijani "January 20" internet p. on the background of the Soviet troop intervention. The p. does not mention the anti-Armenian pogroms which preceded the troop deployment, and served as pretext for the military operation: http://www.january20.net/history.html

89   See http://www.january20.net/victims.htm

(margin note:) Black January – Az victims of Soviet action, not Armenian

In January 1990, Azerbaijani governmental troops "cleansed" Armenian-inhabited villages of the Khanlar and Shahumian districts. In May 1991 Armenian villages to the north of Karabakh, Martunashen and Kedashen, were surrounded by Azerbaijani Interior Ministry troops and the *Spetsnaz*, the special operation units of the Soviet Army. The codename of this operation was Kaltso—Operation Ring. On the pretext of Armenian guerrilla activities, the inhabitants of these two towns and several villages, a total of 10,000 people, were deported to Armenia and their property confiscated.[90] According to Azerbaijani sources, this act of deportation was necessary self-defence:

...[B]andits blocked roads between Azerbaijani villages, established military posts on the highway leading from Khanlar to Kelbajar, and blew up water pipes supplying Ganja with drinking water. Their unpunished activity was a direct threat for the activity of Western Azerbaijan with more than one million inhabitants. In this condition, and to implement the decree of the President of the USSR to disarm illegal military formations, the police of the republic with the support of Internal Ministry Forces of the USSR, in April 1991 started implementing the passport regime in the villages of Chaykend and Martunashen.[91]

In his memoirs, the head of the Soviet KGB notes that Gorbachev wanted to discuss the Kaltso operation with Mutalibov, but the latter refused to go to Moscow: "It is not the first time I oppose you. We *will* continue disarming the bandit formations with our OMON [Interior Ministry troops], since we consider it our internal affair. Inform Mikhail Gorbachev that I will not pay the visit to Moscow."[92] Under Mutalibov, ethnic cleansing had become government policy. In Karabakh itself repression of Armenians increased. Armenian activists were arrested and jailed in Shushi prison, while in Armenian villages self-defence forces were established. The Soviet Army was still present, its role reduced to separating the various fronts in a situation which increasingly looked like an open war. The Soviet armed forces supported the conservative Mutalibov government of Azerbaijan in Baku, which in turn showed loyalty to the

90   *Report on Ethnic Conflict in the Russian Federation and Transcaucasia,* op. cit., p. 74.

91   Ismet Gaibov and Azad Sharifov, *Armianski terorism* (in Russian), Baku, 1991, p. 6.

92   Cyril Stolyarov, *Raspad: Ot Nagornovo Karabakha do Byeloezhskoi Pushchi* (in Russian), Moscow: Olma-Press, 2001, p. 165.

Soviet Union, while at the same time Moscow aimed to punish the Armenian national leadership which was slowly seceding from the USSR.

The Armenian National Movement takes power

The Armenian mobilization around the Mountainous Karabakh issue went through a rapid transformation in its orientation and political philosophy. The movement started as an offshoot of democratization in the Soviet Union, the official policy in the years 1987-88. But the Sumgait pogroms, the ambiguous if not negative position of Moscow towards Armenian demands, and repressive policies towards the popular movement transformed this mobilization from a movement seeing itself as part of the new official policies of reform within the USSR into a movement openly hostile to the Soviet order. The Armenians' faith in Moscow collapsed just like the Soviet-made apartment blocks in the Spitak earthquake on 7 December 1988, which killed over 25,000 people and crippled a third of Armenia's industrial potential. In the meantime the foundations of the Soviet state had been weakened, and Moscow lost control of its provinces to the south of the Caucasus Mountains. Armenia's independence moved swiftly from the realm of the impossible to that of the inevitable.[93]

Although the Karabakh Movement was described in the Western press as nationalistic, its own self-image was often a democratic one. In the words of Levon Ter-Petrossian, "Karabakh was not land, Karabakh was the human being, it was the people (…) For me Karabakh was people who for 75 years lived continuously under national repression. The Karabakh people did not have the same rights as the Azerbaijani people. This repression was killings, unjust trials, cadre policy, deformation of school programmes, and thousand of such things. Individually, those events were not significant, but put together it added up to national repression."[94] Although the mass movement was the result of the passions around the Karabakh problem, it expressed in itself all the desire for change in Armenian society after long decades of Soviet authoritarianism, corrupt social relations and inefficient economy. Ronald Suny

---

93   As in the formulation by Mark Beissinger, *Nationalist Mobilization and the Collapse of the Soviet State,* op. cit, chapter 1.

94   Author interview with Levon Ter-Petrossian, Yerevan, 18 December 2004.

suggested as the best description of the Karabakh Movement's trajectory, "A nationalist struggle for recovery of ethnic irredenta was combined with a broader movement for political reform and ecological survival."[95]

During the spring and summer of 1988, a new leadership was formed known as the Karabakh Committee, which directed the mass movement. At its head were Levon Ter-Petrossian and Vazgen Manukian, who later became the first president and prime minister of independent Armenia. By June 1989, the Armenian National Movement (Hayots Hamazkayin Sharzhoum, ANM) was formed, transforming the Karabakh Committee into an instrument for the struggle of national independence.

Initially, the Armenian activists did not take the existence of the Azerbaijani political factor into account when they raised the territorial issue. They understood their own role to be limited to convincing Moscow about the justice of their cause, and solving the Karabakh problem "in the spirit of *perestroika*". Later, as their anger turned towards Moscow, they saw their struggle in the spirit of national liberation from the repressive Soviet empire. But Azerbaijan as a political actor did not exist then. "Those who took decisions were in Moscow," in the words of Ashot Manucharian, "Azerbaijan as a factor started to take form after January 1990."[96] For the leadership of the political movement in Armenia, it was impossible to imagine that for the Azerbaijanis the demand for unification of Karabakh to Armenia could also cause passionate reaction, mobilize people, and thus sooner rather than later turn the Yerevan-Moscow "dialogue" on Karabakh into a triangular conflict over the control of Mountainous Karabakh and over the control of Baku and Yerevan. The national mobilization in Azerbaijan changed this illusion: the fight was not simply against Moscow and its *apparatchiks* in Baku, as there was soon a symmetrical popular movement developing in Azerbaijan, with at the top of its agenda the preservation of Karabakh within Azerbaijan. The Karabakh issue became by a historical accident the cradle of contemporary Azerbaijani political identity, and even years after the signing of a cease-fire it continues to brew modern Azerbaijani national identity.

---

95   Ronald G. Suny, *Looking Toward Ararat, Armenia in Modern History*, Bloomington: Indiana University Press, 1993, p. 193.

96   Author interview with Ashot Manucharian, Yerevan, 18 December 2004.

The Communist Party in Armenia, destabilized by the popular mobilization on the one hand and multiple pressures from Moscow on the other—in the form of a change of its Brezhnevite leadership, and an unfavourable position on the Karabakh issue—tried to find a difficult accommodation with the ANM. The CP chief Suren Harutunian tried to win public support by liberating the leaders of the Karabakh Committee, arrested in the aftermath of the earthquake, and decided to adopt the 1918 tricolour flag as the national flag, but to no avail. Shooting in border villages escalated, and Armenia and Karabakh were increasingly under a tight blockade. The dissolution of the Volsky Committee brought Karabakh back to its initial political situation, leading to more mass demonstrations in Yerevan. By late 1989, twelve members of the Armenian parliament and the ANM called for the abolition of Article 6 of the Soviet constitution, an end to the CP's political monopoly, and respect for universal human rights.[97]

By that time, both the ANM and the Armenian public were radicalized into anti-Soviet positions. With Moscow's grip over Eastern Europe failing, it was possible in Yerevan to talk about national independence. In an interview given to a Yerevan paper in 1990, Vazgen Manukian, the theoretician of the movement, defined the two main goals of the ANM: "...the re-establishment of independent statehood and the territorial question [Karabakh unification]", and then said: "in order to resolve the territorial problem we must have independent statehood."[98] With the collapse of trust in Moscow and dependence on it for physical security, after the increasing acts of violence in Azerbaijan and the public perception that Moscow had sided with Azerbaijan on the Karabakh issue, the idea of independence was no more taboo, nor politically suicidal in Yerevan. During parliamentary elections in the summer of 1990, the ANM won a majority and its leader Ter-Petrossian was elected the new chairman of the parliament.

The ANM was a revolution in Armenian political culture. It liberated contemporary Armenian thinking from the fixed obsession of traditional Armenian parties: that of fearing Turkey and therefore depending on Russian protection, whether this Russia was Soviet or Tsarist. This was

---

97   *Armenpress*, Yerevan, 22 December 1989.

98   See Gerard Libaridian, *Armenia at the Crossroads, Democracy and Nationhood in Post-Soviet Era*, Watertown: Blue Crane Books, 1991, p. 40.

the position of the Diaspora Hnchakian (Social Democrat) and Ramga-
var (Liberal) parties, while the Tashnaktsutyun (nationalist) opposed the
USSR while being hostile to Turkey. The three Diaspora parties came
up with a joint statement in 1988 to call for calm and prudence, fearing
that weakening Soviet rule would expose Armenia once again to Turkish
danger.[99] The ANM concluded that the Soviet Union was crumbling,
and that the question of liberation of Karabakh could only be achieved
under the conditions of a sovereign Armenian political will—that is,
independence. A major difference from traditional Armenian political
thought was that the ANM considered it possible to have normal relations with Turkey; this was the only way to achieve liberation from Armenia's historic dependence on Russia. In fact, in the late 1980s many
historians and political analysts in Armenia were revising the tradition-
alist thought which was based on the stereotypical fear of Turkey, and
admiration of Russia, overriding historical realities. The new school dug
into the archives to reveal that Moscow's policies in the Caucasus were
never based on "friendship" and similar sentiments, but on *Realpolitik*,
which often happened to clash with Armenian interests.[100]

The ANM's politics brought Armenia into confrontation with Moscow. After Gorbachev had lost control over Armenia, following the
ANM's assumption of power in Yerevan, the only way to influence its
policies was through pressuring Yerevan through the military developments in Azerbaijan and in Karabakh. The participation of Soviet troops
in deporting 10,000 ethnic Armenians from the Shahumian region (north
of Karabakh) in the spring of 1991 was the price of Yerevan's moves towards sovereignty.

The ANM and its leaders could guess the direction of history, and in
spite of suffering Soviet repression in the years 1988-91, they prepared
their nation for the coming independence and for the coming war that
was in the making. Politically, the ANM could unify the Armenians behind the project of national independence, and when the putsch took
place in Moscow in August 1991, they could profit from this opportunity
without having to go through internal political upheavals. They could

---

99   Gaidz Minassian, *Guerre et terrorisme arméniens,* Paris: Presses Universitaires de
      France, 2002, pp. 136-43.

100   Gabriel Lazyan (ed.), *Hayasdane yev Hay Tade, Hayyevrus Haraperutyunneru
      Luysin Dag* (in Armenian), Yerevan: Adana Publishers, 1991.

also build important relations with Russian democrats, which would be decisive for the Karabakh war in 1992-94. Lastly, as Soviet troops sided with Azerbaijanis until 1991, Armenians were forced to develop their self-defence battalions, which played a key role in developing efficient armed forces later in the war years.

Azerbaijan was ready for none of this. Politically, Baku relied on the support of Moscow until very late to preserve the legal status quo in Karabakh. This was the most important element of legitimacy for the Communist *nomenklatura* to stay in power. As a result, when the putsch occurred a destabilized Mutalibov initially supported it, and then, like so many conservative politicians in the USSR that year, had to take confused and confusing steps backwards. Mutalibov had no friends in Moscow with the arrival of the Yeltsin team, and had many powerful enemies at home. Militarily Azerbaijan, which had so much depended on Soviet troops to keep its control over Karabakh, could not hold its positions once the Soviet forces withdrew and their remnants changed sides to support the Armenian fighters. Determined Armenian forces, liberated from Soviet military pressure and facing Azerbaijani police and volunteer groups, went on the offensive.

Most of all, Mutalibov ruled over a country divided and fragmented politically. Two visions of Azerbaijan clashed with each other in this period—a contradiction that persists until the present day. As one scholar emphasizes, "two major competing political discourses" uneasily coexisted with each other, "namely the ideology of *Turkism* of the opposition and the ideology of the *Azerbaijanism* of the government".[101] The ideology of Turkism, popular among the intelligentsia and the vision of the opposition Popular Front of Azerbaijan as well as the Musavat party, came to power for a short period of one year from mid-1992 until mid-1993.

Total war

It was a sunny April day in 1992, the first time I was in Karabakh. On the second day I met Serge Sarkissian, then the Minister of Defence of the Karabakh forces. Then, accompanied by Stefan, a French photojournalist of Armenian descent, and Samvel, a volunteer in the

---

101   Ceylan Tokluoglu, "Definition of National Identity, Nationalism and Ethnicity in post-Soviet Azerbaijan in the 1990s", *Ethnic and Racial Studies*, Vol. 28, No. 4, July 2005, p. 725.

Karabakh army, we went westward from Stepanakert towards Shushi, the second major town of Karabakh. Rising high majestically over a rocky mountain, Shushi was the major stronghold of Azeri troops inside Karabakh, from where they controlled the main road linking Karabakh to Armenia, and regularly shelled Stepanakert with howitzer and Grad missiles. We passed next to Krkjan, a small locality previously inhabited by ethnic Azeris, which was overrun by Armenian forces in February of the same year; all the houses were burnt to ashes. Samvel had a bullet hanging over the belt over his chest: "This one is for me," he said. "I do not want to be taken prisoner." A cruel war was in the making, and there was no way to stop it.

The collapse of the USSR created a power vacuum in Karabakh, a region ready to explode by that time. The 11,000 or so Soviet troops stationed there by 1991 constituted the buffer between Armenian and Azerbaijani paramilitaries, and the removal of this last restraining force led to the eruption of the war. The military positions of the Armenians and Azerbaijanis were difficult on both sides. Armenian positions were vulnerable, since they occupied urban and rural zones within Karabakh, and in Shahumian district to its north. This exclave was cut off from Armenia proper, and in early 1991 Armenian forces did not control the Karabakh civilian airport situated near the village of Khojali, nor the strategic town of Shushi, dominating on the one hand Stepanakert (the district capital) and on the other the Stepanakert-Lachin-Goris pass, on the main road linking Karabakh and Armenia. This meant that the 140,000 or so ethnic Armenians trapped in this region could only communicate with the outside world through the 6-8 helicopters (Mi-8) that Armenia could deploy. This included transporting of people and materials for civilian use: everything from flour to diesel, plus all the necessities for the military effort from fighters to ammunition, as well as evacuation of the wounded.[102]

For Azerbaijani forces the military map was equally problematic. Not only did it have a hostile Armenian population within the mountainous region of Karabakh, but also isolated villages within Karabakh that were

---

102　For a detailed description of the initial period of the war, see the two features by the author after this trip: "Ein Augenschein in Nagorno Karabach", *Neue Zürcher Zeitung*, Zurich, 14 May 1992; "De la guérilla à la guerre totale", *Les Nouvelles d'Arménie*, Paris, June 1992.

home to 40,000 Azerbaijanis. Moreover, it had four districts (Kelbajar, Lachin, Ghoubatli and Zankelan) that were pressed between Karabakh and Armenia proper. This made moving troops from the Azerbaijani heartland to towns such as Kelbajar, Lachin or Khojali very difficult and time-consuming, while by comparison Armenian forces within Karabakh had shorter distances to move to change fronts, which gave them a strategic advantage. To the east, Azerbaijani towns such as Aghdam, Fizuli and Jebrayil were at a disadvantage, being in lowlands below hills dominated by Armenians. Moreover, Azerbaijan had its own exclave of Nakhichevan, cut off from the traditional communication lines by an Armenian blockade, on the border of which there was growing tension and frequent clashes. The situation of military imbalance and dispersion of forces and the long stretch of war front was untenable, and had to lead to a violent clash.

Starting from November 1991, the Armenian side went on the offensive. The first major target was Khojali, where the region's airport was situated. The attack took place on the symbolic date of 26 February, and after the Armenian forces took the village, a terrible massacre followed. As in similar events, here too each side contests the version of the other. For Azerbaijanis, Armenians cold-bloodedly killed several hundred civilians (some sources talk of 1,500), to spread horror among Azerbaijanis elsewhere and force them to leave their villages. Armenians contest this narrative and say they committed no massacre, and that it was Azeri forces themselves who opened fire on civilians who were trying to escape. They quote the Azeri President himself, who laid the blame of the atrocities in Khojali on the APF seeking to try to bring down his regime.[103]

Several hundred civilians were also arrested, among them Meskhet Turks who had escaped earlier pogroms in Uzbekistan and had come to Azerbaijan in the hope of returning to their ancestral lands in southern Georgia. Instead the Azerbaijani authorities, in their efforts to tilt the demographic balance of Karabakh, had settled them in Khojali.[104]

---

103   Few weeks after the event I interviewed Armenian fighters in Yerevan and Stepanakert, in March and April 1992, and what I could conclude is that Armenian fighters did commit a massacre, after the Azerbaijani soldiers and police had surrendered and the civil population was escaping eastwards towards Aghdam.

104   Viktoria Ivleva, "Casualties and refugees, an eye-witness account", *Moscow News*, 15-22 March 1992.

The war in Karabakh had its own rules. In those early months of 1992: while massacres were repetitively perpetrated by the both sides of the conflict; prisoners were often tortured to death. Families who had members held by the other side tried to take hostages from the other ethnic group and keep them until it was possible to identify the captors of their loved ones, and try to negotiate an exchange. Corpses were also exchanged, sometimes in return for cash or a gallon of oil.

There was no shortage of arms and ammunition. The 366th Motorised Infantry Regiment, originally under the command of the Soviet Interior Ministry, which had an initial force of 11,000 soldiers, started its withdrawal from Karabakh in November 1991, and had completed it by February 1992, leaving behind its armament, including heavy weaponry.[105] Thus there was more armament in 1992 in the hands of Karabakh Armenians than ever before. Azerbaijanis had even more, five to six times more armour and ten times more ammunition, after they had taken over the Aghdam and Kirovabad (Ganja) Soviet military bases.[106] Even so, availability of weapons did not mean having an army. Both military knowledge and discipline were very low. Similarly, military hierarchy did not exist in either of the camps in early 1992. Up to then, Armenian forces were composed of localized defence units, or brigades of 10-15 volunteers who had come from Armenia, and they had loose coordination among themselves. The situation was even worse in Azerbaijan. The journalist Kemal Ali says that in Aghdam, which was the centre of the Azerbaijani military command, "in 1992, there wasn't a single army, there were six or seven separate units, fighting the Armenians. (…) But these units were in conflict with each other as well as with the Armenians."[107] Similarly, when I visited the advanced positions near Stepanakert in April 1992, I was told by local commanders that they faced three distinct military groups, and that at that moment they were in a kind of cease-fire situation with two, while continuing to fire on the third.

---

105   This included 10 T-72 main battle tanks (of which five were functional), 3 ZSU-4 mounted anti-aircraft systems (4 barrelled 23 mm machine guns), 8 122 mm field-guns, 70 BMP personal carriers. This information is based on an interview with Serge Sarkisian, the Defence Minister of Karabakh, in Stepanakert on 6 April 1992.

106   Author interview with Monte Melkonian, the commander of Martouni district, in Martouni (Karabakh), 9 April 1992.

107   Quoted in Thomas de Waal, *The Black Garden*, p. 165.

Both sides exaggerated the existence of foreign fighters, their role and importance in the war. Reporters and other "travellers" to war zones often hear about mythical creatures, and in Karabakh there were rumours about women snipers and "black" fighters, supposedly the most redoubtable of all fighters. Other exaggerations were about the role and manner in which Russian (and other former Red Army) soldiers took part in the military operations. During a first visit to Karabakh in April 1992, one could meet several Russian and Bielorussian soldiers, and even an Uzbek soldier with an ethnic Tajik background fighting on the side of Karabakh troops.[108] They were former soldiers of the 366th Motorised Infantry Regiment, who had decided for whatever reason to stay behind instead of return to the uncertainty of their countries. Others, more specialized helicopter, aircraft and tank officers, were highly appreciated by both Armenian and Azerbaijani sides, and were paid as mercenaries to deliver the first punch for the opening of a campaign. Most probably, at this stage Russian soldiers and officers were acting from material motives, and their participation on both sides of the battle lines was in no way the result of a "Russian hidden hand" aiming to re-dominate the Caucasus. If anyone had seen Russian soldiers in those days, completely abandoned by their leadership, having no orders, not even knowing who their superiors were, often without food and protection, and—most important—noted their participation on both sides of the war, he would have found it hard to believe that Russia's Defence ministry had any grasp of, still less a plan for, the Caucasus military developments. Lastly, Armenians often talked about Turkish and even Iranian fighters among Azerbaijani ranks, without any proof.[109] Similarly, Azerbaijanis exaggerated the participation of Diaspora Armenians in the fighting operations. One did play an important part, the legendary Monte Melkonian,[110] the commander of the eastern Martuni district. Overall, not more than few dozen Diaspora Armenians from Iran, France, Lebanon and the USA participated in the fighting, if one excludes the war tourists who passed a couple of weeks in Karabakh.

---

108   Author's notes, Karabakh, April 1992 and February 1993.

109   "We did not kill nor capture any Turkish or Iranian volunteer," Serge Sarkissian, the Defence Minister of Karabakh, told me on 6 April 1992, in Stepanakert.

110   The highly interesting biography of Monte Melkonian is written by his brother Markar. See Markar Melkonian, *My Brothers Road, An American's Fateful Journey to Armenia*, London: I.B. Tauris, 2004.

More important than its role in direct military operations was the political and financial importance of the Diaspora in the Karabakh conflict. While in 1989-90 the ANM leadership in Yerevan refrained from arming various battalions in Karabakh, the Tashnak party was active in distributing money and helped arm Karabakh Armenians. As a result, the party enjoyed great prestige in Karabakh in the early years of the war.

In early 1992 the Armenian forces were on the offensive. Now they had weapons, and the Soviet troops were away. Most important, they sensed that the Azeri leadership in Baku was divided and Azerbaijan did not have a political or military plan for Karabakh. "The Azeris are weak because they do not have a clear political leadership," said Serge Sarkissian, adding, "They (…) don't have a unified military leadership."[111] The Azerbaijani forces also lacked military experience, cadres and discipline. One American journalist who visited Khojali, whose strategic importance cannot be over-emphasized, reported that there was only one armoured vehicle in the town, and from the sixty fighters defending the village and the airport only four volunteers from outside the region had military experience, acquired during the Afghanistan war.[112] Such a force had no military significance, and most Azeri civilians had left towns like Khojali or Shushi, reducing the motivation of the Azeri troops to fight. In contrast, Karabakh Armenian political and military authorities strictly forbade the evacuation of civilians, saying that emptying Karabakh of women and children would reduce the incentive of their men to defend the land.

The battle for Shushi

Following the Khojali victory, after which the Armenian forces ensured an air link with Armenia, they started planning the Shushi offensive to open a corridor to link Mountainous Karabakh with Armenia, to end a three-year-long blockade of the region imposed by Azerbaijan.[113] Shushi, or Shusha in Azerbaijani, was the most populated Azerbaijani-held position within the administrative boundaries of Mountainous Karabakh.

---

111   Interview with Serge Sarkissian, the Defence Minister of Karabakh, Stepanakert, 6 April 1992.

112   Thomas Goltz, *Azerbaijan Diary*, p. 120.

113   *Gharapah yan Azadakragan Baderazm, 1988-1994* ("Karabakh Liberation War", in Armenian), Haygagan Hanrakidagan Hradaragchutyun, Yerevan 2004, p. 529.

It was extremely difficult to take the town, since it was positioned over a rocky structure, with only two roads linked to it: one sliding down eastwards towards Stepanakert, and the second moving to Lachin, the former capital of "Red Kurdistan" (1923-29), still at the time under Azerbaijani military control. Therefore, militarily the Armenians had basically one road to climb up towards Shushi, and the Azeri defenders clearly knew this and expected an attack.

The Azerbaijani forces within Shushi had enough provisions as well as arms and fighters. According to the military commander of the town, Elbrus Orujev, he had "a few hundred" fighters under his command.[114] But they lacked coordination, discipline and morale. Most important, Azerbaijan was in a war without any military planning and military strategy. While the Azerbaijani side was losing one village after the other in central and western Karabakh, its forces were attacking Armenian villages in north and eastern parts of Karabakh, without being able to win territory of strategic significance. In fact, Azerbaijani military attacks had a local nature, armed groups in one village reinforced by volunteers from Baku or elsewhere attacking a neighbouring Armenian village. Even operations coordinated at the highest level failed to achieve any success; for example, in January 1992, Azerbaijani forces led by the Defence Minister Tajedin Mehdiev in person,[115] at the head of a large force of around 500 fighters with three armoured vehicles, attacked the village of Karintak (literally meaning "under the stone"). This village is located just under the rocky structure below Shushi. The 60-70 Armenian fighters defended the village for 12 hours until assistance arrived from neighbouring villages, and Azerbaijani forces withdrew with heavy losses.[116]

The Armenian offensive was planned for 4 May 1992, but for various reasons, such as lack of ammunition and bad weather,[117] it was postponed by several days. General Arkadi Ter-Tadevosian (known as

---

114   Thomas de Waal, *The Black Garden*, p. 178.

115   Mehdiev served as Defence Minister from mid-December 1991 until mid-February 1992.

116   According to Armenian sources, the defence forces lost 20 fighters, while the attackers lost 100 men. See *Gharapaghyan Azadakragan Baderazm, 1988-1994,* op. cit.,p. 664.

117   *Gharapaghyan Azadakragan Baderazm, 1988-1994,* op. cit., p. 531.

Komandos), a career officer who was sent by the Armenian army to Stepanakert on June 1991 to "coordinate and direct"[118] the war effort, was the commander of the Shushi operation. With 1,200 troops, the military operations started in the early hours of 8 May. (This was to create a diplomatic scandal with Iran, as we will see later.) Four attacking and one reserve group took part in the operation, the first moving from Stepanakert uphill; the second moving from the village Shosh from the east on Shushi; the third trying to cut the Shushi-Lachin main road to the south of the town; and the fourth advancing from Stepanakert towards Azerbaijani villages to the north-east of Shushi (Janhasan, Javatlar, Pashkent). The initial Armenian push was thrown back, the Karabakh forces losing one of their T-72 tanks.[119] But by the evening, panic hit the Azerbaijani defenders as the third army succeeded in cutting the Shushi-Lachin main road (this group was led by Samvel Babayan, later Defence Minister of Karabakh), and started evacuating the town. The next morning the first Armenian fighters entered Shushi, and were amazed to discover the quantities of arms and ammunition left behind. They were followed by bands of looters, who after emptying shops and apartments put the rest on fire, causing the destruction of a major part of this historic city.

The fall of Shushi continues to be a subject of polemic. Many in Azerbaijan think that the Baku leadership "sold" this invincible city. There are rumours that the Azerbaijani Defence Minister ordered the withdrawal of armoured vehicles from the town and mine clearing from the front lines.[120] But a careful look at the situation reveals bad organization, confusion and mistrust that led to the fall of this city-fortress. The various military groups in the town did not obey the military hierarchy, and often refused to coordinate among themselves. The inhabitants of the town had left or had been evacuated by the authorities fearing a second Khojali, which gave less incentive for the fighters to resist to defend a civilian population. In the early days of May some of the troops

---

118   *Gharapaghyan Azadakragan Baderazm, 1988-1994*, op. cit., p. 629.

119   Visitors to Karabakh can see this tank, converted to a monument, on the main highway at the entrance of Shushi.

120   See the interview with the former Azeri Defence Minister Rahim Qaziyev, a few days after being freed from prison, in *Ekho*, Baku, 23 March 2005. Qaziyev refutes both charges.

with their equipment seem to have left the town. A final problem for Azerbaijani troops, whose main body was concentrated in Aghdam, was logistic. As the Karabakh troops started their offensive on Shushi, the Azerbaijani troops needed a day or two to start bringing support to Shushi, too late to change the outcome of the battle. On the other hand, the Armenian side showed a high level of discipline and organization skills. As a result of the two-day battle, the Armenian side lost 57 fighters, while Azerbaijani losses were near 200.[121]

In June the Armenian forces continued their offensive, and this time attacked Lachin from the east coming from Shushi, as well as from the west from Goris in Armenia. Azeri forces abandoned Lachin without much resistance. The inhabitants of Lachin were mostly ethnic Kurds, and in spite of Armenian-supported efforts to declare a "Kurdish state"[122] based in Lachin, Kurds had left the town with the departing Azeri fighters. This is not surprising after the treatment the civil population had received from the Armenian fighters in Khojali, since ethnic Kurds had close family ties with ethnic Azeris. Attempts by Karabakh Armenians to create an alliance with ethnic Kurds inhabiting Lachin and in Kelbajar further to the north had had no result.

With the fall of Lachin, for the first time a physical link was created between Armenia and Karabakh, and supplies could move at last to

	Tanks	Artillery	Combat aircraft	Combat helicopters
Armenia	77	160	3	13
Azerbaijan	278	294	50	6

Table 2: Military hardware in Armenia and Azerbaijan in 1992

Source: Roy Allison, *Military Forces in the Soviet Successor States*, Adelphi Paper 280, London: IISS, 1994, p. 86.

---

121   *Gharapaghyan Azadakragan Baderazm, 1988-1994*, op. cit., p. 536. This source puts Armenian losses at 57 dead, while Azerbaijani losses "250-300 killed, 600-700 wounded". The Azerbaijani military commander Elbrus Orujev puts Azerbaijani dead at 159 and 22 missing. See Thomas de Waal, op. cit., note 44 on p. 314.

122   Author interview with Levon Melik-Shahnazarov, head of Karabakh parliamentary committee for foreign relations, Stepanakert, April 1992. See also Suleiman Ali, "Kurdistan: the secret of Lachin", *Moscow News*, 7 June 1992; and Judith Perera, "Azerbaijan: Kurds declare their own state", *Inter-Press Service*, London, 18 June 1992.

Putchist?

encircled Karabakh. The Armenia side thought for the moment that the war was over and celebrated victory ahead of time.

Changing fronts, changing leaders

After the Armenian victories in Shushi and Lachin, and the opening of a land corridor between Mountainous Karabakh and Armenia proper, many in Armenia thought that this was the victory and the main part of the military operations were over. They neglected important ongoing developments in the Azerbaijani political system that were to change that system and the realities of the frontline. Following the fall of Khojalu and the massacre of the Azerbaijani civilians there, Ayaz Mutalibov found himself in a delicate situation. APF-led demonstrations pushed for his resignation, supported by a public opinion infuriated not only because of the Khojali massacre, but also because of the official position which until the last moment was spreading baseless press-releases claiming victories on the front.

Mutalibov's position had been compromised since the August coup in Moscow. In the first hours following the coup, Mutalibov came out with pro-putchist declarations, and the fact that he "corrected" himself a couple of days later did not help erase the initial mistake. More important than the declarations, the August coup had reshuffled the geopolitical equilibrium between Moscow and the Transcaucasus, in which Moscow was trying for a time to preserve the Soviet Union and therefore supported a political system in Azerbaijan, favourable to the status quo, and punished a rebellious, nationalist Armenia that was deconstructing the Soviet order. With the Soviet Union dead, Moscow did not need to preserve the status quo in the Transcaucasus; nor did it have the means to do so. Moreover, the new political leadership in Moscow around Boris Yeltsin was of the same political current as the Armenian leadership, called "democrats" in the context of that time, and both had emerged in opposition to Gorbachev's project of preserving a reformed, federative USSR. The Yeltsin leadership had very close relations with the Armenia of Ter-Petrossian and rejected collaboration with old apparatchiks like those who composed the Mutalibov administration. With the military defeats on the front and the shock of Khojali, the Azerbaijani public was convinced that "only independence from

A2 C? so it propped up Az. govt. be it was best 4 status quo. Moscow was trying to keep USSR afloat

Yeltsin ♡ Armenian govt.

135

Russian military presence (...) would perhaps help Azerbaijan resolve its conflict with Armenia",[123] a conclusion very similar to that of the Armenian leadership a couple of years earlier.

Huge demonstrations in Baku demanded the resignation of Mutalibov. In a stormy session of the Azerbaijani parliament in March 1992, Mutalibov was accused of not having done enough to protect the Azerbaijani population of Karabakh, and was stripped of his post.[124] The parliament nominated as temporary head of state Yakub Mamedov, who was a former rector of the Baku Medical Institute and the speaker of the parliament, and scheduled presidential elections for June 1992. Azerbaijan was clearly in a situation of dual power. On the one hand the influence of the APF was growing in the street with daily demonstrations in Baku, and among the Azerbaijani volunteers fighting on the Karabakh front, and on the other hand the legal power and state administration was still held by the *nomenklatura*. The struggle between the two camps was more about taking power in Baku, and a divided vision of the future geopolitical orientation of Azerbaijan, than about the actual war going on in Karabakh. The military defeats of the Azerbaijani forces were mainly conditioned by this political division within the Azerbaijani elite and public opinion. Two days after the resignation of Mutalibov a Canadian journalist interviewed the leader of the Azerbaijani opposition, Abulfaz Elchibey, and concluded: "For him, the debacle in Karabakh was of lesser import than the opportunity Mutalobov's departure presented for reworking an essentially colonial relationship with Russia."[125]

Following the fall of Shushi and Lachin, Mutalibov tried to organize a come-back to power, on 14 May 1992. The parliament blamed the defeat on the acting President, Mamedov; it cancelled the scheduled presidential elections of 7 June. Mutalibov declared a two-month state of emergency.[126] But mass demonstrations staged by the opposition in

---

123   Leila Alieva, "Reshaping Eurasia: Foreign Policy Strategies and Leadership Assets in Post-Soviet South Caucasus", *Berkeley Programme in Soviet and Post-Soviet Studies*, 2000, p. 21.

124   Elizabeth Fuller, "The Ongoing Political Power Struggle in Azerbaijan", *RFE/RL Research Report*, Vol. 1, No. 18, 1 May 1992.

125   Suzanne Goldenberg, *Pride of Small Nations, The Caucasus and Post-Soviet Disorder*, London: Zed Books, 1994, p. 119.

126   *Report on Ethnic Conflict in the Russian Federation and Transcaucasia*, Harvard

front of the parliament, some of them armed with rifles, forced Mutalibov to resign for a second time and leave the country. The presidential elections of June 1992 gave victory to Elchibey with 59 per cent of the votes. Nizami Suleimanov, a close associate of Heydar Aliev, came second with 38 per cent of the votes. Aliev himself was barred from participating in the elections on the pretext of his advanced age (a limit of 65 years was set for the candidates, with the clear purpose of excluding Aliev). The several months of power struggle cost Azerbaijan dearly on the war front. The Armenian fighters had succeeded in occupying all of the territory of Mountainous Karabakh, and the Karabakh Armenian forces had succeeded in occupying the town of Lachin in Azerbaijan proper, creating a land corridor linking Karabakh to Armenia.

As we will see later, most Armenian military victories coincided with internal strife within Azerbaijan. And power struggle there was a regular phenomenon, reflecting the fractured nature of the Azerbaijani political elite and Azerbaijani identity more generally. This identity was based on regionalist loyalties, in themselves a true reflection of the history of this land, which was either integrated in larger empires, or disintegrated into khanates centred around large cities such as Baku, Shirvan, Ganja, etc.[127]

When Abulfaz Elchibey acceded to the presidency, Azerbaijan got a unified leadership: the state institutions and the former opposition representing large sectors of the public opinion now expressed a unified will. It did not take long for this change to be felt at the front. Elchibey promised to finish with the war "in three months".[128] And indeed, on 4 July 1992, only days after Elchibey's election, a massive Azerbaijani offensive started from the north of Karabakh. According to Armenian sources the former Soviet Fourth Army, which was based near Ganja, took active part in the military operations.[129] Moreover, Azerbaijan had just received its part of the Soviet military heritage, and thus had a large number of tanks and artillery. It could also mobilize larger numbers of

---

University, Strengthening Democratic Institutions Project, Cambridge, MA, July 1993, p. 78.

127   Semih Vaner, "Les Ambitions de l'Azerbaidjan", *Politique Internationale*, No. 57, Autumn 1992, p. 355.

128   Goltz, op. cit., p. 262.

129   *Gharapaghyan Azadakragan Baderazm, 1988-1994,* op. cit., p. 466.

fighters, compared with the limited numbers available for the Karabakh Armenian leadership. The Azerbaijani armed forces first occupied the Shahumian region[130] and later took most of Martakert region, causing a mass exodus of 40,000 Karabakh Armenians towards Stepanakert and into Armenia proper.[131] The wave of Azerbaijani advances was stopped to the north of Stepanakert. Other massive onslaughts to the east and the south, against Martuni and Hadrut, failed to make any change in the front line.

As in the fields of internal politics, management of the economy, and international relations, the Elchibey administration did not show developed skills in the art of military leadership. The initial successes on the northern front of Karabakh proved to be an isolated event in the overall military developments of the Karabakh conflict. In fact the Karabakh Armenians quickly learned from their former failures. In the autumn of 1992 they brought in a State Defence Committee headed by Robert Kocharian which put an end to the volunteer brigade system inherited from the guerrilla phase of the conflict, and created a centralized control and command. It went further and mobilized all resources of Mountainous Karabakh for the war effort. The Lachin corridor also permitted the transport of needed equipment and ammunition from Armenia. Already in that autumn of 1992 the Karabakh Armenian forces were marking slow but regular progress by retaking village after village in the Martakert region. In the spring of 1993 they had already taken the strategic road linking Martakert to Kelbajar, and started advancing west towards Kelbajar, a large mountainous territory that lies between Armenia and Karabakh.

The battle for Kelbajar started on 27 March and ended on 2 April 1993. The Armenian forces advanced from several positions, cutting the Azerbaijani troops in Kelbajar into two. By the time of the Kelbajar battle, the Azerbaijani forces had exhausted themselves. The invasion of the year before had caused huge losses of men and armour. The Azerbaijani defeat also forced some 60,000 ethnic Azeris and Kurds living in the region to cross the Mrav pass and become IDPs (internally displaced people).[132] After the invasion of Kelbajar, the Arme-

---

130   Rechristened as Geranboy region in Azerbaijan.

131   *Azerbaijan, Seven Years of Conflict in Nagorno-Karabakh*, New York: Human Rights Watch/Helsinki, 1994, p. 5.

132   Neil MacFarlane and Larry Minear, *Humanitarian Action and Politics: The Case*

nian forces continued their initiative, taking Martakert in an attack on 26-27 June 1993, less than a year after the town was occupied by Azerbaijani troops. The Karabakh Armenian troops were now determined to deliver a hard blow to the Azerbaijani war ambitions. In the summer of 1993 they occupied several Azerbaijani districts around Karabakh, including Gubatli and Zankelan that lie between Armenia and Karabakh to the south of Lachin, but also Jebrayil, Fizuli and Aghdam to the south-east and east of Karabakh. Serge Sarkissian, the Karabakh Defence Minister, explained the victories of his forces by the huge losses Azerbaijan suffered in 1992-93; these raised morale on the Armenian side: "There were heavy Azerbaijani losses until spring," which he put at 15,000 Azerbaijani soldiers killed against 2,000 on the Armenian side. "Azerbaijan has no tank-armour superiority over Karabakh forces. The air force could never cause any serious military harm, it hurts only civilians."[133] Sarkissian also said that the Azerbaijanis could "reconstruct their forces, but it needs several months", clearly expressing the feeling that he had to make the most of the current confusion on the side of his antagonists.

The military defeats created an atmosphere of uncertainty in Baku, and further weakened the already dwindling popularity of Elchibey. His downfall was triggered by a military rebellion led by the Karabakh war hero Surat Huseinov. The chain of events started with the Soviet Fourth Army suddenly withdrawing from Ganja in May 1993, handing over parts of its weaponry and large stocks of ammunition to the forces of Huseinov. This latter was a former wool factory director in Yevlakh, who had made large financial contributions to the war effort, and had himself led a group of fighters during the various episodes of the war. He had also won medals for his heroism during the capture of Martakert, during which his private army had played a key role. In February 1993, he fell out with the Elchibey government, and was dismissed, along with the Defence Minister, Rahim Qaziyev. Huseinov pulled his 709th brigade from the battle lines, and retreated to his power base in Ganja, creating a vacuum at the front.

To regain the military equipment left behind by the departing Russian troops, the government sent loyal soldiers to Ganja in early

---

of *Nagorno-Karabakh*, Providence: Watson Institute, 1997, p. 17.

133   Author interview with Serge Sarkissian, Stepanakert, 10 July 1993.

June 1993. The forces under the orders of Surat Huseinov resisted, resulting in violent clashes in which up to seventy people were killed. This ignited a rebellion that first took control of Ganja and then started marching eastwards to Baku, demanding the resignation of Elchibey. Although the numbers of Huseinov's troops marching on Baku were small[134] the Elchibey government had no more defences, no one wanted to stand up and fight for him. In the confusion, as the rebel army was 30 kilometres from the capital, Heydar Aliev, the former head of the Azerbaijani Communist Party, returned to Baku from Nakhichevan, and very skilfully took power away from Elchibey. He was first elected member of the Milli Majlis (parliament) and then to head the Majlis, a post that also had the title of vice-president. Fearing the rebel forces would enter Baku, Elchibey left for his native village in Nakhichevan, and a few days later (24 June 1993) the Milli Majlis appointed Aliev to the presidency. The rebel Huseinov became the new Prime Minister. In a Soviet-style election organized on 3 October, Aliev defeated two unknown figures with 98.8 per cent of the votes. Thus ended the Azerbaijani experiment with democracy, and the Soviet-era *nomenklatura* returned to power.

As in the spring of 1992, the power struggle in Baku and the leadership vacuum that it caused had a disastrous effect on the Azerbaijani military. The Armenian side profited from this opportunity as best it could, creating a *cordon sanitaire* around Karabakh. As Aliev was taking power Armenian forces entered Aghdam. Later they took Fizuli to the south-east of Karabakh, and Jebrayil to its south. This left over a hundred thousand civilians in western Azerbaijan trapped by Armenian forces. In a later offensive in November 1993 the region of Zankelan fell to the Armenian fighters without much resistance, and thousands of Azerbaijani refugees crossed the Arax river into Iran, before being settled in refugee camps in central Azerbaijan.

To add to the confusion, a short-lived rebellion hit south-eastern Azerbaijan around the city of Lenkoran, a region inhabited by the Persian-speaking Talish minority. Led by Alikram Gumbatov, an army officer, the rebellion declared the establishment of Talish-Mughan repub-

---

134 Some rumours even suggested that it was just a thirty-man force, see Goltz, op. cit., p. 364. Even if this seems an exaggeration, it reveals how small the rebel army was and how weak Elchibey had become just after a year in power.

lic in August 1992.[135] There was a fear that more minorities would revolt and Azerbaijan as a state would disintegrate. But loyal troops crushed the rebellion, forcing Gumbatov to escape to exile in Russia. Later he was handed back to Baku where he was tried and sent to prison.

Like his predecessors, Heydar Aliev opened his presidency yet with another offensive on the Karabakh front. The offensive started by late November and lasted for four months. This winter offensive was very costly for both sides, as both fighting armies were increasingly organizing their command structures, mobilizing more men, and using sophisticated weapon systems. The offensive was possible after the Azerbaijani army declared a general draft of young men into the national army, and reinforced its ranks with foreign military experts and fighters, who came from various and quite unusual sides: US instructors, former Turkish army officers, Afghan Mujahideen…Several thousand (estimated from 1,500 to 2,500) Afghan fighters from Hizb-i-Wahdat under the leadership of Gulbeddin Hekmatyar were flown to Azerbaijan by fall 1993, after a visit to Afghanistan by the Azerbaijani Deputy Foreign Minister, Rovshan Javadov.[136] They seem to have taken part in several battles in 1993-94. US military experts and Turkish officers took part in military training and advice.[137] The initial offensive concentrated on the south-eastern part of the front, and the Azerbaijani troops tried to recapture Horadiz, an important railway junction. Later in January 1994 the Azeri offensive concentrated on the Mrav mountain chain, in an attempt to take the Omar pass. Initially Azerbaijani forces scored some successes, crossing the pass and entering the villages of Kelbajar region. But soon snow and Armenian counter-attack cut them off from their supply lines.[138] Azerbaijani losses were heavy, many being killed by the

---

135   Hugh Pope, "Azerbaijan may split into two", *The Independent*, London, 18 August 1993.

136   On the use of mercenaries by the Azerbaijani army, see: *Azerbaijan, Seven Years of Conflict in Nagorno-Karabakh*, New York: Human Rights Watch/Helsinki, 1994, p. 46; see also Hayk Demoyan, *Karabakh Drama: Hidden Acts*, Yerevan: Caucasian Center for Iranian Studies, 2003, pp. 34-6.

137   Former American officers turned mercenaries, with experience in the Iran-contra affair and connections with the little known MEGA-oil company, appeared in Baku in 1992 to provide training and mercenaries for the Azerbaijani army. See Goltz, *The Azerbaijani Diary*, pp. 270-9.

138   Idrak Abbasov and Jasur Mamedov, "Azeri Veterans Recall Military Fiasco", Institute for War and Peace Reporting, *Caucasus Reporting Service*, No. 219

cold, with estimates of over 5,000 soldiers killed and over 60 armoured vehicles destroyed.[139] In spite of the fierce fighting, the four-month offensive did not bring about any significant alteration of the war front as established by the autumn of 1993.

By the spring of 1994 the Azerbaijani forces were exhausted, and it was rumoured that the Armenian side was on the point of starting a new offensive to take Yevlakh, an Azerbaijani town on the road between Ganja and Baku.[140] As a result of heavy Russian pressure, a cease-fire agreement was signed by Baku, Yerevan and Stepanakert in Bishkek on 18 May 1994, under the patronage of the Russian Defence Minister, Pavel Grachev. In spite of the absence of peacekeeping troops, this cease-fire has preserved the status quo since 1994.

Why negotiations and mediation failed

I will conclude my discussion of the Karabakh conflict by addressing three questions. The first is whether it was possible to solve the Karabakh problem without violence: was it possible to negotiate a solution, a new format of coexistence between Armenians and Azerbaijanis as the Soviet Union was crumbling? The second is, what role did Moscow or other foreign powers play in the conflict? And the third question, which goes to the essence of my work, is whether nationalism should be seen at the heart of the conflict, and its mobilization as the cause of the political and military developments, or whether nationalism could become an agent of change because of more global shifts in the political-institutional framework. The intention I have here is not essentializing, but rather proposes a new weaving of causes and narratives.

The first remark to be made on the Armeno-Azerbaijani conflict is the radical shift in the geopolitical context as the conflict started in 1988 and developed into a full-scale war in 1992. The conflict started with Armenia and Azerbaijan as sub-entities of the Soviet state, and by the end of 1991 they emerged as independent states. In 1988 the Karabakh conflict was an internal problem of the USSR; it was transformed in December 1991 into an international conflict as Armenia

London, 21 February 2004.

139   Michael Croissant, *The Armenia-Azerbaijan Conflict*, op. cit., p. 96.

140   Author interviews in Yerevan, April 1994.

and Azerbaijan were recognized as independent states which joined the United Nations. As we saw earlier, during the start of the movement the Armenian militants were making demands on Moscow, not Baku, for the rectification of a political error under Stalin—as they saw it at the time. The centre of power of the Soviet state was in Moscow, and any change had to come from there. They thought that once Moscow accepted the idea of change, there would be very little resistance from the Azerbaijani side. "In 1988 Armenians in Karabakh and Armenia tried to solve the question of Karabakh through constitutional ways," according to Vazgen Manukian. "There was some sort of romanticism in our belief that the question could be solved peacefully: no people gives up land without struggle" was his conclusion.[141] The same idea is shared by Anatoly Chernyaev, an adviser to Gorbachev, who said the conflict could have been solved when the Armenian mass mobilization was in its early stage, and before a similar mass movement emerged in Azerbaijan: "To achieve that [peaceful solution to Karabakh conflict] we would have had to give Karabakh to Armenia immediately, as early as 1986, when the crisis there was only beginning and Azerbaijani nationalism was still in deep slumber or at least wasn't yet "organized". (…) In fact that is what actually did happen, only without the process being dragged out over many torturous, hellish years."[142]

It took several months for the leaders of the Karabakh Movement to realize that Azerbaijan was an independent political factor. They started seeing Azerbaijan as an independent player in the Karabakh conflict from November 1988, after the emergence of a popular movement in Azerbaijan itself, well after the Sumgait pogroms. The popular movement in Azerbaijan, as we have seen earlier, was mobilized around the idea of defending Karabakh as part of Azerbaijan. On the other hand, the emergence of the Karabakh movement gave the Armenian side a mobilized force and a political will, which was a source of concern for the Kremlin.

During the Karabakh conflict there were several attempts to create dialogue between Baku and Yerevan. One initial attempt to create links between the Armenian National Movement and the Azerbaijani Popu-

---

141   Author interview with Vazgen Manukian, Yerevan, 16 March 1994.

142   Anatoly Chernyaev, *My Six Years With Gorbachev*, University Park: Penn State University Press, 2000, p. 185.

lar Front took place in Riga, in February 1990. On the agenda were the territorial question, stabilizing the security situation, the return of refugees from both sides, and discussion of the humanitarian consequences of the conflict.[143] This ambitious plan did not take off because of the violent events in Baku at the time, and the meeting did not go further than a basic exchange of views.[144] The defeat of the APF in the September 1990 elections marginalized the Front and led to a break in the negotiations.

A researcher has questioned whether the war was inevitable, and suggested that in summer 1991 "there was a possibility to avert the war at that time, more than three years after the events in Sumgait."[145] The author has the best of intentions, to show theoretically that the Karabakh confrontation was not predetermined, and that at any moment a solution was possible. But in spite of the intention, it is very difficult to project such an analysis on the reality of the Karabakh conflict, and even more so to suggest that a negotiated solution for this complex conflict was possible in, of all years, the fatal year of 1991. He bases his analysis on one episode of negotiations between Baku leadership and a Karabakh Armenian leader, Valerii Grigorian, following Operation Kaltso, during which Armenian villages in Shahumian, Shushi, and Hadrut districts were emptied by a joint Soviet Army and Azerbaijani Interior troops operation. Elsewhere, he says that if the Azerbaijanis had foreseen the outcome of the conflict "they would reasonably have preferred to cut their losses rather than use force to resist Armenian separatism and irredentism."[146] One could argue that even if a small circle of Azerbaijani leaders believed that they had no chance of winning a war (in fact Azerbaijani leaders thought that their superiority in arms and numbers would prevail), they still had to face their population, heavily mobilized around the cause of defending Karabakh within Azerbaijan. Around this notion there crystallized an Azerbaijani mass

---

143   Irina Litviova in *Izvestia*, 31 January 1990, in English in *CDSP*, Vol XLII, No. 5, 1990.

144   Hambartsum Galstyan, "The Riga Meeting", in G.J. Libaridian, *Armenia at the Crossroads*, pp. 47-50.

145   Erik Melander, "The Nagorno-Karabakh Conflict Revisited, Was the War Inevitable?" *Journal of Cold War Studies*, Vol. 3 No. 2, Spring 2001, p. 48.

146   Ibid., p. 50.

movement claiming sovereignty and independence. What Azerbaijani political leader, even a very enlightened one, could have had the courage to tell his people to give up Karabakh in the early 1990s?

The whole political dynamism in Armenia and Azerbaijan was developing towards confrontation, and it was not Sumgait which was an isolated event, but negotiation initiatives: the assassination of Grigorian in the streets of Stepanakert, probably by radical Armenians, put an end to his efforts. The most important misunderstanding in this analysis is the assumption that any agreement could have had serious consequence on the ground: in 1991 the only existing state structure (the USSR) was crumbling, and failed to impose its will on the conflict parties. On the other hand, there was no unified leadership on either side of the conflict that could negotiate a political resolution. The unstable political context made any attempt to negotiate a risky political endeavour, exposing its supporters to accusations of "treason", and the continuous sporadic violence made the role of any negotiator a nearly impossible mission.

A more serious effort of mediation was initiated by the then president of the Russian Soviet Federal Republic, Boris Yeltsin, supported by the Kazakh President Nursultan Nazarbaev. Both heads of state arrived in Stepanakert in September 1991, and their mediation led to the "Zheleznovodsk Declaration" to regulate the conflict. But it did not take long before this agreement turned into a dead letter. In November of the same year Armenian forces shot down an Azerbaijani helicopter which was transporting Azerbaijani officials as well as Russian and Kazakh diplomats, on a mission to implement the agreement. In 1991 the security situation on the ground did not permit any negotiated solution to take root. Formerly mixed Armenian and Azerbaijani regions, towns and villages had gradually polarized, and increasing violence led to mass refugee movement. Roads linking towns and villages were insecure for both sides, since each locality had formed its own guards who blocked the free circulation of the opposite ethnic group. Practically, Armenians were blocking large sections inhabited by Azerbaijani population, while Azerbaijanis had imposed a blockade on the Armenian settlements in and around Karabakh. This explosive situation was kept under control thanks to the presence of the Soviet Army, which accompanied convoys travelling along the main routes of Karabakh, permitting a minimum movement of goods and people. But after the August coup the Soviet

Army had no more leadership, its mission was unclear, it was cut off from its logistic bases inside Russia, and it could not continue its former mission. It started evacuating its positions in November 1991, finishing in a matter of three months. With the disappearance of this last force of interposition a violent clash between the two antagonistic sides was inevitable, and good intentions, whether from within or outside the region, had no chance to stop it.

Iranian diplomacy intensively mediated between Baku, Stepanakert and Yerevan to reach a cease-fire agreement in early 1992. At best, some cease-fire declarations held for a few days, before artillery fire and ground attacks resumed. Despite those setbacks, Teheran succeeded in bringing together the Armenian President Ter-Petrossian and the Azerbaijani head of state Yakub Mamedov. Yet, hours after their arrival in Teheran, the news of Armenian forces entering Shushi spread, making negotiations redundant. This was a heavy blow to Iranian diplomacy, which had invested its energies to bring peace to its northern borders. It was also embarrassing to the Armenian leader, who seemed either to have no control over the ethnic Armenian troops fighting in Karabakh, or to be determined to give a blow to Iranian mediators. The truth could be a third possibility, that the offensive on Shushi, planned to take place on an earlier date, was postponed because of bad weather and logistical difficulties, and was not planned deliberately to foil the Teheran negotiations.

The Russian role, outside intervention and the military outcome

There is not a civil war or separatist conflict in the former Soviet Union without them. They fight alongside Armenians against Azeris in Nagorno-Karabakh and fly bombing missions for Abkhaz rebels in the war against Georgia (…) They are the Russians…[147]

So started Goltz's article that had great impact on shaping American views on the Russian role in post-Soviet space. Goltz thought the Russian policy was to dismember "those states that wish to leave Moscow's

---

147   Thomas Goltz, "Letter From Eurasia: The Hidden Russian Hand", *Foreign Policy*, No. 92, Fall 1993, p. 92.

this dude says it's ALL Russia's fault.

orbit".[148] He went so far as to suggest that the Khojali massacre was the work of Russians, to provoke further conflict between the two nations. In a word, he suggested, the Karabakh conflict was instigated, planned, and fought by the Russians. Such interpretations of the causes of wars in the Caucasus see the local belligerents as simple actors of a script written and a play directed from Moscow.

Goltz' assertions have two problems. The first is that they are very popular in Caucasian capitals, and serve to shift responsibilities away from local actors and leaders. During the war, and since, I have several times heard people in Baku and Yerevan insisting that the changing war fronts were the result of Russian manipulation, of conscious policies in Moscow; and that once the Russian factor was eliminated from the Caucasus, Armenians and Azerbaijanis could find a *modus vivendi*. Just to quote a few examples: the Yerevan based analyst Armen Baghdasarian considered that the Azerbaijani victory in the summer of 1992 could be explained only by Russian military support to the Elchibey regime;[149] the Azerbaijani presidential adviser Vafa Guluzade expressed a similar position, saying, "The current struggle is that of Russia against national independence movements (...) Without Russian protection [of Armenia] Azerbaijan could return Karabakh under its rule";[150] and Isa Gambar, parliament speaker in 1992-93, and one of the leaders of the Azerbaijani opposition, similarly declared: "Russia considers that until it solves its internal problems, it should not permit the normal development of South Caucasus states. If the foreign intervention is eliminated, the resolution of the Armenian-Azerbaijani conflict would be easier."[151]

The second problem with the "Russian Hand" theory is that it came at a time when Western views on a new policy towards Russia were taking shape, and in February 1994 the idea of eastern expansion of NATO while leaving Russia out had won in the policy debate.[152] Therefore, the West saw Russia once again as the potential enemy, and saw its intervention not as a stabilizing force, but as a source of trouble. On

---

148   Ibid.

149   Author interview with Armen Baghdasarian, Yerevan, 10 March 1993.

150   Author interview with Vafa Guluzade, Baku, 28 June 1999.

151   Author's notes of press conference given by Isa Gambar, Baku, 1 July 1999.

152   Gilbert Achcar, *La nouvelle guerre froide*, Paris: PUF, 1999, pp. 72-6.

the other hand, some Russian analysts were worried about a return of dictatorship, in the form of a nationalist ideology and neo-imperialistic policies in the "near abroad", as a result of the failure of the Russian economic reforms and democratization under Yeltsin and Gaidar. Such a shift in Russian policies from pro-democratic reforms to a nationalist backlash could only lead to renewed tensions between Moscow and Western capitals.[153] Perceptions between Russia and the West were changing, and this left a long shadow over the actual role played by Russia in the former Soviet republics.

Apart from perceptions and politically motivated representations, what was the real Russian policy in the Caucasus, and what impact did it have on the Karabakh war? The political reaction of the Kremlin in the initial phase of the conflict (1988-91) was surprise and bewilderment, followed later by an attempt to keep the status quo while proposing large economic investments, since Moscow thought solving socio-economic problems would solve the existing national-political ones. It also introduced the army as a peacekeeping force, to separate the warring factions and bring a minimum of stability to the mountainous autonomy. As the situation worsened Moscow tried to put the region under its direct rule by creating the Volsky commission. By the time that experiment had failed to produce results, Gorbachev was dramatically weakened and his main concern was to keep power and try to reorganize the USSR on federal lines, through constitutional reforms. When Armenia refused to take part in the referendum on the new union (March 1991), the Soviet troops which were deployed as peacekeepers were used to punish the Armenian side (and reward loyal Mutalibov) by Operation Kaltso and by organizing "ethnic cleansing" of Armenian villages to the north of Karabakh and around the town of Shushi.

As the Soviet Union crumbled, Moscow had military forces in the Caucasus region which it hardly controlled. From mid-1991 until the end of 1992, Moscow had little idea about the situation of the former Soviet bases in the Caucasus, and about how it could use them in the future. Nor did the Russian leadership have the means to preserve those bases from a logistic point of view, while the long-term strategic perspective was shrouded in darkness as national movements erupted in various

---

153   Alexander Arbatov, "A New Cold War?" *Foreign Policy*, No. 95, Summer 1994, pp. 90-103.

regions of the Caucasus hostile to Russian rule, calling the survival of those bases into question.[154] Most of those bases were isolated and did not receive either funding or food, and the soldiers were disoriented and starving. In those circumstances, local Russian military leaders had to manage their survival and that of their troops by all possible means, including selling weapons or working as mercenaries.[155] Seeing a conscious, manipulative "hand" behind this is an act of wild imagination.

In the fateful period of November 1991-June 1992, during which the Armenian forces succeeded in taking control of the whole of Mountainous Karabakh and opening a land corridor to Armenia, Russia did not have a clear policy in the Caucasus. Not only did various Russian institutions have contradictory policies—the president's office, the Foreign, Defence and Interior ministries—but even the Defence Ministry did not have control over "its" retreating forces from Karabakh, Armenia and Azerbaijan, leaving behind large quantities of arms and ammunition. Some analysts see in the fact that Russian officers handed arms from the Stepanakert garrisons to Karabakh Armenians, or from the Gumri base to the forces of the local warlord Huseinov, a kind of Russian plot. Let us consider the question whether the Russian officials commanding those bases could have done anything other than hand over those weapons to local fighters. Surely Karabakh Armenians or Ganja fighters would not have tolerated the Russians taking those weapons away. Instead, the Russian officers were happy to cash in a few thousand dollars in return for a tank or a howitzer. Russian military as far away as the Baltic Fleet were selling arms and ammunition, which were later sent to the war fronts in the Caucasus.[156] Russian military assistance in the form of sending arms and ammunition to Armenia

---

154　See the article by Col. V. Kaushansky, "How 'Ours' Become 'Aliens'", *Krasnaya Zvezda*, 22 March 1991, quoted in *Russian Press Digest*, 22 March 1991, describing the difficulties of Soviet troops in Armenia; *Nezavisimaya Gazeta* describes how North Ossets threatened to nationalize military bases on their territory unless the military supplied them with weapons for the fighting in South Ossetia; see *Russian Press Digest* on 23 May 1992.

155　On the condition of the Russian armed forces in 1991-92, see Pavel Baev, *The Russian Army in Times of Trouble*, PRIO/SAGE, London, 1996, pp. 115-20; see also William Odom, *The Collapse of the Soviet Military*, New Haven: Yale University Press, 1998.

156　Julian Borger , "Impoverished Russian troops sell stolen arms for cash", *The Guardian*, 21 May 1992.

was much more important in 1993-94, when the war took the form of confrontation between two regular armies. This assistance was key to creating an air defence system in Karabakh that neutralized the Azerbaijani air superiority, as well as giving the necessary military hardware for the Armenian offensive of 1993. Therefore, Russian policies during the Karabakh war should be seen in a much more nuanced way than by presenting Moscow as the manipulator of the war there for an imperial return to those formerly Tsarist and Soviet colonies. The empire was not returning, it was simply shrinking.

Russian analysts suggest that if manipulation happened, it was a two-way affair. According to Yevgeni Kazhokin, the director of the Russian Institute of Strategic Studies in Moscow, it was not just the Russian policy makers who manipulated the situation in Azerbaijan and Georgia to overthrow nationalist leaders and bring back former Soviet officials; rather it was the old *nomenklatura* figures, Aliev and Shevardnadze, who used their connections with Russia and succeeded in bringing the local Russian military power to support their bids to retake power.[157]

The question remains, how did numerically inferior Armenians, with a difficult geographical position during the initial months of the war, and a big inferiority in arms and ammunition, succeed in winning the war? Many analysts refer to the military tradition of Armenians in the Soviet army, while Azerbaijanis and Muslims in general were discriminated against and did not have specialized military training. Others note the better social organization of Armenians, their discipline and motivation relative to that of Azerbaijanis. On the political level, the Armenian side registered its most dramatic successes when Baku was in a state of turmoil, suffering from a power struggle between various elite factions. Whenever Azerbaijan was united under one leadership it went on to counter-attack, with limited success. Last but not least, the Armenian efforts to build a professional army came much earlier, while Azerbaijan lagged behind. Vazgen Manukian, who was Prime Minister and later Defence Minister of Armenia (September 1992-April 1993), said that he tried to attract ethnic Armenian officers in the Russian Army by offering them wages higher than what they earned in Russia.[158] What has not been remarked so far is that political and military de-

---

157   Author interview with Yevgeni Kazhokin, Moscow, 15 May 1998.

158   Author interview with Vazgen Manukian, Yerevan, 18 December 2004.

velopments in 1988-91 prepared each of the antagonists Armenia and Azerbaijan for a different war.

The presence of the Soviet troops and their pro-Azeri political sympathy and continuous pressure on the Armenian side (Operation Kaltso, April-September 1991) forced Armenian villages to create their self-defence units and fight back. From 1988 until end of 1991 the Armenians of Karabakh not only witnessed direct military pressure but also had the examples of the Sumgait, Kirovabad (later Ganja) and Baku pogroms driving out Armenian populations. The Karabakh Armenians, frightened and encircled, had their backs to the wall. The Azerbaijani side was prepared for another sort of war. In Sumgait and Baku Azerbaijani mobs had numerical superiority and could chase out the ethnic Armenians by the superiority of their sheer numbers. During Operation Kaltso in 1991 they were supported by the superior forces of the Soviet troops against lightly armed Armenian villagers. Their military strategy basically consisted of spreading fear through shelling (as in Stepanakert in 1991-92) and massive attacks that lacked coordination and strategic depth. This military style could not match the organization and determination showed by the Armenian side. Once the Soviet troops withdrew, in the initial year of the war (1992) the Armenian and Azerbaijani self-defence units formed at village level, supported by volunteer battalions coming from Yerevan and Baku, were left to face each other, and on this level the Armenian side was better organized and had more experience.

Causes of war: fear or opportunity?

Stuart Kaufmann proposes an interesting argument on the origins of the Karabakh conflict by criticising the "intellectual conceit that ethnic war is simply the logical result of the pursuit of group interests".[159] He insists that ethnic wars are primarily driven by fear, "which in turn has its sources in prejudice by which ethnic conflicts escalate to war".[160] For Kaufmann, it was the irrational explosion of sentiments that caused the emergence of insecurity and violence, which in its turn eroded the

---

159 Stuart Kaufman, "Ethnic Fears and Ethnic War in Karabagh", Washington: CSIS, 1998, p. 2. Internet address: www.csis.org/ruseura/ponars/workingpapers/008.PDF

160 Ibid.

power of Moscow over the two Caucasian republics, and not conscious elite-led calculations of win-or-lose. "Rather, ideological and prejudice-driven ethnic fears caused conflict and violence that, over time, weakened and finally destroyed the state."[161] But why does such fear erupt at certain moments and not others? Or, why does this fear lead to violence in certain circumstances, and is either repressed or finds different, non-violent, expressions in others? Kaufmann says that just as in the case of Karabakh, "violence may erupt even before extremist elites start to mobilize people".[162] He calls such cases "mass-led", contrasting them with "elite-led" conflicts as in the former Yugoslavia. For example, he remarks that the initial rallies in Armenia in 1988 were mobilized well before the formation of committees at factory and university level. Similarly, mobilization in Azerbaijan, and the imposing of the blockade on Armenian villages within and around Karabakh, had a mass character and were not led by the Baku elite.

Let us put aside expressions like "extremist elites", or dozens of others such as "nationalist", "separatist", or "Christian" Armenians and "Muslim" Azerbaijanis, etc. which are value judgements that hinder our understanding of the political realities, and often are marred by imprecision and misunderstandings. Kaufmann's paper is highly interesting because it helps reconstruct a new argument by rearranging his. We can also see the same equation (nationalism leading to Soviet collapse) the other way around: it was not Armenian nationalism that led to the weakening of the Soviet Union, but the weakening of the Soviet rule that created a huge political space and a demand for the development of a new political legitimacy. Because of reasons proper to modern Armenian history, and because of the specific nature of Soviet policies and more precisely the creation of ethnically defined territories, the new political legitimacy could only be filled by a movement defining itself in national terms. Armenians—or Georgians or Ingushes for that matter—were no less nationalist in 1978 than in 1988, and one can recall the disturbances in Georgia and Abkhazia when Moscow tried to reform the Soviet constitution and questioned the place of the Armenian and Georgian languages in those Soviet Republics. But the Soviet Union

---

161   Ibid., p. 9.

162   Ibid., p. 10.

and its state structures were still intact, and as a result the nationalist outbursts did not develop into alternative political movements.

Gorbachev's reforms proposed new principles for political relations within the USSR, encouraging Armenians to put forward their age-old grievances (loss of land and people) and the territorial question of Karabakh where the majority of inhabitants were still ethnic Armenians. The contradictory policies of Gorbachev, the Sumgait tragedy, the shifts by Communist Party cadres, the rise of inter-ethnic violence and population exchange, all contributed to progressive undermining of Soviet authority in Armenia. As I explained above, Soviet structures were more solid in Azerbaijan, partially because of the weakness of the Azerbaijani popular movement, and because Azerbaijan was supported by Moscow to preserve the status quo. In any case, with the emergence of powerful mass movements and the development of politics outside the framework of the official party and the state institutions, Moscow lost its capacity and role of power broker and mediator, and Armenians and Azerbaijanis found themselves face to face for the first time since the Sovietization of the Caucasus. To conclude, it was the weakening of the Soviet state that led to political nationalism, and its collapse to the war between Armenians and Azerbaijanis to determine who would control the disputed territories.

Svante Cornell looks at the conflicts of the Caucasus from the perspective of the unstable institutional structures, the autonomy structures within the Union Republics. He notes that most secessionist movements took place where autonomy structures existed;[163] that ethnic mobilization takes place "as minority groups perceive themselves subjected to assimilation",[164] and that once conflict erupts minorities do not wish to return to the autonomy arrangement and demand full independence. He concludes:

In a sense, the autonomous status seems to have fuelled rather than diminished minority demands – a factor which is helpful in understanding why Central Asia, where there are few autonomous regions, has witnessed fewer instances of ethnic conflict than the Caucasus.[165]

---

163   Svante Cornell, *Small Nations and Big Powers*, p. 40.

164   Ibid., pp. 41-2.

165   Ibid., p. 45.

While Cornell's remark about the interrelation between minority mobilization and institutional structures of autonomy is highly interesting, I would like to introduce a clear difference between minority mobilization and ethnic conflict. One does not necessarily lead to the other, at least not in a mechanical way. At the time of the Soviet collapse there were dozens of territorial disputes, various forms and levels of ethnic mobilization, and luckily only a few of those led to bloody confrontations. To move from ethnic mobilization to conflict we need a violent intervention to trigger a bloody conflict. This trigger often came in the form of military intervention by republican or central authorities (Baku in the case of Karabakh, Tbilisi in the case of South Ossetia and Abkhazia, and Moscow in the case of Chechnya) to suppress the political movements of minority groups, transforming the conflict from a political level to a military one. This we will see even more clearly in the chapter on Georgia, while discussing the conflict in Abkhazia.

The cease-fire agreement in May 1994 reflected a power equilibrium reached after several years of war. On the one hand the Armenian side could bring its control over Karabakh, and also occupy vast regions of Azerbaijan proper. The dramatic defeat of Azerbaijan, plus the failure of the last offensive in 1993-94, reflected the creation of a military balance difficult to break. Equally important is the leadership of Heydar Aliev, who could repress the power struggle in Baku under his leadership and impose on the country a cessation of hostilities. Aliev knew that the greatest harm his opponents could do him was to attack him on Karabakh issue. But he was also conscious that three leaders of Azerbaijan before him had fallen from power as their forces were beaten on the front. Aliev was already strong enough in May 1994 to sign a cease-fire agreement.

glastnost = publicity: policy that called →
[glasnost] for increased openess/transparancy
in govt. Introduced by gorbachev in
the late 80s.

Perestrokia = restructuring: also done by
Gorbachev in the 80s.
↓
restructuring of soviet political + Economic system.
154
often argued to be cause of 89 revolutions in E-eurp
and end of the cold war.

4

GEORGIA, FROM NATIONAL LIBERATION
TO STATE COLLAPSE AND BACK

Georgia's specific features

Georgia was not an ordinary Soviet republic. It was the country where Stalin or Josef Vissarionovich Jugashvili was born, the person who has shaped the Soviet Union more than any other character. Georgia profited much from the fact that Stalin and several other Soviet leaders who ruled this vast country from the 1920s to the 1950s were of Georgian origin, including Lavrenti Beria, Sergo Ordzhonikidze and Abel Yenukidze. Under Stalin the country enjoyed privileges that other union republics did not have, with living standards higher than elsewhere in the Union, and became the Soviet republic with the highest percentage of its population completing university education. True, Stalinist purges hit the Georgian intelligentsia hard, but nevertheless Georgian attitudes towards the Soviet dictator remained ambivalent even in the age of *glasnost* and heated debates; in spite of his crimes Stalin was Georgian, and was defended by Georgian authors as "a statesman and military leader".[1] Georgia also went through national consolidation under Soviet rule, reinforcing the place of ethnic Georgians in the republic, as a result of out-migration of ethnic Russians and Armenians starting

---

1   Elizabeth Fuller refers to an article by Levan Khaindrava in defence of Stalin published in *Literaturnaya Gruziya*, No. 1, 1989, in her article: "Filling in the 'Blank Spots' in Georgian History: Noe Zhordania and Joseph Stalin", *Report on the USSR*, 31 March 1989, p. 21.

from the 1950s.[2] Rapid urbanization was not accompanied by mass Russification as elsewhere in the Soviet Union, and the central role of the Georgian language was preserved in the cities and the provinces alike.

The fall from grace of Stalin and Beria was a heavy blow to Georgian public opinion, which saw into this event a plot to disgrace the hero of the Soviet Union, and the son of Georgia, by political foes.[3] Zviad Gamsakhurdia, one of the most famous of Georgian dissidents who later became the first freely elected president of Georgia, made the following comment to a Russian journalist in the last months of the USSR: "All in all, the mid-1950's were a time of intellectual ferment in Georgia, associated in part with the Stalinist movement. Young people at the time protested out of a sense of national pride, seeing how Stalin was being reviled."[4] On 9 March 1956, protest demonstrations erupted in Tbilisi as the new Soviet leadership in Moscow publicized the crimes of Stalin, leading to violent clashes with the armed police forces causing the death of 22 with an additional 400 people suffering wounds, according to an official count.

After the 1950s the Georgian economy went through unparalleled liberalization. The central authorities permitted much liberty in Georgia, unseen in neighbouring Soviet republics: "In the immediate post-Stalin years, central political interference in the economy of Georgia was notably reduced. The aim of the central government appeared to be gradual reform, rather than the preservation, of Stalinist practice."[5] This relative economic autonomy led to the development of a parallel or "grey" economy, widespread corruption among the state bureaucracy, the party members and even the local KGB. Retrospectively, Soviet policies are seen as a premeditated effort at the creation of a par-

2 J.W.R. Parsons, "National Integration in Soviet Georgia", *Soviet Studies*, Vol. 34, No. 4, October 1982, pp. 552-3.

3 Apart from the Stalin factor, the Georgians had various other references for their national pride. This includes being an ancient nation, an early convert to Christianity (fourth century), and a feeling of being the easternmost Christians encircled by Islam, having a distinct alphabet and a rich literary tradition.

4 See Pavel Voschanov's interview with Zviad Gamsakhurdia in *Komsomolskaya Pravda*, 21 February 1991.

5 Roland G. Suny, *The Making of the Georgian Nation*, Bloomington: Indiana University Press, Second Edition, 1994, p. 301.

allel economy in Georgia; according to the social psychologist Giorgi Nisharadze, "...in the sixties, after de-stalinization, Communism was dead in Georgia. Georgia was alienated from Communism. The authorities pushed people to put their energy in another direction, in the grey economy."[6] This parallel economy, next to the tourism income of the Black Sea towns such as Sukhumi, Pitsunda and Gagra on the Abkhazian coast, ensured a higher standard of living and the availability of black market consumer goods, which Soviet citizens in other parts of the country had no access to. Georgia also enjoyed cultural freedom unparalleled in other republics. As a result, painting, sculpture, theatre and film production blossomed hand-in-hand with the development of the grey economy and mafia-like structures. Georgia's warm climate and rich earth permitted the development of agricultural products that were in high demand within the closed economy of the USSR: citrus fruits, tea, tobacco, etc. Georgia's Black Sea cost, and especially Pitsunda and Gagra in the Autonomous Republic of Abkhazia, were highly prized tourist destinations. For Georgian public opinion, the Georgian way of life in the Soviet context was one superior to the standard of other Soviet peoples, while for those living in other parts of the USSR, Georgia was equivalent to a privileged land and where sandy beaches and luxury sanatoria carried pleasant memories of past holidays.

De-Stalinization had curious effects on Georgia. Vasili Mzhavanadze, a deputy commander of military affairs in the Kiev military district, who had worked directly with Nikita Khrushchev, was appointed the First Secretary of the Georgian CP in 1953. He was sent to Tbilisi by Moscow to get rid of the close collaborators of Beria, in power in Tbilisi by that time. The fall of Khrushchev in 1964 did not lead to the fall of Mzhavanadze—which proved the development of locally rooted, stable rule of national elite dominating over Georgia. During his rule Georgia witnessed economic progress but also widespread corruption, to a degree that one scholar labels it "capitalist restoration".[7] In the early 1970s corruption had started to have a negative effect on overall economic

---

6   Interview with the author, Tbilisi, 27 February, 1996. For further discussion on the effect of de-Stalinization on Georgian public consciousness, see Theodor Hanf and Ghia Nodia, *Georgia Lurching to Democracy*, Baden-Baden: Nomos Verlagsgesellschaft, 2000, pp. 23-5.

7   R.G. Suny, *The Making of the Georgian Nation*, p. 304.

performance, and Georgian production did not meet the designed targets. A *Pravda* article in 1972 accused the Georgian leader personally of mismanagement, and of economic under-performance. Mzhavanadze was forced to resign in disgrace, probably with some "help" from his Interior Minister eyeing a career move.

The 44-year-old rising star of the Georgian CP, Eduard Shevardnadze, who had spent the last four years (1968-72) heading the Interior Ministry of Georgia, replaced Mzhavanadze. Shevardnadze's rule was characterized by a long fight against corruption and a crackdown on dissidents. As soon as he came to power, massive purges were organized to clean the party and the state from systemic corruption, leading to the arrest of twenty-five thousand people, among them seventeen thousand party members and seventy-five KGB officers.[8] Shevardnadze's rule was characterized by seemingly contradictory policies, on the one hand reacting to the demands of Soviet policies—economic efficiency, action against corruption, Russification and repression of nationalist expressions—and on the other hand reacting to Georgian public opinion, and especially the urban intelligentsia which was demanding increasing cultural autonomy in reaction to Soviet policies of modernization and assimilation.

In the early 1970s, there appeared a small but vocal group of dissidents based mainly in Tbilisi. Among the most famous were Merab Kostava, Valentina Pailodze, and Zviad Gamsakhurdia. The last-named was the son of a famous writer and diplomat of the independent republic of Georgia, Konstantin Gamsakhurdia. Zviad Gamsakhurdia was a lecturer in English and American literature at Tbilisi State University. In 1974, Kostava and Gamsakhurdia formed the Human Rights Defence Group in Tbilisi, and observed human rights violations in the republic and reported to Russian dissident networks and the Western media. The Georgian dissidents, although a small group of a few dozen, were to have a big impact on the development of the political scene in Georgia in late *perestroika* times. Their ideological field was a mixture of two trends which took coherence in their anti-Soviet struggle. On the one hand they followed the human rights discourse, exposing the Soviet regime and its contradiction with the Helsinki Accords, and violations

---

8   Nicolas Jallot, *Chevardnadzé, Le renard blanc du Caucase*, Paris: Belfond, 2005, p. 44.

of basic rights within the Soviet regime; the human rights discourse was oriented more to the external players, whether they were the Soviet authorities, dissidents in Moscow or Kiev, or Western capitals. Then there was a second discourse focused around the defence of the Georgian national symbols, language and culture. More specifically, the Georgian dissidents campaigned for defence of architectural monuments, defence of the natural environment against industrial projects, highways and railways, and defence of the position of the Georgian language against policies of imposing Russian in education and public life. The dissidents were also sensitive towards the question of ethnic relations between Georgians and minorities in Georgia, and often adopted a Georgian nationalist perspective.

For the Georgian dissidents, the Soviet rule in Georgia was illegal and the state institutions illegitimate, going back to its origin which was the armed invasion of 1921 and the overthrow of the Georgian Republic. The dissidents' struggle for the defence of the Georgian culture and language had a large audience and support. For example, by the early 1980s there was strong resistance against the use of Russian in Georgian universities. A decree of the Soviet Ministry of Education in 1975 required that all doctoral dissertations written in the Soviet Union must be submitted in the Russian language. There were several acts of resistance against this decree, including petitions signed by 365 leading intellectuals, protesting that the rule would push out the Georgian language from scholarship and lead to its impoverishment.

The field of vision of the Georgian dissidents' struggle, seen through the prism of the struggle between Soviet "cosmopolitanism" and Georgian national heritage, had a problem: it excluded a third of the population of Georgia by the fact that they did not belong to the titular nation. Those ethnic minorities feared that weakening the position of the Russian language and strengthening that of the Georgian language and culture would undermine their own social status, and political power, within Georgia and in the Soviet context in general. While the Georgian intelligentsia felt threatened by the Soviet-Russian assimilation thrust, minority groups felt the pressure of Georgian policies, but also felt threatened by demographic trends and internal migration. The ethno-linguistic minorities in Georgia feared Georgian nationalism, and considered Moscow the guarantor of the *status quo*.

Acts of resistance and sabotage expressed the malaise in Soviet Georgia; in 1973 the Tbilisi Opera was put on fire, and there followed a series of explosions in administrative offices. In 1977 there was a crackdown on dissidents, and leading figures such as Kostava and Gamsakhurdia were arrested. Gamsakhurdia publicly confessed his "mistakes" on Soviet television: "I sincerely regret what I have done and repent of what I have done and condemn that crime I committed, (...) I want to note that after long reconsideration I understood that I was deeply misled and that my activities were seriously harmful. Materials produced by myself were illegally distributed in the Soviet Union as well as published in the foreign press and broadcast by radio stations abroad, as a result of which I gained 'popularity.' This, for its part, stimulated my anti-Soviet activities," he was reported as saying.[9] As a result, he received a mild punishment; and was exiled to a mountain village in neighbouring Daghestan. He was released after three years. This action by Gamsakhurdia left a deep division among Georgian dissidents, many of whom would never pardon him and considered him a "coward". Kostava, who refused to confess "mistakes", was exiled to Siberia and set free only in 1987 thanks to *glasnost* and the new policies of Gorbachev.

The arrests of Gamsakhurdia and Kostava led to an international outcry; members of the US Congress nominated them for the Nobel Peace Prize, though the prize went to Menachem Begin and Anwar al-Sadat instead. In his memoirs, the leading Soviet dissident Andrei Sakharov writes that he intended to fly to Tbilisi to attend the trial of the two Georgian dissidents, but when he arrived at the airport he "learned that Gamsakhurdia had disavowed his human rights activities" and therefore cancelled the trip. While refraining from criticizing Gamskhurdia's act, Sakharov is full of admiration towards Kostava who "refused to yield, and continued to conduct himself with courage and dignity in camps and exile."[10]

The most important mobilization in the Shevardnadze period took place in 1978, and it presents the essence of the Georgian dilemma. During debates on the new Soviet constitution, a draft constitution for Georgian SSR was prepared which had left out a clause mentioning the Georgian language as the official language in the republic, and replaced

9 Seth Mydans, *Associated Press*, Moscow, 19 May 1978.

10 Andrei Sakharov, *Memoirs*, London: Hutchinson, 1990, p. 483.

it with Russian. This led to demonstrations of up to five thousand, mainly university students, who gathered in central Tbilisi in protest. Shevardnadze first tried to discuss with the demonstrators, was booed, and later returned to inform them that the leading position of the Georgian language would be retained in the new constitution. This popular victory gave the Georgian activists new courage and self-assertion.

The other side of the coin was that ethnic minorities in Georgia also wanted to voice their own concerns. The Abkhaz mobilized strongly in a series of demonstrations in 1978 with demands similar to those of the Georgians: linguistic and cultural rights, political representation, etc. Some Abkhaz leaders went further and demanded the separation of Abkhazia from Georgia, to make it either a union republic or a part of the Russian Federation. Some of their demands were met, especially in the cultural field; the Pedagogic Institute in Sukhumi was enlarged and turned into the Abkhaz State University with three sections (Abkhazian, Georgian, and Russian); Abkhazian TV programmes started (though only two half-hour news programmes per week). But the Kremlin made it clear that it would not revise the status of Abkhazia, and would not alter Abkhazia's territorial subordination. This half victory of the Abkhaz did not calm tensions, but postponed the confrontation in Abkhazia.

The withering away of Soviet power

Gorbachev's *perestroika* and *glasnost* opened new political possibilities in Georgia, the like of which was not seen in seven decades of Soviet rule. One of the early topics for mobilization was the defence of the environment. An old project known as the Caucasian Mountain Railway was reactivated in the 1986-90 five-year plan, a project that aimed at facilitating rail connections between Tbilisi and the North Caucasus, cutting down the journey time by several hours. The planned project included the construction of a new line stretching over 500 kilometres, the piercing of eleven tunnels, and the construction of eighty-five bridges.[11] Georgian intellectuals mobilized and prepared a petition addressed to Moscow with 800 signatures, protesting against this project. They criticized it because of the potential damage to mountain flora and

---

11   Stephen Jones, "The Caucasian Mountain Railway Project, A Victory for Glasnost?" *Central Asia Survey*, Vol. 8, 1989, p. 49.

fauna, but also because of fears that the project would lead to bringing hundreds of workers and engineers from Russia who would eventually settle down in Georgia.

As early as the autumn of 1987, Georgian intellectuals established the Ilia Chavchavadze Society, which initially worked around the familiar themes of the Georgian dissidents going back to the 1970s— the defence of Georgian language and heritage, protection of historic monuments, and the fight against Russification. Later, in 1988, new organizations started appearing, including the Society of Saint Ilia the Righteous, which was led by Zviad Gamsakhurdia, and the National Democratic Party, led by Georgi Chanturia. Those two groups were considered as "radical", because of their views considering the Soviet rule illegitimate, and their demand for Georgian independence, but also because of their uncompromising political positions, whereby any cooperation with the existing political order was regarded as morally unacceptable. Both groups would play a key role in later events. In the autumn of 1988 those societies organized a number of protests in major cities such as Tbilisi and Kutaisi to protest against the destruction of architectural monuments.

The authorities tried to limit the influence of the informal societies by creating yet another society, called the Shota Rustaveli Society after the famous Georgian medieval poet, in March 1988. The new society had aims very similar to those of the informal groups, but differed in being under the control of figures close to the authorities. Yet, with the rise of the political activism of the wider public, this policy did not last long. In one year the Shota Rustaveli Society's membership grew to 30,000 members. But the attempt by the Georgian authorities to impose their candidates at the head of the society at its second congress in March 1989 did not succeed, and several hundred members demonstrated in front of the Tbilisi Opera building to support the candidature of the independent pro-nationalist thinker Akaki Bakaradze.

In November 1988, debates on constitutional changes led to new protests. In Tbilisi 200,000 people demonstrated against proposed changes in the Soviet constitution, whereby the republics would have lost the—so far theoretical—right to secede from the USSR. Moscow rapidly withdrew the proposal, fearing that nationalist mobilization would grow as well as lead to clashes. The capitulation could only reinforce the nationalist camp in Georgia, while the local Communist Party had by now lost all initiative.

There was a sense of urgency in Georgia in these days, a feeling of history unfolding, and the desire to capture the occasion and realize the suspended dream of 1918. For the first time for many decades the independence of Georgia was not just desirable, but possible. In an interview given to a foreign journalist, Akaki Bakaradze said: "I wish for the imploding of the Soviet Empire as soon as possible." When asked whether he was not playing with fire, the Georgian intellectual answered: "It is better to play with the fire than to sit calmly next to the ashes." Then he added: "Today we have the unique occasion, for which we waited seventy years, to realize our national aspirations. Why not seize the occasion?"[12]

In parallel with the Georgian national awakening, the Abkhaz national movement mobilized in its turn around its old themes: the Abkhaz dream of independence from Georgia. This new campaign started when a letter demanding the secession of Abkhazia from Georgia, signed by fifty-eight leading Abkhaz CP members, was addressed to the Nineteenth All-Union Party Conference, held in June 1988. On 17 March 1989 the Abkhaz activists took steps to mark their separatist intentions. On 18 March a mass meeting was organized in Lykhny, a village at the site of the old Abkhaz capital of the Middle Ages, where thousands of people signed the letter of the fifty-eight as a petition demanding Abkhaz sovereignty.[13]

In reaction to Abkhaz demands, mass demonstrations were organized in Tbilisi. Georgians claimed that the Abkhaz, who represented only 17 per cent of the overall population of Abkhazia, already had extensive privileges and discriminated against ethnic Georgians, who composed nearly half the population of the province. In April the demonstrations grew in volume, reaching 100,000 people on 8 April 1989. The day before the tragic events the Patriarch of Georgian Orthodox Church, Ilia II, addressed the crowd demonstrating in Rustaveli Avenue in central Tbilisi, calling them to respect public order, but in vain; the

---

12   Quoted in Amnon Kapeliouk, "La difficile déstalinisation de la Géorgie", *Le Monde diplomatique*, June 1989.

13   Elizabeth Fuller, "New Abkhaz Campaign for Secession from Georgian SSR", *Report on the USSR*, 7 April 1989, pp. 27-8.

patriarch was booed and his message was rejected by the demonstrators. The local authorities seem to have panicked before the massive demonstrations, and decided to use force at an opportune moment to disperse them. The Georgian Communist Party leader Jumbar Patiashvili, with permission from Moscow, introduced martial law. In the early hours of 9 April 1989, as some 8,000 activists continued their vigil on Rustaveli Avenue opposite the Central Committee building, Interior Ministry forces supported by the Soviet Army's 345th Parachute Regiment attacked the crowd with shovels and a toxic gas.[14] This bloody repression, and the attempt by the Soviet leadership in Moscow to escape assuming responsibility, put an end to what was left of Soviet legitimacy in the eyes of the Georgian public.

The 9 April events left 19 dead, and was the last straw that destroyed any legitimacy that Soviet institutions or the Georgian Communist Party still enjoyed among the Georgians. For the Soviet authorities, the fault was to be found among "extremist-minded unofficial groupings who managed to aggravate the situation in Tbilisi"[15] and who shouted anti-Soviet slogans and called for the secession of Georgia from the USSR. Yet, the repression stopped short of crushing by force Georgia's drive for independence, while being ineffective in reviving Soviet authority there. It only led to the total discredit of the Soviet Georgian authorities, who after the events were completely abandoned by Moscow and accused of having ordered the crackdown without the former knowledge of the Politburo.[16] The military were also pointed at as responsible for the casualties; in a meeting between Eduard Shevardnadze and representatives of "the republic's scientific and creative intelligentsia", participants stressed that "there could be no justification" for the tragedy and that the "methods used to disperse the demonstrators ... were unacceptable for a society that has chosen democratization and

---

14　Harold Elletson, *The General Against the Kremlin, Alexander Lebed*, London: Warner Books, 1998, p. 99. The regiment, which was the first to be deployed in Afghanistan and the last to leave, had just been brought back and based at Kirovabad (Ganja) in Azerbaijan. Lebed himself took part in the operation, although he says that he arrived to Tbilisi few hours after the assault had started.

15　*Pravda*, 11 April 1989.

16　Anatoly Chernyaev, *My Six Years With Gorbachev*, University Park: Penn State University Press, 2000, pp. 218-20.

glasnost ... and in essence were a stab in the back of restructuring."[17] The army in its turn refuted charges that it used poison gas, and indirectly put the blame on the Internal Ministry troops, who were also present in central Tbilisi during the repression of the demonstrators. Shevardnadze put the blame for the decision to use force on the head of the Georgian Communist Party, Patiashvili; the latter presented his "voluntary" resignation, and was replaced by Givi Gumbaridze.

The behaviour of the Soviet leadership did not leave any doubt that the driver's seat was vacant: Gorbachev in his memoirs writes: "How many times I have had to withstand 'searching glances', or listen to direct reproaches that 'the General Secretary must have known everything that was undertaken by the Georgian leadership'. In March 1994, Gavril Popov [then mayor of Moscow] declared in an article: 'I will never believe that Gorbachev did not know.' And yet the truth is: the decision to use force was taken without consulting me."[18] An official commission formed to investigate the tragic events, with the Leningrad Mayor and human rights defender Anatoly Sobchak at its head, reached no conclusions and could not give an adequate answer to: "Who gave the order?"

The half-way repressive measures taken after the bloodshed could not calm spirits. Following the April massacre, the leaders of Georgian unofficial movements were arrested, among them Gamsakhurdia, Kostava, Chanturia, Sarishvili, Tsereteli and Khukhunashvili. Strikes spread in Tbilisi and provincial towns, and acts of violence against Soviet army servicemen became sporadic. Young men attacked Soviet bases and plundered weapons, which served for the formation of multiple armed groupings. By mid-1989 nationalist movements were already spreading elsewhere in the Caucasus, and in other parts of the USSR. In the summer of that year inter-ethnic violence erupted in Uzbekistan, in the Ferghana Valley, and later led to clashes between ethnic Kyrgyz and Uzbeks in southern Kyrgyzstan. Similarly, tension was high in Abkhazia in summer 1989 when clashes erupted in Sukhumi between ethnic Abkhaz and Georgians. The idea of the break-up of the USSR and the secession of certain republics was already in the air, and openly discussed by scholars and journalists. As one scholar put it: "[W]ithin a relatively

---

17   *Pravda*, 11 April 1989.

18   Mikhail Gorbachev, *Memoires*, New York: Doubleday, 1995. p. 443.

short but very intense period of history the idea of the disintegration of the Soviet state moved from the wholly unimaginable to the completely inevitable within the popular mind."[19]

The events of 9 April had two dimensions: the struggle against Moscow and the struggle for the unity of Georgia—the demonstration on that day was in favour of the preservation of Abkhazia within Georgia. These two themes were play a pivotal role in the formation of Georgian political current leading to its independence, and continue to play a central role in Georgian politics now, a decade and a half after the fall of the USSR. The lesson Georgian militants drew in 1989 was that to preserve the territorial integrity of Georgia, they had to move away from Moscow and achieve national independence as the only guarantee for self-defence against the repression of the Soviet state.

associated Abkhaz autonomy with Soviet rule.

A triangular power struggle: the Communists, Gamsakhurdia, and the National Council

When Merab Kostava died in a car accident in October 1989, Zviad Gamsakhurdia was left as the leading charismatic leader of Georgian nationalist movement.[20] Gamsakhurdia played a leading role among Georgian dissident movement and left his fingerprints on the political framework of Georgian nationalist movement which led the country into independence as the Soviet system started crumbling. The personal animosity that he shared with a large number of former dissidents who, very much like Gamsakhurdia, became leaders of various political groupings by the late 1980s divided the Georgian national movement into two main fronts, and poisoned the political atmosphere of Georgia on the threshold of building an independent state.

While all the political groups in Tbilisi agreed on their political objectives, severe and often violent competition arose. This division was not ideology-based, like the polarization between Communists and nationalists; the nationalist, pro-independence political currents were divided between "radicals" and "moderates" basically on questions of

---

19   Mark R. Beissinger, *Nationalist Mobilization and the Collapse of the Soviet State*, Cambridge University Press, 2002, p. 5.

20   Gamsakhurdia accused the KGB of organizing the accident, and plotting to kill him as well. See Carey Goldberg, "Prominent Georgian Dissident Dies in Accident Friends Say Was Suspicious", *Associated Press*, 13 October 1989.

political tactics on how to achieve independence. According to Ghia Nodia, the radicals

were led mostly by former political prisoners and joined by young enthusiasts. They thought in moral rather than political terms, and these morals were based on the simple and clear values of Gulag life. There were 'us' and 'them' and the line dividing the two sides was sacrosanct.[21]

Unlike in other Soviet republics where moderates dominated the political movement while the radicals were at the margin, in Georgia the radicals of the national movement were the dominant current. For them, their anti-Soviet struggle and the realization of Georgian independence were more important than certain principles like human rights, democracy, or the political stability of Georgia.

A year after the Tbilisi repression, Georgia was ready to mobilize its forces that would prepare the post-Soviet political field; on 23-25 May 1990 some 6,200 representatives of 150 political groups and organizations met in Tbilisi and formed the National Congress, which was meant to be an alternative national parliament. The main aim of the Congress was to "open negotiations with Moscow on Georgia's secession from the USSR".[22] Among Georgian political formations there was a consensus that all legal documents after 7 May 1920, the date of a treaty between the Georgian Democratic Republic and Soviet Russia, were illegal. A special commission of historians and legal experts, formed by a decree of the Supreme Soviet of the republic, declared the Sovietization of Georgia as military intervention and occupation. The Congress refused any cooperation with local Soviet institutions, since it rejected the foundations of Soviet Georgia, and considered Soviet rule as "occupation" and any collaboration with existing authorities and political institutions as "treason".

Gamsakhurdia, finding himself in a minority position, left the Congress to set up his own Free Georgia Round Table. Soon he changed his previous stand towards Soviet structures and prepared his supporters for the October 1990 Supreme Soviet (parliament) elections. The "radicals"

---

21   Ghia Nodia, "Political Turmoil in Georgia and the Ethnic Policies of Zviad Gamsakhurdia", in Bruno Coppieters (ed.), *Contested Borders in the Caucasus*, Brussels: VUB Press, 1996, p. 75.

22   Elizabeth Fuller, "Georgia Edges towards Secession", *Report on the USSR*, 1 June 1990, p. 14.

potential theme: important players –
Gamsakhurdia, Kostava

refused to take part in elections they considered illegal and illegitimate, seeing their own Congress as the real expression of the independent will of Georgia. As a result, political leaders such as Georgi Chanturia, the head of the National Democratic Party, and Irakly Tsereteli, the leader of the National Independence Party, boycotted the elections. While the radicals stayed out of the parliamentary elections, and while Georgian Communist Party functionaries were completely discredited and disoriented, Gamsakhurdia's Round Table recorded a sweeping victory, receiving 54 per cent of the votes. While the number of political parties and clubs numbered close to two hundred, the 1990 parliamentary elections led to a two-party system in which Gamsakhurdia supporters occupied 155 out of 250 seats, the rest going to the remnants of the Georgian Communist Party and to eleven independent candidates, who formed the nucleus of the future opposition to Gamsakhurdia's rule.

The pre-election contest was marred by violence, which created further divisions between political forces struggling for Georgian independence. The offices of two parties, the National Democrats and the National Independence Party, both on the centrally situated Rustaveli Prospect, were raided and put on fire. On 26 October, two days before the elections, unidentified gunmen opened fire on Chanturia and wounded him. After the elections Chanturia declared:

Zviad Gamsakhurdia and the Helsinki Union he heads [...] are playing the role of a Trojan horse in the national movement. Having earned cheap political prestige from the man in the street, Gamsakhurdia is successfully controlling all the news media in the republic, denying others the right to express their opinion. We must not allow a new dictator to come to power in Georgia.[23]

Similar accusations between Gamsakhurdia and his opponents, each side accusing the other of being agents of the KGB, poisoned the political atmosphere, and destroyed the last bridges of dialogue between the various political forces in Tbilisi.

The Gamsakhurdia leadership, now dominating the parliament and with strong public support, took steps to impose its rule over the republic. Gamsakhurdia appointed Tengiz Sigua as Prime Minister, who in turn made a number of important changes in November 1991, including appointment of a new head of the Interior Ministry and a new di-

---

23   *Izvestia*, 10 November 1990.

everyone thinks everything is the KGB's fault

rector for the Georgian KGB. This latter step drew harsh criticism from Moscow; a letter from Gorbachev demanded an end to "illegal" actions, but nothing more followed. Gamsakhurdia had a two-sided political project: to regain the independence of Georgia from the hegemony of the Soviet power, and to strengthen the ethnic Georgian primacy in the republic, and especially in the regions of ethnic minorities and autonomous structures. To realize his project, Gamskhurdia increasingly used undemocratic political methods, like the appointment of regional prefects which led to the anger of minority elites. Gamsakhurdia did not hesitate to use force and violence to impose his vision of Georgia on ethnic minorities, as well as on Georgian political forces who did not share his policies, including Georgian nationalists who disagreed with his vision or political tactics.

Following the parliamentary elections, the power of the Georgian Communist Party collapsed. Although the GCP had 63 deputies in the new parliament, it formed no opposition to the ruling Round Table. On the contrary: one journalist remarks that the GCP "has so far shown an enviable unanimity with the ruling Roundtable bloc".[24] The new ideologue of the Georgian CP, Vazha Gurgenidze, described the position of his party as a "national party that places Georgia's interests above Party concerns", adding that the Party had promised to declare independence if it had won the elections.[25]

Tbilisi-based Georgian dissidents were conscious of the problem of national minorities in Georgia, and the danger of instability and inter-ethnic clashes in case of any mishandling of relations with them at a time of political change. The events during the first Georgian Republic, and more recent memories of clashes in Sukhumi in 1978, were enough warning of this. Many leaders of the "radical" wing of Georgian nationalist movement tried to establish contacts and dialogue with ethnic minorities, including the Abkhaz and Osset authorities, to ensure their support for the project of Georgia's independence. Yet Gamsakhurdia tried to instrumentalize the ethnic issue and to frame it in a more extreme way for his populist aims: to win popularity and dominate the newly developing political scene. And he was very successful in this. "Ethnic populism" had helped him to become the leader of the

24   Tatyana Nedashkovskaya, *Postfactum*, Moscow, 2 January 1991.
25   Ibid.

independent movement," writes one leading Georgian analyst.[26] The ethnic discourse of Gamsakhurdia found large resonance among the population of Georgia, "fearing" for their status in certain regions of the country or "demographic trends" among certain minority groups. Soon after he came to power, in December 1990 Gamsakhurdia abolished the autonomous status of South Ossetia, a decision that paved the way to the first war in Georgia.

The first armed groups of several dozen people started to form in Georgia in 1989, and one of them, which had legal recognition by the GCP, was formed as early as 1990; holding the status of a "Rescue Corps" under the GCP ruler Givi Gumbaridze in 1990, it was regarded as a nucleus for the future armed forces of Georgia. The Mkhedrioni (Horsemen) group was formed under the leadership of Jaba Ioseliani, who had been convicted of bank robbery and manslaughter in Leningrad, and had later become a playwright and arts professor. On December 1990, under a parliamentary decree, the National Guard was set up, with the objective of defending the country's "territorial integrity". The National Guard was led by another former artist, Tengiz Kitovani, and already in April 1991 it boasted of 12,000 recruits.[27] These two groups were initially in opposite camps; while the National Guard was loyal to Gamsakhurdia, Ioseliani was a member of the National Congress and therefore up to two thousand Mkhedrioni fighters were on the side of the opposition, and formed their central armed structure.

The difficult personality of Gamsakhurdia added a final aggravating factor to an overcharged political atmosphere. Gamsakhurdia thought that Georgia had a messianic role, as a country mediating between East and West. He even claimed that the Holy Grail was in fact in Georgia. Although he described his political orientation as "Christian Democrat", he behaved like an autocratic ruler who did not tolerate negotiations and bargains, creation of alliances and building of consensus, which hindered him developing his political project. When presidential elections were held in May 1991 Gamsakhurdia, having complete domination over "administrative resources" and the mass media, won by a landslide 87 per cent of the votes. Gamsakhurdia had successfully

26   Ghia Nodia, "Political Turmoil in Georgia", op. cit., p. 81.

27   David Darchiashvili, *The Army and Society in Georgia*, Tbilisi: CIPDD, February-March 1998.

Nat Congress ≠ Gam..-

manoeuvred himself to become the leader of Georgia, now a country polarized not between pro-USSR and pro-independent, but between pro- and anti-Zviad Gamsakhurdia.

Conflict in South Ossetia

Yet the first conflict to explode was not in downtown Tbilisi between the former comrades-in-arms of Georgian dissidence, and not even in Abkhazia, where tension had long since been high and acts of violence continuous since the 1989 demonstrations and counter demonstrations. Curiously, the first conflict exploded in the mountainous and agricultural region of South Ossetia, with its "capital" Tskhinvali.[28] In a region deprived of any geopolitical significance, this is an identity conflict *par excellence*.

Descendants of the Alans, Iranian-speaking warrior-tribes who inhabited the northern and eastern shores of the Black Sea and came into contact with the Greeks and Romans, the Ossets were driven to the Caucasus Mountains by further invasions by Turkic tribes (Huns) from Central Asia in the fifth century, and later by the Mongol invasions. Following the Russian Revolution an Osset Autonomous Republic was formed, which was later incorporated into the Mountain Republic. After the Sovietization of Georgia, South Ossetia was declared an Autonomous Region within the Georgian SSR (1922). Most Ossets are Orthodox, while a minority (Digors who were the former noble caste) is Sunni Muslim. Although armed clashes and massacres took place between Georgians and Ossets during the Georgian Republic, after the Sovietization of the Transcaucasus relations between the two sides were calm and peaceful until 1989. Both Georgians and South Ossets share the Christian Orthodox faith (the Digors live the western part of North Ossetia) and the rate of intermarriage between the two groups was high.

---

28   South Ossetia has a surface of 3,900 sq km, and in the 1989 census had a population of 99,000, of which 67 per cent were ethnic Ossets (roughly 65,000), and 29 per cent were ethnic Georgians. Another 99,000 ethnic Ossets lived in Georgia outside the territories of the South Osset Autonomous Republic. In Georgian, the region is considered part of "Shida Kartli", while in Osset it is called "Khosar Iriston".

For Georgian public opinion, political demands from Abkhazia or South Ossetia were seen through the prism of the ongoing Georgian national liberation struggle, and conceived as manipulation by conservative forces in Moscow to apply pressure against Georgia's drive to self-determination. The Georgian public did not recognize the legitimacy of the autonomies, considering their creation as an artificial political manoeuvre by the Bolsheviks to divide and weaken the Georgian nation. Among the Georgian public, other ethnic and cultural groups living in the republic were considered as "guests", and any political demands expressed from them were simply surprising and unacceptable. Stories of abuse and discrimination against Georgians in Abkhazia or South Ossetia were abundant in the Georgian Republic press, while historians published numerous papers and pamphlets about the Georgianness of those territories (see Chapter 2).

In parallel with the Georgian national revival, which in itself was the expression of its times and a reflection of similar national mobilization elsewhere in the Soviet Union, the Osset intelligentsia mobilized around its own national question to reaffirm its group identity. For Ossets, the geopolitical shifts taking place posed two problems. One was the separation of the Osset nation into two political units, the first being North Ossetia, encompassing Osset inhabited regions on the northern slopes of the Caucasus chain, with an Autonomous Republic within Russia, and the second being South Ossetia within Georgia. The second problem, with the rise of Georgian nationalism, was whether independent Georgia would tolerate Osset self-rule, and the form of the Georgian-Osset relations should take as a result.

From an Osset perspective, their drive for separation from Tbilisi and unification with North Ossetia was as legitimate as Georgia's drive for national independence. The revival of Osset nationalism renewed hopes for reunification with their brethren in the north, combined with fears of a Georgian nationalist backlash. South Ossetia feared Georgia's independence from the USSR. Independent Georgia could abolish the status of South Ossetia, which was an Autonomous Region within the USSR. In their struggle for independence, Georgian nationalists were mobilizing to return to the constitution of Georgia of 1920, when Georgia was an independent republic under Menshevik rule. Yet in this constitution neither South Ossetia nor Abkhazia had had its own administrative structures with guarantees to preserve its ethnic character and ethno-cultural institutions. Moreover, during anti-Moscow mobilization the bulk of the Georgian mass movement feared and clashed with the Osset and Abkhaz national movements, instead of creating bridges and negotiating a new deal with them.

Often rumours coming from Sukhumi talked about clashes between ethnic Georgians and ethnic Abkhaz there, with exaggeration of the number of victims. Following such rumours in August 1989 about seventy Georgians killed in Sukhumi, Gamsakhurdia reacted emotionally in front of a foreign journalist: "The Abkhazians are terrorists. They are agents of Moscow, instructed to kill innocent Georgians."[29]

As the nationalist movements grew in strength, clashes between Osset and Georgian armed groups increased in intensity in 1990-91. The region was also put under a state of emergency, and Soviet troops were stationed there to separate the conflicting sides, in an attempt to freeze the conflict. But a political solution within the context of weakening of state (Soviet) institutions, and the instability it unleashed, was simply impossible to reach.

The prospect of losing Moscow as the overlord was a destabilizing factor for Ossets, as in other contexts in the Caucasus. Moscow played the role—among others—of the judge, the mediator, and the reference that preserved the balance during contradictions and conflicts between local entities. In the past, Moscow intervened for the distribution of resources, for solving of land and water conflicts, and for easing of political tensions. Without Moscow Ossets were left face-to-face with their bigger Georgian neighbour, in the absence of traditions of direct negotiations and mechanisms of conflict resolution.

The first expression of Osset nationalism came in the spring of 1989 in the form of a letter published in an Abkhazian newspaper, by Alan Chochiev, a historian at the Tskhinvali Pedagogical Institute, and head of the informal "South Osset Popular Front, Ademon Nykhas".[30] In his letter, Chochiev expressed his support for the Abkhaz call for sovereignty. Although local Osset authorities denied any link to Chochiev's letter, tension started rising between Ossets and Georgians. This was fol-

---

29   Carroll Bogert, "'People Feel No Restraint', Guns, strikes and ethnic feuds in Soviet Georgia", *Newsweek*, 14 August 1989.

30   Ademon Nykhas means "popular shrine" in Osset.

lowed by clashes between those two peoples in Tskhinvali on 26 May 1989, the anniversary of the independence of the former Georgian Democratic Republic, encouraged by Zviad Gamsakhurdia. Further resolutions by the Georgian parliament, such as a law in August 1989 on the introduction of the Georgian language as the only language to be used in public spheres, further angered Ossets as only a minority of them spoke Georgian.[31] Interestingly, in the same period (1989) a similar language law in Moldova making Moldovan (Romanian) the state language and imposing the Latin alphabet instead of the Cyrillic throughout the republic led to the clashes in Transnistria. Ademon Nykhas organized strikes to protest against Georgian policies, and appealed to Moscow to bring South Ossetia into Russian jurisdiction.

But it was Gamsakhurdia's decision to take radical steps in the legal controversy with South Ossetia that was to be fatal for stability in Georgia. As Tbilisi started its legal undoing of Soviet legitimacy, by revising all treaties between Georgia and the USSR after 1921, including the 1922 Union Treaty and the Transcaucasus Federation treaty, it carelessly damaged the position of the Osset and Abkhaz minorities, since those treaties were the legal basis for the autonomous structures in Georgia. In reaction, the South Osset Soviet of People's Deputies adopted a decision to upgrade its status from "autonomous region" to "autonomous republic". This "war of laws" was fuelled by the marginalization of ethnic regions during the October 1990 parliamentary elections; a law barred regional political formations from participating in the elections, practically preventing minority formations from having representatives in the parliament. The Georgian reaction to that step did not wait long; the Georgian parliament passed a law dissolving the autonomous status of the region, on 11 December 1990. And while Georgia boycotted the March 1991 referendum on the future of the Union, Ossets massively participated with 99 per cent of the votes supporting the preservation of the USSR.

A further step towards escalation came when Gamsakhurdia organized a popular march on Tskhinvali under the slogan of defending eth-

---

31   One report puts the number of Ossets who "claimed fluency in Georgian" at 14 per cent. See "Report on Ethnic Conflict in the Russian Federation and Transcaucasia", *Strengthening Democratic Institutions Project*, Harvard University, J.F. Kennedy School of Government, Cambridge, MA, July 1993, p. 95.

nic Georgian rights in South Ossetia. On 23 November 1990, twenty thousand people armed with light weapons but also with armoured vehicles marched on the town. They were stopped at the southern suburbs of Tskhinvali by Soviet Interior Ministry troops. At a meeting with the South Osset party leader Kim Tsagolov, Gamsakhurdia threatened: "I shall bring 200,000-strong army. Not a single Osset will remain in the land of Samachablo [South Ossetia]. I demand that the Soviet flags be removed!"[32] Although the interposition of Soviet troops prevented a bloodbath, the march polarized to the extreme the situation between ethnic Osset and ethnic Georgian villages in the region. Some of the participants in the march, members of the "Merab Kostava Society" loyal to Gamsakhurdia took up positions in the vicinity of Tskhinvali, and a low-intensity war started between Osset and Georgian villages of the region.

South Ossetians created their own national guard, and fighting continued throughout 1991. Tbilisi accused Russian authorities of supplying arms to Osset militants. The unstable situation led to the displacement of Osset civilians from the front line, and over a hundred thousand refugees moved to North Ossetia, where they would later play a decisive role in the Osset-Ingush conflict. Similarly, over ten thousand ethnic Georgians fled Tskhinvali and villages around it. The situation calmed down relatively as tension increased in Tbilisi

	1959	1979	1989
Georgians	2,600.6 (64.3 per cent)	3,433.0 (68.8 per cent)	3,787.4 (70.1 per cent)
Abkhaz	62.9 (1.6 per cent)	85.3 (1.7 per cent)	95.9 (1.8 per cent)
Ossetians	141.2 (3.5 per cent)	160.5 (3.2 per cent)	164.1 (3 per cent)
Russians	407.9 (10.1 per cent)	371.6 (7.4 per cent)	341.2 (6.3 per cent)
Ukrainians	52.2 (1.8 per cent)	45.0 (0.9 per cent)	52.4 (1,0 per cent)
Azerbaijanis	153.6 (3.8 per cent)	255.7 (5.1 per cent)	307.6 (5.7 per cent)
Armenians	442.9 (11 per cent)	448.0 (9 per cent)	437.2 (8.1 per cent)
Jews	51.6 (1.3 per cent)	28.3 (0,6 per cent)	24.8 (0,5 per cent)
Assyrians	...	5.3	6.2
Greeks	7.9 (1.8 per cent)	95.1 (1.9 per cent)	100.3 (1.9 per cent)
Kurds	16.2 (0.4 per cent)	25.7 (0.5 per cent)	33.3 (0.6 per cent)
Others	42.0 (1.0 per cent)	45.0 (0.9 per cent)	56.7 (1.0 per cent)
Total population	4,044.0 (100 per cent)	4,993.2 (100 per cent)	5,400.8 (100 per cent)

Table 3: Population of Georgia by ethnic origin in 2002.
Source: From Britta Korth, Marina Muskhelishvili and Arnold Stepanyan, *Language Policy in Georgia*, Geneva: CIMERA, 2005, pp. 13-14.

---

32   Quoted in Alexei Zverev, "Ethnic Conflicts in the Caucasus 1988-1994", in Bruno Coppieters (ed.), in *Contested Borders in the Caucasus*, Brussels: VUB Press, 1996, p. 43.

between supporters of Gamsakhurdia and the opposition following the attempted putsch in Moscow in August 1991.

The fall of Zviad Gamsakhurdia

Gamsakhurdia's personality, his politics, and the power struggle he caused in Georgia under his rule left their deep mark on Georgian political culture and statehood. Although Gamsakhurdia's Free Georgia Round Table won 54 per cent of the seats in the parliamentary elections of October 1990, and although Gamsakhurdia himself was elected President of Georgia on 26 May 1991 by 86 per cent of the votes, his political manoeuvres, his suspicious character, and his lack of diplomatic skills led to his political isolation in Tbilisi after just a few months of exercising power.

A major problem Gamsakhurdia suffered from, which led to the creation of unnecessary enemies and the loss of allies, was his notorious inconsistency. Although he was the founder and the head of the Georgian section of the Helsinki Union, an organization dedicated to the defence of human rights and therefore the freedom of expression and the press, once taking control of the parliament he closed down all Communist Party publications, but also the independent minded *Molodiozh Gruzii* newspaper. During his campaign for the Supreme Soviet elections, Gamsakhurdia promised preservation of the autonomous status of Abkhazia and South Ossetia, yet barely a few weeks after the elections, in December 1990 the Georgian parliament abolished the autonomous status of South Ossetia. His chauvinistic policies, which earned him a bad press abroad, included a pronouncement about restricting citizenship to those who could prove their ancestors lived in Georgia before the Tsarist Russian invasion, and about distribution of land only to those who had citizenship, practically excluding a large portion of ethnic minorities who made up 30 per cent of the entire population.

The Georgian leader failed to grasp the complex developments in Georgia and the USSR, and had easy explanations: all problems were the result of plots by KGB agents. One analyst has the following description: "...to judge by Gamsakhurdia's rhetoric, any setbacks, whether the defiance shown by the Ossetians or the failure of kolkhozes to fulfil milk delivery quotas, will be interpreted as deliberate sabotage directed

potential theme: ALL KGB'S FAULT

against the new parliament to the detriment of the interests of the people, and those responsible will be considered agents of the Kremlin." [33]

Gamsakhurdia had a personality problem as well. He alienated people, was aggressive to foreign correspondents, rejected dialogue with Georgian political forces. Nodar Natadze, the head of the Georgian Popular Front, a group in opposition to Gamsakhurdia, described him as "a politician who changes his views every twenty-four hours and his principles once a week, who makes fundamental mistakes, who places his own personal interests above those of his party…"[34] Another Georgia observer remarks that "Gamsakhurdia convinced the world that he was a dictator even before he became one."[35] Gamsakhurdia's constant manoeuvring and uncompromising political positions provoked the antagonism of the Tbilisi elite when he had accumulated numerous enemies, such as the ethnic minorities in Georgia and the Soviet authorities in Moscow.

As Gamsakhurdia's political about-turns became increasingly brusque, and as he lost support, more repressive measures were taken by his administration; the first major arrest was of Jaba Ioseliani, the head of the Mkhedrioni paramilitary group, who was followed by Grigori Chanturia, head of the National Democratic Party and a main political rival of the President. As political contradictions polarized the Georgian public, the August putsch in Moscow was the spark to ignite the fire.

On 19 August 1991 high officials and close collaborators of the Soviet President Mikhail Gorbachev, regrouped under the name of a State Emergency Committee, organized a coup d'état in Moscow. Among the putschists were the Vice-President of the USSR, Gennady Yanayev, who was named acting President; the Prime Minister, Valentin Pavlov; the head of the KGB, Vladimir Kryuchkov; the Minister of Defence, Dmitry Yazov; and the Interior Minister, Boris Pugo. Thus the majority of the ruling figures organized a coup against the head of the state! Their aim was to preserve the Soviet Union by establishing a military dictatorship a few days before the signing of a new union treaty, but their

---

33 Elizabeth Fuller, "Gamsakhurdia's First 100 Days", *Report on USSR*, 8 March 1991, pp. 10-11.

34 Elizabeth Fuller, "How Strong is the Georgian Opposition", *Report on the USSR*, 18 October 1991, p. 27.

35 Ghia Nodia, "Political Turmoil in Georgia", op. cit., p. 87.

failure in the matter of two days—thanks to resistance from the head of the Russian Federation, Boris Yeltsin, and the refusal by troops to obey putschist orders—precipitated the collapse of the Soviet Union itself.

Gamsakhurdia's position towards the putsch was highly controversial. On the day it occurred, the Georgian presidential office issued an order to the population to remain calm and continue to carry on their duties. Gamsakhurdia also ordered the National Guard to be put under the authority of the Interior Ministry, seen by his adversaries as a gesture towards the putschists. The hesitant behaviour of Gamsakhurdia could have been justified politically, yet the defeat of the putsch gave his rivals an opportunity to counter-attack. In mid-August, a number of high ranking officials of his government resigned, and joined the ranks of the opposition. Among them were Tengiz Sigua, the Prime Minister, Giorgi Khoshtaria, the Foreign Minister, and Tengiz Kitovani, the commander of the National Guards. Kitovani refused to obey Gamsakhurdia's orders and moved to the Shavanabada military camp on the outskirts of Tbilisi with a thousand of his comrades. In September Vazha Adamia, the head of the Merab Kostava Society, a paramilitary formation which had participated in the clashes in South Ossetia, defected from the government camp and moved to the opposition with a group of armed fighters. Gamsakhurdia now had more enemies than ever before and was completely exposed.

From September onwards Tbilisi descended into chaos. The opposition organized a demonstration calling for the resignation of the government; the police opened fire, wounding several people. The existing embryonic army structure had been divided, between one section led by Kitovani which moved to the ranks of the opposition, and other units which remained loyal to the President. The Zugdidi Battalion was called to Tbilisi for the defence of the parliament building where Gamsakhurdia's offices were situated. Zugdidi is a town in Mingrelia in western Georgia, to the south of Abkhazia. Gamsakhurdia's ancestors were from Mingrelia, and the region remained loyal to him during the civil strife and even long after his defeat and death. Opposition armed groups took control of the state television building, while a hundred metres away were the positions of pro-government armed groups. Busloads of Gamsakhurdia supporters were transported from the country side, and organized demonstrations in support of their President in front of the parliament building. The city plunged into chaos, with clashes between regime supporters and opposition activists increasing in intensity. Armed groups of various political colours or of criminal character took control of Tbilisi. Communal services were interrupted, electric supply in the country became irregular, while the economy came to a stand-still.

As the opposition pressed for the overthrow of Gamsakhurdia, the first freely elected President of Georgia, who had won 86 per cent of the votes in the spring, his popularity remained quite high, especially outside the capital. Even Tengiz Sigua—the renegade Gamsakhurdia Prime Minister—recognized the popularity of the President, as he answered a journalist's question: "At present the alignment of forces is approximately as follows: in Tbilisi, nine to one against Gamsakhurda, and in the countryside, six to four in his favour."[36] Yet armed pressure and the threat of a widespread civil war increased. In December 1991 the opposition regrouped itself in a "Military Council" led by Sigua, Kitovani and Ioseliani, encircled the centre of Tbilisi, and opened fire on the parliament building to dislodge Gamsakhurdia and his supporters. The Georgian President contacted the "Soviet" Transcaucasus troops, whose headquarters were situated in Tbilisi itself, to intervene, but in vain. Moscow preferred not to be part of a conflict where its sympathies were with the Georgian opposition. After 16 days of fighting, which left much of Rustaveli Avenue in ruins, and left 200 people killed, Gamsakhurdia was forced to flee Georgia on 6 January 1992. With some of his supporters he first drove to Azerbaijan, then to Armenia, from where he flew to Groznyy to live in exile in Chechnya as a guest of Djokhar Dudayev.

Gamsakhurdia and his supporters called the rebellion a Russian military coup. For Gamsakhurdia, the rebellion coincided with his refusal to participate in the Alma Ata summit to lay the basis of the Commonwealth of Independent State (CIS).[37] Although it is a fact that the Russian military based in Georgia detested Gamsakhurdia and sympathized with the opposition, and that they did supply the opposition

---

36   Interview by Tatyana Malkina, *Nezavisimaya Gazeta*, 26 September 1991.

37   Zviad Gamsakhurdia, "The Legally Elected and Legitimate President of Georgia, Describes the Evil Revenge of KGB & the Nomenklatura", *Soviet Analyst*, Vol. 21, No. 9-10, 1993.

with arms and ammunition, the coup was entirely due to Georgian political factors.

In the debate on the correct way to Georgia's independence Gamsakhurdia seems to have been right, and Chanturia and Tsereteli wrong. By utilizing Soviet institutions Georgia under Gamsakhurdia acceded to independence, while the National Council remained no more than a political movement without much impact on the events. Yet as Georgia was celebrating the collapse of the USSR and its accession to independence, allies of Chanturia and Tsereteli were raiding the parliament building to chase out the first freely elected, and still somewhat popular, president of Georgia, and to invite the former Soviet boss of Georgia, Eduard Shevardnadze, to return to take power in Tbilisi, this time to rule an independent and much troubled native land. Yet the overthrow of Gamsakhurdia did not put an end to the political divisions within the Georgian elite. "The anti-Gamsakhurdia coalition was as disunited as the nationalist movement from which it emerged."[38]

Worse, Georgia had entered a new historic phase with fractured institutions. In early 1992 the political institutions of Georgia were living a period of political vacuum, its armed forces disintegrating, its territory divided under the rule of multiple warlords loyal to a set of political projects, and its economy in bankruptcy. Without massive humanitarian aid starvation would have been a major problem. In its first year of independence, Georgia presented a classical case of a "failed state".

Shevardnadze returns home

Following the departure of Gamsakhurdia from the parliament building, the Military Council claimed power. It later called itself the State Council, and was formed by the victors Kitovani, Ioseliani and Sigua, unofficially known as the "Triumvirate". Although the State Council was composed of artists-turned-warlords, they were hesitant about assuming the political leadership in the country. The cohesion of the council was another problem, as tension remained high between the men of the National Guard loyal to Kitovani and the Mkhedrioni fight-

---

38   Ronald Grigor Suny, "Elite Transformation in Late-Soviet and Post-Soviet Transcaucasia, or What Happens When the Ruling Class Can't Rule?" in R.G. Suny, *The Structure of Soviet History, Essays and Documents*, Oxford University Press, 2002, p. 503.

ers of Ioseliani, the two major armed groups among others that controlled Georgia in the early 1990s. Kitovani twice travelled to Moscow to meet Shevardnadze and propose that he should return to the country and take the political leadership. Under Gamsakhurdia Georgia had remained isolated, and few countries had established diplomatic relations with it. Shevardnadze, with his extensive international contacts, inspired hope of bringing Georgia into rapid recognition, and receiving much needed support from Western countries and international organizations.

Shevardnadze, marginalized in the new capital of independent Russia, accepted the offer and returned to Tbilisi in March 1992. Shevardnadze promised to upgrade the image of Georgia abroad and receive much needed help from Western capitals. Georgia became a member of the Conference on Security and Cooperation in Europe (CSCE) in March, and in May James Baker, the US Secretary of State and a personal friend of Shevardnadze, whom he knew very well from the days when the latter was Soviet Foreign Minister, flew to Georgia for a visit to Shevardnadze and to show American support to the new-old Georgian leader.

Yet Shevardnadze's internal position was a very difficult one. He had to share power with three new partners, each having veto power over decision making. Having made all his career in Soviet Communist Party structures, now he had to deal in day-to-day matters with a former convict who had spent half of his life in jail (Ioseliani), a sculptor-turned-rebel (Kitovani), and a former-engineer turned nationalist (Sigua). Pro-Gamsakhurdia activists continued to protest against the new regime, while their newspapers were closed down and activists arrested. The most serious problem was the lack of a disciplined military or police force. In the early days of Shevardnadze's rule of the now independent republic, Georgia might have had the form of a state (international recognition) but still needed the development of its content (armed forces, territorial unity, legitimate institutions, etc.). While Kitovani was the Defence Minister, he commanded several thousand badly armed and undisciplined gunmen, whose authority in Tbilisi was challenged by the Mkhedrioni bands. Neither of those armed groups had much influence outside the perimeters of the capital. In April 1992, the State Council adopted a resolution creating unified armed forces out of the National

Guard and the Mkhedrioni, with a total force of 20,000 men, a hasty decision which did not make much headway in creating disciplined armed forces with central command and control. All through 1992 and beyond, Shevardnadze was nominally the head of the state, yet he did not have much real power. Kitovani and Ioseliani did have armed forces, although their control over their own men remained very relative.

Shevardnadze's problems were not limited to the power-sharing arrangements with the triumvirate. He had a legitimacy problem at home, although the image of Georgia abroad improved somewhat. To gain legitimacy, he organized new legislative elections in October 1992, during which mass irregularities were reported. According to official results, 60 per cent of the voters participated and in an uncontested vote Shevardnadze was elected the Speaker of the new parliament with 89 per cent of the votes. Curiously, only a year and a half before a majority of the voters had selected Shevardnadze's rival Gamsakhurdia; this revealed the fragility of the institutions and cast doubts on the reliability of the elections process in a Georgia in the process of independence. The new parliament was heavily dominated by the former Communist Party *nomenklatura* and the new warlords of Georgia. As we will see in more detail later, these elections took place as Georgian troops were at war in Abkhazia, and had just lost the strategic town of Gagra and regions in the north-western part of the province. Under the circumstances, it is improbable that the voters gave massive support to Shevardnadze and his supporters.

The elections did not bring an end to internal turmoil. During the year 1992, the internal contradictions developed on three levels: resumption of hostilities in South Ossetia until the signing of the Vladikavkaz cease-fire treaty; confrontation between "Zviadists" or forces loyal to the overthrown president and others loyal to the State Council, mainly in western Georgia; and the largest military confrontation in Georgia, the invasion of Abkhazia by the National Guard.

The "final march" on Tskhinvali that Gamsakhurdia had called on 28 November 1991 did not materialize, because of internal quarrels within the Georgian nationalist camp. The change of regime in Tbilisi brought new hopes for a peaceful solution. Shevardnadze's declarations introduced a new conciliatory tone, criticizing the policies of his predecessor towards ethnic minorities and especially his encouragement of violence in South Ossetia. Osset prisoners were released, among them Torez Kulumbegov, the Chairman of the South Ossetia Supreme Soviet, who was arrested while negotiating with the Georgian side and imprisoned under orders from Gamsakhurdia. In March 1992 a Georgian delegation travelled to Vladikavkaz, in North Ossetia, and achieved a cease-fire agreement with a South Osset delegation. Events took a downturn in April, as Tskhinvali was once again the target of heavy Georgian shelling from military positions in neighbouring villages, accompanied by attempts to advance towards the town. In May Shevardnadze himself visited Tskhinvali and held direct talks there. Yet even when Shevardnadze and Ioseliani were present in Tskhinvali, the town came under fire from Georgian positions (presumably from uncontrolled elements of the Georgian National Guard). Massive refugee movement of Ossets from Georgia to North Ossetia in the Russian Federation risked destabilizing the situation in the North Caucasus and increasing the pressure on the Russian administration to intervene. Attacks by South Osset militants on arms depots in Vladikavkaz became regular events, often causing casualties, and increasing political tension in the Republic of North Ossetia.[39]

On 15 June Ruslan Khasbulatov, the Chairman of the Parliament of Russia, made a heavily worded threat of military intervention against Georgia. Khasbulatov accused the Georgian side of breaking former engagements with the intention to force a change on the ground, and of organizing "genocide" against the Osset people. He told Georgia to find a negotiated solution, threatening that otherwise "Russia is prepared to take urgent measures to defend (...) the peaceful population and the Russian troops."[40] Three days later Russian helicopters attacked Georgian armoured vehicles, while a column of Russian tanks moved out of Tskhinvali to take positions on its suburbs. For the Georgian side, Khasbulatov's declaration and the military aggression were tantamount to a declaration of war. A few months after the collapse of the USSR, a Russo-Georgian war seemed to be in the making, while wars were flaring up all over the former Soviet periphery, from Karabakh to Tajikistan.

---

39   Mikhail Shevelyov, "War Spreads Northwards", *Moscow News*, 21 June 1992.

40   Quoted in Julian Birch, "Ossetia: a Caucasian Bosnia in Microcosm", *Central Asian Survey*, London, 1995, 14 (1), p. 46.

The tension was defused by a direct call from Yeltsin to Shevardnadze on 22 June, and two days later the two leaders met in Dagomys in Russia. A decision was reached which included a cease-fire agreement effective from 28 June 1992; the withdrawal of Georgian troops and lifting of the siege of Tskhinvali; and the setting up of a peacekeeping force composed of Russian, Georgian, and Osset troops to monitor the contact line between South Ossetia and Georgia. The Osset leaders of North and South were present in the negotiations, yet did not sign the agreement. South Ossetia was demanding the incorporation of the region into the Russian Federation, and considered the agreement between Moscow and Tbilisi as "treason" from the Russian side. Nevertheless, two weeks later the first contingent of the 500 Russian peacekeepers entered the region.

The damage left behind by the two-year conflict was impressive for such a small territory. The number of casualties is put between 700 and over 1,000 dead, the official count of ethnic Osset refugees from Georgia to North Ossetia was put between forty thousand and as high as a hundred thousand people, and the number of the internally displaced ethnic Georgians at 40,000[41] (although those numbers could be exaggerated somewhat by the local authorities for the purpose of receiving larger quantities of international aid, they nevertheless reveal the extent of the tragedy).

The political damage was even greater. From a Georgian perspective, Tbilisi had cancelled the autonomous status of South Ossetia without having an alternative model to propose, had initiated a military struggle and lost South Ossetia, had reached a cease-fire agreement and paid for it by having Russian soldiers as guarantors of stability in South Ossetia. Even worse, the South Osset experience had antagonized other minorities who were highly suspicious of Georgian intentions now, whether the president was called Gamsakhurdia or Shevardnadze. The cease-fire agreement was very successful in suspending the military phase of the conflict, yet no political solution has been found. Clashes occurred in

---

41   Neil MacFarlane, Larry Minear and Stephen D. Shenfield, *Armed Conflict in Georgia: A Case Study in Humanitarian Action, and Peacekeeping,* Thomas J. Watson Institute For International Studies, Occasional Paper Number 21, Providence, 1996, p. 8. On return of refugees and IDP's since, see "Georgia-South Ossetia: Refugee Return the Path for Peace", International Crisis Group Policy Briefing, *Europe Briefing No. 38,* Tbilisi/Brussels, 19 April 2005.

South Ossetia after the Rose Revolution and the coming to power of Mikheil Saakashvili, when Georgian forces tried to advance towards Tskhinvali and were faced by fierce resistance in summer 2004.

War erupts in Abkhazia

In early 1992 the State Council did not have much control outside Tbilisi. Moreover, several armed militias, either groups linked to political movements or simply localized armed groups, divided the countryside into fiefdoms. The State Council faced the serious challenge of putting the country together, a task further complicated by the inconclusive end of the South Ossetia confrontation.

The actions of the State Council in 1992 often led to catastrophic results; they were badly thought out, hardly planned, and chaotically carried out. This chaotic political management led to the tragedy of war in Abkhazia, and the defeat of the Georgian forces with tragic human conseqences. While those events should be scrutinized through a highly critical optic, one should not underestimate the challenge Shevardnadze was facing, and the dilemma of how to bring the bits and pieces of Georgia under a central state. The means available to the Georgian leader were too rudimentary for the difficulties he faced: the State Council did not enjoy legitimacy in the eyes of an important portion of the population of Georgia, perhaps the majority; the embryonic armed forces were fractured, had opened fire on their own parliament and on their own comrades, and had led an inconclusive war in South Ossetia; and the economy was in free fall. In order to go out of Tbilisi and impose the authority of the Georgian statehood, the State Council had neither the means to persuade, nor the means to impose its authority by force.

While the situation in South Ossetia was going through dramatic upheavals, dangerous events were unfolding in western Georgia. Ajaria, Mingrelia, and Abkhazia were all in turmoil in early 1992. Georgia was going through a process of disintegration on the image of the Soviet disintegration itself. The Soviet Union collapsed and as a result various pieces came out of this immense crash like a crystal vase hitting the hard ground, varying according to the texture of the object itself: in some places whole Union Republics came out in one piece, in others the texture was even more fragile and the pieces that came in their turn broke into smaller and much more numerous bits.

Ajaria, an autonomous republic, had an advantageous geographical position, and its main town Batumi was a port city on the border with Turkey. Most of the cargo traffic of Georgia passed through Batumi, making the city an important asset. Tension was first noted in Ajaria under Gamsakhurdia when an Orthodox priest went there to convert the population of Ajaria, of Muslim tradition in the majority, to Christianity. Various influential leaders in Tbilisi, such as Kitovani and Ioseliani, attempted on various occasions to enter Ajaria, but the presence of a Russian military base and the good relations between the Ajaria leader Aslan Abashidze and the Russian military had preserved the status quo.

Several regions in western Georgia remained under the control of "Zviadists", militants loyal to Zviad Gamsakhurdia, including Zugdidi, the main town of Mingrelia, Poti, a seaport on the Black Sea, Abasha, and Khoni;[42] this meant that the rail communications between central Georgia and Russia (which pass through Abkhazia) and with the Black Sea ports in Ajaria, were cut. The population of Mingrelia were staunch supporters of Gamsakhurdia, and did not recognize the legitimacy of the State Council, considered by them an illegal formation that had taken power through a coup d'état. Many of the fighters who had defended Gamsakhurdia in Tbilisi in December 1991 and January 1992 were Mingrelians and had returned to their region of origin at the end of the hostilities. Among them was Gocha Bakhia, the former head of Gamsakhurdia's personal guards, who commanded a force of 250 fighters and operated between Mingrelia and the Gali region of Abkhazia.[43] In early August 1992, Bakhia took hostage the Deputy Prime Minister of Georgia, Alexander Kavsadze, who was in Mingrelia for negotiations with armed Zviadists. When Tbilisi sent a 12-men delegation headed by the Interior Minister Roman Guentsadze for talks for the release of the hostage, they in turn were kidnapped. The Georgian Ministry of Defence sent a force of 3,000 men to Senaki, in western Georgia, and threatened military action if the hostages were not released. While the

---

42   *Yerkir*, 1 April 1992.

43   The Gali region of Abkhazia is the southernmost region of this province, adjacent to Mingrelia, and its inhabitants before the conflict were predominantly Mingrelians.

Georgian National Guard entered Mingrelia to release the hostages and secure the communication lines from the danger of banditry, events precipitated rapidly, leading to what became to be known as the Abkhazia war.

On 14 August 1992 up to five thousand fighters belonging to the Georgian National Guard, supported by five tanks and ten armoured vehicles,[44] crossed the Inguri river and advanced into Abkhazia. They took Gali, the first town on the main costal road, and Ochamchira, and by midday entered Sukhumi, the capital of the Abkhaz Autonomous Republic, and camped in front of the Supreme Soviet building. An amphibious force landed in the Gagra region and brought this town and villages to the north as far as the Russian border at the Psou River under the control of Georgian troops. The central coastal line around the town of Gudauta, and much of the mountainous villages in the north, central, and southern part of Abkhazia (excluding Gali region), were left out of the control of Georgian forces: they simply did not advance towards those regions of dense Abkhaz population. Minor clashes in Sukhumi and Gagra led to several casualties.

The goals of this large-scale military operation were not very clear, and the declared aims were often contradictory. The initial reason given for the operation was the liberation of government officials taken hostage by Zviadist fighters, and suspected to be hidden in the village of Kokhori in the Gali region. Later, Georgian authorities added another mission to their armed forces: to secure the railway and the highway that cross Abkhazia and link Georgia to Russia. In other words, officially the aim of the military invasion was a police operation to bring security to a chaotic region.

The security problems were not the only reason for the Georgian military operation. Relations between the Georgian authorities and the Abkhaz leadership had been tense for several years. The background of the Georgian-Abkhaz conflict and the history of the two nations have already been extensively developed elsewhere.[45] What is relevant for our

---

44. *Nezavisimaya Gazeta*, 15 August 1992.

45. On the history of the conflict, see: Stanislav Lakoba, "Abkhazia is Abkhazia", *Central Asian Survey*, 14(1), 1995, pp. 97–105; Evgeny M. Kozhokin, "Georgia and Abkhazia", in Jeremy R. Azrael and Emil A. Payin (eds), *U.S. and Russian Policymaking with Respect to the Use of Force*, Santa Monica, CA: RAND, 1996; Ghia Nodia, *Causes and Visions of Conflict in Abkhazia*, University of Califor-

analysis is the historic events that led to the antagonism between the Abkhaz and the Georgians, the direct background of the Abkhazian war. In the 19th century the Abkhaz took part in the Great Caucasian Rising, and were last to be put down by the Russian army in 1864, after which several Caucasian tribes kin to the Abkhaz, such as the Ubykhs, were deported in their entirety (45,000 individuals); others so punished were the Sadzians (20,000), the Shapsugs, and various Abkhaz tribes, often of Muslim tradition. The refugees, who left for the Ottoman Empire, became known as *muhajir*s (immigrants or refugees). Two years later the Abkhaz rebelled again, and there was a new wave of brutal repression, and yet another wave of *muhajir*s. A new insurrection in 1877 was punished by the deportation of an additional 50,000 Abkhaz. Half the population of Abkhazia was driven out in this way in the second half of the 19th century. The land being empty, nations loyal to the new rulers were given land to occupy, including Russians, Greeks, Armenians, and especially Mingrelians. According to an Abkhaz author, "a mass of landless peasants from Western Georgia was planted in central Abkhazia, in depopulated villages…" and "because of the endless flow of those resettled from Western Georgia, relations between Abkhazians and Kartvelians were becoming ever more complicated…"[46]

	1897	1926	1959	1979	1989
Abkhazians	53 per cent	27.8 per cent	15.1 per cent	17.1 per cent	17.8 per cent
Georgians	24.4 per cent	33.6 per cent	39.1 per cent	43.9 per cent	45.7 per cent
Russians	5.6 per cent	6.2 per cent	21.4 per cent	16.4 per cent	14.2 per cent
Armenians	6.1 per cent	12.8 per cent	15.9 per cent	15.1 per cent	14.6 per cent

Table 4: The Ethnic Composition of the Population of Abkhazia (in percentage of the total population)

Sources: Roger Caratini, *Dictionnaire des Nationalités et des Minorités de l'ex-U.R.S.S.*, Paris: Larousse, 1992, p. 242 ; George Hewitt, "Abkhazia: A Problem of Identity and Ownership", in John F.R. Wright, Suzanne Goldenberg and Richard Schofield (eds), *Transcaucasian Boundaries*, UCL Press, 1996, p. 192; Viacheslav A. Chrikba, "The Georgian-Abkhaz Conflict", op. cit., p. 53.

---

nia, Berkeley, CA, 1997; Bruno Coppieters, Ghia Nodia, and Yuri Anchabadze (eds), *Georgians and Abkhazians, The Search for a Peace Settlement*, Cologne: Bundesinstitut für Ostwissenschaftliche und Internationale Studien, 1998; Jurij Anchabadze, "History: The Modern Period", in George Hewitt (ed.), *The Abkhazians: A Handbook*, New York: St. Martin's Press, 1998.

46   Stanislav Lak'oba, "History: 18th century-1917", p. 85, in George Hewitt (ed.), *The Abkhazians: A Handbook*, op. cit.

For the Abkhaz mass psyche, the events of the 19th century left a deep trauma, similar to the effect of the mass killing and deportations of 1915 on the Armenians, or the deportations of 1944 on the mass consciousness of the Chechen people. The Russian massacres and deportations reduced the number of the Abkhaz to a point where the survival of the Abkhaz has become a delicate issue. But from the late 19th century the danger for the existence of the Abkhaz identity did not come from the Russians—who had already conquered and pacified the Western Caucasus—but from the Georgians; it took the form of mass colonisation and the increase in the percentage of the ethnic Georgian (more precisely Mingrelian) population, but also Georgian pressure to assimilate the Abkhaz culture and identity.

Politically, Abkhaz-Georgian relations went through various changes as a result of the new demographic reality, and as a result of the political ambitions in Tbilisi and Sukhumi. In the period of the Georgian Republic (1918-21) relations between the two sides were turbulent, occasionally leading to violent clashes. After the Sovietization of Georgia, from 1921 to 1930 Abkhazia was a Soviet Republic linked to Georgia in a federal union (within the Transcaucasus Federation), and after that its status became an autonomous structure within the Georgian Soviet Socialist Republic. The Abkhaz contested their political status, wishing to have a different accommodation that dispensed them from being under the political hierarchy of Georgia. They did this through petitions sent to the Kremlin, or mass demonstrations on various occasions: 1957, 1964, 1967, 1977, 1978, and 1989. The collapse of the Soviet system led to a legal puzzle: what could the political status of Abkhazia be now that the Soviet Union had collapsed, and who was entitled to decide it? Under Gamsakhurdia—who considered the Abkhaz as autochthonous people and recognized their rights, unlike the Ossets whom he considered as "newcomers" and "guests"—a power sharing compromise was found, according to which the parliament of the republic was to have a quota system, with 28 seats given to the Abkhaz, 26 to Georgians, and 11 to other ethnic communities.

The Georgian side often alleges Abkhaz "separatism" to be the main reason that caused the conflict. The Abkhaz side denies this interpretation. According to Vyacheslav Chirikba, between 1990 and 1992 Abkhazia did not seek independence: "All acts undertaken by Abkhazia, beginning in 1990, were designed to protect its autonomous political status, deemed necessary in view of numerous statements made by leading Georgian politicians that they doubted the legal character of Georgia's autonomies and even threatened to abolish all of them and transform Georgia into a unitary state."[47] To counter the "accusation" of separatism, this analyst coins the concept of "aggressive integrationism"—meaning the use of military means in an attempt to impose territorial integrity, leading to large scale bloodshed—to explain the causes of not only the Abkhazia war but equally those in South Ossetia and Chechnya. In other words, for the Abkhaz side the root cause of the war was not Abkhaz separatism, but the Georgian aggression to deny them their political rights and the autonomy they previously enjoyed.

In early 1992 Tbilisi substituted the Soviet constitution of 1978 with the Georgian constitution of 1921. This posed a particular legal problem for Abkhazia, which lost its autonomous status and the legality of its institutions under the new-old constitution. As a response, the Abkhaz Supreme Soviet in its turn suspended the 1978 constitution, and adopted the 1925 Soviet constitution which gave Abkhazia state attributes. Beneath this legal battle lay a political one: the State Council leaders were not very keen on respecting the power-sharing deal in Abkhazia, which they considered was unjust for the local Georgian population and strengthened the hands of the Abkhaz leadership. They also wanted to tear up an agreement devised by Gamsakhurdia and show it to have failed to serve the interests of the Georgian nation, at a moment when Gamsakhurdia was still highly popular in Abkhazia (among the Mingrelians) and in neighbouring Mingrelia.[48] In Abkhazia itself local Georgian militant organizations developed, often armed, rejecting the authority of the Abkhaz parliament and its Speaker Vladislav Ardzinba. Neither were they loyal to the new rulers in Tbilisi; they were often supporters of the former President Gamsakhurdia. For example, in February 1992 Georgian National Guard detachments of "250-300" soldiers entered Sukhumi with the agreement of the Ardzinba government to

---

47   Viacheslav A. Chirikba, "The Georgian-Abkhazian Conflict: In Search for Ways Out", in Bruno Coppieters, Ghia Nodia and Yuri Anchabadze (eds), *Georgians and Abkhazians, The Search for a Peace Settlement*, 1998, p. 54.

48   Ghia Nodia, *Causes and Visions of Conflict in Abkhazia*, University of California, Berkeley, 1997, 52 pp., p. 33.

put an end to the rail blockade imposed by Zviadists.[49] The conflict setting was ready, and it needed a small provocation. The Georgian military action of 14 August, the "original sin" of the conflict, provided that and even much more.

The military logic of the Abkhazia war

While reviewing and recognizing the historical background of the Georgian-Abkhaz conflict, it must be stressed that the explosion of the Georgian-Abkhaz conflict was not "determined" as a fatality, but it was just one possibility out of many. Several other developments in the difficult relations between Georgia and Abkhazia could have been equally possible. But it was the introduction of the military element on 14 August 1992 that put an end to the possibility of negotiations or a new political arrangement, and polarized the situation into a state of no return. It is difficult to imagine the exact calculations of the Georgian leadership, yet the chronology of events suggest that the operation was planned to take place two months before parliamentary elections, with the aim of boosting the popularity of Shevardnadze and forces supporting him. A "small victorious war" in Abkhazia would have strengthened the hand of the leadership that issued from the January coup. Abkhazia seems to have been chosen as the easiest target; the Abkhaz were a small minority within their own republic, and could not count on the support of an Abkhaz state outside Georgia (in contrast to a military operation against the Armenians or the Azerbaijanis of southern Georgia). The bellicose declarations of the Georgian leadership reveals a high degree of confidence in Tbilisi in the early days of the Abkhazia adventure. Three days after the operation, in a televised speech Shevardnadze "said that as of today the jurisdiction of the Republic of Georgia has been restored throughout the territory of Georgia and that the authorities intend to continue resolute actions to restore order…"[50]

There was a large discrepancy between the (various) objectives of the 14 August military operation and the deployment and the actions of the Georgian troops on the ground. This reflected lack of strategic thinking

---

49 Source: Russian Television, reported by *BBC Summary of World Broadcasts*, 8 February 1992.

50 *Izvestia*, 17 August 1992.

and planning, as well as lack of material capability to reach the objectives through military means. If the aim was a security operation for liberating hostages from Zviadists active in Gali region, there was no point in sending troops to Sukhumi and Gagra; if the aim was to bring the railways and communication lines under governmental control, then it is strange that Georgian troops left large sections of the same lines, from the northern suburbs of Sukhumi to the southern entrance of Gagra, outside their control; and if the real objective was to hinder separatism in Abkhazia, then it is not clear why the Georgian forces were deployed on portions of the Abkhazian coast, leaving large sections of Abkhazia under rebel control—or why they used military means at all, since the Abkhaz authorities feared to lose the autonomy they enjoyed, and did not call for secession at the time.

While the invasion was equivalent to murder of the Georgia-Abkhaz dialogue, it was also a military suicide, for the following reasons:

(a) The geography of the Georgian military invasion: the invading Georgian troops took most of the coastal shore, stretching from Gali to Sukhumi, and from Gagra to the Russian border; but they did not overrun the central part of the coast around Gudauta, with its dense ethnic Abkhaz population, and where the rebel Abkhaz government moved. Moreover, the mountainous villages remained under Abkhaz control. Militarily, this was a very bad position, to have a long, coastal-line exposed to higher mountainous positions.

(b) The Georgian troops did not have any further military initiative after the initial invasion, while their positions were completely exposed to Abkhaz guerrilla style attacks;

(c) While the Georgian National Guard was well equipped relative to the Abkhaz militia, thanks to the Soviet military hardware that Georgia inherited according to the Tashkent Treaty, it was ill disciplined, did not have a well structured control system, did not have enough logistic means and ammunition for a protracted conflict, and did not have qualified officers to run their operations;

(d) Tbilisi miscalculated the role that the Russian military would play in the conflict, although Russia's political sympathy towards the Georgian State Council had already disappeared in the South Ossetian crisis in June. The direct intervention of the Russian forces in the fighting in South Ossetia should have rung alarm bells;

(e) The war mobilized the Caucasus People's Confederation (KNK) and several thousand North Caucasian volunteers to come to the support of the Abkhaz side. The KNK, which had its headquarters in Sukhumi, was forced to move to Groznyy after the Georgian invasion, and from there mobilized North Caucasus resources to support the Abkhaz war effort;

(f) The bandit-like behaviour of the National Guard antagonized the population of Abkhazia of different ethnic backgrounds, including the "ethnic Georgians" there who were Mingrelians and often supporters of Gamsakhurdia, and often were suspicious towards the National Guardsmen and Mkhedrioni sent to Abkhazia from central Georgia and the Tbilisi area;

(g) Last but not least, the Georgian troops had to cross through Mingrelia, controlled by Zviadists, before reaching the front-lines in Abkhazia. This stretched the logistics of the Georgian troops from their bases in Samtredia across hostile Mingrelia to volatile Abkhazia, and led to disruption of Georgian military movements during decisive periods of the war.

The Georgian leadership, then, ordered the military adventure in Abkhazia while being in a state of civil war against Zviadists, while knowing that the Russian military would intervene as they had just done weeks earlier in Tskhinvali, while knowing that they would not control the mountainous part of Abkhazia and therefore face a guerrilla war, and all this without having a proper army!

There is one controversy concerning the start of the war, and more specifically the nature of the operation: whether there was an agreement between Shevardnadze and Ardzinba concerning the introduction of Georgian troops to the Autonomous Republic. In the days preceding 14 August there seem to have been intense contacts between Tbilisi and Sukhumi on the entry of Georgian troops to Gali and Ochamchira districts, with the objective of repressing Zviadist armed groups there. The night before the operation, Shevardnadze and Ardzinba discussed once again the next day's operation, and according to Ardzinba the head of the State Council gave guarantees that the National Guard would not enter Sukhumi itself.[51] In spite of an agreement between the two sides, the National Guard violated the agreement by entering the capital of Abkhazia. Tbilisi went further by creating an "Abkhaz Military Council" composed of figures loyal to Tbilisi as the state organ recognized by

---

51   Author interview with Vladislav Ardzina, Sukhumi, 22 April 1994.

the Georgian authorities, headed by Tamaz Nadareishvili, the former Vice-Chairman of the Abkhaz Supreme Soviet. What was supposed to be a police operation turned into a military conflict with broad political aims: Tbilisi was clearly trying to press the Abkhaz leadership to agree to new political terms, in which the ethnic Abkhaz leadership in Sukhumi would lose its dominant position in the Autonomous Republic. As a result, ethnic Abkhaz members of the Abkhaz Supreme Soviet and their allies moved to Gudauta, 45 kilometres north of Sukhumi, and prepared for a major war.

In August, days after the Georgian invasion, the Abkhaz were already starting to form their own National Guard, from parts of the local police force of ethnic Abkhaz origin or elements loyal to the Abkhaz leadership. Georgia in its turn adopted a law on military conscription on December 1992, as a temporary measure for the security needs linked to the war in Abkhazia. Yet this decision was never seriously enforced, and six years after the adoption of the law the Defence Ministry put the size of the army at 30,000, which in reality meant less. Although the Georgian side had numerical and material superiority it suffered from chronic lack of discipline at the individual and the battalion level. According to a detailed report of the war prepared by Human Rights Watch:

Warfare in the Abkhaz conflict was characterized on both sides, most particularly in the beginning months and in rural areas, by a lack of formal, central military control over the operations of the rival forces. The command and control structures vital to military discipline and accountability were all but absent. Volunteers, mercenaries and other "outsiders" involved in combat in notable numbers collaborated with, but operated outside traditional military structures.[52]

Moreover, different military units had different political affiliations, which translated into a highly pluralistic military behaviour on the battleground. "Kartvelian forces were never able to become a cohesive fighting machine (…). A lack of unit and individual discipline not only cost them on the battlefield, but also made the Kartvelian troops exceedingly unpopular amongst the local inhabitants."[53]

---

[52] "Georgia/Abkhazia: Violations of the Laws of War ad Russia's Role in the Conflict", *Human Rights Watch* Vol. 7, No. 7, March 1995, p. 2.

[53] Dodge Billingsley, "Military Aspects of the War: the Turning Point", in Hewitt,

On the other hand although the Abkhazians had fewer resources, both human and material, they showed high level of discipline and a unified will. They compensated for their numerical inferiority by receiving volunteers from abroad, including some from the North Caucasus through the Congress of the Mountain Peoples of the Caucasus (later renamed the Confederation of Peoples of the Caucasus), from the Abkhaz Diaspora in Turkey, Syria and Jordan, and finally through volunteers from Russia, mainly Cossacks, and former Soviet Army officers. Most important, the Abkhaz were able to integrate all those fighters with different origins into a unified fighting force.

The Georgian threat and the Abkhaz trauma

A highly controversial declaration by a Georgian military leader was to have a profound effect: the commander of the Georgian military in Abkhazia, Colonel Giorgi Karkarashvili, in a televised address broadcast by the local Sukhumi channel on 25 August 1992, hardly two weeks after the invasion, gave the following warning: "We are ready to sacrifice 100,000 Georgians to annihilate 97,000 Abkhazians. We will leave the entire Abkhazian nation without descendents."[54] As the total number of ethnic Abkhaz residing in the autonomous republic was just a bit above 97,000, Karkarashvili's statement was received by the Abkhaz as a threat of genocide. The statement was not an isolated event, and did not reflect the opinion of the military only. Goga Khaindrava, Georgian Minister of Abkhazian Affairs, declared: "The Abkhaz have an interest to finish this war rapidly (…) They are just 80,000, that means that we

---

The Abkhazians, op. cit., p. 147.

54 *Report on Ethnic Conflict in the Russian Federation and Transcaucasia*, Harvard University, Strengthening Democratic Institutions Project, Cambridge MA, July 1993, p. 103. This often quoted declaration of Karkarashvili takes different forms in different sources. Viacheslav A. Chirikba puts it in the following form: "Even if the total number of Georgians – 100,000 – are killed, then from your [Abkhaz] side all 97,000 will be killed." See Chirikba, "The Georgian-Abkhazian Conflict: In Search for Ways out", in Bruno Coppieters, Ghia Nodia and Yuri Anchabadze (eds), *Georgians and Abkhazians*, op. cit., p. 50, footnote 1. The Russian *Ostankino Channel 1*, on 26 August 1992, quoted Karkarashvili as saying he was ready "to leave the entire Abkhaz nation without descendants, and (…) to sacrifice 100,000 Georgians to annihilate 97,000 Abkhazians" in case of resistance. Quoted by *BBC Summary of World Broadcasts*, 27 August 1992.

can easily destroy the genetic basis of their nation by killing 15,000 of their youth. And we are perfectly able to do that."[55]

Although the Georgian declarations sound like a threat of genocide, the Georgian leadership was not inclined to organize massacres in Abkhazia and destroy the Abkhaz nation. The Georgian fighters did commit mass violations of human rights, and in some localized cases ethnic cleansing, but there is no evidence that their objective was mass annihilation of the Abkhaz people. The leading Georgian scholar Ghia Nodia gives a somewhat different interpretation to those words. He says:

I happened to watch the interview of Karkarashvili which was quoted and, although I do not remember the exact wording myself, can say that what he meant was that it is silly on the Abkhaz side to fight, that Georgians will never give up Abkhazia, so the Abkhaz are putting their very existence in danger – even if one hundred thousand people died in the war on each side, Georgians would still be there, but not the Abkhaz. This may have been nasty statement, but Karkarashvili was merely expressing in his own way the idea that was always reiterated by Georgian officials at the time – that it was the radicalism of the Abkhazia's leadership, not Georgia's, that endangered the existence of the Abkhaz as a group.[56]

The fact that those words were meant to be a warning rather than a threat does not make much difference, at least not for the Abkhaz audience, and still less after the Rubicon was crossed and the war erupted. For the Abkhaz mass psychology, wounded by the memories of the losses of the 19th century, faced with the threat of cultural assimilation and demographic marginalization, it was not necessary to recall so openly about the dangers with which they were surrounded. In a speech given in London Stanislav Lakoba, the Deputy Chairman of the Parliament of Abkhazia, said: "We are lost between life and death – to be or not to be, because defeat in this war is tantamount to the annihilation of a whole nation. We have proved to be a very 'inconvenient' people, but despite our small numbers it is not so easy to do away with us right away."[57] It needed less

55   Karel Bartak, "Moscou dans le bourbier caucasien ", *Le Monde diplomatique*, April 1993.

56   Ghia Nodia, *Causes and Visions of Conflict in Abkhazia*, University of California, Berkeley, 1997, p. 10, footnote 8.

57   Stanislav Lakoba, "Abkhazia is Abkhazia", *Central Asian Survey*, London, 14 (1), 1995, p. 97. The paper was presented in London at a conference entitled "The Contemporary North Caucasus" at the SOAS on 22-23 April 1993.

than a hundred thousand dead on each side to destroy the Abkhaz people. The recent disappearance of the last surviving community of the Ubykh people in Turkey, who had left their ancestral lands after their defeat in the Caucasian War of the 19th century, reminded the Abkhaz and other peoples about the dangers of the conflict.

The practices of the Georgian fighters, often lacking discipline, only worsened the situation. Abkhaz institutions suffered under Georgian occupation. The burning down of the Abkhaz National Library and the State Archives in Sukhumi in October 1992 was seen by the Abkhaz as an attempt by the Georgians to destroy their historic memory and cultural institutions. Ethnic Abkhaz who had stayed behind under Georgian military rule also suffered physical aggression, and damage to their property, as well as other ethnic groups including Russians, Armenians and Greeks. The brutality of the Georgian irregular fighters did not even spare the ethnic Georgian civilians of the occupied province.

Georgian defeat

After their initial thrust, the Georgian forces lost the military initiative. They did not undertake a single major military operation in the 14-month-long war that followed. The Abkhaz on the other side regrouped their forces, mobilized all men capable of bearing arms, organized their logistics, and received volunteers from the North Caucasus and to a lesser degree from the Diaspora in the Middle East. They were motivated to fight, and had one objective: to restore the former boundaries of Abkhazia and chase out the Georgian forces.

The obvious target of the Abkhaz military activities was the town of Gagra, a pleasant town decorated with palm trees and squeezed between the waters of the Black Sea and the rocks of the Caucasus. Gagra had a strategic position since the distance between the sea and the mountains is very narrow here. The Georgian positions in this town blocked Abkhaz overland communication lines towards Russia and the North Caucasus (although they could use secondary mountain passes to transport volunteers and limited arms and ammunition). Moreover, Gagra was an isolated pocket of Georgian forces, where up to 1,000 Georgian fighters were stationed. Therefore, it was the most suitable ground for the Abkhaz side to test the force of their arms.

The Abkhaz offensive did not wait long. On the night of 24 August Abkhazian forces attacked Gagra, only ten days after Georgian troops entered Abkhazia. The fighting continued for some five days, and after receiving reinforcements Georgian troops went on the counter-offensive and repelled the Abkhaz. A cease-fire agreement was reached under Russian patronage on 26 September, calling for the withdrawal of heavy weapons from inside urban centres to their peripheries. According to some sources, following this agreement the Georgian troops withdrew their military hardware and most of their fighters from Gagra. A Russian officer, Lt-General Sufiyan Bepayev, the Deputy Commander of the Transcaucasus Military District which was based in Tbilisi, was quoted by *Izvestia* saying that following the cease-fire agreement, and two days before the Abkhaz assault on the city, the Georgian side withdrew its weapons and 1,200 fighters from Gagra, leaving only 200 soldiers armed with light weapons for its defence.[58] Yet this does not make much sense, because even after the signing of the agreement exchange of fire continued all along the lines of contact, from the Ochamchira region up to the suburbs of Gagra.[59] Withdrawing troops and heavy weapons from Gagra meant its doom. The second Abkhaz offensive against Gagra started on 2 October, in three directions. The Georgian defences collapsed in a matter of hours, and the Abkhaz controlled the town on the following day. A Georgian counter-offensive failed miserably, leading to a badly organized retreat of fighters and civilians from Gagra and from the villages up to the Russian border. According to Human Rights Watch, the number of the dead was between 100 and up to 300 in the battle of Gagra, and the Russian troops evacuated the rest of the Georgian fighters and their military commander, Karkarashvili, to nearby Russian territory.[60] In Tbilisi the press and politicians accused the Abkhaz fighters of massacres of Georgian civilians. Nine days before the parliamentary elections in Georgia (11 October 1992), Gagra fell to Abkhaz forces.

The battle of Gagra was a turning point in the war. It showed the determination of the Abkhaz and the disorder among the Georgian

---

58   *Izvestia*, 5 October 1992.

59   Dodge Billingsley, op. cit., p. 149.

60   "Georgia/Abkhazia: Violations of the Laws of War and Russia's Role in the Conflict", *Human Rights Watch*, Vol. 7, No. 7, March 1995.

troops. The outcome of this battle cast a long shadow over the next and the decisive battle for the control of Sukhumi. The Georgian authorities immediately accused the Russian side of being responsible for the outcome of the Gagra battle, although there is no clear evidence of immediate involvement of Russians there. Massive Russian military support, both in arms and military officers, started arriving to support the Abkhaz side after the battle of Gagra, after the Abkhaz had proved to be a fighting force. There is ample information about Russian support to the Abkhaz during 1993, both supplies of arms and ammunition and employment of Russian aircraft in direct military operations. The Gagra battle was also a warning about things to come; under Georgian control houses of Abkhaz, but also of other minorities such as Armenians and Russians, were looted and then put on fire. When the Abkhaz forces entered the town, the entire ethnic Georgian population of Gagra, as well as the villages north up to Leselidze to the north, was displaced, and its houses put on fire.[61]

The downing on 14 December 1992 of a Russian military helicopter, which was evacuating civilians from the besieged town of Tkvarcheli in south-east Abkhazia, caused relations between Moscow and Tbilisi to fall to a new record low. According to Russian sources, the helicopter was shot down by a Georgian surface-to-air missile, killing all 30 civilians and the Russian pilots on board.[62]

A major Abkhaz military offensive against Sukhumi took place in mid-March 1993. Abkhaz forces crossed the Gumista river and initially succeeded in breaking through the Georgian defences. The battle lasted two days and the Georgian defenders threw back the assault. Artillery duels between Abkhaz positions in Novi Esher village and Georgian troops positioned in the northern suburbs of Sukhumi continued. Under heavy Russian pressure, mainly by the Defence Minister Pavel Grachev, a new cease-fire agreement was reached by the belligerent sides in the Russian town of Sochi on 28 July 1993, in which the Georgian side made substantial concessions including the withdrawal of much of its military equipment from the frontline and expression of readiness to recognize Abkhaz autonomy. The cease-fire was meant to lead to a political resolution of the conflict, yet five rounds of direct Georgian-

61   Personal observations, Gagra, 10 May 1993.
62   *Izvestia*, 15 December 1992.

Zviadist?

Russian negotiations did not lead to a conclusion, because of Georgian rejection of Russian demands which included Georgia's joining the CIS and the legalization of five Russian military bases in Georgia.

The failure of the State Council in Abkhazia strengthened Gamsakhurdia's popularity in Georgia. As a result, Zviadist activities increased in western Georgia in summer 1993. Several battalions in Sukhumi and Gali declared that they were withdrawing their allegiance from the State Council and joining Kobalia's forces after the "shameful" cease-fire agreement signed by Shevardnadze, which provided for withdrawal of armed forces of the two sides from urban areas. By the end of August, Kobalia's forces took control over a number of towns in Mingrelia, including Senaki, Khobi, and Abasha.[63] The government troops in Abkhazia were in complete isolation, politically disoriented, while facing a determined enemy.

On 16 September the Abkhaz broke the latest cease-fire on the pretext that the Georgian side had not respected its provision for the withdrawal of heavy equipment from Sukhumi, and launched a major offensive. An amphibious force of several hundred fighters landed in the Ochamchira district, to the south of Sukhumi, cutting down Georgian communication lines and besieging the city. The assault on the city itself from three fronts followed. A rebellion in Mingrelia after calls from ex-President Gamsakhurdia further complicated the situation of Georgian troops in Abkhazia. On 17 September a speech by Gamsakhurdia was broadcast by Abkhaz TV in Gudauta, in which he urged his supporters in Mingrelia to take up arms against the Tbilisi authorities.[64] Yet it was not clear how much the orders of Gamsakhurdia were followed. According to news reports, Kobalia, the head of the pro-Gamsakhurdia militia in Zugdidi, moved towards Ochamchira on 17 September with the aim of supporting the Georgian forces trapped in the Sukhumi area.[65] At this stage the Georgian forces in Abkhazia found themselves in complete chaos, and under a heavy attack from a vengeful enemy.

In the confusion Shevardnadze flew to the besieged Sukhumi, and later met Grachev in Adler, a small town north of the Georgian-Russian frontier where a civilian airport is situated, on 17 September. Shevard-

---

63   *The Georgian Chronicle*, CIPDD, Tbilisi, August 1993, p. 6.

64   *Moscow News*, 24 September 1993.

65   *Izvestia*, 22 September 1993.

nadze demanded Russian military intervention to return the fighters to their pre-16 September positions. Shevardnadze even consented to the positioning of Russian troops on the Inguri river, separating Abkhazia from Georgia. Shevardnadze was making last minute concessions to the Kremlin while in a desperate situation. At this meeting Grachev made bold promises in his typical style to the Georgian leader, promising to send two paratroop divisions and a brigade which would "after landing, separate, cut off and disarm the opposing sides and end the conflict in two or three days."[66] Later, similar declarations by General Grachev were to lead to even greater tragedies in the North Caucasus. Yet no Russian troops were sent, because the Russian parliament was against positioning troops in a situation where house-to-house fighting was destroying Sukhumi and devastating battles were raging in the villages of Ochamchira and Gali districts.

After the Georgian side had put up a last desperate resistance, Sukhumi fell on 28 September. The Abkhaz advance continued towards the towns of Ochamchira and Gali, and Abkhaz fighters reached the Inguri river on 30 September. The advancing Abkhaz fighters showed no pity; they executed the numerous Georgian fighters trapped in isolated buildings of Sukhumi, including the Chairman of the Council of Ministers of the pro-Tbilisi government in Abkhazia, Zhiuli Shartava. Abkhaz fighters burned down those houses in Sukhumi that belonged to Georgians, or to individuals of other ethnic groups who had collaborated with the pro-Tbilisi government in Abkhazia. Similarly, entire villages in the south were torched, and the Georgian population of those villages was pushed out of Abkhazia. The displaced people escaped in two directions, one southward towards Zugdidi, and the other through mountain passes through the Kodori gorge towards Svaneti. The displacement of over 200,000 people created an acute problem in Georgia, at a time when the authorities could hardly feed and provide the basic services for the population of the capital. The destruction left behind by this 14-month war had turned the pearl of Soviet holiday resorts, with its villas, sanatoria, hotels and beach resorts, into a miserable, depressing heap of debris. The Abkhaz had lost 2,800 people, around two thousand of them ethnic Abkhaz, "over two per cent of the entire Abkhaz

---

66   *Sevodnya*, 21 September 1993.

population" in the words of an Abkhaz official, who continued: "This is a tragedy for a small nation!"[67] Georgian casualties were three times higher than the Abkhaz losses.

The enormous mistake of the Georgian leadership—what I called earlier "the original sin"—transformed a difficult political situation between Tbilisi and Abkhazia into a complicated knot that poisoned the relations and erected a wall of separation between the two neighbouring nations. The conflict further destabilized Georgia, and the entire Caucasus region. Thousands of Caucasian volunteers fought in Abkhazia, who acquired military experience and were later visible elsewhere, especially in Chechnya. The Abkhazia conflict also blocked communication lines, hampering trade and economic normalization: one of the two railway connections between Russia and the South Caucasus passes through Abkhazia, and still remains shut down a decade after the end of the armed conflict. This situation harms Georgia but also Armenia, a major economic partner of Russia in the South Caucasus. Last but not least, the Abkhazia conflict transformed and deformed Russian-Georgian relations, as we will see in more details below.

In the last days of the Sukhumi battle, during which Shevardnadze was himself in the besieged town, he made the ultimate capitulation: he sent a telegram to Moscow accepting that Georgia would join the CIS, which Shevardnadze defined as "Georgia's kneeling down", a desperate attempt to save the city from an assault planned "in the General Staff of the Russian Army".[68] Although this desperate political step did not save Sukhumi from falling to the Abkhaz fighters, in a few days Shevardnadze would appreciate Russian military help, saving his regime and saving Georgia from further dismemberment. A cease-fire agreement was finally signed between the two sides in Moscow on 14 April 1994, which included the separation of forces and the introduction of CIS peacekeeping forces on the border of the former administrative limit that marks the southern borders of Abkhazia.[69]

---

67   Leonid Lakerbaya, Vice-Prime Minister of Abkhazia, author interview, Sukhumi, 22 April 1994.

68   *The Georgian Chronicle*, September 1993, p. 4.

69   The English translation of the agreement can be found at: http://www.usip. org/library/pa/georgia/georgia_19940514.html

War in Mingrelia

The defeat of the Georgian governmental forces did not end the internal conflict in Georgia. "Zviadist" forces, led by Vakhtang Kobalia, had regrouped, received arms and ammunitions during their participation in the war in Abkhazia on the side of the National Guards, and confiscated additional heavy weapons from the governmental forces retreating from Abkhazia. During the months of August and September 1993, they took control over most of Mingrelia. With the collapse of the government forces in Abkhazia, Zviadists felt it was the moment to push towards Tbilisi and reinstall Gamsakhurdia at the head of the Georgian state.

Zviadist forces continued their assault; on 2 October 1993 they took control of the strategic Black Sea port of Poti, where they took control of additional military equipment that the Georgian troops had evacuated from Sukhumi. Then they turned eastwards, and on 10 October attacked Khobi, which they brought under their control seven days later after violent clashes. They took control of Samtreda on 18 October, and continued their advance in the direction of Kutaisi, the second major town of Georgia.

The situation on the front line changed dramatically at the end of October. Governmental forces launched a counter-offensive and retook town after town from pro-Gamsakhurdia rebels. This change of fortunes was attributed to the newly established alliance between Georgia and Russia, and to considerable Russian military support to the Georgian side. Unofficial reports noted the arrival of much needed arms and ammunition from Russia, and the participation of Russian tank crews on the side of the Georgian government forces. Russian warships also patrolled the shores off Poti, to block any possible assistance to the rebels. Rebel positions fell one after the other, and on 6 November 1993 troops loyal to Shevardnadze entered Zugdidi, the stronghold of Gamsakhurdia, without a fight. Certain armed groups loyal to Gamsakhurdia laid down their arms and surrendered to the government, including those under the command of Soso Zhghenti and Akaki Eliava.[70]

---

70   The life and death of Akaki Eliava illustrate the state of the Georgian armed
      forces in the 1990s. Eliava joined the Georgian National Guard in 1992,
      and later joined the Zviadist revolt in autumn 1993. He was amnestied a few
      months after the death of Gamsakhurdia, and he and his men joined the Geor-

Gamsakhurdia himself was found dead in obscure circumstances in the village of Jikhashkari, to the east of Zugdidi, on 31 December 1993, thus turning a page to a tragic period of Georgian history.[71]

Russia's role and changing image after Abkhazia

For the Georgian national liberation movement Russia—and not just the Soviet system—was the "enemy". It was the Russian empire that had put an end to the last Georgian kingdom in the early 19th century. It was the Bolsheviks (in an invasion that was initiated by a certain Sergo Ordzhonikidze[72]) who had invaded Georgia to put an end to the short-lived independent republic in 1921. The anti-Russian antagonism took a deep character after the Tbilisi repression of 9 April 1989. For Georgian nationalists, the Soviet/Russian Army was a force of occupation, and Georgia could only achieve its full independence after the departure of the last Russian soldier from its territories. The Georgian parliament even passed a law, following the failed putsch in Moscow, considering the Soviet troops in Georgia as "occupation forces". Yet both Gamsakhurdia and Shevardnadze tried to co-opt and use the Russian military when this suited their agenda. During the days of confrontation in Tbilisi between the opposition and Zviadists, Gamsakhurdia had tried to get support from the Soviet military to suppress the Mkhedrioni militia.[73] Shevardnadze's Russia policy was even more contradictory and constantly oscillating.

Following the overthrow of Gamsakhurdia, and the coming to power of Russia-friendly forces led by Shevardnadze, Russian-Georgian relations seemed to be on the way to improvement. Shevardnadze back-

---

gian armed forces. Colonel Eliava led an army mutiny in October 1998, triggered by delays in pay, and took over the Senaki barracks. With 200 soldiers and 17 tanks he advanced towards Kutaisi, where he clashed with loyalist forces. After several casualties, the mutiny disintegrated, and the Colonel was on the run hiding in the Zugdidi region. He was arrested and shot in the Zestafoni police station in July 2000, ending the life story of the last of the Zviadist field commanders.

71   The official version of Gamsakhurdia's death was "suicide", while supporters of the former president accuse government forces of having him executed.

72   Jeremy Smith, "The Georgian Affair of 1922. Policy Failure, Personality Clash, or Power Struggle?" *Europe-Asia Studies*, Vol. 50, No. 3, May 1998, pp. 519-44.

73   David Darchiashvili, *The Army-Building*, op. cit., p. 27.

tracked the former Georgian parliament decision that considered the "Soviet" troops as occupying forces. Although the relations between the two sides reached a new low point in June 1992 over violent events in South Ossetia, direct negotiations between Yeltsin and Shevardnadze led to a cease-fire agreement and the introduction of peacekeeping troops there.

In May 1992 Georgia joined the CIS Tashkent Treaty on the division of Soviet conventional weapons between the newly independent states. Following this agreement, the Russian military started delivering to the Georgian armed forces their quota of Soviet weaponry.[74] (Abkhaz officials refer to those arms transfers to accuse Russia of having supplied the necessary means to the Georgian side for the invasion of Abkhazia.)

Russian-Georgian relations entered a new phase of difficulty after 14 August 1992, with Georgian troops entering Abkhazia. Initially, Moscow seemed to have been surprised by the events and did not have a clear policy. On the other hand, several factors on the ground were already shaping the "unofficial" Russian policy. The unlawful activities of the National Guard members and Mkhedrioni militias caused thousands of Russian-speakers to become refugees in southern Russia. Several thousand native North Caucasians crossed the Russian-Georgian border to join the struggle on the Abkhaz side. In addition, the local Russian officers sympathized with the Abkhaz and provided them with weapons even before the ministries of Foreign Affairs and Defence in Moscow had come to a policy conclusion on the conflict.

After the battle of Gagra, in which the Abkhaz forces supported by North Caucasian volunteers drove the Georgian troops from the northernmost coast of Abkhazia, a clear policy emerged in Moscow. By supporting the Abkhaz side and increasingly putting pressure on Tbilisi, the Russian leadership tried to impose political and military demands on Georgia. This including forcing Tbilisi to join the new Commonwealth

[74] In the months of June-August 1992 the Georgian army received 109 T-55 Main Battle Tanks, 169 armoured vehicles, and 76 artillery systems, from the former Soviet military base of Akhaltsikhe. Although the equipment was rather old, it nevertheless provided the Georgian troops with armour and firepower enabling them to launch the Abkhazia operation. See David Darchiashvili, "The Russian Military Presence in Georgia: The Parties' Attitude and Prospects", in *Caucasian Regional Studies*, Brussels, Vol. 2, Issue 1, 1997.

of Independent States (CIS), to legalize the Russian armed presence in Georgia under the mantle of "peacekeepers", and to reach an agreement for turning the former Soviet bases into Russian military bases in several strategic places such as Batumi, Akhalkalaki, and Vaziani.

Yet, while Russia was supporting the Abkhaz side of the conflict with arms, ammunition and mercenaries, including officers and pilots of the Russian military base in Gudauta, Moscow was also seeking to mediate between the two belligerents. Russia brokered cease-fire agreements in September 1992, and afterwards the cease-fires of May and July 1993. While being the guarantor for the cease-fire and the mediator for a political solution, Russia did not make any effort to stop the Abkhaz assault to take Sukhumi. On the contrary; many accounts, and even more so the chronology of events, suggest that the Russian side did not respect its engagements vis-à-vis the Georgian side, and in September 1993 it simply let the Abkhaz fighters regain their heavy weapons and facilitated their multiple movements to encircle the remaining Georgian forces in Sukhumi and southern Abkhazia.[75]

The war in Abkhazia was a turning point in the West's view of Russia. After the initial Western sympathy towards democratizing and still anarchic Russia, now a new image emerged, that of the new-imperial, militaristic Russia imposing its weight over its smaller neighbours. Western analysts, who up to then had seen the role of Russia in the chaos of the Caucasus as a stabilizing factor, revised this script so as to show Russia as contributing to escalation of conflict.[76] Analysts in neighbouring countries also read the military developments in the war fronts of the South Caucasus as the result of Russian decisions, and a sign of a return of Russian military hegemony over the Near Abroad through the manipulation of inter-ethnic conflicts and civil wars from Karabakh to Transdniestra and Tajikistan. This image of a powerful Russian manipulator was to be somewhat corrected only a short while

---

75   *The Georgian Chronicle*, *CIPDD*, Tbilisi, September 1993, pp. 1-4 ; "Back in the USSR", op. cit., pp. 49-57; for a Russian point of view see Evgeny M. Kozhokin, "Georgia-Abkhazia", in Jeremy Azrael and Emil Payin (eds), *U.S. and Russian Policymaking with Respect to the Use of Force*, Santa Monica, CA: RAND, 1996.

76   Thomas Goltz, "Letter From Eurasia: The Hidden Russian Hand", *Foreign Policy*, No 92, Fall 1993; Charles Fairbanks, "A Tired Anarchy", *The National Interest*, Spring 1995.

later, with the direct Russian military intervention in Chechnya and its miserable defeat.

Russia's biased position confirmed the "enemy" image that Georgians had developed of Russia. On the official level, Shevardnadze tried to distinguish between the Russian civilian leadership's and President Yeltsin's policies towards Georgia, which respected country's territorial integrity, and conservative military elements seeking to take revenge against the former Soviet Foreign Minister, or neo-imperial elements trying to extend a new type of military hegemony over strategically positioned Georgia. Shevardnadze stubbornly kept thinking that reaching an agreement with the Russian leadership and satisfying Russian demands would be enough to stabilize the situation in Abkhazia. Yet although the Russians were a powerful actor in the Abkhazia conflict, they were not in a position of hegemony over the Abkhaz and North Caucasian forces on the frontline, nor could they change the Abkhaz political objective in the war, which was to bring Abkhazia under their total control by expelling the Georgian troops.

Moscow did score temporary success out of its ambivalent role in the Abkhazia conflict. Georgia was defeated and humiliated, and asked Russia for help. Politically, Shevardnadze eventually agreed to join the CIS, Russia's political instrument intended to extend its new-old hegemony over the former Soviet republics. Militarily, it gained important influence in Georgia, by having its soldiers as peacekeepers separating the Abkhaz and the Georgian sides. It also gained wide influence over the Georgian military by the appointment of Vardiko Nadibaidze, a Russian-speaking officer of Georgian ethnic background from the Soviet army, as Defence Minister of Georgia, replacing Giorgi Karkarashvili, in 1994. It also took over the role of equipping and training the Georgian armed forces.

On the strategic level, through its role in Abkhazia Russia lost Georgia.[77] The Georgian elite, while collaborating with the Russian military in the period after 1993, stayed deeply anti-Russian. The Georgian anti-Russian position was not simply the result of ideological antago-

---

77   On Russian policies in the Caucasus, see Vicken Cheterian, "Russia and the Caucasus: Divide and Don't Rule", in Frédéric Grare (ed.), *La Russie dans tous ses Etats*, Brussels: Bruylant, 1996, pp. 147-69; Pavel Baev, *Russia's Policies in the Caucasus*, London: Royal Institute of International Affairs, 1997.

nism of the Georgian leadership influenced by the national liberation movement, but reflected political realities: by its divide-and-rule policies, Russia could offer no solution to the main problems of Georgia, either the problems of territorial integrity or those of the emergence of a central and efficient government. On a more general level, Russia had no model to propose to Georgia, nor to other post-Soviet countries, being itself in a "transition" period whose objective was to copy Western models in the political system and a market-based economy. Moreover, Russia had neither the necessary capital nor the technological means to propose solutions for the necessary economic modernization, infrastructure works, and industrial transformation that were necessary for post-Soviet states. As a result, Georgia had to look elsewhere, and this elsewhere could only be the West. As early as 1996, Georgia looked for military partners to replace Russia, and especially to the United States where it sent its young officers for training. And when the opportunity was presented after September 2001, this cooperation turned into a major alliance, and through a "Train and Equip" programme the US military, with the presence of over 200 military specialists on Georgian soil, replaced the Russians in military cooperation, including military reform and training and equipping of the Georgian armed forces.

From a failing state to a weak one

In 1992, following the collapse of the USSR and the coming of Shevardnadze to power, Georgia was recognized as an independent state and admitted to a number of international organizations and regional associations. Considering Georgia as a member of clubs of states, and from the perspective of an international law founded on the principle of state sovereignty and territorial recognition, the conflicts in South Ossetia and Abkhazia are seen, and often described, as "separatism". In other words, Ossets and Abkhaz were seen as having developed nationalist tendencies and, after reaching an extreme position, declared their separation from the Georgian state.

Although this interpretation makes sense from a legal point of view,[78] since the international community admitted Georgia and the other four-

---

78   Legal experts defending Abkhaz or Osset perspective argue that they declared their "separation" or sovereignty not from the Georgian state but from the Soviet Union.

teen Union Republics of the USSR, within the borders defined under
Soviet administration, it fails to reflect the historical events. If one looks
at the developments in Georgia over the period 1990-94 and wants to
learn more about the causes of the conflicts, their development, and
their results, this schema of separatism versus Georgian statehood fails
us. Similarly, interpretations that see the source of the conflicts coming
from Russia, in an attempt to weaken the emerging newly independent
states and to bring them under the new hegemony of Moscow again,
obscure much of the history of the Georgian-Abkhaz war and the history of the South Caucasus. Although it is true that the Russian military on the ground and some of the Moscow leadership did interfere in
the development of the events, whether in the wars between the ethnic
minorities against the central authorities or during the two rounds of
Georgian power struggle, the Russian role remained limited to intervening in developing events, and not causing and containing them.

In the moment of Soviet collapse and the emergence of the independence of Georgia, the country was struggling to define its new political identity and impose it on the country. In this period, Georgian
statehood was a political project, and at times one doubted whether
it was achievable or not.[79] The Georgian project of building sovereign
statehood clashed with several other forces. The most important clash
was the internal division of this political project, between its various
wings, one led by Zviad Gamsakhurdia and the other initially regrouped
around the umbrella of the National Congress (Chanturia, Tsereteli),
and led by the Military Council (Sigua, Ioseliani, Kitovani) and eventually by the State Council under Shevardnadze. The second major challenge came from Abkhazia and South Ossetia, with their own national-
statehood projects that were the mirror-image of the Georgian project
itself. Yet the Abkhaz and Osset movements were defensive in their
essence, trying to defend their institutional framework and local rule
from a mounting Georgian national project that tried to incorporate
them into a centralized state project. The third force that challenged the
Georgian national project was Moscow. In the Soviet period Moscow's

---

79   Stephen Jones, "Georgia: A Failed Democratic Transition", in Ian Bremmer and
      Ray Taras (eds), *Nations and Politics in the Soviet Successor States*, Cambridge
      University Press, 1993; Paul B. Henze, "Was Georgia Ready for Independ-
      ence?", *Caspian Crossroads Magazine*, Volume 3, Issue No. 3, Winter 1998.

Moscow's resistance to Georgian nationalism was weak and incoherent, and after the inefficient repression of the 9 April 1989 demonstration the central Soviet authorities, and their local instrument the Georgian Communist Party, simply had no Georgia policy any more, and surrendered their authority to the newly rising national movement there. Later, Russia was to find a new way of regaining influence in Georgia, through interfering in the little wars in South Ossetia, Abkhazia and Mingrelia.

Following the Russian military intervention and the crushing of the Zviadist rebellion, Georgia entered a period of relative stability. In late 1993 Shevardnadze created the Citizens' Union of Georgia, a coalition of forces that became the political base of his rule and the ruling party in Georgia, composed by former *nomenklatura* members as well as young, Western-educated reformers: former Communists, the Green Party, and a wing of the Republican Party. Through various manoeuvres he weakened the warlords and eventually imprisoned Kitovani in early 1995, after this latter prepared armed formations to march on Abkhazia. Later that year, and after an assassination attempt, Ioseliani and dozens of Mkhedrioni fighters were arrested and imprisoned. At the same time the Georgian authorities accused Igor Gogsadze, the head of the Georgian National Security, of masterminding the assassination attempt. Gogsadze escaped to Moscow where he found refuge. Shevardnadze reinforced the police detachments but the Georgian army never became a real force under his rule.

But the dynamics of positive development ended there, and Georgia stagnated after 1997. Shevardnadze played the role of mediator between several power centres and economic groups that divided influence and resources among them. The control of the state over vast territories was no more than nominal: apart from the conflict-ridden Abkhazia and South Ossetia, the government had no control over Ajaria, Mingrelia, Samtskhe-Javakheti, Svanetia. The relative stability of Georgia was perturbed in February 1998 with an assassination attempt against the President, carried out by Zviadist fighters with probable Chechen support. Fighting erupted once again in May 1998 in the southern Gali district of Abkhazia as Georgian guerrilla troops tried to advance in the region, causing scores of dead and the expulsion of those refugees who had by then returned to their villages. The collapse of the Russian economy in the summer of the same year was yet another blow to the economic stability of Georgia. Another attempt to attack Abkhazia, this time from the Kodori gorge with a multi-ethnic force led by the Chechen field commander Ruslan Gelayev in October 2001, was yet another sad chapter in Georgian-Abkhazian relations. The state structures were deeply corrupted, and the economy did not succeed in taking off. Shevardnadze failed to reveal a long term strategy to take his country out of the crisis. "Without that, his balancing act began to look like an exercise in opportunism."[80] Shevardnadze did avert the danger of disintegration of his country in 1992-93, but Georgia remained a weak state under his rule.

Ghosts of nationalism

The 2003 "Rose Revolution" revived hopes that Georgia would re-emerge like a phoenix from the ashes of a failing state and advance on the path of modernization. A group led by Mikheil Saakashvili and Zurab Zhvania, two former collaborators of Shevardnadze known to be leaders of the reformist wing of the ruling Citizen's Union of Georgia, broke with the regime of the "White Fox" by late 2001, when it was clear that staying with Shevardnadze would led to a dead-end in their political careers. The parliamentary elections of November 2003, and the fraud associated with it, provided the appropriate moment to launch a mass movement to bring down the corrupt regime. In mobilizing of the masses the opposition discourse focused on the failures of the Shevardnadze administration, attacking his corrupt, semi-criminal regime as the source of all the ills of Georgia; the revolution promised to solve the problems of the Georgian society by toppling the criminal regime. Corruption, economic failure, unemployment and poverty would find their conclusion once the post-communist elite of Shevardnadze went. The national question, the issue of Georgia's territorial unity, was not a part of the political discourse of the opposition to Shevardnadze during the mobilization in the spring and summer and on to November in 2003. Nor was the question of a new policy towards ethnic minorities.

It did not take long to bring the national question to the central stage of Georgian politics. Two months after the Rose Revolution, in

---

80   Ghia Nodia, "Georgia's Identity Crisis", *Journal of Democracy*, Vol. 6, No. 1, January 1995, p. 114.

his inaugural speech following his victorious election to the presidency, Saakashvili promised "unification, security and well-being".[81] He promised to make Georgia "attractive" to the secessionist regions, and integrate them through its charm rather than use force to achieve the unification of Georgia.

The first area to test the new policies was Ajaria, an Autonomous Republic on the Black Sea shores. Ajars are ethnic Georgians, but of Muslim religion. After the collapse of the Soviet Union Ajaria was ruled much like a medieval fiefdom by Aslan Abashidze. Without declaring any secessionist ambitions, Abashidze made sure that the vast revenues that he collected thanks to the region's favourable geographical position—situated on a major overland route between Turkey and the heart of Eurasian continent, besides having in Batumi a major port on the Black Sea—would stay with him to reinforce his clientelist and corrupt regime, and not a cent would go to the central authorities in Tbilisi. In April 2004 a combination of external pressure and opposition demonstrations in Batumi led to the fall of Abashidze regime. Tbilisi was lucky for once: Aslan Bek did not fight back, his police did not open fire on the crowds, and Russia tried to mediate instead of pushing for a military solution, avoiding a major bloodshed. After Ajaria was brought under the rule of Tbilisi, Saakashvili emptied the term "autonomy" of all sense by taking full control over the province. If the goal was to make Georgia attractive to other secessionist regions, than the policy in Ajaria sent the wrong message to Abkhazia and South Ossetia.

Next it was the turn of South Ossetia. There too Saakashvili aimed at combining external military pressure and provoking an internal "colour" revolution. First the market at Ergneti, a Georgian village few kilometres to the south of the Tskhinvali, where trade of all sorts took place, was closed down. The idea was that if the economic resources of the South Ossetian regime were cut off, then it would not take long to collapse. Instead, the external pressure led to military clashes in August 2004 with dozens of casualties, in the absence of a popular movement demanding a peaceful, pro-Georgian revolution. Saakashvili had badly miscalculated this time, and he stopped the confrontation at the right moment before it could get out of control. The 2004 clashes in

---

81   Quoted in Peter Slevin, "Saakashvili takes office after protests ousted Shevardnadze", *The Washington Post*, 26 January 2004.

South Ossetia had shown how complicated ethnic conflicts are, and how counter productive military solutions could be. Twelve years after the 1992 cease-fire, while Ossets and Georgians were slowly building a new and peaceful life together, Saakashvili's plan to unify Georgia had rekindled the old fires of inter-ethnic antagonism.

These two experiences reinforced belief in Tbilisi about the possibility of achieving unification in the near future. Once again the reasons for failure were seen in Russian interference in the internal affairs of Georgia: "If Moscow stops supporting the separatists in Abkhazia and South Ossetia, these two regions would simply return to Georgia" seemed to be the line of thinking among the Georgian policy making elite. As a result, Georgia gave top priority to its integration into NATO, as the only way to neutralize Russian influence over Georgian territory. It also started a vast project of military modernization, by increasing its military spending tenfold in a matter of four years.[82]

Emphasis on the issue of territorial unification has given a heavy nationalist overtones to the Rose Revolution, which otherwise would like to see itself as a democratic revolution and a Westernizing experience. Saakashvili initiated a youth movement called the "Young Patriots", which organizes youth camps from among all the places near the fronts with the secessionist regions. Another example of the new nationalism of post-revolution Georgia is the rehabilitation of Zviad Gamsakhurdia. As early as 2004 Saakashvili, in a number of speeches, rehabilitated Gamsdakhurdia as the "first president" of independent Georgia. In April 2007 Gamsakhurdia's remains were transferred from Groznyy to Georgia and, after an official procession through the streets of the Georgian capital, were buried at the Mtatsminda Pantheon, where prominent Georgian figures rest. It is easy to analyze the political calculations behind this act: by rehabilitating Gamsakhurdia the Georgian leadership is questioning the legitimacy of Shevardnadze, against whom they organized an extra-legal coup. Moreover, Saakashvili is returning the favour of pro-Zviadist supporters from western Georgia, who participated massively in the 2003 revolution.

---

82   In 2007, Georgia was spending a quarter of its state budget on defence, that is 513 million GEL (423 million euros) from the total state budget of 3.7 billion GEL. See Vicken Cheterian, "Georgia's arms race", *Opendemocracy*, June 4, 2007. http://opendemocracy.net/conflicts/caucasus_fractures/georgia_military

What is left out from the equation is the public opinion in both Abkhazia and South Ossetia. By considering its main adversary to be the Kremlin Tbilisi is simply ignoring them. In the words of the President of North Ossetia, Alexander Dzasokhov, the rehabilitation of Gamsakhurdia "cannot but cause anxiety". He added: "Nothing has been done for nearly 14 years to overcome aftermaths of the conflict so as to raise gradually confidence between Georgia and South Ossetia. (...) I mean full rehabilitation of the first Georgian president who had been at the head of all 1991 dramatic events, (...) Of course this provokes concern. What is this line like, and will it help to settle the conflict?"[83]

By rehabilitating Gamsakhurdia without the slightest debate about his controversial role in starting an unnecessary war with the Ossets, Georgia is revealing that it is not yet ready to face its past. Post-Rose-Revolution Georgia continues its strong references to nationalist symbolism, and continues to reproduce the mistakes of the late 1980s and early 1990s: to ignore the Abkhaz and the Ossets as the main sides of a conflict, and to consider them as simple expressions of the will of the Kremlin. Is modern Georgian history following a cyclical mode? Fifteen years after the events Eduard Shevardnadze recognized Georgian responsibility in starting the war in Abkhazia. On 14 August 2007, Georgian television Rustavi-2 broadcasted the following interview with him:[84]

[Presenter] Was it possible to avoid the armed confrontation in Abkhazia 15 years ago? Fifteen years later, the then-commander-in-chief [of the Georgian army] speaks about insubordination. He says refusal to obey his order grew into an armed confrontation.

[Eduard Shevardnadze] I phoned and if I am not mistaken, it was Goga Khaindrava who answered or, no, it was Ivliane Khaindrava. Ivliane Khaindrava answered and I told him to tell [then Georgian Defence Minister Tengiz] Kitovani that on behalf of the military council, on behalf of the government I categorically forbade him from entering Sukhumi. Well, they told him this, but Mr Kitovani took a decision and said that he would still enter Sukhumi.

---

83   *Tass*, Moscow, 30 June 2004.

84   Rustavi-2, 14 August 2007, English text distributed by *Georgian News Digest*, Georgian Foundation for Strategic and International Studies, Tbilisi, 15 August 2007.

And he did. If our army, our national guard, had not entered Sukhumi, the war might not have started at all.

[Correspondent] So Kitovani did not obey you?

[Shevardnadze] No, he did not. Kitovani did not obey me, because the actual commander-in-chief was Kitovani and not Shevardnadze.

5   *Chechnya*

THE SECOND CAUCASIAN WAR   *94-b + 2nd war*

When the Russian Federal troops crossed the administrative boundaries of Chechnya, a Moscow based weekly entitled its leading article "The Second Caucasian War".[1] For many observers in late 1994, the Russian military intervention in Chechnya aiming to put down the rebellious Caucasian republic recalled fears of an earlier Caucasian War, which erupted in the early 19th century as the Russian armies were expending the borders of the empire to the mountains of the Caucasus. This fear had two dimensions: one was that military confrontation in Chechnya could spread and ignite the entire North Caucasus; the other, that the conflict could last for decades, as in the 19th century.

More than a decade later, the alarmist calls of Russian liberals of the early 1990s seem to be largely justified. The December 1994 invasion led to a 20-month war, with catastrophic consequences, and eventual Russian defeat and withdrawal. Three years of chaos in Chechnya were followed by another invasion, now known as the "Second Chechnya War". Russia's policy of supporting the Kadyrov regime in Chechnya seems to have succeeded in pacifying the resistance there—but at what price! The situation remains precarious in Chechnya and volatile in neighbouring Daghestan, Ingushetia and Kabardino-Balkaria. Repression and guerrilla attacks continue. With the two wars in the Caucasus, the Russian political system itself evolved into a new authoritarian model where political descent and media freedom had no place. In a word, the global result of the war is catastrophic. This war is evidently the most horrific, violent, and long lasting of post-Soviet wars.

---

1   *Moscow News.* No 50, 16-22 December 1994.

Although the war in Chechnya does seem to be a long-term war, it differs from the earlier war there in various ways. No Caucasian alliances came to the support of the Chechens, no inter-ethnic or tribal alliance was set up, nor did other localized rebellions try to imitate the Chechen fight for liberation from Russian rule. In this sense, the "Second Caucasian War" is limited to a Russo-Chechen confrontation. The idea of pan-Caucasian solidarity, of an alliance or even a confederation of mountain peoples, which had much following in the early 1990s, failed to materialize in any political sense after the Russian military invasion in Chechnya. The anti-Russian resistance in the North Caucasus in the 19th century was possible largely because of the imposition of a state structure, especially the Imamate under Sheikh Shamil, giving the resistance the institutional support of a structure going beyond what had previously been a tribal alliance; this permitted long-term resistance. What Imam Shamil succeeded in doing in the early 19th century was not possible for Dudayev and Maskhadov to achieve in the 1990s: to move from resistance to statehood. The wars of the 19th century were a clash between an expanding Russian empire and a resistance that relied on a new ideology and organizational structure that was developed in response in the North Caucasus—the political Islam of the day and the state (Imamate) that it permitted to develop. The contemporary conflicts described in this book are the result of decline; the decline of the Russian power, and its retreat from the South Caucasus and elsewhere, but also the decline of Chechen society and its disintegration: both Russia and Chechnya were part of the USSR, and with its collapse both went through severe social, economic, political dislocation.

This conflict, which was largely caused by the instability due to the Soviet collapse, became in itself an additional source of instability and further disintegration. The war in Chechnya has caused severe problems for neighbouring Daghestan, cutting its communication lines from the rest of the North Caucasus and Russian provinces, and causing waves of security problems, acts of violence and terrorism. The Chechen conflict has also destabilized Ingushetia, pushing it away from Vaynakh[2] unity

---

2   Vaynakh is the common name regrouping the Chechens and the Ingush. The development of a separate Chechen and Ingush identities goes back to the Russian invasion of the North Caucasus in the early 19th century, when a group of elders representing a minority of the Vaynakh accepted Russian rule and later became known as Ingush, while the majority did not recognize Russian rule and

to look for a separate course, and eventually contributing to the Ingush-Osset clashes. The continuous conflict, now lasting over a decade, has led to large scale military operations, terrorist acts, and population displacement that have destabilized the entire North Caucasus and shifted Russian popular perception towards xenophobic attitudes to "blacks" or "peoples with Caucasian features", "Muslims", and other components of *rossiyani*.[3]

Before turning to Chechnya, we need to look at the situation in the North Caucasus in general in the last years of the USSR, and the effect developments in the Transcaucasus[4] were having on the northern part of the region. The conflicts in the North Caucasus have three main sources: the struggle for sovereignty, to upgrade their status and political independence against the central authorities, which brought a radical-nationalist movement to power in Chechnya; the struggle for pan-Caucasian federalism uniting the peoples of the North Caucasus, and separating them from the Russian state; and finally territorial conflicts within the peoples of the North Caucasus that led to separation of the Ingushes from the Chechens in peaceful manner, but to bloodshed among the Ossets and Ingushes.

The parade of sovereignties

The regions of the South Caucasus were not the only area where ethnic groups associated with administrative entities (union republics, autonomous republics, autonomous regions) were mobilizing against the centre of Soviet power to achieve their sovereignty. In 1989-90 similar movements mobilized in Baltic countries, and later in Ukraine and Moldova. In reaction to the desire of the centres of the Union Republics to distance themselves from the Union centre, certain entities mobilized against this movement, fearing to lose their own status and autonomy as

---

became known as Chechen.

3   In Russian there is a distinction between *russky*, meaning ethnic Russian, and *rossiyani*, which includes non-Russian components of the Russian Federation, with multiple ethnic, linguistic, religious and cultural backgrounds.

4   In Soviet times the three republics of Armenia, Azerbaijan and Georgia were called *Zakavkaziya*, translated into English as "Transcaucasus". Since independence, the term "Transcaucasus" has gone out of favour because it contained a Moscow angle (Transcaucasus from Yerevan is what lies behind the Caucasus, and that is Russia!), and it has been replaced by the term "South Caucasus".

a result. For example, ethnic Russians in the Baltic republics, the region of Crimea in Ukraine, and Transnistria (a region of Moldova east of the Dnestr river) all witnessed reactive mobilizations.

The Russian mobilization for sovereignty, the Russian entity's change from supporting a project of a reformed Union to adopting a separatist project, was the decisive and the final blow to the existence of the Soviet Union. For the Russian liberal elite, Gorbachev's policies were leading towards anarchy and chaos, reforms had reached a dead-end, and Russia was facing growing resistance in the republics. Many Russians were weary of supporting and subsidizing the economies of poorer regions of the USSR, such as Central Asia, and argued that economic reforms and modernization in Russia had a better chance if Russian statehood was dissociated from its colonial past. Strong currents within Russia led to the Congress of People's Deputies of the RSFSR adopting a declaration in favour of "sovereignty" as early as in June 1990. The election of Boris Yeltsin as RSFSR President in June 1991 further strengthened Russian "separatist" trends; while in opposition to the head of the Soviet state and the ruling Communist Party, Yeltsin created a dual-state situation pitting Russia against the USSR. This struggle was in a few months to put an end to the tormented history of the Soviet Union.

Yeltsin used the struggle of minorities, non-Russian ethnic groups and the Union Republics against the Soviet centre to achieve his own political aims. In March 1991, before he had been elected President of Russia, he made a statement often quoted since, encouraging sovereignty structures within RSFSR to "take as much sovereignty as they can administer."[5] This was a signal that every political entity within the Russian Federation understood differently, but it created an unmistakable dynamic towards political self-assertion, especially in the central Volga region,[6] and even more so in the North Caucasus.

Not everyone agreed with this strategy. The fate of ethnic Russians left outside the frontiers of the Russian Federation was a major

---

5   John Dunlop, "Russia: Confronting a Loss of Empire", in Ian Bremmer and Ray Taras (eds), *Nations and Politics in the Soviet Successor States*, Cambridge University Press, 1993, p. 53.

6   On the drive for sovereignty in Tatarstan, Bashkortoastan, Chuvashia and Khakassia, see Dmitry Gorenburg, "Regional Separatism in Russia: Ethnic Mobilization or Power Grab?", *Europe-Asia Studies*, Vol. 51, No. 2, March 1999, pp. 245-74.

problem. One Party expert on international affairs, Alexander Tsipko, warned against Russian "sovereignty" which "would eventually lead to the split the historical core of the state", and added: "I understand and support the Balts, who have begun their own struggle for sovereignty. But what gain is there for millions of Russians in striving for independence from Moscow and destroying their own state?"[7] Political developments put an end to this debate, and pronounced a final judgment on the Soviet-Russian competition. The attempted putsch in Moscow in August 1991, and its failure, put an end to the situation of dual power. Yeltsin and his supporters emerged as the core of opposition to the putschists, and once these had failed to receive enough support from the armed forces and failed in their Kafkaesque coup d'état, the choice for Russia's sovereignty ended up imposing itself.

For Moscow, in the months before the collapse of the Soviet system, Chechnya did not emerge as the major problem of secessionism on the Russian territories. A more serious challenge was posed at the time by Tatarstan, an Autonomous Republic with a strategic position on the middle Volga, largely industrialized, with important oil deposits, and sizeable population.[8] In August 1990 the President of Tatarstan, Mentimer Shaimiev, declared the "sovereignty" of the autonomous republic, giving political space for the development of radical nationalist formations, under the umbrella of a "Tatar Public Centre" and other groups, which were calling for the proclamation of Tatarstan's independence.

The contrast between developments in Tatarstan and in Chechnya will help us understand why in one case calls for sovereignty led to redistribution of power between Moscow and a provincial capital, and in another they led to the most bloody of post-Soviet conflicts. Curiously, one can also find many parallels between developments in Groznyy and Moscow, as we will see below.

---

7   Original article in *Izvestia*, 1 October 1991; English translation in *CDSP*, Volume XLIII, No. 39, 30 October 1991, p. 1.

8   Tatarstan has an area of 68,000 square kilometres, with a population of 3,658,000 in 1989, of which 47 per cent were ethnic Tatars and 43 per cent ethnic Russians. Although Tatarstan is situated in the heart of European Russia, to its east lies Bashkortistan, another Autonomous Republic with a titular Turkic speaking nation, and with its southern frontiers not far from the northern borders of Kazakhstan.

Before that, let us have a look at Chechen specificities, and see why Chechnya emerged as the most difficult political issue and the most complex security challenge after the Soviet collapse.

The Chechen trauma

Many authors have looked back to Chechen history to understand this conflict. Very often the Chechen resistance to the Tsarist armies in the 19th century is evoked, and current Russo-Chechen confrontation is pictured as part of a historic process going back three or four hundred years.[9] The first important uprising against the Russian advances to the Caucasus was led by Imam Mansour (Ushurma), a Chechen from the *aul* (village) of Aldi, who led a rebellion from 1785 to 1792, until he was arrested when the Ottoman fortress at Anapa fell to Russian soldiers. He later died in a Russian prison. The three following major Caucasian rebellions were led by non-Chechens: Ghazi Muhammad (1829-32), Hamzat Bek (1832-34), and the legendary Imam Shamil (1834-59), all three Daghestani Avars. Under the banner of Islam, and the leadership of Imam Shamil, Chechen tribes joined the Great Caucasian Rebellion and fought fiercely against the Russian armies, until the defeat and surrender of Shamil in the village of Gunip (in central Daghestan) in 1859. Yet there are vast differences between the conflicts of the 19th century and the wars of the 1990s in the North Caucasus. Although the Chechens formed "the elite of Shamyl's army",[10] the "Caucasian Wars" of the 19th century were a rebellion of a tribal alliance, under the banner of Islam that cemented together the North Caucasian tribes against the expansion and colonial policies of the Russian army.[11] Although the Chechens played an important part in this resistance, they were not

---

9   See for example Marie Benningsen Broxup, *The North Caucasus Barrier,* especially the Introduction; Michael Fredholm, "The Prospect for Genocide in Chechnya and Extremist Retaliation against the West", *Central Asian Survey,* London, 2000, 19 (3/4), pp. 315-27.

10   Lesley Blanch, *The Sabres of Paradise, Conquest and Vengeance in the Caucasus,* London: Tauris Parke Paperbacks, 2004, p. 94.

11   Some authors have given the Chechens the central place in the 19th century Caucasian Wars, going as far as substituting them for various other peoples of the north Caucasus in the war against Russia. See Matei Cazacu, *Au Caucase, Russes et Tchétchènes, Récits d'une guerre sans fin,* Geneva: George Editeur, 1998.

alone: Avars, Dargins, Lezgins, Laks, and other peoples of Daghestan played just as central a role, as did Kabardin, Cherkess, Adyghes and Abkhaz in the west who resisted Russian armies for five years longer following the collapse of the rebellion in the eastern part, and suffered harsher repression.

In contrast, the rebellion of the Chechens under Djokhar Dudayev was part of national mobilization at the moment of the collapse of the USSR. While the Chechen national movement had a lot in common with that of its neighbours in the south—the Armenian, Georgian, Abkhaz and Azeri national movements—it remained largely isolated within the context of the North Caucasus.

A more relevant historic experience for understanding of the Chechen rebellion in 1991 was the 1944 deportation of the entire Chechen population under the orders of Stalin. "To the Chechens, the so-called 'deportation' is the worst catastrophe in their collective memory. It is also the most recent (or was until the war of 1994-96 and the one which started in 1999)," writes Moshe Gammer, a specialist in North Caucasus history.[12] A similar view of the relevance of the 1944 deportations and not the "Great Caucasian War" of the 19th century for understanding of the 1991 Chechen revolution is expressed by Valery Tishkov.[13] Those deportations played an essential role in the construction of new identities in the North Caucasus. The Soviet policy which started with the breaking up of the Gorskii Respublika (Mountain Republic) in 1921, only a year after its formation, by creating administrative structures that separated the mountain peoples on the basis of ethnic division, finally took the form of banishment. In some cases, such as that of the "Meskhet Turks" from south-west Georgia, their national identity was created in exile; the Meskhets were the only group among the eight deported "peoples" who did not have their own autonomous structure prior to the deportations, "since there was no such nation at the time. Only after the deportations were the Meskhetians forged into a nationality from diverse ethnic groups such as the Muslim

---

12   Moshe Gammer, "Nationalism and History: Rewriting the Chechen National Past", in Bruno Coppieters and Michel Huysseune, *Secession, History and the Social Sciences*, Brussels: VUB Brussels University Press, 2002, p. 130.

13   Valery Tishkov, *Chechnya: Life in a War-Torn Society*, Berkeley and Los Angeles: University of California Press, 2004, p. 20-21.

Georgians and Armenians, the Azeri Karapapakhs, the Turkic Kurds, and other Muslim turkicized groups living in the south-western corner of Georgia, known as Meskhetia."[14] Similarly, exile to the steppes of Central Asia and Siberia defined the clear limits between who was a Chechen and who was an Avar; instead of being united by the anti-Russian resistance of the past, they were divided not only by linguistic differences, but also by the fact of one being exiled to Central Asia and the other not. Moreover, after their return from exile in 1957, villages of Akins (or Chechens of Daghestan) occupied by various Daghestani groups since 1944 (mainly by Laks and Avars) were never returned to their previous owners. Since then the issue of return of the land of Akins remains a source of discord between Chechnya and Daghestan.

On Red Army Day, on 23 February 1944, the entire Chechen people, as well as the Ingushes, the Karachais and the Balkars, were forced into trains and trucks, and sent into exile for "treason". Even Chechens serving in the Red Army at the front were arrested and deported. In total, over four hundred thousand of them were deported to Siberia, Kazakhstan, and Kyrgyzstan.[15] The punishment of an entire nation for the presumed crimes of some of its members made some observe that the Stalin regime was practicing "racial politics without the overt concept and ideology of race."[16] Only two decades after the creation of ethno-territorial entities in the North Caucasus, as elsewhere in the USSR, came the forced deportation of entire nations. This led to what some scholars call the "paradox of the last two decades of Stalin's rule: the simultaneous pursuit of nation building and nation destroying."[17] The consequences of the deportations were catastrophic; there are no precise statistics, but it is believed that a quarter of the deported Chechens perished on the road to exile. A Chechen historian, Yavus Akhmadov, writes, "Of the half-million Chechens and Ingush who were sent into

---

14 Isabelle Kreindler, "The Soviet Deported Nationalities: A Summary and an Update", *Soviet Studies*, Vol. 38, No. 3, July 1986, p. 389.

15 In the 1939 Soviet census, 407,690 Chechens were registered.

16 Eric D. Weitz, "Racial Politics Without the Concept: Reevaluating Soviet Ethnic and National Purges", *Slavic Review*, Volume 61, Number 1, Spring 2002, p. 3.

17 Terry Martin, "The Origins of Soviet Ethnic Cleansing", *The Journal of Modern History*, Volume 70, Number 4, December 1998, p. 816.

exile, not even 300,000 were still alive a few years later."[18] Other sources put the number of the Chechens who perished under horrible conditions of transportation (in the back of trucks or in cargo trains), from the harsh conditions in Central Asia where there was no infrastructure ready to receive them, and from the cold and deprivations in the early years following the deportations at over a hundred thousand.[19]

The Chechen generation which led the revolt of the early 1990s was deeply influenced, if not completely conditioned by the experience of deportations and return. Dudayev himself was born in 1944 in Chechnya and grew up in exile in Kazakhstan. Similarly, his comrade-in-arms and successor as President of Chechnya, Yandarbiev, was born in 1952 in Kazakhstan; Aslan Maskhadov, the chief of staff of the Chechen armed forces during the 1994-96 war, later elected President of Chechnya, was born in Kazakhstan in 1951. The deportations, the suffering, and the humiliation made the Chechens feel they were vulnerable and distinguished from others, and had a cause to rebellion.

The deportations were followed by the liquidation of Checheno-Ingush ASSR, the distribution of its land over neighbouring republics, the resettlement of Slavs in the northern lowlands and urban areas and peoples of Caucasian origin in the mountain villages. All traces of the Chechens and the Ingushes were erased, references in publications censored. Most shocking for the Caucasian populations was the use of tombstones for construction purposes, an extreme humiliation for a people and a culture that venerate ancestors and identify *teip* (tribal) belonging as far back as 12 generations. For the Chechen consciousness, the deportations were the most horrific in a series of genocidal acts initiated by Russia to eradicate Chechens physically and culturally. In the contemporary Chechen memory, the massacres by Russian soldiers in Chechen villages during the Great Ghazavat, the deportations that followed the 1859 defeat, the deportations of 1944, and the more contemporary wars were parts of a chain of events in a war of "three hundred years" that continues, a war in which the Russian state has tried to crush

---

18   Quoted in Inga Prelovskaya, "New Data on 1944 Exile of Chechens", *Izvestia*, 12 March 1992; translated into English in *CDPSP*, Volume XLIV, No. 12, p. 17, 22 April 1992.

19   Comité Tchétchénie, *Tchétchénie, Dix clés pour comprendre*, Paris: La Découverte, 2003, p. 25.

the Chechens and resistance and rebellion are seen as the only way to guarantee a future without the danger of annihilation.

One anecdote reveals how deep an impact the deportations left on the Chechens: following the start of the war in Chechnya in 1994, and its catastrophic failure to yield the results expected by the Yeltsin administration, scarcely eight weeks before the presidential elections of 1996, the Russian leadership asked the Chechen resistance leadership to start direct talks to put an end to the war. The Chechens could have rejected this and chosen to support the Communist Party candidate Zyuganov, with the fair assumption that this could be an effective move because the war was a major source of public dissatisfaction with the Yeltsin regime and opinion polls gave Zyuganov real chances for victory. Yet, they decided to give a positive response to the talks, and here is one interpretation as to why:

> Here is the most curious part of the scheme because effectively, by agreeing to talks, the Chechen rebels are endorsing Yeltsin for re-election. The Chechen commander [Aslan Maskhadov, the chief of Chechen General Staff] explained this by saying he could never trust the communists for what they had done to his people, especially the deportation of the entire Chechen nation to Central Asia in 1944.[20]

The Chechen revolution

What distinguished Chechnya from Tatarstan and many other autonomous entities striving for "self-determination" was that in August-September 1991 a revolution took place in Chechnya, and a radical Chechen political formation overthrew the local Soviet authorities by force and took command in the republic. This revolution was unlike the power transfer in Armenia or Georgia, where the local Communist elite abandoned power as a result of growing popular mobilization in support of the national movements through parliamentary elections; it conditioned the Chechen-Russian relations that led to violent confrontation.[21]

---

20   Thomas de Waal, "Chechnya talks set to avoid sovereignty", *The Moscow Times*, 25 May 1996.

21   For detailed description of the Chechen Revolution, see Marie Benningsen Broxup, "After the Putsch, 1991", in Marie Benningsen Broxup (ed.), *The North Caucasus Barrier, The Russian Advance towards the Muslim World*, Lon-

As we have seen earlier, much of the struggle between the centre and the ethnic territories happened parallel to the weakening of the Soviet regime and the Gorbachev-Yeltsin struggle for power. In 1990, as it became evident that the Soviet Union could no longer be reformed even at the rapid pace of *perestroika*, various projects with different visions about what could replace the USSR clashed. While Gorbachev continued to insist on a reformed federation of republics replacing the Soviet Union, Boris Yeltsin put forward the idea of sovereign Russia and the dissolution of the USSR, thus undermining Gorbachev's authority and also undermining central rule. In this struggle Yeltsin encouraged political independence for the union republics. For Yeltsin and Russian democrats, this was not just a cynical way to get rid of Gorbachev and take power, but to a large degree reflected genuine belief that Russia had no other choice but to get rid of the heavy Soviet heritage if it wanted to become a "normal" nation and integrate into the Western world. Nevertheless, a bitter power struggle developed in which the Russian democrats encouraged sovereignty for the Union Republics while Gorbachev tried to stir trouble to Yeltsin by encouraging the autonomous republics within the RSFSR, such as Tatarstan and Chechnya, to achieve more self-rule. As the struggle reached a dramatic height with the attempted putsch of August 1991, internal political life in Chechnya was boiling and ready to explode.

In this period, the Chechens were living a new kind of national self-assertion. Since the return of the Chechens and the Ingushes from deportation in 1957-58, the Autonomous Republic had been under strict Russian rule. Yet Russian presence in the republic was weakening: between 1979 and 1989, while the ethnic Chechen population of the Autonomous Republic increased by 20.1 per cent, the ethnic Russian population decreased by 12.6 per cent.[22] In 1989, the candidacy of Nikolai Semyonov, a party cadre from Groznyy, to succeed another ethnic Russian, the republic's party chief Vladimir Foteyev, met resistance from ethnic Chechen and Ingush members of the local party. As a

---

don: Hurst, Second Edition, 1996, pp. 219-40; see also Flemming Splidsboel-Hansen, "The 1991 Chechen Revolution: the Response of Moscow", in *Central Asian Survey*, Vol. 13, No. 3, 1994, pp. 395-407, and Valery Tishkov, *Ethnicity, Nationalism and Conflict in and After the Soviet Union*, pp. 198-206.

22   L.A. Belyaeva (ed.), *Chechenski Krisiz*, Moscow: Tsentr Kompleksnikh Sotsialnikh Issledovanyi i Marketinga, 1995, p. 9.

result Doku Zavgayev, an ethnic Chechen party cadre, and a descendent of two important Chechen *teips*, became the new party leader. This led to popular celebrations in Groznyy and elsewhere in the republic, for in contemporary memory it was the first time an ethnic Chechen had acceded to such a high post. Yet Zavgayev, a career party cadre, was not well equipped to cope with the shifting political forces in the republic, and he was to make way for two other ethnic Chechens who were also rising to prominence. One was the Soviet air force pilot Djokhar Dudayev, who had received the rank of army General, the first ethnic Chechen who reached such a post in the Soviet armed forces. The second was Ruslan Khasbulatov,[23] an economy professor and close collaborator of Yeltsin, who was elected to the Russian parliament in 1990.

Rapid growth of political activity led to the formation of a number of new, unregistered political parties. The first among them was the Vaynakh Democratic Party, created by a poet and schoolteacher, Zelimkhan Yandarbiev, in 1990.[24] Another organization was called the Islamic Path and was led by a former officer of the Interior Ministry forces, Beslan Gantemirov; it was a paramilitary structure that later evolved into armed units self-proclaimed as the "National Guard". The new political formations came together in the first National Congress of the Chechen People, held on 25 November 1990 in the Chechen capital, where over a thousand delegates attended. Among the organizers were figures who later played key roles in the historic developments, including Yandarbiev and Gantemirov, Yusup Soslambekov, who later became the leader of the Caucasus Peoples' Confederation, and Yaragi Mamodayev, a rich businessman who financed much of the activities of the Congress in those early days. Djokhar Dudayev was among many guests invited from abroad, including the Chechen Diaspora in Turkey and Jordan, to attend and take part in the debates. A resolution was adopted focusing on ending discrimination against Chechens, on ter-

---

23   Khasbulatov also played a key role in Russian politics, as he became a close associate of Yeltsin in 1990-91 and served as Deputy Speaker and later Speaker of the Russian Parliament, before becoming one of his arch-rivals, by joining Vice-President Alexandr Rutskoi in the legislative struggle with Yeltsin that led to the October 1993 power struggle.

24   Zelimkhan Yandarbiev was later elected Vice-President of Chechnya, and became acting president after the assassination of Dudayev in 1996. He himself was killed in a car bomb in Doha, the capital of Qatar, on 13 February 2004.

ritorial disputes with neighbouring Daghestan, and on the need to re-store the Ingush Republic, separate from Chechnya.[25] In line with other national formations which had already developed in the Transaucasus (Armenian National Movement, Azerbaijani Popular Front, Georgian National Congress), and now developing among the peoples of the North Caucasus including the Cossacks, the first Chechen National Congress also adopted resolutions for the preservation of the national language and culture, as well as furthering of religious education. The conclusions of this congress were not especially radical in their context, but its significance was in the creation of a political movement with a large base in Chechnya autonomous from the official institutions. The Congress also took a leaf from Soviet practice in historiography, by publicly demanding that the local historian Vitaly Vinogradov, the au-thor of a concept on "voluntary union" between Chechnya and Rus-sia, should be stripped of his prizes and even his "citizenship" of the republic.[26]

The second National Congress of the Chechen People (NCCP) was held in July 1991, and witnessed further radicalization. The Congress proclaimed its executive committee to be the only legitimate state insti-tution in the republic, very much in the spirit of the Georgian Nation-al Congress two years earlier, and declared its intention to "separate" Chechnya from both the USSR and the RSFSR.[27] It also elected Du-dayev as its president. Dudayev, a Chechen who had spent most of his life outside the republic, with a career in the Soviet military establish-ment that could only inspire respect from ordinary Chechens, was the best suited person to guide such a political movement. The "alternative" political structure was now mobilized and armed with resolve at a time when the Soviet leadership in Moscow seemed unable to handle simi-lar revolts in the Transcaucasus and the Baltic states, and Gorbachev's project to create a new federation was failing to mobilize support. In a short few months the political situation in the republic had polarized

[margin handwritten note: Dudayev elected as president in 91.]

25 Valery Tishkov, *Chechnya: Life in a War-Torn Society*, London: University of California Press, 2004, p. 58.

26 Carlotta Gall and Thomas de Waal, *Chechnya, A Small Victorious War*, London: Pan Original, 1997, p. 82; Tishkov, op. cit., p. 59.

27 Emil Payin and Arkady Popov, "Chechnya", in Jeremy Azrael and Emil Payin (eds), *US and Russian Policymaking with Respect to the Use of Force*, Santa Mon-ica, CA: RAND, 1996; Tishkov, op. cit., p. 60.

to extremes, and needed a single spark to ignite a revolution. The Soviet and Russian Federation leaders in Moscow, preoccupied with even more dramatic changes, hardly noticed the events developing in this far away Caucasian province.

The putsch attempt in Moscow, here too, was the spark that transformed the historical trajectory.[28] Zavgayev was in Moscow during the events, and made a public declaration in support of the coup. In Groznyy, Dudayev and the militants of the National Congress called for disobedience and strikes to oppose the coup. As it became clear that the coup was failing, thousands of people came to support the few who had earlier gathered in the main square of Groznyy. The failure of the coup did not put an end to mobilization in Groznyy; on the contrary, the taste of victory created a euphoric feeling and the movement took a new dynamism. The leadership of the National Congress wanted to put an end to the local leadership of Zavgayev, discredited for having supported the failed putsch. It saw itself as the legitimate leadership of Chechnya, representing the wishes and opinions dominant in Chechnya at this historic moment. On 22 August 1991, the newly formed armed volunteers loyal to the National Congress took over the local television building, and later the radio station, as well as the offices of the Council of Ministers. The local law enforcement forces, the KGB and the MVD, lacking orders from their superiors in Moscow,[29] did not interfere or show any signs of resistance. Both politically and militarily, the road was open for a change in power. On 1 September 1991, the leaders of the National Congress declared the local Supreme Soviet dissolved. As the local authorities refused to be disbanded, the armed wing of the National Congress, the National Guard, attacked the building of the Supreme Soviet, on 6 September.

Khasbulatov flew to Groznyy on 14 September, and took part the next day in the meeting of the local Supreme Soviet during which the

---

28   The August 1991 events precipitated the Karabakh conflict into an open war, and led to political crisis in Tbilisi where the authority of Gamsakhurdia was challenged by the armed Georgian opposition, leading to the civil war of December 1991-January 1992.

29   The Speaker of the Russian Supreme Soviet, preoccupied with bringing down pro-Gorbachev loyalists in Chechnya, had ordered local law enforcement forces not to intervene against the National Movement militants.

ruling body in the republic declared itself dissolved.[30] A Provisional Supreme Soviet was set up with 32 members to supervise new elections planned for November. A deal seems to have been agreed between Khasbulatov and Dudayev, to get rid of the old party bureaucracy in Chechnya. The role of the Russian leadership was key to the outcome of the struggle in the Groznyy streets: the Yeltsin leadership supported the Chechen National Congress to get rid of Doku Zavgayev, seen as a rival provincial leader allied with Gorbachev and the Yanaev-led putschists. A Provisional Supreme Soviet was set up to organize new legislative elections. One Russian analyst wrote later about the role played by Ruslan Khasbulatov that he "had done more than the others to bring Dudayev to power in the hopes to lean on him as his own deputy in Chechnya, also miscalculated and was later branded as a 'traitor to the Chechen nation'".[31]

But the militants of the National Congress did not intend to be dictated to by Moscow. Soon, the militancy of the Chechens in the streets of Groznyy, and the radical declarations of their leadership, alarmed Moscow. Their "democratic" ally did not behave according to the rules of the game fixed by Moscow. The NCCP activists continued their armed assaults on government buildings and took control of the local KGB headquarters, increasing their arsenal of light weapons. This last act alarmed the new head of the Russian KGB, Viktor Ivanenko, who flew to Groznyy in the company of the Russian Vice-President Alexandr Rutskoy. After the meeting, Rutskoy declared that he was afraid "that Chechen-Ingushetiya will become a second Karabakh".[32] The meeting did not produce the results desired by Moscow, which were the return the KGB building and the stolen weapons and the transfer of the leadership of the republic to the Provisional Supreme Soviet.

A cascade of events starting with the putsch in Moscow and a fight against the Communist party bureaucracy in Checheno-Ingushetia soon evolved into an anti-Russian struggle for the independence of Chechnya. Both for the Chechen nationalists of the NCCP and for the new

30   Flemming Splidsboel-Hansen, "The 1991 Chechen Revolution: the Response of Moscow", *Central Asian Survey*, 13 (3), 1994, p. 396.

31   Emil Payin, "Chechnya and Other Conflicts in Russia", *International Affairs*, Moscow, Vol. 44, No. 6, 1998, p. 154.

32   "'Revolutionary' Events in Chechen-Ingushetiya", *Tass*, 6 October 1991.

leadership in Moscow, Dudayev seemed a good alternative to the corrupt party bureaucracy in Groznyy. For Yandarbiev and Gantemirov, the general who had spent all his career outside the republic and belonged to a minor Chechen *teip,* seemed to be the ideal leader they needed to mobilize the Chechen people, traditionally divided around clan allegiances, around a charismatic leader, whom they thought they could control. For the Yeltsin leadership and Moscow Chechens such as Khasbulatov and Salambek Khajiev, Minister of Chemical Industries in the last Soviet cabinet and one of the two ministers who condemned the August putsch, Dudayev talked like a democrat; he seemed resolved to oppose the local bureaucracy, and his past career in the Soviet army and his ethnic-Russian wife seemed enough restraints from developing into a Chechen nationalist hero. The genie was now out of the bottle. Dudayev did not play the role others projected onto him, but went further in writing his own script.

Dudayev and the Executive Committee of the NCCP pushed to disband the Provisional Council and organize early elections. On 27 October 1991 elections were organized and Dudayev was declared the new President of Chechnya. According to Chechen figures 72 per cent of the electorate voted, with Dudayev receiving 90 per cent of the votes. The Kremlin contested both the legitimacy of the elections and the results, saying that there had been only a small turnout, 10-12 per cent of the voters.[33] Five days after the elections Dudayev declared Chechnya an independent republic, in line with the positions expressed within the Chechen National Congress, but an open act of defiance of Moscow.

In Moscow there was a fear that Russia might follow the fate of the USSR, that ethnic conflicts would cause the collapse of the Russian Federation. Rutskoy clearly expressed these fears in an interview after his return from Groznyy: "What has happened recently, so to speak, is particularly incomprehensible. Why? Because, when I met Dudayev, he told me very clearly that the independent Islamic Chechen state is not a part of the Russian Federation, nor of the USSR."[34] Rutskoi also

---

33   Sebastian Smith, *Allah's Mountains, The Battle for Chechnya*, London: I.B. Tauris, 2001, p. 127.

34   In an interview given to Russian Television on 9 October 1991, reported by *BBC Summary of World Broadcasts*, "Vice-President Rutskoy interviewed on Chechen-Ingushetiya", 11 October 1991.

warned against the policy of Yeltsin, who had advocated finding compromise in Chechnya and in the 16 other autonomous republics of the Russian Federation; he criticized this policy as "giving out sovereignty" to ethnic regions.[35]

On 8 November the Russian President declared a state of emergency in Chechnya, and dispatched up to 2,500 Interior Ministry and KGB troops to Groznyy. But those forces could not move out of the Groznyy airport, where they were besieged by demonstrations of several thousand people, some armed with automatic weapons, while downtown Groznyy witnessed further demonstrations of up to 50,000 people.[36] The Russian parliament overwhelmingly voted against a military solution to the Chechen crisis, and the troops were called back from the Caucasus.[37] The first military showdown between Moscow and Groznyy was avoided by a Russian retreat, at least for the moment. Chechnya was out of the control of the new Russian authorities, a *de facto* independent, albeit unrecognized state-project.

[handwritten: Close call in '91]

Territorial conflicts: Prigorodnyi Rayon and the Osset-Ingush War

Rebellion against the central authorities in Moscow was not the only source of conflicts in the North Caucasus. As in the Transcaucasus, numerous territorial conflicts pitted one nation against another; according to one count, in the early 1990s there were "at least 20 actual or potential disputes in the North Caucasus region."[38] But while in the Transcaucasus those territorial conflicts were the result of border fixing in the early Soviet era (in Karabakh for example), in the North Caucasus there was an additional acute problem arising from the 1944 mass deportations of "punished" peoples.[39] After the "pardon" of those peoples by

[handwritten: transcaucasus: early soviet border fixing > foundation of problem.]

35 Deborah Seward, "Russia threatens blockade of defiant Muslim region", *Associated Press*, Groznyy, 14 November 1991.

36 *New York Times*, "Enclave resists Russian crackdown", 10 November 1991.

37 AFP, 11 November 1991.

38 Anna Matveeva, "Territorial Claims in the North Caucasus", in Martin Pratt and Janet Allison Brown, *Borderlands Under Stress,* The Hague: Kluwer Law International, 2000, p. 297.

39 Other "punished peoples" included Koreans, who were deported from their historic regions in the Far East as early as 1937, and the Volga Germans, the Crimean Tatars, the Meskhets, and the Kalmyks.

Khrushchev in 1957 they could return from exile, to homelands where either new Russian migrants or peoples from neighbouring regions had taken over villages and fields, which had to be emptied and returned back to their original owners. Yet certain territories were not returned; for example the Novolakski Rayon in Daghestan, initially inhabited by ethnic Chechens, was occupied by Laks and Avars of Daghestan; certain originally Balkar villages were kept by Kabardin, and the Prigorodnyi Rayon of North Ossetia was not returned to the Ingushes. The resulting land conflicts continue to poison the relations between various ethnic groups in the North Caucasus. Moreover, the Balkars complained of the domination of the Kabardin over the republican leadership posts, concentrating most of the resources in their hands. "In 1991 the Balkars decided to create their own autonomous republic within the Russian Federation, but the central authorities refused to study the case", according to Sofyan Bipayev, the leader of the National Council of the Balkar People.[40]

Another source of territorial conflict was the division of ethnic groups as a result of the emergence of international borders dividing the Caucasus into two: Russia in the north and Georgia and Azerbaijan in the south. As we have already seen, the Ossets found themselves divided; in the north there was the North Osset Autonomous Republic which made part of the Russian Federation, and in the south the former South Osset Autonomous Region, which was one of the major sources of the Georgian-Osset conflict. Another people divided into two as a result of the new international frontiers were the Lezgins. A Caucasian people speaking an east Caucasian language, they were living in southern Daghestan and in north-eastern Azerbaijan. A Lezgin national movement formed in 1990 called Sadval (Unity), especially active in Daghestan, called for the creation of a Lezgin autonomous structure bringing together Lezgin-inhabited lands in southern Daghestan and northern Azerbaijan, as an entity within the Russian Federation.[41] The movement did not mobilize enough support and its importance declined from the mid-1990s.

---

40   Author interview with Sofyan Bipanyev, Nalchik, 15 May 1995.

41   "The Lezgins: A Situation Assessment", *International Alert,* London 1997, pp. 14-15.

The North Caucasus was divided into ethnically based entities after the dissolution of the Mountain Republic in the early 1920s. Daghestan was an exception, with its over 30 ethnic groups. North Ossetia had its one titular nation giving its name to the republic, while there was a strange mixture in the Karachayevo-Cherkess and Kabardino-Balkar ASSRs, which were combinations of Turkic peoples living in the mountainous regions (the Karachays and the Balkars), and Adyghe peoples living in the plains (the Cherkess and the Kabardin). Checheno-Ingushetia was composed of two related peoples belonging to the Vaynakh nation, differing in tribe and dialect.

The conflict between Ossets and Ingushes is a contemporary one resulting from the 1944 deportations and their consequences. The territorial units of North Ossetia and Ingushetia were first defined in the early 1920s when the Gorskaya Respublika was finally dissolved in 1924. The Prigorodnyi Rayon was in Ingushetia, while Vladikavkaz[42] was the capital of both republics: one bank of the Terek River was the Ingush part, while the North Ossetians had the other for their capital. In 1934 Ingushetia was merged with Chechnya, the Checheno-Ingush Autonomous SSR being created in 1936. In both cases the contested territory remained with the Ingushes until their mass deportation in 1944. Several thousand Ossets from South Ossetia and elsewhere in Georgia were forced to move to villages emptied after the deportation of the Ingushes. After their return in 1957, the Checheno-Ingush ASSR was restored, but the Prigorodnyi Rayon—with an area of 978 square kilometres—was left out and stayed within North Ossetia. Instead, three regions of Stavropol Krai were added to the Checheno-Ingush ASSR. Yet the Ingush tried desperately to return to Vladikavkaz or to their villages of origin in Prigorodnyi Rayon. The North Osset authorities did all they could to limit the Ingush return by using administrative restrictions, such as freezing the issuing of *propiska* (residency permit), and applying a policy of discrimination against the Ingushes in jobs and education.

---

42   Vladikavkaz, which literally means "rule the Caucasus" in Russian, was one of the first Russian fortresses in the North Caucasus, built in 1784. It had a significant strategic importance, being the starting point of the Caucasian Military Highway, which crossed the mountains and ended up at Tbilisi. In 1931 the city was named Ordzhonikidze, after Georgian Bolshevik leader Sergo Ordzhonikidze, and regained its first name shortly before the collapse of USSR.

Discrimination led to tensions and explosions. In 1973 a demonstration erupted in Groznyy, then still the "capital" of the Checheno-Ingush Autonomous Republic, and lasted four days, demanding the return of the Prigorodnyi Rayon to the Ingushes.[43] For the Ossets, a region situated on the eastern suburbs of their capital Ordzhonikidze (now Vladikavkaz) was impossible to relinquish, and for the Ingushes, a region where old and important cemeteries were found was impossible to forget. Tension rose again in 1981, leading to clashes between the two communities in Prigorodnyi Rayon, and calmed down only after the intervention of Interior Ministry troops.

In the age of independent political movements, the Ingushes naturally mobilized around the cause that troubled them most, the situation in Prigorodnyi Rayon. Niiskho (Justice) was the first among several political organizations that were formed, which made the return of the territories central to their platform. But what gave boost to Ingush mobilization was a law "On the Rehabilitation of Repressed People" that the Russian Supreme Soviet passed in April 1991. The law intended to render justice to the various ethnic groups that had suffered deportations under Stalin, but also to Cossacks repressed by the Bolsheviks in the early 1920s, including territorial compensations. But the law failed to establish precise procedures for the promised compensation, and what to do with people living on contested territories. This law created hope among the Ingushes who were left to think that Moscow finally supported their demands; both Yeltsin and Rutskoy, on separate occasions, promised to Ingush public meetings to implement the law as soon as possible.[44] On the other hand it caused alarm among the Ossets, and had the effect of sharpening the already tense relations to a dangerous degree. As one report puts it, "[t]he Ingush contend that the law itself is good, but that North Ossetia's militant behavior made it a dead letter…"[45] Ossets, while agreeing to discuss the return of Ingushes to their villages of origin, refused territorial change; Yuri Biragov, Deputy Chairman of the Osset Supreme Soviet, was on the record declar-

---

43　Alexandre Grigoriantz, *La montagne du sang, histoire, rites et coutumes des peuples montagnards du Caucase*, Geneva: Editions George, 1998, p. 256.

44　Irina Dementyeva, "A people lost", *Moscow News*, 26 February 1992.

45　"The Ingush-Ossetian Conflict in the Prigorodnyi Region", New York: Human Rights Watch/Helsinki, 1996, p. 20.

ing: "Ossetia will put up with any law that does not presuppose border changes."[46]

The conflict in South Ossetia aggravated even further the situation in Pregorodnyi Rayon. Up to 100,000 ethnic Ossets fled Georgia, most finding refuge in North Ossetia, and particularly in villages in Prigorodnyi Rayon where most had relatives because of the 1944 forced resettlement. Those refugees had gone through traumatic experiences and were in a desperate situation. Many of them played key roles in the violent events that followed.

Another catalyst of the clashes was the Chechen Revolution. In the Checheno-Ingush Autonomous Republic the Ingushes were a minority,[47] and as the Chechens' nationalism awoke they took over key posts from ethnic Russians, and in the process marginalized even further the Ingush minority.[48] The Chechen national movement, embodied by the National Congress of the Chechen People, did not seek to accommodate the interests of the Ingushes, and created a dynamism of ethnic separation. When the Chechen revolution broke out the Ingushes did not share its aims, did not want a confrontation with Moscow, and were forced still more to look for their separate way. Promises from the Russian leadership to compensate for the territorial losses of the repressed peoples played an important role in Ingush aloofness towards Chechen anti-Russian militancy; on the other hand Chechen radicalism posed the question of separation between the Chechens and the Ingushes and the creation of an Ingush republic, and thus the territorial issue was put strongly on the agenda. The three Ingush-inhabited regions to the west of the Checheno-Ingush ASSR, Nazran, Malgobek, and Sunzha, declined to join the Chechen drive for independence, and in June 1992 the Supreme Soviet of the Russian Federation founded the Republic of Ingushetia as part of the Russian Federation, but without defined borders. At this stage both the Ingushes and the Ossets started to arm

---

46   Lyudmila Leontyeva, "Another Autonomous Republic inside Russia", *Moscow News*, 21 June 1992.

47   According to the last Soviet census (1989), the Checheno-Ingush Republic had 1,290,000 inhabitants, of whom 52.9 per cent were ethnic Chechens, 29.1 per cent Russians, and 11.7 per cent Ingushes.

48   Valery Tishkov, *Ethnicity, Nationalism and Conflict in and After the Soviet Union*, SAGE, 1997, p. 163.

themselves, and skirmishes between the two groups and sporadic killings increased.

The situation exploded on 31 October 1992, when armed Ingush groups from Ingushetia attacked the village of Chermen, with a mixed Osset-Ingush population, in the northern part of Prigorodnyi Rayon.[49] Violent clashes erupted in the next days among Osset and Ingush villages, and in less than a week over 500 people were killed and the Ingush inhabitants of North Ossetia were expelled, with the exception of one village.[50] South Ossetian armed formations showed particular brutality during the clashes, deliberately destroying Ingush houses and villages. The Russian authorities played a negative role; at the outbreak of the hostilities, the Russian Interior Ministry transferred arms to the North Ossetian authorities, which were later distributed to the North Ossetian police and illegal paramilitaries. When the clashes started Russian forces intervened to repress Ingush armed resistance, but did not oppose military action from the Osset side, leading to the expulsion of between 34,000 and 64,000 Ingushes from North Ossetian territory.[51] This was the first, massive bloodshed on the territory of the Russian Federation after the break-up of the USSR.

The Osset-Ingush confrontation and the Russian military intervention there once again brought the North Caucasus to the precipice of war. Russian Interior Ministry (MVD) troops deployed to stop the clashes entered Ingushetia, reaching territories claimed by the Chechen authorities in Groznyy. Dudayev warned Moscow not to expand its deployment over Chechen territory: "Russia must not forget where the Chechen borders are", he threatened, otherwise "both Nazran and Vladikavkaz will blow up."[52] Chechen military forces were put on alert.

---

49   Serge Schmemann, "Russian troops arrive as Caucasus flares up", *New York Times*, 11 November 1992.

50   According to the Human Rights Watch quoted above, the clashes led to 583 confirmed deaths, Ingush and 192 Osset, and by 1994 over 200 people were still missing.

51   Vicken Cheterian, "North Ossetia: Under the Volcano", *Swiss Review of World Affairs*, Zurich, May 1994. Different estimates of the number of the displaced depend on the different sources: Osset sources have put the number of the Ingush displaced at 34,000, while Ingush sources have mentioned the higher number.

52   "Osset-Ingush Conflict – Details", Itar-Tass, Moscow, 10 November 1992.

The Caucasus People's Confederation (KNK) made a similar threat of sending detachments of Caucasian volunteers in case Russian forces invaded Chechnya. War seemed inevitable. But once again Moscow backed down, when Yeltsin ordered Russian troops back to Ingush territories.[53]

To conclude, one can make a number of remarks on the Osset-Ingush conflict. First, the Ingush desire to return to their lands of origin was mass driven, and opposed by the North Ossetia administration which tried to fight this by administrative and sometimes repressive policies. Second, the Osset-Ingush clashes might not have happened—at least not in the violent explosion that occurred in October 1992—without two other conflicts: a hundred thousand Ossets fled from Georgia, and the Chechen conflict with Russia led to the exclusion of Ingushes from the administrative framework in which had been included since 1957. And third, there was the shifting nature of Russian statehood, and the impact of its policies in the Caucasus region. Between April 1991 and October 1992 the Russian leadership changed profoundly. The law "On the Rehabilitation of Repressed People" reflected an attempt to correct past prejudices, albeit in a clumsy, disorganized manner that led to more tragedies rather than correcting past ills. In late 1992 the Russian leadership was no more preoccupied with moral questions, but rather with how to restore its rule over a potentially explosive borderland of new Russia, and manipulation of inter-ethnic conflicts, "divide and rule" policies, and even outright military intervention were among the possible means. For the second time the Yeltsin leadership renounced using force thinking that it was not yet the right moment to do so.

The Confederation of Peoples of the Caucasus

A third force that was taking form in this time, aiming at political and territorial change, was the Confederation of Peoples of the Caucasus, known as KNK. This movement was a contemporary reflection of the former Gorski Respublika, and aimed at the creation of a large confederal structure for the mountain peoples of the northern Caucasus, stretching from the Black to the Caspian Sea. The KNK simultaneously

---

53   Fiona Hill, *"Russia's Tinderbox", Conflict in the North Caucasus and its Implementation for the Future of the Russian Federation*, Strengthening Democratic Institutions Project, Harvard University, September 1995, p. 84.

looked back to the past and projected a certain vision of a future: its aim was to revive a unity of Caucasian nations, similar to the Gorski Respublika of the early 1920s, incorporating Daghestan, Chechnya, Ingushetia, Ossetia, Kabardino-Balkaria, Karachai-Cherkessia, Adyghe and Abkhazia, with Sukhumi its capital.[54] The KNK expected further decrease of Russian power in the North Caucasus, permitting the emergence of a federal structure and eventually a sovereign state independent from Moscow.[55]

The founding conference of this movement was held in Sukhumi in August 1989, bringing together political movements representing thirteen ethnic groups in the North Caucasus. Here the Assembly of Mountain Peoples of the Caucasus was established. At its second conference in Nalchik in October 1990, the organization changed its name to the Confederation of Peoples of the Caucasus (Russian initials KNK). Musa Shanibov, a former history professor from Nalchik, and a Kabardin national movement activist, was elected its president. At the Nalchik conference the KNK declared itself the legal successor of the 1918 Mountain Republic, and called for its restoration.[56] Thus the KNK aimed to establish a "state" from territories of what still was the Soviet Union, territories that were soon to be divided among two separate states, most being in the Russian Federation, while Abkhazia was in Georgia. Both Moscow and Tbilisi took the threat of the Confederation seriously, and Moscow tried to limit its influence by creating parallel inter-ethnic organizations, directed by figures loyal to the Kremlin.

At its second conference the KNK developed two institutions; the first was the "Caucasian Parliament" in which 16 of the North Caucasus ethnic groups were represented, each group having three seats, and it was headed by Yusup Soslanbekov, a Chechen militant who would later play a key role in the Chechen revolution. The second was a "defence committee", organized from volunteers from various regions of the Caucasus, the armed branch of the movement. The vision of the KNK leadership was to establish a multi-ethnic Caucasian state: accord-

---

54   Arkady Popov, "'Wild geese' in the Caucasus", *Moscow News*, 8 November 1992.

55   Vakhtang Dzhanashiya, "No problems with weapons over here", *Russian Press Digest*, 2 September 1992.

56   Fiona Hill, "Russia's Tinderbox", op. cit., p. 26.

ing to Musa Shanibov, the aim was to transform the KNK: "from the confederation of peoples we want to advance towards confederation of states."[57]

But after the collapse of the USSR and the spread of inter-ethnic conflicts, the KNK proclaimed a different role by creating a new structure, the Committee of National Accord, to keep inter-ethnic peace and regional stability. According to Shanibov:

The Confederation has internal contradictions on the ground of nationalism. Nationalism has brought the struggle for the definition of national borders, and the return of lost territories. The Osset-Ingush conflict created a passage to introduce the Transcaucasus syndrome to the North Caucasus. From Derbent to Sukhumi, the creation of the house of the Caucasian peoples will make borders irrelevant.[58]

The KNK was however full of romantic idealists with little political experience and contradictory ambitions. It did not play any visible role until the Georgian National Guard invaded Abkhazia. Many North Caucasian ethnic groups, such as the Adyghes, Kabardin and Cherkess, are related to the Abkhaz. As a result, mass mobilization took place from the early days of the Abkhazia war, and several thousand KNK volunteers travelled through mountain passes to join the struggle. According to media reports, 3-5,000 Caucasian volunteers joined the Abkhaz forces in the autumn of 1992. The Caucasian volunteers played a highly important role in the military developments in the Georgian-Abkhaz war. For Shanibov and many in the KNK, the war in Abkhazia was a Russian imperial war against indigenous Caucasian peoples, carried out by Georgians. "Today, young folks of the Caucasus peoples, including Russians and Cossacks are valiantly trying to prevent genocide by the two empires - Russia and Georgia - against a 100,000-strong nation,"[59] said Shanibov in an interview.

Moscow was alarmed by the increasing capacity of the KNK to mobilize and the radicalization of its discourse. The arrest of Shanibov was arranged in Nalchik, the capital of Kabardino-Balkaria, in late September 1992. As Shanibov was being transferred to a police facility in Rostov-

---

57   Author interview with Musa Shanibov, Sukhumi, 21 April 1994.

58   Ibid.

59   *BBC Summary of World Broadcasts*, 14 July 1993.

on-Don, demonstrations organized by the Congress of Kabardin People gathered over 30,000 demonstrators in central Nalchik. Valery Kokov, the President of Kabardino-Balkaria, introduced emergency rule in the republic on 26 September, and federal troops surrounded the crowd in Nalchik. This did not calm the situation, as some militants tried to storm the local television building and attacked the airport. The clashes led to 40 victims. Another revolution on the Chechen model seemed in the making in Kabardino-Balkaria.[60] During negotiations between local opposition leaders and Kokov, Kabardin militants demanded the lifting of the state of emergency, the withdrawal of troops and the release of Shanibov. On 28 September the Russian authorities declared that Shanibov had "escaped" from detention, and he arrived in Nalchik the same evening to address to the crowd, after which the situation calmed down in the capital of Kabardino-Balkaria.[61]

At the end of the next month, when clashes started between Ossets and Ingushes (31 October 1992), the KNK took a neutral position in this conflict. When Russian troops approached Chechen territory, it made threatening declarations of mobilizing volunteers in case of a Russian invasion of Chechnya. But when the real Russian invasion took place in December 1994, the KNK was already in a period of decline and failed to come to the assistance of the Chechen resistance, as we will see later. There can be different explanations for this: the first is that there is a huge difference between mobilizing volunteers living in the territories of the Russian Federation against Georgian irregular forces and doing the same against the Russian armies. Many political movements such as national movements of the Adyghes or Avars in Daghestan have easily mobilized for the first cause, and refrained from doing so in the Chechnya war. Second, many North Caucasian ethnic groups were ready to come to the assistance of the Abkhaz, hoping that the liberation of Sukhumi would give them access to the sea and direct contacts with Turkey with its large Caucasian Diaspora, while for many Chechnya did not have a similar geographical importance. Third, many

60   Lyudmila Leonteva, "The Chechen scenario in Kabarda?" *Moscow News*, 1 October 1992.

61   Natalya Pachegina, *Nezavisimaya Gazeta*, 30 September 1992; English translation in *Current Digest of Post-Soviet Press* (CDPSP), Vol. XLIV, No. 39, p. 6, 28 October 1992.

why other Caucasun volunteers were down to help in Abkhazia but not so much in Chechnya.

peoples of the North Caucasus feared the Chechens, and did not like the idea of replacing Russian rule with the domination of the Chechens over the region. Most important, the Confederation was formed in a special period of euphoric discovery of independent political mobilization, in the last years of Soviet collapse, when utopian ideas were needed. This mobilized force was instrumentalised in the war in Abkhazia, against the Georgian forces. In December 1994 political realities had changed, the popular support for national movements was in free fall, and the Confederation itself was a used force. The war in Chechnya declared the end of the romantic idealism of Caucasian unity. After a rapid increase in strength the KNK weakened following the victory in Abkhazia, and with the start of the Chechnya war, it became "impotent as a military and political power in the North Caucasus."[62]

Chechnya under Dudayev, 1992-94

Euphoria was high after the success of the Chechen Revolution, and seeing Soviet/Russian troops depart for the first time in living memory was surely an extraordinary event. The revolutionaries took the leading posts: Dudayev became President, Yandarbiev Vice-President, Yaragi Mamodayev Deputy Prime Minister in charge of the economy, Yusup Soslanbekov headed the parliamentary commission on foreign relations and later became its Speaker, and Beslan Gantemirov headed the City Soviet of the Chechen capital.

Yet this euphoria had a shorter life-span than happened in other revolutions. In a few months Chechnya was already transformed into a failed state, where the old institutions were disintegrating faster than elsewhere in Russia and the former Soviet Union, while the new did not appear on the mental horizons. The result was a total institutional collapse: budget allocations from Moscow were interrupted, links between industries in Chechnya and their former partners elsewhere in the ex-USSR were broken, and production came to standstill. State employees received no wages, resulting in mass impoverishment. Electricity supply, gas and heating were irregular at best. Criminality increased, while the court system was marginalized, reviving old traditions of vendetta.

---

62   Amjad Jaimoukha, *The Circassians, A Handbook*, London: Curzon, 2001, p. 86.

As popular discontent over the misfortune caused by the new regime increased, so did the internal competition within the ruling elite: while the economy was kept under "state" control a struggle for large chunks of cash illegally appropriated, especially from the oil industry, led to schisms within the new leadership.

Chechnya became not only a danger in itself, but also a danger for itself. Trains travelling in the region and crossing Chechen territories were regularly victims of looting. Even having trains escorted by armed Interior Ministry troops did not solve the problem. One railway security officer in Mineralniye Vody in the Russian North Caucasus reported: "Over 50 carriages have been completely looted in the past two months. This is considering only the trains which have reached us. No fewer carriages were plundered before reaching the Makhachkala station. During the first nine months of this year [1993] about 200 cases of robbery were registered…"[63]

More preoccupying was the growing criminal economy that developed in Chechnya, often in close collaboration with official circles and economic interests in Russia. There was an important oil refinery near Groznyy, and a pipeline carrying Caspian oil from Baku to the Black Sea port of Novorossiysk. According to Yusup Soslanbekov, Chechnya exported in 1992 only the equivalent of $130 million worth of oil products to Russia.[64] Since Russia imposed a total blockade on rebellious Chechnya, neither crude oil pumped to Chechnya nor refined products exported were officially accounted for. The benefits were pocketed at the highest levels in Groznyy and Moscow. Similarly, the legal limbo in which Chechnya found itself made banks in Groznyy ideal places for money laundering. As former Soviet republics introduced their national currencies, large quantities of old Soviet roubles were flown to Chechnya and reinjected into the Russian market, where the Soviet rouble was used until mid-1993. According to one report, two Tupolev-134 flights from Tallinn transported over ten tons of old Soviet roubles, out of circulation in Estonia but still in use in Russia.[65] Such transactions enriched a select few but caused much harm to the Russian economy.

---

63   Lyudmila Leontyeva, "Dangerous roads", *Moscow News*, 26 November 1993.

64   Sebastian Smith, *Allah's Mountain*, p. 131.

65   *Chechenskiy Krizis,* op. cit., p. 22.

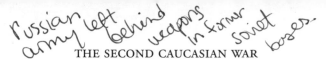

Another controversy which later became a subject of heated debate in Moscow was the weapons and ammunition left behind by the departing Russian armies. The Russian forces stationed in the former Soviet military bases came under increasing pressure after the Chechen Revolution, when Chechen youths started raiding arms depots to steal arms and ammunition. In mid-1992 Grachev negotiated with the Chechen leadership and reached an agreement to divide the military equipment and weaponry fifty-fifty, half to be taken by the departing Russian troops while the other half was handed over to Chechen authorities. Most probably the Russian side left most of its part back in Chechen hands as well. While Grachev was later heavily criticized for having "sold" Soviet weaponry to the Chechen "enemy", probably he and the Russian military had no other choice except for a bloody confrontation with Chechen militants to withdraw the Soviet weaponry from the Chechen territories. As a result, forces loyal to Dudayev were now in possession of heavy armament and large quantities of rifles and ammunition.[66]

Dudayev also made foreign policy moves that did not bring Chechnya any profit other than media coverage, often negative. First he offered asylum to the former dictator of East Germany, Erich Honecker. After Honecker turned down the offer, Dudayev offered to receive another high-profile asylum seeker, Zviad Gamsakhurdia. "By giving a home to Gamsakhurdia, Dudayev only succeeded in angering the new regime in the only other country with which he shared a frontier: Georgia."[67] In those years the Chechen leader made numerous visits to Arab and Islamic countries seeking recognition. Although he was received at high levels in many capitals, and managed to open a semi-official representation in Ankara in early 1994, those trips did not bring much to Chechen foreign policy: no state recognized Chechnya's independence. After each foreign visit and after each interview with a foreign journalist Dudayev aroused more scandal, revealing his growing psychological imbalance; after a visit to Iraq and a meeting with Saddam Hussein, he announced his support for "the fight of Islam against Russia, the United States and the West in

---

66   According to V. Tishkov, the volume of arms left behind in Chechnya by the Russian troops amounted to 42 tanks, 153 cannon and mortars, 18 Grad multiple rocket systems (40 tube, 122 mm), 55 armoured personal carriers, 5 fighter planes and 2 helicopters, 130,000 hand grenades, and over 40,000 semi-automatic rifles. See *Chechnya*, op. cit., p. 64.

67   Gall and de Waal, *Chechnya*, op. cit., p. 109.

general."[68] Groznyy's problem was with Moscow, and Dudayev's gestures abroad were not helping to establish a dialogue with the Russian leadership, let alone develop a sympathetic audience in the West.

The internal political situation showed initial signs of tension as early as in April 1992, when an unknown group tried to storm the television building in central Groznyy. Things got even worse in early 1993 when the political situation became completely polarized between the opposition dominated parliament, which demanded the resignation of the President, and the head of the state.[69] In April 1993 visitors to the Chechen capital could see two rallies, one organized by the opposition demanding the immediate resignation of Dudayev, and the other ten minutes' walk away in support of Dudayev. Each gathered between 5-10,000 people. By now Dudayev had succeeded in turning his closest collaborators into his fiercest enemies. The opposition counted among its leaders former collaborators of Dudayev such as Soslanbekov, Gantemirov and Mamodayev. Ruslan Labazanov, a former convict who for a time headed the personal guards of Dudayev, was also with the opposition, with his private armed formation. Dudayev dissolved the parliament and dismissed his cabinet in April 1993, and introduced presidential rule. The opposition-dominated parliament declared that the Dudayev decree was illegal and amounted to a coup. On 19 April the Chechen Constitutional Court similarly ruled the President's decrees unconstitutional.[70]

The parliament continued to meet and started a process to impeach Dudayev. The opposition planned to organize a referendum in early June, and asked people whether they preferred a presidential or parliamentary system. But a day before the referendum, armed formations loyal to Dudayev attacked opposition offices and disrupted the work of the electoral commission. There were up to fifty casualties as a result of the clashes, including Shamil Dudayev, a nephew of the Chechen president, and the brother of Labazanov. Now not only there was personal animosity and political antagonism between the hero of the Chechen

---

68   AFP, Groznyy, 25 November 1993.

69   Nikolai Troitsky, "The Chechen crisis as the mirror of Russian Revolution", *Megapolis Express*; English translation in *Russian Press Digest*, 24 February 1993.

70   Timur Muzayev and Georgy Melikyants, "Political Crisis in Chechnya", *Nezavisimaya Gazeta*; English translation in *Russian Press Digest,* 20 April 1993.

revolution and his closest comrades, but also a blood feud and vendetta. Only months before the showdown between the Russian President Yeltsin and his parliament led by Khasbulatov, Chechnya went through a similar political crisis that was resolved by the President dissolving the parliament and using force to crush its resistance. But after this "mini civil-war" Dudayev lost control over certain regions of Chechnya, and especially of three northern districts: the Nadterechny, Gudermess and Urus-Martan regions announced their dissidence, and were controlled by armed formations of various opposition groupings. In fact, from mid-1993 the authority of Dudayev did not go beyond the limits of Groznyy.[71]

The situation continued to degrade further in 1994. Chechnya under Dudayev was a *de facto* independent entity lacking state institutions, with the central authorities highly unpopular and even illegitimate in the eyes of part of the political elite and local population, where state institutions such as parliament or the cabinet of ministers did not function, where the authorities did not control much of the territory of the country, and finally where the collapse of social services and economic activities led to widespread discontent. Chechnya in 1992-94 resembled very much neighbouring Georgia under Gamsakhurdia and in the early years of Shevardnadze rule. Yet there was one fundamental difference: Chechnya was not recognized by the club of nations, and the Kremlin did not agree to let it go. While Georgia had a historic chance to reorganize its political set-up, Chechnya did not have time for that. In this sense, Djokhar Dudayev bears a double responsibility: first for leading the Chechen masses into open rebellion against Moscow, with all the risks such a rebellion involved in view of the past record of Russo-Chechen relations; and second for failing to find an arrangement with the Russian leadership to save his land from the backlash.

The "Tatarstan model" and the negotiations that did not take place

Several developments in Russia by early 1994 increased pressure on the Yeltsin administration to find an adequate response to the challenge

---

71   Yakov Nikolayev, "The Chechen opposition is getting armed", *Megapolis Express*, reproduced in *Russian Press Digest*, 16 June 1993.

of the Dudayev leadership and the security problems of the growing chaos in Chechnya. Unfortunately, the change of political context in Russia and the shift of public opinion towards the nationalist right, the hard-line positions of a number of key decision-makers in Moscow, the disintegration of the Chechen leadership and its infighting, and the personality clashes between Dudayev and Yeltsin created an atmosphere of uncertainty, doubt, and lack of trust towards a process of political negotiations—in itself difficult to realize. As a result, military escalation was seen in Moscow as a possible and even desirable option, before a process of negotiations even started.

While Chechnya was undergoing a breakdown of the political forces that came to power as a result of the 1991 revolution, similar political developments were taking place in Moscow. Against the background of the devastating social cost of the "shock-therapy" reforms applied by the Prime Minister Yegor Gaidar, two camps were formed within the Russian leadership, with conflicting visions of Russia's future, clashing over the path to take for economic reforms and monetary policies, as well as the new constitution. The schism was between Yeltsin, supported by the executive and especially the loyal Minister of Defence Grachev, and on the other Yeltsin's closest allies of not long ago who had fought with him against the hardliners trying to reinstall the old Soviet power in August 1991. The leaders of the anti-Yeltsin dissent were Vice-President Rutskoy and Speaker of the Parliament, Ruslan Khasbulatov. They criticized the economic policies of Yeltsin, saying they had "enriched a narrow band of people, criminalised the economy, and debauched hungry officials".[72]

After much tension and political paralysis, Yelstin went on the offensive in September 1993 by sacking his Vice-President.[73] The situation deteriorated further when on 21 September a televised speech of Yeltsin declared "Step-by-Step Constitutional Reform", which basically dissolved the existing Supreme Soviet and called for new elections and voting on the constitution in December. Although the actions of Yeltsin were unconstitutional, and can be described as a coup d'état, the

---

72   David Hearst, "Yeltsin's coup: the economy: parliament's leaders favour third way", *The Guardian,* 23 September 1993.

73   John Lloyd, "Yeltsin tells rival he is sacked: Dismissal of vice-president Rutskoi raises constitutional doubts", *Financial Times,* 2 September 1993.

Russian President had the support of the power ministries and the mass media—notably the central television, which gave him the possibility to manipulate the public opinion throughout the country.[74] Yeltsin also enjoyed widespread support in the West, which still considered him as a democrat fighting against conservative forces. In retaliation the parliament called an emergency session and named Rutskoy as President.[75] But the balance of power was on Yeltsin's side; as the Supreme Soviet did not receive any support from military divisions—in spite of Rutskoy's efforts—and no mass demonstrations came to support the anti-Yeltsin forces, they had little chance to win the fight. After being besieged in the White House for 12 days, supporters of the Supreme Soviet moved out of the building to attack the city mayor's office and the building of Ostankino (the main offices of Russian Channel One). This badly calculated move gave the Supreme Soviet the image of an "aggressor", providing the necessary pretext for Yeltsin to send army tanks to shell the White House to dislodge rebel deputies and their armed supporters. Rutskoy and Khasbulatov, isolated in the White House, lacking popular support and opposed by the military, had no other choice but walk out of the buildings, their hands up.[76] The elimination of Khasbulatov from the political scene in Moscow created a new opportunity for negotiations between Yeltsin and Dudayev.

In the same period another event came to focus attention on Chechnya. In February 1994 the Russian and Volga Tatar leaders reached an agreement to put an end to the ambiguity in the relationship between Kazan and Moscow.[77] Tatarstan was the autonomous republic within the Russian Federation which was the first to come with a declaration of sovereignty, and passed a referendum in March 1992 in which 61

---

74 Roy Medvedev, *Post-Soviet Russia, A Journey Through the Yeltsin Era*, New York: Columbia University Press, 2000, pp. 107-108.

75 Helen Womack, "Yeltsin ignites power struggle", *The Independent*, 22 September 1993.

76 Serge Schmemann, "Showdown in Moscow" *New York Times*, 4 October 1993.

77 The treaty was called "Treaty on Delimiting the Jurisdictions and Mutual Transmission of Authorities Between the Organs of State Power of the Russian Federation and the Republic of Tatarstan", and was signed in Moscow between Yeltsin and the Tatar President Mentimir Shaymiev on 15 February 1994.

per cent of the voters answered positively about its "state sovereignty".[78] After three years a treaty was signed between Moscow and Kazan in which Tatarstan dropped the expression "sovereign state" and "subject of international law", but obtained the right to have foreign diplomatic representation, and to have direct foreign economic agreements abroad without passing through Moscow.[79]

Bashkurtistan and Yakutia had already signed the new Federal Treaty, with appendices added to regulate certain specificities. As a result, after the agreement between Moscow and Kazan, Chechnya was the last oddity sticking out of the "parade of sovereignties", and therefore the focus of attention of the Kremlin. Most important in this issue was that while other republics such as Azerbaijan, Georgia, Moldova and Tajikistan went through bloody conflict to reshape the new political hierarchies, Moscow revealed a high level of political maturity by reaching agreements with various republics and autonomies without the use of force. The Russian Minister of Nationalities, Sergei Shakhrai, said that the Treaty would "serve as an example" towards normalizing relations with Chechnya.[80]

In the spring of 1994 Yeltsin seemed ready to negotiate with Dudayev to find a political solution to the Chechen case. Many republican leaders, like Shaimiev of Tatarstan, offered their mediation. In March, a Kremlin spokesperson announced preparations for a Russian-Chechen "summit". Later in May, the Kremlin still insisted that preparation for a summit was underway, and that Yeltsin was ready to meet with Dudayev. Another mediator was Kirsan Ilyumzhinov, the President of Kalmykia: "On April 28, 1994, I met Yeltsin who asked me to contact Dudayev, he wanted to avoid bloodshed (...) But all the papers were eventually thrown to the basket. I felt Yeltsin's circles had made

---

78   The question of the referendum was formulated in the following way: "Do you agree that the Republic of Tatarstan is a sovereign state and a subject of international law which develops its relations with the Russian Federation and the other republics on the basis of bilateral treaties?" quoted in Raphael S. Khakimov, "Prospects of Federalism in Russia: A View from Tatarstan", *Security Dialogue*, Vol. 27 (1), 1996, p. 74.

79   Radik Batyrshin, *Nezavisimaya Gazeta*, 16 February 1994; in *CDPSP*, Vol. XLVI, No. 7, p. 11.

80   Jean Raffaelli, "Tatarstan signs treaty normalizing relations with Moscow", AFP, Moscow, 15 February 1994.

the military choice."[81] But a car bomb in Groznyy on 27 May 1994, which hit a convoy escorting Dudayev, disrupted the attempts at direct talks between the two leaders. The Chechen leader himself was unhurt, but three people were killed—the Interior Minister Magomed Eldiyev, his deputy and their driver. Chechen authorities blamed Russian secret services for the attack.[82] Even worse, in an interview given to a major Russian television station, Dudayev personally attacked Yeltsin, even insulting his dignity by describing the Russian President as a "drunkard". In the words of Shakhrai, this was the last straw and put an end to Yeltsin's timid attempts to meet with Dudayev: "Dudayev simply insulted the president, called him a sick man, an alcoholic. After that a personal meeting again failed to happen."[83] The breakdown of negotiations that did not even start increased the pressure on Yeltsin to listen to the hardliners in his cabinet who were calling for an immediate military intervention to "solve" the problems in Chechnya.

Failure of the Chechen opposition

In the summer of 1994 Yeltsin had an opportunity to consider a military solution for the crisis in Chechnya. After removing his arch-rivals Rutskoi and Khasbulatov, now Yeltsin could claim to have unified the Russian state structures under his leadership and stopped its disintegration. The same events convinced him that he had the support of the Russian military, especially through the loyal support of Pavel Grachev.[84] With the "sovereignty" issue clarified with Bashkurtistan, Yakutia, Tatarstan and others, Chechnya was now an isolated case in the Russian Federation. Yeltsin also felt that Dudayev was isolated and weak, and Chechen opposition against him growing.

But there was also cause for urgency. In the Duma elections of December 1993, the party of the eccentric nationalist Vladimir Zhirinovsky's Liberal Democratic Party of Russia (LDPR) got a surprising 22.9 per

81 Author interview with Kirsan Ilyumzhinov, Elista, 19 May 1995.

82 "Chechnya Blames Russia for Assassination Attempt", *AP*, Moscow, 30 May 1994.

83 Gall and de Waal, *Chechnya*, op. cit., p. 147.

84 The Russian armed forces had once again failed to come to the support of "putschists" accused of trying to restore a Soviet Union. But in the days of October 1993, their support for Yeltsin was equally slight, since the Defence Minister had difficulties in bringing four tanks to shell the White House.

cent of the votes, ahead of the pro-establishment Russia's Choice which got only 15 per cent.[85] As a result of combined proportional and direct votes, Russia's Choice became the largest group in the Duma, followed by the LDPR, leaving the Russian Communists in the third position.[86] Following the crushing of the patriotic-leftist opposition to Yeltsin's policies in the October 1993 events, the success of the LDPR was simultaneously a result of it and a warning. Western analysts did not hide their fears of "unappeasable popular anger, the collapse of public order and eventually dictatorship."[87] The Russian administration felt it had to do something before the 1996 elections to bolster the image of Yeltsin. Changes in key government positions in the summer of 1994 brought hard-liners into decision-making posts around Yeltsin.[88]

There were also geopolitical shifts on the regional level, in which the situation in Chechnya looked like hurting Russia's position. The growing interest of Western oil industries in the Caspian hydrocarbon resources increased the geopolitical profile of the Caucasus region. In September 1994 a consortium of Western oil companies and the Azerbaijani government signed the "deal of the century", a project worth an estimated $8 billion for oil production in offshore regions off the Azerbaijani Caspian coast.[89] The Russian Foreign Ministry opposed the deal—even though Russia's Lukoil had a minority share of 10 per cent in the project—arguing that an agreement for the delimitation of the

---

85   The LDPR was the second party registered in the Soviet Union, in March 1990, the first being the Communist Party of the Soviet Union—this was one cause of rumours about Zhirinovsky's association with the KGB. Even if he was a political agent of the KGB, the growth of the nationalist vote and the weakness of the party in power were enough signs of regime instability.

86   Russia's Choice got a total of 70 seats, the LDPR 64, and the Communists 48, out of a total of 450 seats. For a detailed description of the 1993 elections see Richard Sakwa, "The Russian Elections of December 1993"; *Europe-Asia Studies*, Vol. 47, No. 2, 1995, pp. 195-227.

87   Stephen Sestanovich, "Russia Turns the Corner", *Foreign Affairs,* January/February 1994, p. 83. In the article the author makes analogies between Russia under Yeltsin and Weimar Germany, with the shadow of fascism hanging over Russia as a possible threat.

88   Gail W. Lapidus, "Contested Sovereignty, The Tragedy of Chechnya", *International Security,* Vol. 23, No. 1, Summer 1998, p. 17.

89   Daniel Southernland, "Azerbaijan, Western firms agree on Caspian Sea oil drilling plan", *The Washington Post*, 20 September 1994; Agis Salpukas, "Huge-scale Caspian oil deal signed", *New York Times*, 21 September 1994.

Caspian had not yet reached. In the next years the interest of Western oil interests, but also of Western diplomats, academics and the media in the Caspian Sea and its (often exaggerated) energy resources reached a dramatic height, and exerted influence on the conflict zones of the Caucasus. The chronology of events suggests that the competition between the West and Russia over the division of the Caspian region might have influenced the Russian leadership's decision to accelerate events in Chechnya.

Yet, Moscow did not initiate an outright invasion of Chechnya, but tried to overthrow Dudayev's rule by arming and supporting the Chechen opposition. Dudayev seemed weak and isolated, losing control over Chechnya. By this time, seven out of fourteen regions (*rayons*) of Chechnya were under opposition control:[90] all the lowlands to the north of Groznyy were under the control of the various opposition formations, while support for Dudayev came mainly from the mountainous regions, reflecting historic divisions between the steppe, which was easily conquered in the past by Russian forces, and mountainous regions with traditions of resistance and anti-Russian sentiments.

The Chechen opposition to Dudayev gathered in the "Provisional Council of Chechnya" created in December 1993 was an impressive but very heterogeneous group. The opposition headquarters was at Znamenskoye in the northern Nadterechnaya region, and was headed by Umar Avturkhanov, a former head of the regional administration. Avturkhanov called for Russian help to overthrow Dudayev, demanding arms and cash, but opposed direct Russian military intervention. Avturkhanov also promised to drop separatist calls if the opposition took power in Groznyy.[91]

While the political demands of the opposition were understandable (to overthrow Dudayev and reach a deal with Moscow), its military approach was more confused and confusing. With their forces alone they knew they could not conquer Groznyy. Their position regarding the kind of support they expected from Moscow reveals a deep dilemma:

90   C. W. Blandy, *Chechnya: Two Federal Interventions, An Interim Comparison and Assessment* , Conflict Studies Research Centre, Royal Military Academy Sandhurst, January 2000, p. 11.

91   John Lloyd, "Moscow backs rebel power bid in Chechnya", *Financial Times*, 3 August 1994.

while they asked for Russian material support, they opposed an outright Russian military intervention. They knew that any Russian invasion of Chechnya would rally the Chechens not so much around Dudayev, but around the idea of anti-Russian resistance. In the words of Gantemirov, the head of the "Joint Forces", the military wing of the opposition: "I was, am and shall remain opposed to bringing Russian troops into Chechnya. We will be able to settle accounts with Dudayev's supporters on our own, although recently it seems to me that I would not mind taking command of several battalions of Russian troops. Then we would teach Dudayev a lesson."[92]

The Chechen opposition was a strange mixture of personalities, "united" by their antagonism against Dudayev. Next to Avturkhanov and Gantemirov were characters like Doku Zavgayev, the former Soviet Party boss of Checheno-Ingushetia, Salambek Khadzhiyev, a former Soviet Oil Minister and leader of the Daimokhk opposition party, and Yaraghi Mamodayev, a former businessman and former ally of Dudayev.[93] At Russian insistence the former arch-enemy of Yeltsin, Ruslan Khasbulatov, who had moved to Tolstoy Yurt, his village of origin in Chechnya, since his release from prison in early 1994, meddled in the murky waters of Chechen politics. Khasbulatov tried to stay above the political divides of Chechnya by seeking to play the role of mediator between the Dudayev government, the opposition, and Moscow—but without much success.

The opposition was deeply divided, and did not project any image of an autonomous political force. Labazanov hated Gantemirov, and there was no coordination on military level between the two largest military formations under the umbrella of the Provincial Council. Mamodayev in his turn openly criticized Avturkhanov, the head of the Council, calling the Provisional Council "an impostor structure", and stated that "no more than 1,000 people stand behind the Provisional Council".[94]

In the summer of 1994 the security situation deteriorated dramatically. An opposition demonstration in Groznyy, organized by Ruslan Labazanov, degenerated into armed clashes causing scores of casual-

---

92   Dmitry Balburov interview with Beslan Gantemirov, *Moscow News*, 30 September 1994.

93   Dmitry Balburov, "Chechen opposition leaders make strange bedfellows", *Moscow News*, 15 September 1994.

94   TASS, Moscow, 26 June 1994.

ties.[95] Dudayev also increased his criticism of Khasbulatov, calling him a traitor and stripping him of "Chechen citizenship",[96] thus breaking the last possible contact between the Kremlin and Groznyy.

Government troops attacked armed formations led by Labazanov and drove them out of Argun, the third main urban centre in Chechnya. The weakness of the opposition against the pro-Dudayev forces was shown once again. Labazanov found refuge in Tolstoy Yurt, near Ruslan Khasbulatov, but pro-Dudayev troops attacked the village and put the opposition militias on the run. This attack meant that Dudayev did not want Khasbulatov to interfere in Chechen politics, as mediator or not. In spite of the failures of the Dudayev regime, many Chechens rightly considered the Provincial Council as an instrument of Moscow, representing the interests of the remnants of the old Soviet bureaucracy in the republic. Any outside (that is Moscow) initiated pressure on Dudayev led to most Chechens closing ranks, and thus increased support for the Dudayev government. To increase the tension in an already complicated situation, Chechen military sources spread information saying that there were 24 nuclear warheads left behind in the republic after the departure of the Russian forces.[97]

Moscow, instead of waiting for a further degradation of the situation in Chechnya, making its intervention necessary to pacify a region falling into civil war and anarchy—which would have eventually led to louder calls for intervention to put an end to an inter-Chechen war—opted for increasing direct Russian military involvement. In fact, the Russian leadership in 1994 was not aiming to find a solution to the growing violence in Chechnya and the North Caucasus, but to impose its will over the region. Under the cover of the "opposition", specially recruited Russian Defence Ministry personnel equipped with heavy armour and with air support were sent to take Groznyy and throw Dudayev's government out of power. On 26 November 1994 the "opposition" troops advanced into Groznyy. After a day-long battle with forces loyal to the

---

95   The Chechen opposition put the number of the dead up to 300, while Chechen authorities put the number "between 10 and 60 at the most". See "Up to 300 dead in fighting in Chechnya opposition", *AFP*, Moscow, 15 June 1994.

96   Leonid Sergeyev, "Situation in Chechnya deteriorates sharply", in *Rossiskiye Vesti*, published in *Russian Press Digest*, 16 June 1994.

97   *Covcas Bulletin*, Geneva, Vol. 4, No. 17, September 7, 1994, p. 1.

Russian forces went in as "oppositas" to overthrow Dudayav.

Dudayev government, the opposition was beaten back leaving behind several tanks, and of a total of 200 prisoners from among the invaders, 70 were identified as regular servicemen of the Russian Armed Forces.[98] This humiliation was one too many for the Yeltsin administration. After nourishing illusions of a hasty change of power in Groznyy through the armed groups of the opposition, it abandoned the weak and inefficient opposition; but the idea of a rapid change was not dropped. Following the failure of the initial efforts, the logical continuation in military escalation was outright invasion.

On 29 November Yeltsin broke his silence and demanded that the Chechen side should free the prisoners and disarm within 48 hours. He added: "All forces and resources which are at the disposal of the state will be used to put an end to the bloodshed, to defend the life, rights and freedoms of the citizens of Russia and to restore constitutional legality, law and order, and peace in the Chechen republic."[99] On 6 December Generals Grachev and Dudayev met in Ingushetia. Although the meeting led to the release of the Russian prisoners, it did not solve any other pending issue. Meanwhile the Russian air force was bombing targets at Groznyy airport, destroying planes, radars, and communication facilities. The war machine was activated. A tragedy started unfolding, leading to one of the cruellest wars in the post-Cold War era. It was also a war that was entered precipitately, a war which lacked any serious planning, resulting in gross military mistakes, dissidence within the Russian armed forces, and catastrophic results for the troops—and unimaginable suffering for the civilian population, trapped between the fire of the Russian army and the wrath of the Chechen fighters.

The Russian military intervention: an army close to collapse

The invasion of Chechnya was hardly prepared. The Russian Security Council ordered Grachev on 29 November to prepare the invasion in merely a week. Although Grachev could put together an impressive

---

98   "Chechnya threatens to execute captured Russians", AP, Groznyy, 28 November 1994.

99   Larry Ryckman, "Yeltsin issues ultimatum to Chechnya; jets bomb Grozny", AP, Moscow, 29 November 1994.

[handwritten: no one expected such xtreme Chechen Resistance]

force[100] compared with the Chechen forces loyal to Dudayev,[101] and superior to the Soviet troops sent to crush demonstrations in Tbilisi (1989), Baku (1990) and Vilnius (1991), the military leadership were unprepared for the kind of operation they were to face in Chechnya, and no one among the planners of the operation expected fierce resistance from the Chechens. During one interview Grachev, denying the participation of regular Russian troops in the 25 November assault on Groznyy, said: "One airborne regiment would be enough to solve all the questions in two hours." [102]

In the early hours of 11 December 1994, Russian troops from three directions started their advance towards Groznyy. Their objective was to move rapidly on the city and to capture Dudayev's Presidential Palace on 13 December.[103] The troops from the west, crossing Ingush territories, advanced slowly as villagers in Ingushetia organized demonstrations and blocked roads in front of their movement. The same happened

---

100 The initial invading Russian forces had a strength of 23-25,000, armed with 80 tanks and 200 fighting vehicles, and supported by air cover with Sukhoi-25 bombers and Mil-Mi 24 helicopter gunships. They were opposed by a Chechen regular force of 3,000 including 800 in the battle hardened "Abkhaz battalion", with an estimated 40 tanks and 60 fighting vehicles. See Pavel Baev, *The Russian Army in a Time of Troubles*, PRIO, Oslo, 1996, p. 143; and "Grozny Forces no Match for Moscow", *AFP*, Moscow, 28 December 1994.

101 According to an official Kremlin International News Broadcast on 27 January 1995, the Chechen forces had the following strength: "T-62 and T-72 tanks – from 40 to 50; - BMP-1 (infantry assault vehicles) and BMP-2 - from 40 to 45; - BTR-70 (armoured personnel carriers) and BRDM-2 (armoured scout vehicles) - from 30 to 35; - anti-tank weapons - from 90 to 100; - grenade launchers of various types - from 620 to 630; - artillery pieces and mortars - from 150 to 160; - Grad multiple rocket launchers - more than 20-25; - D-30 122 mm howitzers - 30; - small arms - about 42,000 units; - tank machine guns - 678; - heavy machine guns - 319; - anti-aircraft weapon complexes of various types - about 40; - ammunition: cartridges, artillery shells, bombs, mortars, grenades - in quantities sufficient for 6-7 months of intensive combat by an army of 40,000 men." These data were based on Russian military information about the quantity of weapons left behind in Chechnya as Russian troops departed in mid-1992. They do not necessarily mean that all this weaponry was under the control of the Chechen forces opposing the Russian invasion, nor that it was all in functional state by late 1994.

102 See Peter Ford, "Russia threatens a splinter state", *Christian Science Monitor*, 30 November 1994.

103 See the notes of the former Minister of Interior of Russia Anatoly Kulikov, "The First Battle of Groznyy", in *Capital Preservation, Preparing for Urban Operations in the 21st Century*, Santa Monica, CA: RAND, Appendix B, p. 14.

to troops moving from the east, from Daghestan. Only those forces that started from Mozdok in North Ossetia, and crossed Chechen provinces under the control of the opposition, advanced rapidly and deep into Chechen territory. If this was meant to be a *Blitzkrieg*, as the Russian Defence Minister had earlier boasted, it was a bad copy of the German original.

The Russian army, having wasted the element of surprise, gave the Chechen defenders precious time to set up hasty defence positions. The Chechen defences of Groznyy had three rings: the first, central ring was put around the Presidential Palace; the middle ring consisted of defences across Sunzhe River bridges, and Minutka square; the outer ring was positioned on the highway network of Groznyy, the southern, industrial suburb of Neftyianka, around Khankala airport, and Staraya Sunzhe.

The order given by the Russian President to the invading troops was to "restore constitutional order", which is to say the least a vague phrase for the launching of a military operation on a massive scale. The opposition from within the military establishment reveals better the gap between the political leadership—the presidency and Defence ministry—on the one hand, and the army General Staff. Opposition to the operation spread widely within the army, and among its senior officers: General Boris Gromov, Deputy Defence Minister, openly voiced his criticism, saying that after a decade of budgetary cuts and the collapse of the Soviet Union with all its consequences for the military, the Russian army was unprepared for a large-scale military operation in the Caucasus;[104] General Eduard Vorobyev, deputy head of the ground forces, refused to lead the invasion.[105] More than anything else, the Russian military loathed to be sent once again into action and then see the politicians who ordered them in the first place not assuming responsibility. This had already happened with a series of military adven-

---

104   In a televised interview, the Deputy Minister of Defence, General Gromov, said that he himself learned about the invasion of Chechnya "from the press", and that the "whole military campaign had been prepared spontaneously", while the planning was done not by military people, since "major decisions are not being taken by military people"; interview with General Gromov on Ostankino TV Channel 1 in Moscow, *BBC Summary of World Broadcasts*, 6 February 1995.

105   Pavel BAEV, *The Russian Army in a Time of Troubles*, Oslo: Prio, 1996, pp. 64-6.

[handwritten margin note: Russian military action in the south Caucasus]

tures in the last years of the Soviet Union, almost creating a tradition: the military repression of demonstrations in Tbilisi in April 1989, the Red Army's entry to Baku in January 1990, and the repression in Vilnius, where Gorbachev had distanced himself from the events, diverting the blame for the repression onto the army generals. Similarly Yeltsin, after giving the order to the military to restore "constitutional order" disappeared for a whole week for a "nose operation".

In the early months of the intervention, up to early February 1995, it was the generals of the FSB—the intelligence services—who were obliged to lead the military operations, with catastrophic consequences. Certain elite troops "refused" to take part in the operation, and according to one Western military expert over 20,000 troops participating in the operation were Interior Ministry troops, specialized in domestic security operations, but unsuitable for major warfare.[106]

There was equally important political opposition to the war. Yegor Gaidar, former Prime Minister and the leader of Russia's Choice, the biggest parliamentary faction, called the invasion of Chechnya "a crime".[107] The public in its turn was highly divided about the military invasion of Chechnya. In an opinion poll conducted by the All-Russia Centre for the Study of Public Opinion (ARCSPO) on 16-19 December, 31 per cent "blamed" Dudayev for the crisis, and 25 per cent Yeltsin and his associates. To the question "what is to be done", 36 per cent chose "search for a peaceful solution to the Chechen problem", and 30 per cent supported "decisive measures to re-establish order" in Chechnya.[108] To conclude, neither the Russian political elite, nor the public, nor even the media were ready for, or convinced of the necessity of, a war in the Caucasus.

---

106   Mark Galeotti quoted in Bruce Clark and Chrystia Freeland, "Elite troops 're-fusing to fight in Chechnya'", *Financial Times*, 6 January 1995. Galeotti is quoted as saying that "the commanders of the airborne divisions refused categorically to put their full weight behind the Chechen operation." Similarly, tmilitary intelligence seems to have refused the operation, and withdrawn from the North Caucasus before the invasion.

107   John Thornhill, "Gaidar calls Chechnya war 'a crime'", *Financial Times*, 4 January 1995.

108   Yury Levada, *Izvestia*, 23 December 1994, English translation in *CDPSP*, Volume XLVI, No. 51; p. 11.

New Year's Eve: the battle for Groznyy

There were several Russian parliamentarians in Groznyy on the New Year's Eve, trying desperate last minute mediation between the Chechen leadership and the Kremlin. Among them was Sergei Kovalev, the famous human rights defender, as well as Viktor Kurochkin, Gleb Yakunin, with several journalists, a Russian clergyman, and others. In the early morning of the New Year, as the sky was glowing from the blazing fire of the Groznyy oil facilities, they walked past abandoned streets of central Groznyy and gathered in the basement of the colossal Presidential Palace. Wounded soldiers and civilians, as well as prisoners, were brought into the basement of the building. Kovalev recalled, "Of course, no one had expected an assault on the palace or set up a field hospital in basement. We lent a hand in clearing the premises to make room for wounded Chechens and Russians alike..."[109]

In spite of the political conflict, in spite of Chechen nationalism, the debate about Russia's colonial past, and the call for independence, it was still possible until then to imagine a common project, to initiate a peace mission, to clean a basement to tend wounded soldiers and civilians, Russians and Chechens alike. But once violence exploded, those intermingled, cosmopolitan communities shattered, polarized. Political conflicts like those that have occurred and are still going on in the Caucasus differ qualitatively from conflicts where one side, at a certain moment of the political crisis, decides to use violence. Once blood starts flowing, the same conflict takes on a totally different dimension, as fear takes the place of enthusiasm and commitment is mixed with anxiety.

On New Year's Eve the Russian army moved in three columns into Groznyy. By now, the army's strength in the theatre of operations had increased to 38,000 soldiers;[110] the number of forces sent into the city was put at 6,000. Again, the idea was to surprise the forces defending the

---

109   Sergei Kovalev, "Offensive on New Year's Eve", *Moscow News*, 29 January-4 February 1998. Kovalev describes the lack of preparation of the Russian units, most of the Russian captured servicemen he interviewed in the Presidential Palace basement were conscripts, who had joined the army only two months prior to the invasion and had no experience of handling arms. The few experienced officers lacked basics: for example, they had no military maps of Groznyy. Instead, they were supplied with tourist maps...

110   Pavel Felgenhauer, "The Russian Army in Chechnya", *Central Asian Survey*, Vol. 21, No. 2, 2002, p. 158.

city on this New Year's Eve. Again, the Russian Army failed to achieve surprise. It started advancing in Groznyy before even bringing the city under siege, with the southern suburbs of Groznyy under Chechen control and able to move fresh reinforcements from mountainous areas to the south. According to Kulikov, "If the failure to move at 0500 on December 11 was the first mistake made by the Russian forces, the failure to initially wait until the blockade was complete was the second mistake."[111] Another basic failure was that the Russian military planners did not expect fierce resistance to the three forces moving towards the centre of Groznyy; in fact, most of the advancing units were engaged in fierce fighting in the suburbs of the city, and failed to carry out their plan. The few units which succeeded in penetrating the town were even less lucky; those advancing from the north reached the vicinity of the Presidential Palace but met fierce resistance there. The 131st Motorized Rifle Brigade, which surprisingly advanced to the south of the city and reached and captured the main train station, was soon surrounded by Chechen fighters and decimated under a hail of anti-tank rockets and sub-machine gun fire.

Once a modern army enters an urban region, it loses most of its advantage against a lightly armed enemy: its use of armour and domination of the skies, which play such a crucial role in open fields. The Chechen forces were divided into small group of 10-20 fighters, with good knowledge of the city, often composed of members of the same family, clan, or village of origin. Either they were mobile, on foot or in small cars, or they had taken positions in large buildings with good field vision.[112] Mobile groups armed with light weapons including RPG-7 anti-tank rockets, or youngsters with petrol-bombs positioned in buildings, set deadly traps for the advancing Russian tanks and armoured vehicles.

The attack on Groznyy on New Year's Eve led to a disaster when tank columns which lacked the protection of infantry forces were cut off from behind after reaching the Presidential Palace and around the railway station. "The Russians hoped to scare the Chechens into surrender but that has clearly failed," said one commentator.[113] As if the Russian mili-

111   Kulikov, op. cit., p. 29.

112   Sean Edwards, *Swarming and the Future of Warfare*, Santa Monica, CA: RAND, 2005, pp. 269-70.

113   Christopher Bellamy, "Top Brass Ripe for Fall after Fiasco", *The Independent*, 5

tary planners thought that taking the Chechen capital would progress according to their previous experience in Prague! Aslan Maskhadov, who was commander of the Chechen military units at the time, recalls that two Russian motorized units penetrated Groznyy and practically surrounded him in the Presidential Palace without much resistance. It was only then that mobile Chechen fighters armed with RPG-7 rocket propelled grenades started attacking Russian armour, which were like "sitting ducks".[114] The Russian forces' losses in men and material were colossal: up to two thousand Russian servicemen died that night, while their supreme leader was sipping champagne on the first channel of Russian television, without uttering a word about the developing events in the Caucasus.

The military mistakes were so huge, the preparation so chaotic, and the results so depressing that politicians or analysts alike looked for exotic explanations other than "human stupidity". According to General Alexander Lebed, illicit arms trafficking was the reason of the Chechnya war, and explained why the Russian military leadership sent tank columns to Groznyy without the protection of infantry:

> …at the time of the liquidation of the Western Group of Forces, [Grachev] and Burlakov [Grachev's deputy] had stolen 1,600 tanks and sold them in Riga… The procurator was investigating it. The late journalist Kholodov got close to the truth. (…) Therefore, a military conflict was necessary. In Russia there is a saying – war writes off everything.[115]

Following this initial failure, the Russian army intensified its attacks, increasing its rate of shelling and carpet-bombing the entire city. The railway station was taken, after successive tank attacks, only on 9 January, the Presidential Palace was taken on 19 January, and Groznyy was

January 1995.

114 Maskhadov claims that in the three days following the New Year misadventure, his forces destroyed up to 400 Russian armoured vehicles. See Maskhadov interview on: http://urbanoperations.8media.org/chechnya1.htm

115 Harold Elletson, *The General Against the Kremlin, Alexander Lebed*, London: Warner Books, 1998, p. 222. The journalist Dmitry Kholodov was killed when a booby trapped briefcase exploded in his hands in October 1994; the briefcase was believed to contain top secret military documents sent by an unidentified military contact, since at the time Kholodov was investigating corruption among top military officials, including the Defence Minister Pavel Grachev. *Moskovskiy Komsomolets*, for which the journalist worked, accused the military of being behind the contract killing.

[handwritten margin note: So R eventually took hold of Groznyy.]

finally surrounded only on 23 February.[116] Resistance in Groznyy practically ended by the end of that month, turning the city that was once the home of 400,000 people into post-World War II-like debris.[117]

The catastrophic military results of the Chechnya campaign reflected the dire situation in which the Russian army had found itself, a shadow of its Soviet past. A decade of reforms—which in Gorbachev's period aimed at modernizing the economy by basically shifting investment from the defence budget to other, productive sectors of the economy—and three years of complete neglect under the Yeltsin administration had brought the Russian armed forces to near collapse. Investment, repairs and procurement were so low that in 1994 only a fifth of the Russian army's tanks were serviceable. Russian pilots were test flying a mere 25 hours a year—compared with 180 hours in the US forces—because of lack of fuel and funding.[118] In those conditions, many of the more skilled military cadres had left the army for better paid jobs in the booming private sector, to a point where one journalist compared the situation in 1994 to that of 1941, when the Soviet Army was not ready to face Hitler's forces, after being decapitated in the Stalinist purges.[119] Was this the heir of the mighty Soviet armed forces which had threatened all Western Europe with invasion? How could it fail to pacify one of its own provinces, which was not even that big in surface and population size? One observer of the Russian armed forces could not hide his surprise:

[handwritten margin note: (6) Yeltsin, Gorbachev disconnect brought armed forces to their collapse.]

NATO's military posture was configured on the reasonable assumption that if war came, Western forces would have to fight badly outnumbered and from a defensive and a reactive posture against a massive, combined-arms military machine that retained full control over nuclear weapons option and was pre-

---

116   Maj. Gregory J. Celestan, "Wounded Bear: The Ongoing Russian Military Operation in Chechnya", *Foreign Military Studies Office,* August 1996. Available online: http://www.globalsecurity.org/military/library/report/1996/wounded.htm

117   "(T)he highest level of firing recorded in Sarajevo was 3,500 heavy detonations per day. In Groznyy in early February, a colleague of mine counted 4,000 detonations per hour", writes Frederick C. Cuny, "Killing Chechnya", *The New York Review of Books*, 6 April 1995, p. 15.

118   Dave Carpenter, "Chechnya operation plagued by mistakes, morale, disarray", AP, Moscow, 5 January 1995.

119   Pavel Anokhin. *Rossiiskiye Vesti*, 30 December 1994, English translation in *CDPSP*, Volume XLVI, No. 52, p. 4.

(7) the military personelle were legit in shambles.

pared, as a matter of doctrinal principle, to trade high casualty rates for victory. The clash in Chechnya revealed a military of a sadly different sort: a ragtag band of hastily assembled conscripts who were not resourceful enough to evade the draft, led by underequipped, undertrained, and demoralized officers, who freely admitted that they did not understand why they we there.[120]

The Chechens' choice to stand and fight in Groznyy came with a price tag. The Russian army destroyed the city before taking it, causing a high rate of casualties. Most of the civilian victims of the war (that is the 1994-96 war) are believed to have fallen during the battle of Groznyy. Some put the number of the dead between 25,000 and 29,000.[121] One explanation is that Groznyy was largely a Russian city, and until the late 1980s two-thirds of its population were Slavs and only one-third Chechens. Although many Russians, Ukrainians and other Slavs left it in the early 1990s, nevertheless Groznyy stayed largely a Russian town. Moreover, many Chechens left the city for villages as military activities intensified from November, finding refuge with relatives or moving to their villages of origin, leaving behind Russians who did not have similar opportunities. It is believed that most of the civilian casualties of the battle of Groznyy were from this ethnic Russian population, old Russian pensioners who were left with no choice and neither protection.[122]

every juncture Russia amps up its military involvement.

Terrorism and guerrilla warfare

Following the Groznyy debacle, the Russian forces upgraded their tactics, especially the use of infantry, added reactive armour[123] to protect

120   Benjamin S. Lambeth, "Russia's Wounded Military", *Foreign Affairs*, March/April 1995, p. 91.

121   John Dunlop, "How many soldiers and civilians died during the Russo-Chechen war of 1994-1996?" *Central Asian Survey*, 2000, Vol. 19, No. 3/4, pp. 334-5.

122   One estimate is that 60 per cent of the civilian casualties of the 1994-96 war were ethnic Russians of Groznyy. Valery Tishkov, "Political Anthropology of the Chechen War", *Security Dialogue*, 1997, Vol. 28, No. 4, p. 426.

123   Reactive armour is added to tanks and armoured vehicles to protect them from anti-tank weapons, such as rockets and missiles. It was first used by the Israeli Army in 1982. When the reactive armour is hit by a rocket it explodes and therefore decreases the impact of the projectile. The Soviet army started using itself reactive armour from mid-1980s, in Afghanistan. The Russian tanks sent to Groznyy were heavily armoured in their fronts, but completely vulnerable from their sides and their rear to rockets, and from their tops to petrol bombs,

the rear and the sides of their tanks, and used smaller groups for house-to-house fighting. Yet the reliance of the Russian Federal troops on heavy (and often indiscriminate) firepower continued. They showed a better performance in the spring of 1995. Following their success in Groznyy, the other major population centres fell to the advancing Russian troops by mid-March: Gudermes, Argun, Shali. By mid-April all the plains were under the control of the Russian forces. The Chechen fighters put up fierce resistance in each of those towns, and then evacuated the lowlands and moved their bases to mountainous regions. In the spring of 1995 the Russian troops, better organized and, with fresh reinforcements, went on the offensive towards the mountainous strongholds of the Chechen rebels: Vedeno in the east, and Bamut in the west, where Chechen fighters were positioned in a former Soviet Strategic Missile Forces facility.

Although it took the Russian forces two months to take Bamut, the Russian military campaign seemed to have destroyed the organized Chechen resistance. The Chechen military structure was completely disorganized as a result, arms and ammunition were low, and morale was on the downturn. Russia seemed to be winning the war, in spite of the heavy losses it had suffered in the initial phase of the campaign. The Russian military analyst Pavel Felgengauer noted the failure of the Chechen resistance to organize efficient guerrilla warfare, because the Chechen fighters "are still unable to put up a lengthy resistance to regular troops that has dug in at a strategically important point. The Chechens have many grenade launchers, but neither the long-promised Stingers nor any artillery have been seen in their possession." Here, clearly, the comparison is with the guerrilla warfare the Soviet army faced in Afghanistan, and fears of a second Afghanistan still haunted Russian analysts and the military alike.[124] However, it should be noted that Afghanistan had an area of 647,000 sq. km. and a population of 15.5 million when the Soviets invaded, while Chechnya had a mere 19,300 sq. km. and a pre-war population of slightly over one million.

often dropped from second or third floors of residential buildings.

124 Pavel Felgengauer, *Sevodnya*, 26 December 1995; English translation in *CDP-SP*, Vol. XLVII, No. 52, p. 13.

It was a Russian hospital

It was in this desperate moment for the Chechen fighters that a group of them, probably 200 armed men,[125] led by the already notorious Shamil Basayev organized a raid outside the administrative boundaries of Chechnya, reached the town of Budyonnovsk in Stavropol Krai, attacked the city hospital and took around 1,500 people inside the hospital building as hostages. The Chechen leaders' threats to take the war into Russian territory itself had materialized. Basaev demanded an end to the military operations in Chechnya, the withdrawal of all federal forces from there, and the immediate beginning of talks between the Russian leadership and Dudayev, as a precondition for release of the hostages.

After two failed attempt by the Russian security forces to storm the hospital, which caused the death of thirty hostages, the Russian Prime Minister Viktor Chernomyrdin entered into direct negotiations with the Chechen hostage takers. Four days after the hostage taking started, an agreement was reached in which the Russian Prime Minister agreed on the cessation of hostilities in Chechnya and safe passage for the hostage takers back to Chechen territory.[126] Basayev and his men returned to Chechnya in buses, shielded by several hundred hostages and other volunteers such as Russian journalists and parliamentarians. At the end of the crisis of Budyonnovsk, Chernomyrdin declared, "A great thing has been done. The war is in fact over". Afterwards, Russian political leaders made a habit of declaring the end of the war at each cease-fire agreement. But Chernomyrdin refused to continue political negotiations with Dudayev ("Russia does not need Dudayev's signature, our opinion on him is known")[127] and insisted that Chechnya stayed within the Russian Federation, and proceeded with organizing new presidential elections.

The halt in Russian military operations after Budyonnovsk gave the Chechen fighters valuable time to reform their ranks and organize logistics, and, probably most important, it gave a strong boost to their morale. Resistance operations resumed, and the Chechen fighters carried out not only guerrilla attacks in mountain areas but also daring and vast

---

125   Grigory Sanin, *Sevodnya*, 16 June 1995, in *CDPSP*, Volume XLVII, No. 24; p. 3.

126   Sergei Shargorodski, "Rebels release hostages after deal to halt fighting in Chechnya", AP, Budyonnovsk, 18 June 1995.

127   Ibid.

266

operations into the urban centres in the northern part of the republic, taking control of cities for a day or two, and causing many casualties among the Russian military forces. In August 1995 Chechen fighters attacked Argun, the third major urban centre of the republic, taking control of its centre. In December 1995 they attacked Gudermes, the second major city of Chechnya and a strategic town dominating the railway lines linking Russia with the Azerbaijani capital. It took the Russian forces a week to expel the rebels from Gudermes, with heavy losses.[128]

A third major operation was carried out in January 1996, when a large Chechen armed group led by Salman Raduyev attacked the Daghestani town of Kizliar. Raduyev was a close relative of Djokhar Dudayev, and declared that the attack was carried out under the orders of the Chechen President.[129] Their objective was to take the airport of Kizliar, where, according to information the rebels had, eight helicopters armed with guided missiles were supposed to be based. Yet their operation failed as police forces in Kizliar put up an unexpectedly stubborn resistance.[130] Instead, the fighters attacked a hospital and took several hundred people hostage. After negotiations the Chechen group agreed to release most of the hostages, keep a hundred as human shields, and retreat to Chechnya. On the way they were attacked by Russian troops, and took up positions in the village of Pervomayskoye, near the border with Chechnya. The Russian troops encircled the village and threatened to storm it.

It seemed that the Budyonnovsk tragedy was being repeated. There was a serious danger of the Chechen conflict spilling over into neighbouring Daghestan. The Daghestani Minister of Nationalities, Magomed Gusayev, threatened: "If they want blood to spill here it will spill forever."[131] Chechen fighters launched a large offensive inside Groznyy on 15 January, to divert the attention of the Russian troops from Per-

---

128   Pavel Felgengauer, *Sevodnya*, 26 December 1995, English translation in *CDP-SP*, Vol. XLVII, No. 52, p.13.

129   See interview of Dudayev in *Obshchaya Gazeta*, Moscow, in Russian, No 1, 11-17 January 1996.

130   Valery Yakov, *Izvestia*, 13 January 1996, English translation in *CDPSP*, Volume XLVIII, No. 2 p. 7.

131   Michael Specter, "Strife in Chechnya embroils a neighboring people", *New York Times,* 14 January 1996.

vomayskoye.[132] The Russian troops surrounding the village pounded Raduyev's fighters with heavy artillery for three days. The fighters nevertheless succeeded in breaking through the encirclement by the Russian elite Alfa group, and most of the Chechen fighters survived the action and reached their positions inside Chechnya.[133]

On 21 April 1996, a missile launched by a military plane exploded near Gekhi-Chu, a village in south-west Chechnya, and killed the Chechen rebel President Djokhar Dudayev. The missile homed into the satellite telephone of Dudayev, who was connected to a Duma member Konstantin Borovoi.[134] What an irony: the former Soviet air force general was killed by a Russian air force missile. The death of Dudayev removed a major obstacle to negotiations between the Kremlin and the Chechen resistance, since his bellicose declarations had made direct negotiations with him unacceptable to Yeltsin. In his long interviews, sometimes spending as long as four hours with foreign journalists, he made extreme declarations, going as far making veiled threats of using nuclear weapons.[135] If the Russian leadership had been ready to change the course of the already catastrophic war, the death of Dudayev could have offered a pretext.

From the start of the Russian military campaign, Dudayev was no more than a symbolic figure, and increasingly the chief of staff of the Chechen forces, Aslan Maskhadov, a former Soviet Army artillery officer, had emerged as the military leader of the largely decentralized armed groups led by charismatic field-commanders. Dudayev was succeeded by Zelimkhan Yandarbiev, a former literature professor, who

---

132   Natalya Gorodetskaya and Maria Eismont. *Sevodnya*, 16 January 1996; in *CDPSP*, Volume XLVIII, No. 3; p. 2.

133   Over 200 people, including 78 Russian servicemen, were killed as a result of the operation. See Andrei Magomedov, "Russia jails Chechen warlord Raduyev for life", AFP, Makhachkala, 25 December 2001.

134   Sharip Asyuev, "Dudayev died in missile attack on the outskirts of Gekhi-Chu", *Tass*, Moscow, 23 April 1996; Tony Barber, "Obituary: Dzhokhar Dudayev", *The Independent*, London, 25 April 1996; see alsoYulia Kalinina, "Dudayev's Last Words", *Kommersant-Daily*, Moscow, 26 April 1996.

135   In one interview he boasted of having a "secret weapon [which was] capable of bringing a continent to its knees within a few hours". Then the general added: "No one has any protection against these weapons. There are no missile fields, no land defences, nothing." See David Hurst, "Dudayev Accuses 'Third Force'", *The Guardian*, 9 April 1996.

was Vice-President before the Russian military intervention, and one of the founders of the Chechen national movement. *[handwritten: why the war happened: urges to end talks of sovereignty.]*

Chechen fighters retake Groznyy

As the start of the Chechnya conflict in 1991 was closely linked with the disintegration of the USSR, the launching of the Chechnya campaign was dictated by the urge to end demands for sovereignty among the subjects of the Russian Federation. But developments within the Russian political system increased pressure on Yeltsin to put an end to the "open wound" in Chechnya. In the December 1995 parliamentary elections the Communist Party won over 22 per cent of the votes, while the pro-establishment Our Home is Russia formation led by Prime Minister Chernomyrdin got a mere 12 per cent in spite of all the resources invested. Yeltsin, candidate for the 1996 presidential elections, had ratings even below that: opinion polls in December 1995 gave him 5 per cent of vote intentions, while his most serious rival, the Communist Party candidate Gennadi Zyuganov, had 20-22 per cent of vote intentions.[136] The ongoing war in Chechnya was seen as a major factor favouring a potential Communist victory in 1996. In this context Yeltsin took the initiative to launch a new "peace plan". Even negotiations with Dudayev, or after his death with his successor, although through mediators, were no more taboo. *[handwritten: Yeltsin started this "peace plan"]*

In a public speech on 31 March 1996, the Russian President announced a three-stage peace plan: an end to military operations, followed by organization of parliamentary elections, and finally defining of the status of Chechnya "within the Russian Federation".[137] He also said that he had started indirect negotiations with Djokhar Dudayev. Following this initiative, in a letter sent to Dudayev, Yeltsin assured the rebel Chechen leader a few days before the latter's assassination that "regular checks have shown that military activities by the federal forces have stopped. You will no longer find that our forces have initiated military adventurism anywhere."[138] Yet the Russian military leadership *[handwritten margin: bc an election was coming up!]*

---

136   Roy Medvedev, *Post-Soviet Russia*, op. cit., p. 216.

137   Yeltsin's speech was published by *Rossiiskaya Gazeta*, on 2 April 1996; reprinted in English in: *CDPSP*, Volume XLVIII, No. 13, p. 1, 24 April 1996.

138   David Hearst, "Chechen ceasefire hands Yeltsin election coup", *The Guardian*, 28 May 1996.

did not want a repetition of the 1995 events, when following the Budy-onnovsk hostage taking operation the Russian Prime Minister ordered the cessation of military operations in return of the release of hostages. The contradictory strategies of the political leadership and the military, already seen at the start of the military campaign in December 1994, were to continue. This time, it was the politicians in Moscow who were in haste to put an end to military operations, while the generals leading a difficult war in Chechnya saw this as unnecessary manoeuvring which caused them loss of time and energy, and hindered them from accomplishing their mission.

Yandarbiev's radical rhetoric after his inauguration did not prevent him from accepting a Kremlin invitation in May 1996, through the mediation of the OSCE head of mission in Chechnya, the Swiss diplomat Tim Guldimann. On 27 May just before the Russian presidential election, Yeltsin received Yandarbiev for cease-fire talks. An agreement was signed that day between Chernomyrdin and Yandarbiyev, in the presence of the Russian-appointed head of the Chechen administration, Doku Zavgayev. Yeltsin hailed this agreement as a "historic moment in the restoration of peace in Chechnya and the end of war".[139] Yeltsin skilfully made the withdrawal of the Russian troops from Chechnya by early September 1996 (after the presidential elections!) one of his major electoral promises. How far the Russian leadership was committed to end the hostilities is not clear, but the announcement of the Russian Defence Minister commenting on the signing of the agreement was expressive: "There is nobody who can formulate the position better than our own president who said bandits, murderers and professional mercenaries must be incapacitated."[140] But even without such a negative attitude from the Russian military leadership, it was simply impossible to implement a cease-fire agreement, after eighteen months of heavy conflict, with intermingled positions and without a clear troop separation and withdrawal.

Another stunt that the Russian President used to boost his popularity days before the second round of elections was to strike a deal with

---

139   Maria Eismont, Tatyana Malkina, "Boris Yeltsin and Zelimkhan Yandarbiyev have agreed to stop war on June 1", *Segodnya*, 28 May 1996, reported in *Russian Press Digest* of the same day.

140   David Hearst, *The Guardian*, 28 May 1996.

270

another presidential candidate who was a harsh critic of the Chechen war, General Alexander Lebed. Lebed, a career officer who had served in Afghanistan, was discharged from the military a year earlier, because of increasing disagreement with the Defence Ministry. On 16 June 1996, the Kremlin announced the appointment of Lebed, who had come in the third position in the first round of presidential elections, to the post of National Security Adviser.[141] The appointment gave Lebed the power of supervision of the entire armed forces. Yeltsin also hinted that he saw in the General a successor of his in the year 2000.[142] The Defence Minister Pavel Grachev, an old friend of Lebed who had turned into his bitter enemy, was now replaced. Among Lebed's top priorities in his new post was to put an end to the Chechnya crisis. Once again, it was internal politics at the top of the Russian leadership which had to define change of course in a Caucasus War.

A day after the signing of the agreement, Yeltsin flew to Groznyy, accompanied by his generals. In a speech he delivered in front of a military unit, the Russian President mixed his promises of peace with false claims of victory: "Victory is already behind us. We have defeated the mutinous Dudayev regime (...). Their resistance has been practically broken. The road to restoring peace and constitutional order in Chechnya is open..."[143] On the first day of the cease-fire, fighting was raging in Chechnya with vast military operations simultaneously taking place on several fronts. The Russian military commander of Chechnya, General Tikhomirov, made the following declaration on Russian TV: "I will order troops to destroy, resolutely and with hatred, all those bandit groups that do not want peace..."[144]

On 6 August 1996 several hundred Chechen fighters infiltrated Groznyy, Gudermes, and Argun, the three main urban centres of Chechnya, and started fierce battles for their control. They attacked Russian army posts and fortifications, strategic points, and administrative build-

---

141   In the first round of the 1996 presidential elections, Yeltsin received 34.8 per cent of the votes, Zyuganov 32.1 per cent, and Lebed 14.7 per cent.

142   Harold Elletson, *The General Against the Kremlin, Alexander Lebed*, London: Warner Books, 1998, p. 256.

143   Robin Lodge, "Yeltsin in Chechnya: the war is won", *The Moscow Times*, 29 May 1996.

144   Lee Hockstader, "Sides violate Chechen truce on first day", *The Washington Post*, 2 June 1996.

ings. By the end of the day Russian forces were surrounded, cut off from each other, and in a desperate situation. In the next days more Chechen men armed with rifles and grenade-launchers came down to the cities to increase the thrust of the attack on the Russian forces.[145] Boris Yeltsin, just recently re-elected on the promises of an end to the war in Chechnya, and suddenly allied with General Lebed, had yet again to deal with a major problem in the Caucasus: losing Chechnya.

The Russian political and military leadership seemed completely surprised by the Chechen successes. While Lebed flew to Groznyy and tried to meet Maskhadov, calling for separation of forces, local Russian military leaders such as the commander in Chechnya, General Vyacheslav Tikhomirov, as well as the Interior Minister Kulikov, were giving ultimatums to the Chechen fighters. Yet the Russian army was completely exhausted, suffering great losses in two weeks of fighting (according to one estimate given by a Russian military spokesperson by late August, 406 soldiers had been killed and 1,264 injured and 130 were missing, huge losses in a few days).[146] Retaking Groznyy and the other towns would have cost the Russian military thousands of additional casualties, not counting the losses that the 120,000 civilians trapped in Groznyy would have suffered. Eventually, Lebed and Maskhadov concluded a cease-fire, saving Groznyy from yet another Russian assault, and promised a Russian military withdrawal from Chechnya. By end of the month, on 31 August, in the Daghestani town of Khasavyurt, Leben and Maskhadov signed a cease-fire agreement, putting an end to what later became to be known as the "First Chechen War". The two main points of the Khasavyurt agreement were Russian military withdrawal from Chechnya by the end of the year, and deferment of the issue of Chechnya's status until 31 December 2001.[147]

deferment of status.

---

145 James Meek, "Chechens jubilant as the great bear staggers", *The Guardian,* 17 August 1996.

146 James Meek, "Yeltsin's gripe erodes Grozny peace deal", *The Guardian*, 23 August 1996.

147 *Khasavyur Truce Agreement Between the Russian Federation and the Government of the Chechen Republic*, signed by A. Lebed, A. Maskhadov, S. Kharlamov, S-Kh. Abumuslirnov, in the presence of the Head of the Special Task Group of the OSCE for Chechnya Ambassador T. Guldimann, 25 August 1996, in Moshe Gammer, *The Lone Wolf and the Bear*, London: Hurst, 2005, pp. 221-3.

THE SECOND CAUCASIAN WAR

The last of the Russian troops withdrew from Chechnya by end of 1996. This was a humiliating defeat for Russia, to its newly elected but ailing president, to its huge but crumbling military. Very soon Chechnya was consigned to oblivion: no one was asked to present an explanation for the thousands of dead, for the havoc and destruction. Lebed lost his usefulness and was sacked after his first political mistake; Chechnya was left to survive in ruins; and the generals plotted their vengeance. The lack of comprehension of the calamity of the First Chechnya War was to lead inescapably to a new round of violence, a new war that continues until now.

But before going further, there are a number of interesting questions that I would like to discuss on the 1994-96 conflict: first, how can we explain that the rag-tag army of Dudayev could resist, harass and force out the Russian military machine? Second, how relevant is history , and which page of history should be considered, when looking at the causes of the Russo-Chechen confrontation? And third, was Chechnya a threat to the Russian Federation—could it cause its collapse?

"Military democracy": explaining Russian defeat and Chechen victory

little guy beats the big

In Chechnya, as in the Karabakh and Abkhazia wars, a small nation mobilized enough force to put up a strong resistance against the armed forces of a larger nation, and eventually score military victory and impose a cease-fire. Yet, while the Karabakh Armenians or the Abkhaz were facing the newly created, badly structured and undisciplined National Guards of Georgia, or the volunteers of the Azerbaijani Popular Front, the Chechen fighters themselves were facing a qualitatively different military institution, the heir of the once superpower Soviet Army.

There can be different explanations for the Russian failure—or the Chechen victory. From the military perspective, we have seen how the Russian army was in a serious condition; while it had a large number of soldiers, officers, and equipment, the servicemen had not received the necessary training and equipment, funding, logistical support and were not in combat-ready conditions. Moreover, the planning of the military operation of 11 December 1994 was done in a rush, and failed to achieve its objectives, on the way suffering huge losses.

- big guys in Georgia + Azerbaijan were big but lame, unorganized, indisciplined, qualitatively less strong than Moscow's army

273

The Russian forces, which had inherited their former Soviet formations, suffered from basic structural weaknesses as well. The Soviet Army was based on the Second World War experience ("armies are always preparing for the last war" is often repeated, yet was very true in this case) and structured to fight similar conventional armies, relying on large motorized formations, heavy artillery and air support, to overrun NATO positions in Western Europe. In Chechnya, as well as in Afghanistan, the Russian army and its Soviet predecessor lacked the necessary units trained for mountain warfare or large scale urban operations. Nor did the Soviet and later Russian army have adequate equipment to cope with long-term guerrilla resistance, and the Soviet Army in Afghanistan had to adapt its tactics and improvise its material for the new challenge.[148] Those shortcomings that were so obvious in the 1994-96 war[149] continue to haunt the Russian military in the "second" Chechnya war that started in 1999.

Other interpretations looked beyond the military sphere to the larger political context in which the war took place. Some observers found fault in the basic objectives of the Russian military campaign that started in December 1994. The announced objective was "to restore the constitutional order" in Chechnya. The political agenda was to boost the failing popularity of the Yeltsin administration. A Chechen researcher remarks that the war in Chechnya coincided with the large-scale redistribution of Soviet property among a handful of oligarchs in Russia.[150] This echoes the accusations of General Alexander Lebed, referring to the vast corruption within the Russian military as the main reason for the war, and reflecting doubt, mistrust, and incomprehension towards the immensity of the collapse, and the misappropriation caused by privatizing a state-dominated economy in such a short time as happened in Russia in 1993-96.

---

148 Among the most typical tactics in Afghanistan as well as Chechnya was an attempt to stay at least 300 metres away from the enemy, to reduce the efficiency of guerrillas relying on light arms, and increase the efficacy of Russian long-range fire-power.

149 Robert M. Cassidy, *Russia in Afghanistan and Chechnya : Military Strategic Culture and the Paradoxes of Asymmetric Conflict*, Strategic Studies Institute, US Army War College, Carlisle, PA, February 2003. See especially pp. 14-17.

150 Musa Yusupov, " Une opération de politique intérieure russe", *Le Monde diplomatique*, June 2003.

In searching for explanations for the Russian defeat in Chechnya, Anatol Lieven looks at the larger picture, at the state of Russia and its society in the early 1990s: "The Russia that went to war in Chechnya (...) was both a weak state and one in the throes of a liberal capitalist revolution..."[151] The Russian elite in those years was caught in a deadly struggle to privatize large chunks of former Soviet property—which included everything from oil fields to airports to banks—while the population was struggling to adapt to rapid changes in society and an equally rapid decline in their living conditions. As a result of the new hardships—and structural changes of modernization and urbanization under the Soviets—Russia's population had suffered decline in a physical sense as well: the Russian health care system had nearly collapsed, causing a decline in life expectancy and a rapid demographic decline; in the period of one year, from 1992 to 1993, life expectancy of the Russian male population dropped from 62 to 59 years, or 13 years less than American men.[152] Not only was Russian society demoralized as a result of those profound changes, it was largely indifferent towards the political status of Chechnya, and whether Russian "constitutional order" was imposed on the Caucasus Mountains or not. For a Russian citizen from Volgograd or Khabarovsk, the Chechens did not threaten their livelihood, their security, and their way of life. For the young Russian recruit, often from an underprivileged family, armed with an AK-74 rifle and a tourist map and sent to conquer Groznyy, the war failed to inspire patriotic feelings.[153] Moreover, the organization and logistics of the Russian forces in the Chechen war zone, and the Russian Defense Ministry's finances, were in such a bad shape that often recruits were forced to trade their weapons for food or vodka.

---

151   Anatol Lieven, *Chechnya, Tombstone of Russian Power*, New Haven: Yale University Press, 1998, p. 150.

152   Life expectancy in Russia began declining in 1988-89, when it was on average 67 years for men and 74 for women. Russia's birth rate fell to 9.2 per 1,000 people in 1993, from 10.7 in 1992. In real numbers, Russian women bore 1.4 million babies in 1993, compared with 1.6 million in 1992. See Alan Cooperman, "Amid Economic Woes, Life Expectancy Is Falling in Russia", AP, Moscow, 3 February 1994.

153   In spite of the overall Russian superiority in arms and men, at the unit level the Chechen fighters were better armed compared to the heavy but inadequate armament of the Russian forces.

In spite of those Russian shortcomings, neither the Russian political leadership nor foreign observers expected much resistance from the Chechen side. This was mainly due to the (correct) appreciation of the decline of Dudayev's popularity starting from early 1993, the defection of some of his former close collaborators, and the growing civil war of 1994; all this convinced many experts and observers (wrongly) that the Chechen pro-independence forces had no resources for much resistance against a Russian onslaught. Military observers compared the Chechen fighters with the Georgian National Guard, although a more correct comparison would have been with the Karabakh Armenians or the Abkhaz fighters. Another mistake was to evaluate the military capabilities of the pro-Dudayev Chechen fighters during their clashes with Chechen opponents. A set of social norms and traditions, personal and clan links, and the fear of vendetta, prohibited a total war during the Chechen civil war. But Chechen resistance against the Russian armies could not be anything but a total war, until the withdrawal of Russian troops from Chechnya. Although Chechnya looked and was largely chaotic in 1993-94, any traveller would have not failed to see that there at least one consensus among the Chechens, and that was to exclude Russian intervention, and especially Russian military intervention, to sort out the problems of the republic.[154]

The Chechen war of 1994-96 has become a classical example of asymmetric wars, in which a great military power fights—and loses—against a pre-industrial enemy. In such a confrontation, the strategic aims, tactics, technologic means, and will to fight and bear sacrifices differ between the two warring parties. In modern times, most colonial wars such as those of the French in Algeria, the US in Vietnam, and the Soviet Union in Afghanistan can be described as asymmetric wars. More recent examples are the Israeli army's actions in South Lebanon and the occupied Palestinian territories, and the US Army's in Somalia and more recently in Iraq. Strategically, the big power tries to limit the effectiveness of the resistance by imposing its political agenda and dominating the given country even partially, while the resistance sees its survival dependent on the outcome of the confrontation. The strategy of the big power is control of the territory, and that of the resistance is

---

154   Authors notes from several discussions in Groznyy, February 1994.

to make the occupation costly, through a long-term guerrilla campaign, to erode public support for the war and make the foreign military occupation politically unbearable. The great power tries to respond by punitive raids, often causing larger casualties among the civilian population, paradoxically increasing the chances of guerrilla recruitment. While most territory is impossible to "control" when the local population is hostile to a force of occupation, the military "successes" of punitive operations increasingly cause a loss of popular support. In a remark on the reasons why the US lost the war in Vietnam, Henry Kissinger writes, "We lost sight of one of the most cardinal maxims of guerrilla war: the guerrilla wins if he does not lose. The conventional army loses if he does not win."[155] The will to resist and the readiness for unlimited suffering provide the strategic strength of native forces facing a colonial force superior in number, armament, finances, and technology.

The Chechen resistance against the Russian forces displayed a skilful capacity to blend guerrilla and conventional tactics, and to choose the best situations to use limited human resources and armament to confront a bigger force. From the start of the war, Chechen fighters challenged the Russian army in pitched battles as during the battle for Groznyy in January-February 1995, or in Bamut later that summer. After they were driven out of the urban centres and mountain towns, the Chechen fighters stubbornly returned to challenge Russian control for a week over Gudermes in December 1995, and attacked Groznyy in January 1996 and again in March 1996. The most remarkable operation was the attack of August 1996, when Chechen fighters took control of Groznyy, Gudermes, and Argun. In Groznyy alone, 12,000 Russian soldiers were cut off from each other, and encircled in their strongholds and behind their reinforced positions, by Chechen forces numbering initially a few hundred, which after the third day of the operation increased to a couple of thousand fighters. The Russian forces had already lost the will to fight and now lost the control over the city.

The Chechen men went to the battlefield in a spontaneous manner that is unseen elsewhere. In the past, Chechens had distinguished themselves from their neighbours by the largely classless nature of their society, and the equality that conditioned the relations between them.

---

155   Henry A. Kissinger, "The Vietnam Negotiations", *Foreign Affairs*, January 1969, Vol. 47, No. 2, p. 214.

According to Professor Sergei Arutyunov, an anthropologist who has large field experience in the North Caucasus:

Chechnya was and is a society of military democracy. (...) Quite unlike most other Caucasian nations, there had never been any feudal system in Chechnya. Traditionally, if it was ever governed at all as a distinct entity, it was done by a council of elders on the basis of consensus. But like any other military democracy, such as the Iroquois in America or the Zulu in southern Africa, Chechens retained an institution of a supreme military chief. In peacetime, that chief had no power at all. No sovereign authority was recognized, and the nation might be fragmented in a hundred of rival clans.[156]

As a result, the Chechens fought their war without needing a strictly hierarchical military command; the general staff that Aslan Maskhadov led did carry out planning, coordination, and logistics, but did not coerce young Chechens to join his armed forces to got to the battlefield. This was done spontaneously out of the social tissue of the Chechen towns and villages, in the form of small groups loyal to their field commanders. Although this "military democracy" proved impressively effective against a larger and heavy war machine, enabling the Chechen fighters in the field to adapt to changing circumstances and take the initiative, compared with a hierarchical Russian army slow to react to changing realities, it became the main obstacle for the Chechens building their institutions in the inter-war period of 1996-99: without a centralized military command Aslan Maskhadov failed to build state institutions in the war-torn land, while the numerous armed groups controlling various parts of Chechnya made sure that the country would not see either stability nor security. Chechens have a long tradition of resistance, but too short an experience in state-building.

Disintegration of Russia?

On 27 December 1994, President Yeltsin addressed the Russian and international public, to explain the ongoing military operations in the

---

156   Sergey Arutiunov, "Possible Consequences of the Chechnya War for the General Situation in the Caucasus", in Mikhail Tsypkin (ed.), *War in Chechnya: Implications for Russian Security Policy*, Naval Postgraduate School, Monterey, California, 1995, available on the internet: http://www.globalsecurity.org/military/library/report/1995/con-nps.htm

North Caucasus. He put forward his arguments, starting with: "What is happening in the republic, why are Russian troops in Chechnya? First, I will answer the main question: Russian soldiers and officers are defending the unity of Russia. This is an indispensable condition of the existence of the Russian state. The Chechen Republic is part of the Russian Federation whose composition has been sealed in the Constitution. No territory has the right to secede from Russia."[157]

Following the collapse of the USSR, there was a fear that Russia, a multi-ethnic federal structure composed of ethno-territorial entities very similar to the Soviet Union, could follow the fate of its predecessor and end up collapsing along ethno-territorial lines. There were two reasons for this fear. The first was the acute struggle to control the political leadership within the Kremlin, between Yeltsin on the one hand and Vice-President Rutskoy and the Speaker of the Supreme Soviet, Khasbulatov, on the other. This struggle peaked in October 1993, and was eventually resolved by the use of tanks, which shelled the White House into surrender. The second reason for fearing collapse of the Russian Federation was the demands for sovereignty and self-determination from the ethno-territorial entities such as Tatarstan—the most important from the perspective of population, economic weight, and position as a communications hub—and Chechnya, which lacked a similar weight to Tatarstan but was relevant with its radical leadership and its geographical position in the volatile Caucasus.

This fear of the collapse of the Russian Federation played a key role in igniting the war in Chechnya. While many analysts have insisted on the desire of the Russian leadership to score a "little victorious war", this aspect of a fear of collapse has often been marginalized in the debate about the causes of the Chechnya war.[158] As one expert put it, "Moscow feared Chechnya would become Russia's Nagorno Karabakh."[159] That

---

157   "Address by Boris Yeltsin" reported by *Official Kremlin International News Broadcast*, Moscow, 27 December 1994.

158   Modern analysts who have studied history of warfare, and the emergence of war, have switched focus from "man the hunter" and the projection of power to "man the hunted", a creature living most of its existence in fear, making fear and irrational reaction due to it the root cause of wars. See Barbara Ehrenreich, *Blood Rites, Origin and History of the Passion of War*, New York: Metropolitan Books, 1997.

159   Alexei Malashenko, in a conference organized by the Swiss Peace Foundation

risk of the additional weakening of the Russian Federation was largely diminished in 1994. Following the confrontation with the parliament, Yeltsin emerged weakened and largely unpopular, yet succeeded in ending the duality of power in Moscow. Moreover, the agreement between Moscow and Kazan in February 1994 broke the trend of autonomous republics' efforts for increasing sovereignty. Therefore, the fear of collapse was not the direct cause of the Russian leadership to launch the Chechnya invasion, but it was very much present in the back of the minds of Russian decision-makers.

While Russian fears of state collapse are understandable, the events in Chechnya and the North Caucasus went beyond this preoccupation. Both during the first war and later in 1999 during the "second" war in Chechnya, this threat of Russia's disintegration was used for larger political purposes. "...Russian leaders have overreacted to the threat of secessionism triggered by the wars in Chechnya. The domestic implications of Chechen secessionism were hardly as threatening as Yeltsin and Putin portrayed them."[160] The war in Chechnya in 1994 (and the same can be said for the 1999 war) was launched to reinforce the hand of the Kremlin leader before elections, and to boost Russia's geopolitical positioning in the competition to access Caspian Sea resources. Moreover, the conflict in Chechnya served to reinforce "vertical powers", that is presidential authority over the subjects of the Russian Federation, and therefore limiting possible debate on the nature of the federation and its essence. While it is hard to deny the Kremlin's concerns about Russia's unity, or its attempts to find remedies to the security problems that were posed by the anarchy in Chechnya after the revolution in 1991, yet it seems that the Russian strategy in 1994 (the same can be said about 1999) was an attempt to address political problems back in Moscow (Yeltsin's re-election in 1996, and the transition from Yeltsin to Putin in 1999) rather than to address the strategic problems in the North Caucasus. The political objectives of the Chechen wars should be looked for in Moscow, not in the Caucasus.

A final problem in the discussion on preservation of Russia's territorial integrity is the lack of proportionality between the perceived threat

political objectives in Moscow

on the theme "Searching for Peace in Chechnya", Berne, 8 November, 2005.

160   Matthew Evangelista, *The Chechen Wars, Will Russia Go the Way of the Soviet Union?* Brookings Institution Press, 2002, p. 8.

and the means to counter it. The destruction of Groznyy and other urban centres in Chechnya, the massacres committed against civilians during military operations, as in Samashki,[161] the large number of civilian victims, all this amounts to a conflict looking less like a police operation to deal with internal problems of a state than the colonial wars of the past, such as the Russian experience in the same North Caucasus in the 19th century, or the Soviet intervention in Afghanistan. It is precisely the means used by the Russian leadership under two administrations that might eventually undermine the initial publicly declared aim of the military intervention: the conflict is increasing the schism between a Russian population among which xenophobia towards Caucasians and Muslims in general is on the rise, and those populations which feel that their essential rights are violated by large segments of the Russian society, and the Russian state.

One of the most interesting and thought-provoking works on Chechnya and the Caucasus conflicts comes from Valery Tishkov an anthropologist who served as Minister of Nationalities in Yeltsin's cabinet. It is highly important to consider his arguments because they question issues taken for granted by Western scholars when they discuss Chechnya. Tishkov has since long criticized certain "Western" authors who take a biased position in analyzing the Chechen conflict. He is equally critical towards those outsiders who take up the separatist cause while having little knowledge of the complexity of the Chechen society, and frequently express a certain political agenda, often reflecting older Cold-War reflexes: "Emotional and political involvement in evaluating the events in Chechnya has been demonstrated by many foreign experts, among whom a pro-Chechen position has become linked up with an unexpectedly strong recidivist ant-Russian position."[162] Tishkov also refuses to see the conflict on Chechnya as a part of a "four hundred

---

161   On 7 to 12 April 1995, Russian Federal troops attacked the village of Samashki, after the village elders negotiated the departure of the fighters. According to Russian press reports "hundreds" of villagers were killed. See Dmitry Balburov, "Samashki Massacre Shows Grim Reality of War", *Moscow News*, No. 15, 21-27 April 1995. According to a report by Human Rights Watch, 120 people were killed in Samashki. "Russia, Partisan War in Chechnya on the Eve of the WWII Commemoration", *Human Rights Watch*, Vol. 7, No. 8, May 1995; see the report on-line: http://www.hrw.org/reports/1995/Russiaa.htm

162   Valery Tishkov, *Ethnicity, Nationalism and Conflict in and After the Soviet Union*, p. 185.

years war", and the Chechens as the "eternal rebels", and rightly points out that the most vivid historic experience for Chechens and the closest historic reference remains the mass deportations under Stalin, and the trauma linked to this memory.[163]

Tishkov goes further to criticize the instrumentalization of past grievances by Chechen militants for political purposes. He rejects the use of such terms as "Chechen people" as an entity: "Our analysis shows that the Chechen people, or Chechen society as a collective body, no longer exists as an agent or locus of social action."[164] Tishkov insists that wide differences between Chechens and Russians, so much emphasised to justify the conflict, are not real, since Chechens have largely adopted modern, urban culture, especially in late Soviet times, and says that the majority of the Chechens are atheists, to underline their similarity with the rest of the Russian population. Every revolution mobilizes the masses and captures their imagination, and is eventually followed by a period of inevitable disillusionment. Tishkov relies on interviews showing this post-revolution disappointment to criticize the revolution itself, and question the real motives of its leadership.[165]

Tishkov is especially critical towards the notion of self-determination. "The rhetoric of self-determination has been the chief legal and emotional argument underlying disintegration and violent conflict."[166] Self-determination, therefore, is not the expression of the will of the majority of the Chechens, but the political project of a small group of nationalist militants. For Tishkov, self-determination can be only negative, aggressive and destructive. This argument (that self-determination can only lead to violence) excludes the possibility of a Chechen majority finding a political arrangement with the Russian leadership by its own free will. Moreover, it also excludes the possibility of Moscow agreeing to Chechen independence: after all, Belarus and Kazakhstan arguably have closer links with Russia than Chechnya does, and still they acceded to independence not long ago, in 1991. To conclude Tishkov's thought provoking arguments, he proposes four reasons for the outbreak of the

---

163   Valery Tishkov, *Chechnya: Life in a War-Torn Society*, pp. 17 and 20-21.

164   Ibid., p. 13.

165   Valery Tishkov, "Political Anthropology of the Chechen War", *Security Dialogue*, 1997, Vol. 28, No. 4, p. 428.

166   Tishkov, *Chechnya: Life in a War-Torn Society*, p. 12.

conflict in Chechnya: first, "the profound trauma of deportation", second, social problems in Chechnya including a high rate of unemployment, third, rapid modernization in the two decades preceding the conflict (including the emergence of a social urban group with higher education), and last, the availability of large stocks of weapons as a result of the withdrawal of the Russian army.[167] And: "The idea of Chechen self-determination as a form of nonnegotiable secession first arose under Mikhail Gorbachev's policy of perestroika, when nationalism on the periphery overpowered the process of democratization…"[168]

Yet self-determination does not necessary intend to be polarized, extreme, "non-negotiable", and lead to violence. Looking at the Chechen past—the trauma of the deportation is the key period here, and not the anti-colonial struggle of the 19th century—one can understand the radical nature of Chechen nationalism, itself a child of the failure of *perestroika* to reform the USSR. Yet the Russian political leadership did not exhaust all the ways of negotiation and mediation before deciding that the Chechen drive for self-determination was "non-negotiable". It was the 11 December 1994 Russian military invasion that put an end to all possible negotiations, and introduced a new level into this conflict, the military dimension. By putting the blame on "self-determination" and a "small faction of people", Tishkov is blaming the Chechen side as responsible for the conflict, as if the only option following the tectonic changes of 1991 was for Chechnya, as well as other regions of the Russian federation, to wait for Moscow to decide their fate, and not to be actors of politics—and why not also history—on their own terms. The Chechen demand for independence in 1991 created a political crisis. The Russian invasion of 1994 turned a political crisis into a war.

---

167   Ibid., p. 73.
168   Ibid., p. 57.

6

SOURCES OF CONFLICT: MASS TRAUMA, MOBILIZATION, REPRESSION

State collapse and state building

The collapse of the USSR was part of a dramatic, accelerated phenomenon already taking form in different shapes and expressions on a global level: the retreat of the state. After several centuries of growth in size, and domination of global politics, the state started its retreat in the last decades of the twentieth century, both in its military dimension, and in its role as provider of social welfare.[1] In the West and in the Third World the state was retreating with mass privatization of the state sector and the abandonment of conscript armies. While the shrinking of the state led to the emancipation of private capital, often with the side effect of growing poverty and social polarization, in most of the countries of the Third World the state started its retreat before it achieved its metamorphosis and reached the stage of development of the original model, the Western state. As a result we have the phenomenon of the state abandoning large sections of its territory to local elites, some of its functions to civil society actors, and its former economic monopoly to multinationals. Those changes have effected states and political systems differently, which made one observer warn: "The danger in taking the state for granted is that we begin to assume states in all times and places have had a similar potential or ability to achieve their lead-

---

1   Martin Van Creveld, *The Rise and Decline of the State*, Cambridge University Press, 2004 (fourth edition). See the sixth chapter of the book which discusses the decline of the state, pp. 336-414.

ers' intentions; the varying roles states have played in different societies may be lost".[2] Externally, weak states gave way to outside intervention, with sovereignty contested by major powers and international organizations.[3] The Soviet Union, the "largest, most centralized, and militarily most powerful state that the world had seen",[4] went through an accelerated process, and instead of shrinking, it fell apart. For the newly independent state-projects, building up their own institutions out of the debris of the USSR at a time when globally the state was challenged by multilateralism and by multinational corporations, the challenge was immense. As in the post-colonial condition, post-Soviet countries faced huge difficulty in appropriating an institution that in the past was imposed from the outside. Ghia Nodia refers to the "foreign-ness" of the state to explain the fragility and the weakness of post-Soviet Georgia.[5]

The state-building process had additional complications for states emerging from the USSR compared with post-colonial nations that gained their national independence after World War II. For post-Soviet countries, the challenge of independence was threefold:

(a) To build viable state institutions on the debris of the Soviet institutions, including army and police, an efficient taxation system, a bureaucracy, a diplomatic corps, etc.

(b) To face the challenge to the state's territorial control by centrifugal forces;

(c) To manage the systemic change from a highly centralized state structure with heavy and obsolete industrial infrastructure to the new requirements of international economics, through massive privatization and monetarization.

The international community recognized the fifteen union republics of the USSR as legitimate independent states. The fifteen states became members of international and regional organizations, such as

---

2   Joel S. Migdal, *Strong Societies and Weak States, State-Society Relations and State Capabilities in the Third World*, Princeton University Press, 1988, p. 17.

3   Stephen D. Krasner, "Sharing Sovereignty, New Institutions for Collapsed and Failing States", *International Security*, Vol. 29, No. 2, Fall 2004, pp. 85-120.

4   Martin Van Creveld, *The Rise and Decline of the State*, p. 375.

5   Ghia Nodia, "Putting the State Back Together in Post-Soviet Georgia" in Mark R. Beissinger and Crawford Young (eds), *Beyond State Crisis? Postcolonial Africa and Post-Soviet Eurasia in Comparative Perspective*, Baltimore: Johns Hopkins University Press, 2002, p. 434.

the United Nations and the Conference on Security and Cooperation in Europe—later named Organization for Security and Cooperation in Europe (OSCE)[6]—and were recognized by major international and regional powers, such as the US, EU states, Turkey and Iran. This outside recognition of the fifteen new countries as *independent* should not shroud the fact that those independences were still *state-projects* and lacked many of the attributes of statehood.[7] Even fifteen years after the collapse of the USSR, only a few of the fifteen republics would pass the test of a functioning state if one chose one or two basic criteria such as control of territory, effective capacity to raise taxation, or capacity to organize free and fair nationwide elections, the necessary condition for legitimate political representation. The waves of coloured revolutions in the early years of the new century reveal the weakness of the state-structures in both their legitimacy and even their limited capacity to repress dissent, while the revolutions should be seen as a new mobilization to reform inefficient institutions, and a new attempt at state- and nation-building.

To understand the origins of the conflicts in the Caucasus, therefore, we should first define the political mobilization that took place at the moment of the collapse of the USSR, and the conditions in which the clash between those emerging forces took place. As we have seen in the preceding chapters, various political forces independent of the official ruling party structures emerged in the Caucasus in the 1987-91 period. These forces referred to the idea of the nation, as defined and nourished within the Soviet system, and wanted more rights, freedoms, and power in the name of the nation from the Soviet authorities. Such were

---

6 On the debate within the CSCE on whether all of the new republics emerging from the USSR should join the organization or not, see Victor-Yves Ghebali, *L'OSCE dans L'Europe Post-Communiste, 1990-1996*, Brussels: Bruylant, 1996, pp. 109-11. The organization first admitted the three Baltic countries on 10 September 1991, Russia took the vacant seat of the USSR on 8 January 1992, and on 30 January 1992 the OSCE accepted ten new members: Armenia, Azerbaijan, Belarus, Kazakhstan, Kyrgyzstan, Moldova, Tajikistan, Turkmenistan, Ukraine, and Uzbekistan. Georgia, in a state of civil war, gained accession only on 24 March 1992.

7 Some even questioned the role of the OSCE in mediating between conflict sides, criticizing the organization for favouring territorial integrity against the aspirations of minority ethnic groups. See Moorad Moordaian, "The OSCE: Neutral and Impartial in the Karabakh Conflict?" *Helsinki Monitor*, 1998, No. 2, pp. 5-17.

they wanted freedom within the current framework.

the national movements in Armenia, Georgia, and Chechnya in their initial stages. When their demands were frustrated—either because the centre could not satisfy them, as in the case of the Armenian demands concerning Mountainous Karabakh, or because the authorities tried to repress their independent mobilization, as in the case of Georgia as well as Armenia and Azerbaijan—the national movements under the shock of repression felt that the Soviet Union could no more guarantee their national security, and turned against the Soviet authorities. It was in this dynamic political context that the idea of self-determination and detachment from the USSR was put forward.

Simultaneously, the weakening of the authority of Moscow, and its incapacity to play a decisive role in making political decisions in the Caucasus, led to a power vacuum within which the various national movements of the Caucasus clashed. Most of the sources of friction—such as the status of Mountainous Karabakh, political power arrangements in Abkhazia, etc.—were there well before the coming of Mikhail Gorbachev to power and the launching of his reform project. Yet these were not "ancient hatreds" that had resurfaced. As one observer has put it, "nationalism reflects a need to establish an effective state to achieve a group's economic and security needs. The most aggressive nationalist movements arise when states fail to carry out tasks, spurring people to create more effective states."[8] It was the attempt at reforms that destabilized the existing political arrangements, marginalized the former ruling elite within the hegemonic party, and opened up space for new political forces to emerge and eventually to clash first with Moscow and then with each other.

The nature of the various national mobilizations needs to be examined. From the perspective of international law they have been divided into recognized states and rebellious "separatism". The nature of the two, from both historic and sociological perspectives, remains the same: political movements invoking the right of the nation—whether Georgian or Osset, Azeri or Chechen—to self-determination and statehood, over the ruins of the collapsing USSR.[9] In this sense, calling the

---

8   Jack Snyder, "Nationalism and the Crisis of the Post-Soviet State", *Survival*, Vol. 35, No. 1, Spring 1993, p. 7.

9   Hratch Tchilingirian, "Nagorno Karabagh: Transition and the Elite", *Central Asian Survey*, Vol. 18, No. 4, 1999, pp. 435-61.

[handwritten margin note: wasn't really separatist bc what they were separating from wasn't well established.]

Karabakh, South Osset, Abkhaz, or Chechen movements "separatist" makes sense in legal and political terms, but does not help us understand their essence: both were trying to establish a new national political entity emerging from a crumbling mega-state, the Soviet Union. Refocusing our analysis on the common nature of "nationalism" and "separatism"—movements of titular nations against the Soviet centre, and movements of ethnic minorities against the titular nations—helps us better understand the conflicts and their military outcome.

Next to the challenges of state building were the difficulties associated with nation building. As already discussed in chapter 2, it was especially difficult for Azerbaijan to define itself in the terms specific to a nation, since it lacked specific delimitation proper to national groups as they emerged by the 19th century in contrast to empires, religious communities, and regional identities. The debate on national identity in Azerbaijan is highly political: the Popular Front of Azerbaijan pushed while in power for the idea of *Turkism*, Heydar Aliev after returning to power switched back to the idea of *Azerbaijanism*. Such ideological changes had also policy consequences, extending to cultural policy: under the Popular Front the official language spoken in Azerbaijan was called "Turkish", while after the return of Aliev to power it was renamed "Azerbaijani" as in Soviet times. Until today, this schism between two visions of Azerbaijan divides the political elite in the country. According to an unidentified scholar close to the Azerbaijani opposition, "the term Azerbaijani as it is used by the government today does not have a historic root or a scientific base. In his view, there is no such nation as Azerbaijan since Azerbaijan is a geographic name and consequently, the concept of Azerbaijani refers to all those who live on this piece of land".[10]

Similarly, the North Caucasus went through changes in identity in which tribal specificities developed into ethnic distinctions, as in the separation between the Chechens and the Ingushes. Even peoples with long distinct identity like the Armenians and the Georgians, with their specific languages, literary traditions, even alphabets, had to go through

---

10   Ceylan Tokluoglu, "Definition of National Identity, Nationalism and Ethnicity in post-Soviet Azerbaijan in the 1990's", *Ethnic and Racial Studies*, Vol. 28, No. 4, July 2005, p. 736.

a process of defining who made part of the nation and who did not.[11] In the Georgian example, the Ajars were generally considered as being part of the mainstream Georgian nation, although being of Muslim religion, while the Meskhets, who were deported en masse by Beria to Central Asia, were not.[12] To add to an already complex context, the Caucasus went through population movements, exchanges, and deportations starting from the 1917 Revolution, reaching a conclusion with the cycle of violent conflicts at the moment of the Soviet collapse (1988-96). The former cosmopolitan cities of Tbilisi and Baku, metropoles with large communities of ethnic Armenians and Russians by the late 19th and the early 20th century,[13] have increasingly come to resemble capitals of nation-states with ethnic Georgian domination in the first case and ethnic Azerbaijani in the second, the migration of ethnic Russians from Azerbaijan and Georgia northwards to Russia, and population exchanges between Armenian and Azerbaijan. It is yet to be seen whether the situation has stabilized, or whether there are new population exchanges and mass migration movements on the horizon.[14]

Self-determination and conflict

The context of Soviet collapse, although a necessary condition for generalized uncertainty and insecurity, is not sufficient to explain the Caucasian conflicts. Many observers have noted that the collapse of the USSR has been relatively bloodless, in comparison with the fall of Yugoslavia

---

11   For example, see the case of the Hemshins in Hovann H. Simonian, "The Vanished Khemshins: Return from the Brink", *Journal of Genocide Research*, Vol. 4, No. 3, 2002, pp. 375-85.

12   On the Meskhetians, see Oskar Pentikäinen and Tom Trier, "Between Integration and Resettlement: The Meskhetian Turks", *European Centre for Minority Issues*, Working Paper, No. 21, September 2004. Available on the internet: http://www.ecmi.de/download/working_paper_21b.pdf

13   See Ronald Grigor Suny, *The Baku Commune 1917-1918, Class and Nationality in the Russian Revolution*, Princeton University Press, 1972, chapter one, in which he recalls the ethnic division in the city with 95,000 Muslims, 90,000 Russians and 63,000 Armenians (p. 20); on the multi-ethnic character of Georgia during the same period, see Stephen F. Jones, *Socialism in Georgian Colors, The European Road to Social Democracy 1883-1917*, Cambridge, MA: Harvard University Press, 2005, pp. 1-29.

14   A collection of recent articles on patterns of migration in the Caucasus can be found in Alexandr Iskandaryan (ed.), *Migratsii Na Kavkazye, Materiali Konferentsii*, Yerevan: Caucasus Media Institute, 2003.

in the same period.[15] Yet, one needs to explain further why there were wars in Karabakh, Abkhazia, and Chechnya, and inter-ethnic clashes in North Ossetia? Why were there no other conflicts? One explanation put forward was the drive to self-determination by ethnic groups which were the source of the problem.[16] The fear of the contagion of national mobilization and proliferation of new independent states through ethnic mobilization haunted observers in the aftermath of Soviet and Yugoslav disintegration. "If there is one lesson to be learnt from the terrible tragedy in Yugoslavia, it may be that the principle of self-determination of peoples, as it stands now, is dangerous foundation for international relations", some argued.[17]

Andre Liebich points to the fact that the number of recognized states has continued to grow, and argues against the standardization of nations or cultural entities acceding to statehood. "Taking only language as a defining criterion, one could count some 6,000 linguistically defined groups. (…) An international system consisting of many hundreds, possibly even thousands, of state units would function along different lines from the one we know."[18] The author exposes various schools of thought that have tried to define the conditions in which nations should become states, including, in the words of Liebich, definitional arguments (nations and states are interchangeable), causal arguments (nations become states through modernization, that is the cultural community and the state institutions correspond to each oth-

15   Gail W. Lapidus, "Contested Sovereignty, The Tragedy of Chechnya", *International Security*, Vol. 23, No. 1, Summer 1999, p. 5.

16   Criticism of the idea of self-determination came from various angles; see for example the article of Viktor Alksnis, a deputy in the Soviet parliament from Latvia, and a founder of the Soyuz (Union) caucus, "Suffering from Self-determination", *Foreign Policy*, No. 84, Autumn 1991, pp. 61-71; see also the article of Charles Tilly, "National Self-Determination as a Problem for All of Us", *Daedalus*, Summer 1993, Cambridge, MA, p. 29; a recent paper arguing against secession see Donald L. Horowitz, "The Racked Foundations of the Right to Secede", *Journal of Democracy*, Vol. 14, No. 2, April 2003, pp. 5-17; Strobe Talbott, "Self-Determination in an Interdependent World", *Foreign Policy*, No. 118, Spring 2000, pp. 152-63.

17   Reneo Lukic and Allen Lynch, *Europe from the Balkans to the Urals, The Disintegration of Yugoslavia and the Soviet Union*, New York: Oxford University Press, 1996, p. xiii.

18   Andre Liebich, "Must Nations Become States?" *Nationalities Papers*, Vol. 31, No. 4, December 2003, p. 453.

er) and moral arguments (nations must be free, and therefore have the rights for self-determination). Liebich convincingly reveals the limitations of the arguments that define conditions in which nations must become states, and instead prefers "historical examination" that takes "the international system as a reference point rather than those based on an ethical discourse of rights".[19]

The international system today, with the principle of territorial integrity of states clashing with and in most cases overriding national self-determination, is a conservative force to guard the status quo. When faced with monumental change such as the collapse of the largest state on the surface of the earth, the question of how to mange its succession cannot be restrictively addressed by legal considerations. Whether in 1991 nations, ethno-cultural groups and administrative entities had to be automatically attributed to the fifteen recognized successors of the USSR without the formal and explicit agreement of the populations involved remains a difficult question. The Soviet authorities tried to slow down the process of disintegration by trying to provide a legal exit from the Union; a law on secession ratified on 3 April 1990 laid down conditions: any secession needed two-thirds of votes in a republic-wide referendum, and there must be a five-year exit period in which separation should be negotiated between the given republic and the central authorities. The Baltic republics immediately rejected this law, considering that it did not apply in their case, and accelerated their measures to assert full independence.[20]

Whatever position the international community could take in the matter, the fact remains that the collapse of the USSR led to fifteen recognized, but also four additional non-recognized states, three of which are in the region of the Caucasus.[21] As one study puts it, "the territorial

---

19   Ibid., p. 460.

20   Martha Brill Olcott, "The Soviet (Dis)Union", *Foreign Policy*, No. 82, Spring 1991, p. 125.

21   The three unrecognized states are Mountainous Karabakh, South Ossetia, and Abkhazia, all three situated in the South Caucasus. We also have the Pridnestrovyan Republic occupying the eastern stretch of Moldova. Chechnya could have qualified as unrecognized state between 1991 and 1994, and again from the summer of 1996 until 1999, and currently is pacified only thanks to a huge Russian military presence, and at a heavy financial and political price, besides the military sacrifices. For a discussion on the current situation of the unrecognized states and European security, see Dov Lynch, *Managing Separatist States:*

separatists of the early 1990s have become the state builders of the early 2000s, creating de facto countries whose ability to field armed forces, control their territory, educate their children, and maintain local economies is about as well developed as that of the recognized states of which they are still notionally a part."[22]

It is important to remember that the right to self-determination does not automatically lead to separation and state formation: elites may prefer negotiating a new political deal reflecting the changes and stay within the same state structure, or in some cases political leaders calling for self-determination and the formation of an independent state may fail to mobilize support. When Tatarstan, Bashkortistan, Yakutia and others had the chance to decide, they settled for agreements with Moscow to preserve their presence within the Russian Federation, yet insisting on certain rights and self-rule. The same is true for Ajaria, an autonomous republic within Georgia, which did not demand separation from Georgia in spite of difficult relations between its long-time ruler Aslan Abashidze and the political leadership in Tbilisi. The same is true in Azerbaijan, where ethnic Lezgins, Kurds and Talishes did not express any desire for national-independence, although they were never formally asked to express their feelings whether they wanted to be part of independent Azerbaijan or not. Yet, when an army colonel in the Talish inhabited region of southern Azerbaijan declared a separatist Talish-Mughan republic, he received no support from the local population, and his attempt was soon crushed by regular troops.

One more clarification: even in the case of "separatism", one should not equate the drive for national self-determination with armed conflict and prolonged war. For example, the Armenian and Georgian national movements succeeded in their goal and achieved independence from the USSR and recognition from the international community without a "national liberation war", because of the changing political context. From the same historic period, we have the example of the separation of Slovakia from the Czechoslovak Federation without bloodshed, and, on the other hand, the recognition of the independence of Eritrea by

A Eurasian Case Study, Institute for Security Studies – Western European Union, Occasional Paper 33, November 2001, 34 pp.

22   Charles King, "The Benefits of Ethnic War, Understanding Eurasia's Unrecognized States", *World Politics,* No. 53, July 2001, p. 525.

Ethiopia in 1993, after a long and bloody struggle. The point made here is that the existence of a political force calling for separation, self-determination and the establishment of a nation-state on a part of another internationally recognized state is not enough in itself to ignite war. In the case of the wars of Soviet succession, and as we will see in more detail later, the decision of central authorities to repress ethnic and regionalist political movements has often led to both radicalization of those movements and the start of an armed conflict.

per precipitation factor.

Territorial autonomy and violence

In an effort to look for the causes of conflicts, one author has looked at the interrelation between autonomous republics and political mobilization leading to armed conflicts. Svante Cornell in two articles looks at "autonomy" as a primary source of conflict.[23] The author starts with expressing his surprise: the usual model of minorities calling for independence and finally settling for an autonomous status does not seem to work in the case of post-Soviet conflicts. "What we see there is that, quite to the contrary, it is the state that advocates autonomy for the minority, which in turn refuses to accept any solution short of independence."[24] As a result, in post-Soviet situation we are left without one of the classical forms of compromise between a state and national minorities searching for self-accretion. Cornell comes to the conclusion that although numerous minorities live in the Caucasus, "only those that were holders of an autonomous status actually rebelled."[25] Then the author adds that in the Soviet system, although certain entities enjoyed autonomous status, in reality real autonomy was never practiced on account of the highly centralized nature of the Soviet state. As a result, now that the former autonomies have achieved self-rule as a result of the conflicts, they are extremely reluctant to go back to the previous arrangement about which they have large doubts and long decades of negative experience.

23   Svante Cornell, "The Devaluation of the Concept of Autonomy: National Minorities in the Former Soviet Union", *Central Asian Survey*, Vol. 18, No. 2, 1999, pp. 185-96; and "Autonomy as a Source of Conflict, Caucasus Conflicts in Theoretical Perspective", *World Politics*, Vol. 54, January 2002, pp. 254-76.

24   Cornell, "The Devaluation…", p. 185.

25   Ibid., p. 192.

Svante CORNELL, 1999 & 2002

In a later article Cornell develops further his study of the interrelation between autonomies and conflicts, and starts by generalization: "Autonomous regions, by their very nature, are conductive to secessionism."[26] The author emphasizes that all the conflicts in the Caucasus took place between central governments and *autonomous* minorities" [in italics in the original text] while numerically important minorities, such as ethnic Armenians and Azerbaijanis in Georgia, also had grievances yet did not develop secessionist movements—both being without autonomous structures.[27] Convincingly, the author emphasizes the existence of a leading elite, symbolically potent elements such as borders, political institutions such as local parliaments (soviets), police forces, mass media which could mobilize the local population, and local soviets that could counter republican laws by issuing local laws and thus provide both legitimacy and capacity for ethnic minorities to revolt.

Cornell raises an important issue: the autonomy status of Mountainous Karabakh, South Ossetia, and Abkhazia clearly gave those three entities the means, institutions, and leverages to mobilize. For example, the first step taken by Karabakh Armenians that brought the territorial issue out to the open was its Supreme Soviet resolution on 20 February 1988, demanding to be transferred to the jurisdiction of the Armenian SSR. Similarly, it was the head of the Abkhaz Supreme Soviet, Vladislav Ardzinba, who moved from Sukhumi to Gudauta in August 1992 as the Georgian National Guards advanced on the regional capital, and called for mobilization and armed struggle. Without his position as the head of the Abkhazian Soviet the orders of Ardzinba would not have had the same weight. Yet looking at the autonomous status of a region does not help us understand why certain conflicts took place, and others not. Nakhichevan had a superior status to that of Mountainous Karabakh within the Azerbaijani SSR (being an Autonomous Republic), yet it did not witness any violent conflict, nor did it go through a separatist movement against the central rule of Baku.[28] In the North Caucasus,

---

26 Cornell, "Autonomy as a Source of Conflict", p. 251.

27 Ibid., p. 258.

28 Nakhichevan is an Autonomous Republic within Azerbaijan, and an exclave with long borders with Armenia to its east and Iran to its west, and a short crossing to Turkey in its north-western corner. The region has traditionally provided Azerbaijan with its ruling elite. During the rule of the Popular Front of Azerbaijan, Heydar Aliev was the President of Nakhichevan, running the region

from the various examples we can simply say that it was not the Autonomous Republic of Checheno-Ingushetia that drove for separatism, but the Chechen National Congress, and in the process it undermined and broke apart the Checheno-Ingush autonomy. Looking more widely at other post-Soviet conflicts, neither the war in Moldova nor the intra-Tajik war was characterized by autonomous formations. If the issue of existing autonomy played a role in the Caucasus conflicts, it was a secondary role indeed. The Karabakh Armenians, the Ossets, Abkhaz and Chechens had their distinct identity well before the Soviet "gift" of presenting them with territorial autonomy. Their distinct group identity, and their drive for self-determination, can be traced to periods prior to the October Revolution.

Another pitfall of this argument is to look at the conflict dynamics through the political ambitions of ethnic minorities enjoying "autonomous" status. The conflict dynamics were different in each of the cases. In Abkhazia, the compromise around the Abkhaz autonomy was being challenged as a result of Georgian national mobilization. In Karabakh and Chechnya, it was the ethnic minorities that challenged the status quo, demanding a different political arrangement: for Karabakh Armenians union with Soviet Armenia, and for Chechens self-determination (which meant different things at different times). "The Soviet Union was a totalitarian state that showed little respect for the human or political rights of its citizens, thereby making it difficult to determine whether specific groups or the entire population were the targets of state abuse. Who was to blame for discrimination – the republics or the central Soviet state? Blaming republican governments would actually be somewhat illogical if major decisions were taken in Moscow..."[29] Such abstract viewpoints reflect the discourse popular among Caucasian elites delegating responsibility for all the problems including their own acts to the Soviet authorities, and later the Russian leadership. While such mechanisms are useful in easing inter-Caucasian enmity (since Moscow was "responsible" for the problems between the Abkhaz and the Georgians, then finding a solution could be somewhat easier "once Moscow stops meddling in our affairs"), they are not helpful on the level of

---

in an independent political course, yet never demanding secession from the rest of Azerbaijan.

29   Ibid., pp. 258-9.

analysis. There is a vast literature about how the Soviet authorities lost the control of the "periphery" to local ethnic elites and clan structures,[30] which reached the summit of their power under Brezhnev. The attempts under Gorbachev to reassert central rule over the republics, by sacking local party bosses such as Dinmukhammad Kunaev in Kazakhstan and Heydar Aliev (removed from his position in the Politburo in Azerbaijan), or by the mass rotation of cadres in Uzbekistan and elsewhere after the "cotton affair", turned out to be insufficient:[31] local elites had already developed deep roots and cadre reshuffling was insufficient to change the new power relations.

If it was the central authorities who were to blame for the discrimination suffered by the minorities, as Cornell suggests, then how should we explain the fact that both ethnic Ossets and ethnic Abkhaz overwhelmingly voted for the preservation of the Union, while ethnic Georgians in Abkhazia and throughout Georgia refused to participate in the referendum? Both Abkhaz and South Osset saw in the Soviet centre as a guarantee for preserving the status quo, the relative political and cultural autonomy they enjoyed under the Soviet rule, and feared change coming from Georgian nationalism. This was no abstract fear: leaders of the Georgian nationalist movement rejected all autonomy in South Ossetia (saying their homeland was in "North Ossetia" and they were "guests" in Georgia), and while recognizing Abkhaz specificity they were ready to concede "cultural autonomy" to the Abkhaz but not "territorial autonomy". On the other hand, Karabakh Armenians did not support the preservation of the USSR, seeing in Soviet policies and Soviet legality an obstacle to their self-determination. As a result they paid dearly when Soviet troops and Azerbaijani police attacked ethnic Armenian villages to the north of the administrative border of Karabakh, killing and deporting thousands in 1991.

---

30   To suggest some, see Ronald G. Suny, *The Revenge of the Past*, Stanford University Press, 1993; Gregory Gleason, "Fealty and Loyal: Informal Authority Structures in Soviet Asia"; *Soviet Studies*, Vol. 43, No. 4, 1991, pp. 613-28; Alisher Ilkhamov, "Nation-State Formation: Features of Social Stratification in the Late Soviet Era", *International Journal of Middle East Studies*, Vol. 34, 2002, pp. 317-35.

31   One estimate puts the number of cadres imprisoned for corruption under Gorbachev in Uzbekistan and Kyrgyzstan at 30,000! See Kathleen Collins, "Clans, Pacts, and Politics in Central Asia", *Journal of Democracy*, Vol. 13, No. 3, July 2001, pp. 137-52, p. 144.

The factor of the autonomous entity is important to understand the conflicts. Without it, it is rather unlikely that the Abkhaz would have come to clash with Tbilisi. But it was not the autonomous status of Abkhazia that was the trigger for conflict. The key problem was that with the weakening of the Soviet authorities and the rise of Georgian nationalism, the previous political arrangement in Abkhazia was threatened. The Abkhaz feared to lose the little autonomy they enjoyed (which was real in domains such as cultural rights, education, mass media, resource distribution, etc.) and mobilized in its defence. As Abkhaz authors and politicians have stressed several times, they did not put forward any demand for secession until the onset of military operations, and after Sukhumi was under the occupation of the Georgian National Guard. "We never demanded secession from Georgia before the war, but Georgia was not ready for compromises," in the words of the Abkhazian Foreign Minister Sergei Shamba.[32]

While discussing the conflicts in detail, we saw how the use of violence by the leadership of titular nations precipitated a political conflict over territorial status (Karabakh and Chechnya) or limits of autonomies (South Ossetia and Abkhazia) into violent conflicts. Without the use of force, we can imagine the possibility of a compromise solution on power sharing (as in Abkhazia under Gamsakhurdia), or even acceptance by the central power of the right of the minority group to secede. Theoretically, there is nothing to suggest it was impossible for Moscow to agree to Chechen independence, only a short period after it had agreed to let go the whole of Eastern Europe, the Baltic States, Ukraine and Belarus, Central Asia and the South Caucasus. And one should not exclude the possibility of development of Chechen political forces which, in opposition to Dudayev's policies, called for close links with the Russian Federation and eventually succeeded in convincing Chechen public opinion about the merits of the Tatarstan model. But Moscow gave Chechnya neither the time, nor the right to choose. Moscow wanted to impose its own will on Chechnya, and the result was—still is! —a long and painful conflict.

---

32   Author interview with Sergei Shamba, Sukhumi, 12 May 1997; see also Viacheslav Chrikba, "The Georgian–Abkhazian Conflict: In Search for Ways Out", in Bruno Coppieters and Yuri Anchabadze (eds), *Georgians and Abkhazians, the Search for a Peace Settlement*, Cologne: Bundesinstitut für ostwissenschaftliche und internationale Studien, 1998, p. 54.

It was not the autonomous status of Karabakh, South Ossetia, Abkhazia, or Chechnya which caused the conflicts in the Caucasus. It was the drive of those ethnic groups for self-determination, and the will of the leaders of the titular nations to suppress this drive by force that caused the wars. A central fact in the mechanism of starting the conflicts, which has been surprisingly absent from the literature analyzing post-Soviet conflicts, is the fact of the first use of force: without Moscow ordering the invasion of Chechnya in December 1994, without the Georgian National Guard invading Sukhumi in August 1992, without the pro-Gamsakhurdia armed militants marching to take control of Tskhinvali, without the series of anti-Armenian pogroms in major Azerbaijani towns in 1988-1990 followed by ethnic cleansing in the Kaltso operation in 1991, there would not have been the initial explosion that caused the series of chain reactions and precipitated political conflicts into armed conflicts. An author who has studied the disintegration of the USSR, Yugoslavia, and Czechoslovakia comes to the following conclusion: "the conditions under which secessionist struggle becomes violent (...) is, when the centre uses force to defend existing state boundaries..."[33]

If we agree that the fact that some ethnic groups had autonomous status is in itself not enough to explain the conflicts, and also that the trigger of *violent* conflict (war, or armed conflict) came from the will of the leadership of titular groups to repress by force any independent expression of ethno-regional groups, we still have the question of the strong political mobilization of certain groups leading to a *political* conflict. Why did the Karabakh Armenians, Abkhaz and Chechens mobilize earlier, more widely throughout their societies, and take more radical positions than their neighbouring ethnic groups? The particular history of those groups, their past memories and historic traumas, is key to understanding their strong mobilization in a period of uncertainty and sudden change.

Now, after the resort to violence and the eruption of war, it is difficult to negotiate "autonomy" as a compromise to come out of the crisis situation. The Azerbaijani authorities propose to Mountainous Kara-

---

33 Valerie Bunce, "Peaceful versus Violent State Dismemberment: A Comparison of the Soviet Union, Yugoslavia, and Czechoslovakia", *Politics and Society*, Vol. 27, No. 2, June 1999, p. 218.

bakh "the highest degree of autonomy", in the words of the Heydar Aliev.[34] Similarly, Georgian negotiators for a political solution a year after the conflict agreed to provide Abkhazia with such state attributes as "Constitution and legislation and appropriate State symbols, such as anthem, emblem and flag".[35] Yet, after a history of violence and fear of destruction, neither Karabakh nor South Ossetia nor Abkhazia has so far gone for a compromise solution that would bring their territories and population under the rule of their antagonists.

Mass trauma and political mobilization

The collapse of the Soviet ideology and political system necessitated the development of new definitions and new group identities. Nationalism, whether the nationalism of the titular nations or that of the minority groups, was the best positioned to take on this role, as argued in chapter 2. The Caucasian groups developed new political myths based on the traumatic experience of the past, a strong tool of political mobilization. In the words of Tirza Hechter, "perceived and traumatic shared experiences under certain conditions might lend themselves to divergent interpretations and conceptualizations. In such situations, it is possible that major ideologies that were dormant in the specific society would be rediscovered and eve born anew."[36] Such myths link past sacrifices with the contemporary struggles in a common narrative. A psychologist working on trauma related to conflict regions remarks that: "Croatian psychiatrists then working with captured Serbian military found an unexpectedly high frequency of 'old', World War II trauma-related issues." And continuing remarks on the Balkan Wars, he adds: "the worst

---

34   Author's notes from press conference given by Heydar Aliev, Baku, 1 July 1999.

35   *Declaration on Measures for a Political Settlement of the Georgian/Abkhaz Conflict*, signed by A. Kavsadze for the Georgian side, S. Jinjolia for the Abkhaz side, E. Brunner from the UN, B. Pastukhov from the Russian Federation, and V. Manno from the Conference on Security and Cooperation in Europe, on 4 April 1994, in Moscow. The English text is available on the internet: http://www.usip.org/library/pa/georgia/georgia_declar_19940504.html

36   Tirza Hechter, "Historical Traumas, Ideological Conflicts, and the Process of Mythologizing", *International Journal of Middle East Studies*, Vol. 35, 2003, pp 439-60, p. 455.

atrocities in the 1990s were exactly in the areas most affected by the World War II."[37]

Authors looking at the root causes of the wars in the Caucasus, and the post-Soviet context, have underlined the element of "fear" as an important mechanism of explanation. Rogers Brubaker has talked about the security dilemma emerging from the triangular relationship between nationalizing states, national minorities, and external national homelands.[38] Similarly, in his discussion of the Karabakh conflict, Stuart Kaufmann insists that "ethnic war is driven primarily by fear, which in turn has its sources in prejudice rooted in nationalist ideology."[39] His conclusion is that "prejudice, fear and extremist ideology" have caused security problems in otherwise "apparently stable states",[40] leading to the destructive war.

Yet, studies looking at the causes of the wars in the Caucasus have by and large failed to see the key role played by *historic trauma* among Karabakh Armenians, Abkhaz and Chechens, in the three major conflicts in the Caucasus in the 1990s. Although this much neglected subject needs a thorough study, I will nevertheless try to give a concise presentation on how past trauma has played an important role in ethnic mobilization and in the radical demands of the three major conflicts in the Caucasus. Moreover, I will emphasize that the past was not only present in the mass consciousness of aggrieved groups, but was constantly present as a potential threat used by the governments trying to repress ethnic mobilization. To put it another way, in a moment of historic change and uncertainty, ethnic groups with historic trauma have mobilized to defend themselves against the repetition of past genocides, massacres, and mass deportations, while simultaneously dominant groups have threatened—either implicitly through certain repressive policies or explicitly through clear threats—either to force surrender or to go through similar mass repression.

The Karabakh Armenians, the Abkhaz and the Chechens, each in an individual way, share a deep trauma related to historic events, during

---

37   Malvern Lumsden, "Breaking the Cycle of Violence", *Journal of Peace Research*, Vol. 34, No. 4, 1997, p. 377.

38   See chapter three in Rogers Brubaker, *Nationalism Reframed*, pp. 55-78.

39   Stuart Kaufmann, "Ethnic Fears and Ethnic War in Karabakh", *op. cit.*, p. 2.

40   Ibid., p. 36.

which each *ethnos* came close to annihilation. The relevance of those traumas is even stronger since none of the three nations has received full recognition and symbolic reparation to comfort them. Moreover, recent events in the last decades of the Soviet Union have made the mass trauma present in the daily experience of the three groups. The political opening that accompanied the Gorbachev reforms has simultaneously inspired hope and caused uncertainty and insecurity, both opportunity and fear, which explains on the one hand mass mobilization and on the other the radical demands of the groups. Similar traumatic experience can be found at the source of Ingush mobilization and territorial demands from North Ossetia. In the case of the Ossets in Georgia, although they do not have a traumatic past like the Armenians or the Chechens, they nevertheless went through heavy repression during the Georgian Republic of 1918-21. Moreover, there were moments during the conflict in South Ossetia when the Ossets felt that their presence to the south of the Caucasus Mountains was threatened. It was such perceived threats that radicalized the positions of minority ethnic groups. "If a group believes that there is even a small chance that it may become a target of genocidal attack, it may choose conflict over compromise and the risk of future destruction. To provoke conflict, one group need not believe that the other group really is aggressive, only fear that it might be."[41]

In the case of the Armenians, the spill-over of mass demonstrations from Stepanakert to Yerevan was a somewhat naïve expression of historic frustrations, combining specific Armenian suffering with what was common with other Soviet peoples. In the words of Rafael Ghazarian, one of the members of the Karabakh Committee,

The liberation movement of 1988 was the explosion to empty from our hearts the negative charges of historic injustice accumulated in our heart. (…) The inquisitive sociologist, by deconstructing those charges, will discover there the Genocide [*yeghern*] and the forced separation of Karabakh and Nakhichevan....[42]

---

41   David A. Lake and Donald Rothchild, "Containing Fear, The Origins and Management of Ethnic Conflict", *International Security*, Vol. 21, No. 2 Fall 1996, p. 51.

42   Rafael Ghazarian, *Hashvedou Yem...* (in Armenian: "I am Accountable"), Yerevan, 2003, p. 9.

For that author, frustrations accumulated in relation with the Genocide, the decision of Soviet authorities to place Nakhichevan and Karabakh—both with substantial Armenian populations—within the Azerbaijani SSR in 1923, and the Soviet repression, all of that found expression in the mass movement under the banner of *Miatsoum* (unification).

For the Karabakh Armenians, their initial mobilization was addressed against decades of political repression and discrimination exercised in daily politics by the Soviet Azerbaijani authorities. It also expressed the long-term fear of losing control over the territory, with the increase in the ethnic Azerbaijani population of Mountainous Karabakh, and the example of Nakhichevan testified to that. The anti-Armenian pogroms in Sumgait in the last days of February 1988 sent a shock wave throughout the nation ("It was like putting salt on our wounds" in the words of Vazken Manukian), and magnified the fears, transposing them to the huge suffering of the Armenians in Turkey during and after World War I. "The terms "massacre", "pogrom", and even "genocide" became current, and immediate, spontaneous association with 1915 was made everywhere. The Azerbaijanis, related by race, language and culture to the Turks, became in Armenian minds the same heartless people who had participated in the genocide of 1915".[43] Sumgait transformed a past trauma into an immediate threat. The repetition of the pogroms in Kirovabad and Baku, and the mass deportations from Martunashen and Ketashen, turned the threat of pogroms and massacres into an official policy in Azerbaijan, whether in the hands of the radical opposition (the Baku pogroms) or the official policy of the Azerbaijani SSR (Martunashen and Ketashen). The official Turkic ideology in Azerbaijan under the PFA only added to Armenians' mental amalgamation of the Turkey of 1915 with the Azerbaijan of the Karabakh war. It was this fear of a threat of annihilation which explains more than other factors the strong mobilization and militancy of Karabakh Armenians, and their determination in the battlefield against an enemy which was not moved by similar instincts, similar fear, and past experience of near annihilation.

---

43   Richard Hovannisian, "Historical Memory and Foreign Relations, The Armenian Perspective", in S. Frederick Starr (ed.), *The Legacy of History in Russia and the New States of Eurasia*, Armonk: M. E. Sharp, 1994, Volume I, p. 241.

The historic fear, or threat, of genocide did not come just from one side. It was not just Armenian fears. By the pogroms in Sumgait and Baku Azerbaijani authorities were talking the same language, and were sending a message equivalent to a threat: either end the Karabakh demands or take the risk of massacres, deportations, and the loss of the historic land. Even years after the end of the hostilities, it remains part of the Karabakh discourse. In the words of Samvel Babayan, at the time the head of the Karabakh military forces:

Today, they [Azeris] are hurting our fatherland, we should not swallow this. Having separated us for more than 70 years, they have hurt us, insulted us. Perhaps, they committed the Genocide [of Armenians] because we did not fight, we were defeated, we were spread all over the world. Today, we do not have the right to behave like that. We must unite and fight. If we do not defend our lands today, a new Genocide will take place; we cannot turn and blame others for that; generations will scorn us for losing a chance.[44]

The case of the Abkhaz people's historic experience, and the fear of losing group identity, were central in their mobilization in defence of their political autonomy. Like the Karabakh Armenians', the Abkhaz historic trauma was the interposition of various layers, coming from different epochs of history. As we have seen in some detail in chapter 4, the Abkhaz had become a minority in the land called after their name, as a result of the Caucasian Wars against Tsarist Russia in the 19th century and the massacres and mass deportations that followed. Yet, in the last part of the 20th century, the Abkhaz saw the threat to their survival coming from Georgian policies, in the form of increasing migration of Mingrelians to Abkhazia, often encouraged by official policies of Tbilisi, and not from Russia (it should be recalled that, according to the 1989 census, 45 per cent of the population of Abkhazia were ethnic Georgians, and only 17 per cent were ethnic Abkhaz). Unlike the Karabakh Armenians or the Chechens, there was no "revolution" taking place in Abkhazia: it was the former leadership in place that was suspicious about Georgian nationalism, and determined to preserve the relative political independence they enjoyed. The Abkhaz saw the role of Moscow as that of a guardian of the status quo, and that was why the Abkhaz sided with the preservation of the USSR in whatever form, and

---

44   *Aztag* (Beirut), 11 August 1997.

not any imagined Abkhaz loyalty to communism or collaboration of their leadership with Soviet officials. The Abkhaz feared that Georgian nationalism, often armed with "historians" negating Abkhaz specificity and separate historic identity, would overrun the last institutional that guarantees their group survival.

The continuous rhetoric by Georgian intellectuals questioning the "autochthonous" nature of the Abkhaz, the introduction of Georgian troops to Sukhumi, Gagra, Ochamchira, and other major towns of Abkhazia, the wanton behaviour of the Georgian militiamen including the destruction of the Abkhaz National Library and other symbols of culture, and the threatening declarations of the Georgian National Guard commander Karkarashvili about the possibility of sacrificing 100,000 Georgians to win a war against 97,000 Abkhaz—the accumulation of all this meant that the future existence of the Abkhaz, in a material and not a metaphoric sense, was being questioned. Georgian authors tend to underestimate the existential problems of the Abkhaz, and often see cold calculations in their behaviour, even the choice of war to reverse the demographic superiority of the Georgian (Mingrelians) in Abkhazia itself. The Georgian nation could have continued to live and develop its culture and preserve its identity, even after a defeat in Abkhazia. Whether the Abkhaz could continue preserving their culture and group identity after a defeat in the war started by the invasion of the detachments led by Tengiz Kitovani is very difficult to answer, whether in perspective or from the angle of 14 August 1992.

In the Chechen case, I agree with those authors who focus on the Stalinist deportations of the "punished peoples", the deportation of the entire Chechen people in 1944, and not the legendary resistance of the Caucasian tribes under the leadership of Shamil to look for the root causes of Chechen rebelliousness growing by the late 1980s and early 1990s. This traumatic experience, and the memories of coming close to the precipice as a group,[45] remained vivid among the Chechens when the policies of "New Thinking" were introduced in Moscow: most

---

45   According to Soviet official records (NKVD and MVD), of the over two million deported peoples, by June 1948 246,086 deaths were registered, of which 144,704 were North Caucasians, the highest rate of death among the deportees, meaning that 23.7 per cent of all North Caucasian deportees died in the first four years in exile. See Otto Pahl, "Stalin's Genocide against 'Repressed Peoples'", *Journal of Genocide Research*, Vol. 2, No. 2, 2000, pp. 267-8.

Chechens born before 1957 were born in exile. Even though the Soviet authorities prohibited any public expression of Chechen memory and grief over the losses, privately Chechens developed "a countermemory of the events surrounding the deportations" according to Brian Glyn Williams, who adds:

Chechens are brought up on ritualized narratives of this tragic event. In the tales of "the Deportation" the role of the Chechen collaborators with the Nazis is usually downplayed, Stalin's treachery in surprising the loyal Chechens and deporting them is stressed, and the brutality of the actual deportation and re-settlement in Central Asia is recounted. Lost family members, such as an uncle who was shot for moving too slowly towards collection points, a grandmother who died of a heart attack on the trains to Central Asia, or a cousin who died on the frozen steppes of Kazakhstan, are commemorated at this time. The older generation which survived the deportations became in effect a living memorial to this people's communal tragedy and a repository of memories and grievances which were handed down to new generations.[46]

Even after their "pardon" under Khrushchev, the Chechens, like the other "punished peoples", received neither material nor moral compensation. Their neighbours continued to consider them as having collabo-rated with Nazi Germany, and treated the Chechens and the Ingushes with distrust. And, even if the Russian parliament recognized the de-portations of 1944 as "genocide", in the "Law on the Rehabilitation of the Repressed Peoples" signed by Boris Yeltsin on 26 April 1991, there were no concrete steps taken to follow up on this initial recognition. Russian society did not go through a profound debate about the crimes committed under the Stalinist regime, including the racial crimes against the "punished peoples"; nor did the Chechens receive moral satisfaction and recognition of the suffering they had gone through. Consequently, Russian society was ready to repeat past injustice towards the Chechens, and the Chechens themselves had every reason to feel insecure within such a society, and look for other arrangements to secure their future.

Similarly, the Soviet Georgian authorities, or those who came to power after independence, never recognized the discrimination suffered by the Abkhaz and the ethnic policies practiced under Lavrenti Beria.

---

46   Brian Glyn Williams, "Commemorating 'The Deportation' in Post-Soviet Chechnya", *History and Memory*, Vol. 12, No. 1, Spring/Summer 2000, p. 106.

True, after the death of Stalin, in 1956 the Central Committee of the Georgian Communist Party criticized former "errors" in official policies towards ethnic minorities: "In Abkhazia and South Ossetia, the conflict between Georgians, Abkhazians, Armenians and Ossetians was artificially fomented and a policy leading to the liquidation of the national cultures of the local Abkhazian, Ossetian and Armenian peoples and their forced assimilation was deliberately pursued."[47] But while after the mass demonstrations on 24 April 1965 Armenians in the Armenian SSR could openly commemorate the genocide of 1915, Karabakh Armenians under Soviet Azerbaijani rule were forbidden from organizing any such commemoration, or even mentioning the genocide in books, journals, or fiction.[48]

The destruction of memory is not necessarily limited to the more distant past. After their return from deportation, the Chechens collected the tombstones scattered by the Russian settlers and built a huge memorial out of thousands of tombstones at Alkhan-Kala in Groznyy, the Garden of the Dead. When the Russian troops broke into Groznyy, "they fired their tanks from the memorial, (...) the soldiers took stones from the graveyard there and built toilets for their camp."[49] Once again a Russian assault threatened to destroy the memory of the Chechen past, to destroy its culture and traditions. For what did the Russian soldiers or their leaders understand of Chechen culture? The same offence can be found in the case of the Armenian memory, with continued Turkish denial of the Armenian Genocide.[50] In Azerbaijan, the last remnants

---

47   Quoted in Bruno Coppieters, "In Defence of the Homeland : Intellectuals and the Georgian-Abkhazian Conflict", in Bruno Coppieters and Michel Huysseune (eds), *Secession, History and the Social Sciences*, Brussels: VUB Press, 2002, p. 92.

48   In Armenia itself the memory of the Genocide was publicaly commemorated only after the mass demonstrations of 24 April 1965, fifty years after the tragedy. See H. Simonian (ed.), *Hayots Batmutyan Himnahartser* [in Armenian: "Basic Questions of Armenian History"], Yerevan State University, 2000, p. 436.

49   In the words of Shamil Basayev, reported in Sebastian Smith, *Allah's Mountains*, p. 2.

50   A classical example is the work of Turkish diplomat Kamura Gürün, *The Armenian File, the Myth of Innocence Exposed*, Istanbul: K. Rustem and Brother, 1985.

of a past Armenian presence, the medieval *khachkar*s in Nakhichevan, continue to be destroyed by Azerbaijani Army soldiers.[51]

The trauma of past repression, massacres, deportations and Genocide, as we have seen, was a primary factor leading to mass mobilization among ethnic minorities in the Caucasus. The response of the political leadership of titular nations was repression of the mass movements, threats of pogroms, massacres and deportations, reinforcing the past trauma and further mobilizing the minorities around the idea of resistance and self-determination in the form of a separate state.

The military outcome of the conflicts

What was the decisive factor that led to the conclusion of the wars, which made one side win, and the other lose? The answer depends not only on who answers this question, but on when, but also where. From a distance—whether this distance is geographical or a factor of time—we tend to formulate geopolitical analysis, historic factors, plots and intrigues as narration to wars and conflicts. While all this is fine, we should also not forget the human factor. As one approaches the heat of the battle, such explanations as courage, solidarity, patriotism, organization skills, logistics, knowledge of the terrain, become dominant in the explanation of the men—and sometimes women—who try to explain the outcome on the battlefield.[52] When asked why the Azerbaijanis in their massive attack of summer 1992 succeeded in overcoming the defences in Shahumian and Martakert regions, and their numerous attacks on Martuni failed to record any advance, the commander of Martuni forces had the following answer: "Those in Martakert abandoned their posts and ran away, we in Martuni we kept our ground and fought back."[53]

The Caucasus conflicts were fought by irregular armed groups recently formed out of the radical wings of national movements or out of self-defence units in neighbourhoods and villages. Their performance on the battlefield depended less on the numbers of the titular nation

---

51   As recently as 10 December 2005, over 200 Azerbaijani soldiers were sent to destroy the cemetery of Old Jugha.

52   Author's notes from Karabakh in April 1992, February 1993, and July 1993, and from Abkhazia in March 1993, and April 1994.

53   Author interview with Monte Melkonian, Martuni, February 1993.

they claimed to be defending, or the potential of its economy, than on the capacity of officers to build up a disciplined fighting force, and the motivation of the units to brave dangers and face the battle. Not all the military formations that emerged in the Caucasus excelled in discipline, in planning, logistics, and courage. As one observer of the armed groups that emerged in the Balkans and the Caucasus puts it: "many existing 'armies' are more dangerous to their countries than to the enemy."[54]

Now, looking at the outcome of the wars, how can we explain the fact that "small is victorious?" How can we explain that the Karabakh Armenians, admittedly with the support of neighbouring Armenia, and the South Ossetians could defend their ground? How could Abkhazia, admittedly with outside support again (from the North Caucasus and the Russian military), win a war against Georgia, and Chechnya win a war against the Russian army?

The answer to this question is at the same time complex and multiple. It also differs from one case to the other, while one can also find certain common features. There were varying relations and balances among fighting, groups that could include various armies, militias, clans, and political trends. The Karabakh Armenian forces, as well as the Armenian army, revealed better organization and discipline than the Azerbaijani army they fought against. Another key point in the Armenian victories and Azerbaijani defeat is the relative political stability in Armenia, and popular support for the national movement contrasted with elite power struggle in Baku and the changes of regime between the *nomenklatura* embodied by Mutalibov, the nationalist forces led by Elchibey, and the return of the former Soviet elite under Aliev. Armenian military victories profited from the power vacuum in Baku and coincided with severe power struggles in Azerbaijan, leaving the front line defenceless.

In the case of the Abkhazia war, there was no power struggle at that particular time in Tbilisi, although there was the Gamsakhurdia-Shevardnadze rivalry in the background. Another specific feature of the Abkhazia war is the complete Georgian military inaction after the initial intervention in Abkhazia. Contrast this with the successive invasions the Azerbaijanis launched, especially after the coming to power of each new president. Similarly, the Russian invasion of Chechnya was charac-

---

54   Charles H. Fairbanks, Jr., "The Postcommunist Wars", *Journal of Democracy*, Vol. 4, No. 3, October 1995, p. 33.

terized by constant military operations as far as Vedeno high up in the mountains. The Georgian forces never tried to move their troops up to Abkhaz mountain villages. Even though the Abkhaz received substantial support from North Caucasus volunteers and Cossack formations, they succeeded in creating a disciplined, integrated fighting force, which the Georgian side failed to do. Lastly, while the political objective of Shevardnadze was unclear after the initial invasion, the Abkhaz strategy was highly focused.

The most complicated case is that of the war in Chechnya. Before the armed conflict erupted between the Russian Federal forces and the Chechen resistance, there were contradictory indications of how this conflict could evolve. First, there were the examples of the Karabakh, South Ossetia and Abkhazia wars. In those conflicts, the armed resistance of the secessionist entities showed a huge capacity of resistance, while the military performance of the loyalist troops was very poor. On the other hand, the Chechen troops had participated in the war in Abkhazia (the notorious "Abkhazian Battalion" led by Shamil Basayev) and had proved to be a fighting force. There was also the uncertainty about whether a major war in Chechnya would have a spill-over effect, engage volunteer troops from the rest of the North Caucasus, and eventually lead to massive unrest throughout the region. On the other hand the inter-Chechen conflict, the fall in Dudayev's popularity, and the chaotic situation in Chechen politics could give then impression that Chechen separatism was close to collapse. Even if the Russian forces were weakened, it was commonly thought that they could still field enough forces to crush Dudayev's regime.

In spite all that, the Russian army faced initially huge difficulties, as we have seen in the battle for Groznyy, and later had to face a humiliating defeat. Again, after three years of chaos from 1996 to 1999, the Russian army intervened again, this time with superior means, with Russian forces outnumbering the rebels fifty to one, leaving aside their possession of aircraft, armour, long range artillery and surface-to-surface missiles, all used to conquer Chechnya.[55] Now, even after the huge

---

55   For a detailed military analysis of the "second" Chechnya war, see Mark Kramer, "Guerrilla Warfare, Counterinsurgency and Terrorism in the North Caucasus: The Military Dimension of the Russian-Chechnya Conflict", *Europe-Asia Studies*, Vol. 57, No. 2, March 2005, pp. 29-290.

price Russia paid for this war, and in spite of the immense side effects of the conflict on the military level (thousands of Russian servicemen and officers dead and wounded), on the political level (the establishment of a "vertical" political system and the complete suffocation of any independent political expression), and on the social level (censorship of the media), the outcome of the struggle remains uncertain, and Chechnya continues to plague the whole region's stability and the fragile political arrangements in the North Caucasus. But as a result of the Chechnya war, and as a result of stigmatizing the Chechens and the Caucasians in general in negative stereotypes, xenophobic tendencies in the Russian public and racial attacks in Russian cities continue to grow.[56]

The war in Chechnya is rich in lessons. First, it sheds light on the processes in the post-Soviet Caucasus, and helps us better understand the real forces that led to the conflicts. The Chechen war underlines once again the disintegrative nature of post-Soviet states, the weakness of the political entities that succeeded, and the continuation of centrifugal tendencies. It puts an end to the senseless debate which attributes the conflicts in the Caucasus to a mythical "Russian manipulation", so much in fashion in Baku and Tbilisi, at times also in Yerevan, to explain the catastrophic political decisions taken, and the military consequences reached. True, the Russian leadership intervened in all of those conflicts—it would have been surprising if it had not intervened—but Russian policies were neither central in igniting the conflicts nor pivotal in conditioning the outcomes. Both the causes of the conflicts and the conditions determining the outcomes should be found in the region, its geography, history, and political culture: the Caucasus conflicts were the clash of local political projects that were mobilized to fill the space of the collapsing Soviet empire, and their outcome was the result of the forces mobilized and led by local actors.

Chechnya has exposed the difficulties, for even such a massive force as the Russian army had during its operations there, of launching an invasion against a population determined to resist, with refuge in mountainous areas. This means that for Azerbaijani or Georgian troops, lacking the experience, the fighting force, and the mechanised and airborne

---

56   John Russell, "Terrorists, Bandits, Spooks and Thieves: Russian Demonisation of the Chechens before and since 9/11", *Third World Quarterly*, Vol. 11, No. 1, 2005, pp. 101-16.

capabilities of the Russian forces, it is even harder to launch a military invasion against Karabakh or Abkhazia, in similar mountainous terrain, against people similarly determined to resist, with military capabilities comparable to the Chechens'.[57] If the political leaderships in Baku and Tbilisi had come to a similar conclusion, they would have dropped the military choice for conflict resolution, and taken diplomatic efforts more seriously.

The military victories of the Karabakh Armenians, the Abkhaz, and the Chechens (in August 1996 in the Chechen case) turned their previous role of minority and victim upside down. Now, for the first time in memory, the Karabakh Armenians, the Abkhaz and the Chechens were no more minority groups ruled by "foreign" powers, but had established self-rule, and were trying to build up institutions imitating state structures elsewhere. This was done with varied success: while the Karabakh Armenians have proved capable of organizing disciplined armed forces and state structures,[58] the Chechens failed to develop a semblance of normalcy in the period of *de facto* independence in 1996-99. Moreover, the victors in the conflicts did not show any particular tolerance or understanding towards the other ethnic groups, and thus with their military victories changed their previous identity of victim to that of repressor of other groups. The Karabakh Armenian military drove out the entire ethnic Azerbaijani and Kurdish population not only from Karabakh, but also from six Azerbaijani districts outside the former administrative regions within Azerbaijan which they occupied during the war (from Lachin district in 1992 to Zankelan in late 1993). More than ten years after the signing of the cease-fire agreement[59] the Karabakh

---

57   For much of the time, the anti-Russian Chechen forces were estimated to have a basic corps of 2-5,000 fighters. Both the Abkhaz forces and the Karabakhi forces had similar numbers of fighters, and superior organization and armament, though a smaller pool of reservists. The Karabakhi military leadership can count on military support from Armenia to compensate for the numeric superiority of the Azerbaijani Army. For example, during military manoeuvres on 19 April 2005 the Abkhazian forces that took part included 1,500 soldiers, 2,500 reservists, armed with ten tanks, artillery, warships, and modern Su-27 warplane The ISN report can be found at: http://www.isn.ethz.ch/news/sw/details.cfm?ID=11135

58   Ara Tatevosyan, "Nagorno-Karabakh's New Army of 'Iron Will and Discipline'", *Transition*, Prague, 9 August 1996, pp. 20-3.

59   *Bishkek Protocol*, [Cease-fire agreement document to end hostilities in Moun-

authorities have made no gesture to bring back the original Azerbaijani population of those occupied regions, linking this with the final peace agreement and the regulation of the Karabakh conflict.

Similarly, the Abkhaz forces have forced out the entire population of Abkhazia of ethnic Georgian (Mingrelian) identity, and in the same way link those people's return to a final peace agreement. The only exception is in the southernmost Gali region where refugees from the neighbouring Zugdidi region have returned, or return on seasonal basis (linked with agricultural work), but often in a highly unstable security context. The Chechen armed groups have often terrorized the non-Chechen inhabitants of the republic, causing a mass exodus from Chechnya of over 200,000 "Russian speakers", including ethnic Russians, Ukrainians and Armenians, as well as the majority of ethnic Ingush inhabitants of Groznyy, the former centre of the "Checheno-Ingush Autonomous Republic". These unresolved conflicts, combined with huge refugee problems and a complete misunderstanding and polarized narrations about the reasons, the development and the history of the conflicts, make the region dangerous for future generations.

Was it avoidable?

Considering the literature on causes of war, nationalism, and nation building, there are many instances when a direct link is made between war and nation building, between war and state building. For Kenneth Waltz, states threatened by internal divisions tend to go to war: "War most often promotes the internal unity of each state involved."[60] Although Waltz was referring to *external* wars, this fits very much the analysis followed in this study, considering the recognized states as state projects in the process of attempting territorial unification. Anthony Smith argues that "war has been a powerful factor in shaping, not society or ethnicity *per se*, but certain crucial aspects of ethnic community and nationhood."[61] In other words, states facing certain internal prob-

---

tainous Karabakh Conflict], signed by S. Sarkissian, Defence Minister of Armenia, M. Mamedov, Defence Minister of Azerbaijan, and S. Babaian, the Army Commander of Mountainous Karabakh, in Bishkek, 9 May 1994.

60   Kenneth N. Waltz, *Man, the State and War*, New York: Columbia University Press, 2001 (first published in 1954), p. 81.

61   Anthony D. Smith, "War and Ethnicity: The Role of Warfare in the Formation,

lems have a tendency to look for unity through military adventures outside, and in this process shape the identity and draw the boundaries of the nation.

Were the conflicts in the Caucasus avoidable? In my attempt to answer to this question, I will start by trying to divide the conflicts into two parts: political conflicts and violent conflicts. As we have seen, there have been numerous conflicts which stayed on a political level—like the conflict between the Georgian central government and Ajaria under Aslan Abashidze—and did not necessarily degenerate into a violent conflict. There have also been the five conflicts that took a very violent turn, in chronological order the Karabakh, South Ossetia, Abkhazia, Osset-Ingush and Chechnya conflicts. So the question to ask here is, what was the mechanism that transformed a political conflict into a military, violent one?

Before trying to give an answer, it is important to make yet another distinction. Some of the violent conflicts spiralled out from popular mobilization, from clashes between emerging and contradictory nationalist projects with mass popular support. Others were the result of political decisions by a few leaders ordering (more or less) regular armed forces to crush opposing parties and ethno-political movements. Now, as we will see, it is difficult to draw a clear line and make a distinction between the "popular clashes" and "armed repression" cases, but it is helpful in understanding the nature of the conflicts.

Concerning Karabakh, the initial explosion of Armenian mobilization, and the radical demands it put forward, were unavoidable in view of past Armenian history, the discrimination suffered under Azerbaijani rule, and the feeling that the new opening in Soviet politics and the new leadership in Moscow would eventually mean favourable attention to Armenian demands. Yet, such an attitude was completely oblivious of the Azerbaijani perspective, and not just the official policies in Baku: as Soviet society was moving towards democratization, which was a precondition for the Armenian mass mobilization, the issue of Karabakh had to be a source of popular mobilization. I have described at some length the controversy surrounding the tragic events in Sumgait: were they a spontaneous explosion of mob anger, or an

---

Self-Images and Cohesion of Ethnic Communities", *Ethnic and Racial Studies*, Vol. 4, No. 4, 1981, p. 375.

act planned and guided by either republican Azerbaijani leaders, and/
or with the collaboration of key figures in Moscow? Regardless of the
answer to this question, by looking at the development of the cycle of
violence between Armenians and Azerbaijanis in the years 1988, 1989,
and 1990, until the Baku pogroms and the Soviet troop intervention
to suppress the collapse of the local Party authorities, I would characterize the violence as coming from mobilizing, antagonistic popular
movements which escaped all guidance, control and leadership. Sym-
pathizers of the APF attacked trains and convoys transporting fuel and
construction material on their way to Armenia, Armenian self-defence
groups formed at village and neighbourhood level attacked neighbouring Azerbaijani posts. Certainly, key intellectuals in Baku and Yerevan
could have done very much more to calm the agitation, to quote from
peaceful pages of common history instead of recalling the dark pages;
they could have made more efforts and organized more public events in
their attempts to find non-violent solutions for the crisis, and eventually
they could have built additional bridges for post-conflict rehabilitation,
doing more than what a handful of activists from the two sides. did Yet,
looking at the trajectory of the Armenian and the Azerbaijani national
movements, a violent clash was difficult to avoid.

The conflict in South Ossetia developed on similar lines. The power
vacuum left behind by the sudden collapse of all Soviet authority in
Georgia, after April 1989, created favourable conditions for clashes between newly rising forces. The surprise here was that the clash between
the nationalism of the titular nation, the Georgians, and minority group
nationalism, took place in South Ossetia, even though Abkhazia had a
longer record of inter-ethnic tensions and even clashes. One can convincingly argue that Gamsakhurdia, the first popularly elected President
of Georgia, played a very negative role here, by encouraging anti-Osset
actions, even violent ones. Yet Gamsakhurdia was not a unique phenomenon in the Georgian society of this historic epoch, and even those
Georgian forces that were in bitter struggle against him often shared
his views on the necessary policies to be followed towards the ethno-
territorial autonomies and the rights of minority groups in Georgia,
including the imposition of Georgian as state language.

The third conflict that I would characterize as a clash of mass mobilization and anger is the Osset-Ingush conflict over Prigorodiy Ray-

on. The Ingush deportations, and the fact that the returned deportees could not recover their houses, cemeteries and villages in the region east of Vladikavkaz in North Ossetia, now mainly inhabited by ethnic Ossets who were transferred there from South Ossetia and other parts of Georgia, followed by the decade-long official discrimination against the Ingushes in North Ossetia, and the civil war in South Ossetia and the movement of up to one hundred thousand Osset refugees to the north—all this made the situation highly explosive.

I would describe both Abkhazia and Chechnya as military operations that started as a result of political orders coming from heads of state. Therefore, Eduard Shevardnadze in Abkhazia and Boris Yeltsin in Chechnya bear the responsibility for initiating a war, and I conclude that if they had reached a different analysis and taken different political decisions on the eve of 14 August 1992 or 11 December 1994, the political conflict between Abkhazia and Georgia on the one hand, and Chechnya and Russia on the other, could have taken a very different trajectory. I disagree with the otherwise very fine analyst of Georgian developments, Ghia Nodia, regarding his remarks on Shevardnadze, saying that "he had little choice but to use force against an array of fairly well armed enemies who openly defied his rule, including Zviadists militants in western Georgia and secessionist rebels in Abkhazia and South Ossetia."[62] One cannot lump together all those events, the repression of Zviadists holding government officials as hostages, with the invasion of Abkhazia. The war in Abkhazia, clearly initiated by Tbilisi, was wrong by all possible standards: politically, it led to the loss of Abkhazia, a very valuable and strategically situated territory on the Black Sea coast; militarily, it was a catastrophe, not planned, badly organized, employing irregular forces which antagonized the Abkhaz and other minorities, and leading to a defeat making over 200,000 ethnic Georgians refugees; and morally, since by taking the political decision to go to war the head of the state was responsible for all the casualties and losses, military as well as civilian. The Abkhaz war and its catastrophic consequences were among the heaviest blows to the young Georgian statehood—as the failure to analyze it remains a major obstacle to future Georgian-Abkhaz normalization.

---

62   Ghia Nodia, "Georgia's Identity Crisis", op. cit., p. 114.

Following the initial explosion of the conflicts in the Caucasus, from Karabakh to South Ossetia, North Ossetia, Abkhazia and finally Chechnya, no new conflicts erupted; a line was drawn around the destabilization of the Soviet state, its fall, and wave of instability and conflicts this caused. No new conflicts erupted in spite of continuous political fragility, tensions, and even economic meltdown, as in the financial crisis with the devaluation of the Russian currency in the summer of 1998. Since then, the old conflicts have heated up again, like old volcanoes going active; Georgian paramilitaries and Abkhaz forces clashed once again for a few days in May 1998, replaying the original 13-month war on a smaller scale; in March 2004, Georgian troops clashed with Osset fighters, without succeeding in bringing about any change on the ground. And, most significant, there was the new Russian invasion of Chechnya following the incursion of Chechen and other North Caucasian and Arab fighters into Daghestan in the summer of 1999. But there is a major difference in the quality of those conflicts compared with the earlier ones: the original conflicts that exploded in late 1980s and early 1990s were conditioned by an initial historic event, the collapse of the USSR, a massive earthquake that caused mass mobilization of popular, nationalist movements in search of a future to correct past injustices; the conflicts and little wars since are the result of political decisions, ordering troops or paramilitaries to march and bring solutions to political disorder, and in the process often creating new ones.

7

FAILURE OF DIPLOMACY

It was 28 June 1999, when I boarded a small UN aeroplane in Yerevan with six journalists from Armenia and Mountainous Karabakh, heading for Baku. We were all nervous; it was the first group of Armenians heading to the capital of Azerbaijan since the cease-fire agreement in the Karabakh conflict. Upon landing, as the organizer of the event I approached the airport security officers to announce the arrival of the Armenian journalists, but they seemed not to have been informed. Our contact in Baku, the journalist Kemal Ali, was nowhere to be seen. Nevertheless the airport authorities invited us to a special lounge, and provided us with a telephone to contact our Azeri colleagues. An airport worker in her 40s said to her colleague: "Before, we had so many Armenian friends in Baku. They were very nice people." Forty minutes and many cigarettes later Kemal appeared accompanied by three security officers, and we were swiftly taken out of the airport and driven to downtown Baku.[1]

The trip to Baku was part of a project on which I was working, with financial support from the Swiss Federal Department of Foreign Affairs, to create a network of journalists in the South Caucasus and develop more balanced reporting about the conflicts in the region. Already in 1997 a group of Azerbaijani journalists had come to Yerevan, and in 1998 I had taken a similar group to Mountainous Karabakh. Besides a two-day conference among journalists discussing the evolutions in the sector and possibilities of cooperation, we organized meetings with local politicians, opposition figures, intellectuals, etc. The idea was granting

---

1   I have described the trip in details in "Six Days in Baku", *Armenian International Magazine*, Los Angeles, August-September 1999, pp. 24-7.

such possibilities would give journalists a more balanced view about the "other side", better realizing the fears and hopes of their neighbours, and reflecting this understanding in their work. It took me over a year and a half of efforts to get the "OK" of the Azerbaijani authorities for this trip. After our conference, we met high-level officials including President Heydar Aliev, the Foreign Minister Tofik Zulfugarov, the presidential adviser Vafa Guluzade, the leader of the opposition Musavat Party Isa Gambar, and others. This trip, highly publicized, had a considerable impact on public opinion in Azerbaijan. Two weeks later the first face-to-face meeting took lace between the two presidents, Aliev and Kocharian, in Versoix near Geneva, starting a process of intense negotiations that would lead to the Key West meeting, the most serious attempt in the course of the conflicts in the Caucasus at conflict resolution through negotiations.[2]

The road to Key West

Before discussing the negotiations framework, it is useful to recall the balance of forces that emerged after the signing of cease-fire between Baku, Yerevan and Stepanakert, under Russian pressure, in May 1994. The cease-fire was signed because the two warring sides realized that continuing military operations would be enormously costly and would not lead to their political objectives: the massive Azerbaijani military operations in the winter of 1993-94 led to thousands of casualties among both armies (many more among the Azerbaijani Army),[3] without producing any significant change in the front line. As a result, hostilities ceased while Karabakh Armenians, with the support of the Armenian Army, had most of the Soviet era Mountainous Karabakh administrative region under their control.[4] The Armenian side considered the occupied

---

2   I suspect that the Azerbaijani authorities agreed to the visit of our group to Baku only weeks before the Versoix meeting, as a way to prepare Azerbaijani public opinion for the upcoming and highly secret negotiations.

3   According to Azeri sources 4,000 Azerbaijani and 2,000 Armenian soldiers and officers were killed during the unsuccessful "winter offensive". See Idrak Abbasov and Jasur Mamedo, "Azeri Veterans Recall Military Fiasco", IWPR *Caucasus Reporting Service*, London, No. 219, 21 February 2004.

4   Certain portions of Martakert and Marduni districts of Karabakh remain under Azerbaijani control, as well as Shahumian district, which had a majority of ethnic Armenians in its population but was situated to the north of Karabakh's administrative borders.

Azerbaijani districts—seven in all[5]—as a security guarantee against possible future Azerbaijani attacks, while at the same time declaring that they did not have claims to Azerbaijani territory and were ready to return the occupied districts under a peace treaty. For the Armenian side the occupied districts were thus a security guarantee, a military buffer zone, and a negotiating chip.

The responsibility for mediation in the conflict in Karabakh fell to the Organization for Security and Cooperation in Europe (OSCE), at the time still known as CSCE ("Conference" instead of "Organization").[6] In 1992 the CSCE called for a special conference to address the Karabakh conflict, to be held in the Byelorussian capital Minsk. To this day the conference has not convened, yet the OSCE became the institutional framework to mediate over Karabakh, and has set up the "Minsk Group" as a sub-structure of the OSCE in charge of Karabakh negotiation process.[7] The Minsk Group went through some changes in its structure, while the OSCE was challenged by Russian diplomacy over its mediating role. To put an end to this competition, the OSCE Budapest summit of 1994 decided to establish a co-chairmanship to head the Minsk Group, initially headed by Sweden and having one rotating position, while Russia had a fixed seat. In December 1996, the OSCE Chairman-in-Office nominated a French diplomat to succeed the Finnish co-chair, which led to Azerbaijani protests demanding an American representative instead. Since then, the Minsk Group has been headed by a "troika" of French, Russian and American representatives. This composition is believed to represent the interest of the great powers, France representing the EU. Local observers have ironically remarked that managing the conflicting interests of the various countries repre-

---

5   The seven Azerbaijani districts occupied by the Armenian forces are: Lachin, Kelbajar, Ghubatli, Zankela, Aghdam, Fizuli, and Jebrayil. The Armenian side is ready to give back the last five districts, but insists on keeping Lachin and Kelbajar under its control for a longer period, in order to have a land-link between Karabakh and Armenia proper.

6   At the time still known as Conference for Security and Cooperation in Europe (CSCE). The organization changed its name following the Budapest conference in 1995.

7   The Minsk Group is composed of the following states: Armenia, Azerbaijan, Belarus, Finland, France, Germany, Italy, Portugal, the Netherlands, Russia, Sweden, Turkey, and the US.

senting the Minsk Group was at least as complicated as the effort to find a solution to the conflict itself.

When the Minsk Group was set up the Karabakh conflict was at its height, and finding a cease-fire arrangement was its most urgent task. From 1994, when a cease-fire was reached by the mediation of the Russian Defence Minister Grachev, the task of the Minsk Group focused on facilitating a political settlement to the conflict. During the OSCE Lisbon summit, the mediators proposed a formula for the conflict resolution based on three principles: the territorial integrity of Azerbaijan, extensive autonomy for Mountainous Karabakh, as well as security guarantees and unimpeded access to Armenia.[8] The Armenian delegation vetoed this document, arguing that the final status of Karabakh would be decided during the Minsk Conference, and that the declaration of principles predetermined the outcome of the negotiations by declaring support for the territorial integrity of Azerbaijan. Mediation efforts intensified and from 1997 several conflict resolution principles were proposed. The first proposal, known as a "package solution" was presented by the co-chairs in May 1997. It was a comprehensive solution looking at the security as well as political aspects of the conflict, to be agreed by the three conflict parties Armenia, Azerbaijan, and Nagorno Karabakh.[9] It had two parts: the first dealt with military aspects, including withdrawal of armed forces and the introduction of peacekeeping forces under the OSCE banner, and the second concerned a political solution, the final status of Nagorno Karabakh. The initial reactions from Baku and Yerevan seemed positive, but Stepanakert rejected the proposal.

Later, in September of the same year, the OSCE presented a "step-by-step" approach in which the security aspects of the conflict would be resolved in an initial stage—including military withdrawal from the conflict zone and return of refugees—before the political status of the region was discussed in a second stage. Karabakh rejected this proposal, arguing that once its forces lost control over the Azerbaijani districts they currently occupied, it would lose any negotiating means to ob-

8   Terhi Hakala, "The OSCE Minsk Process: A balance after five years", *Helsinki Monitor*, 1998, No. 1, pp. 9-10.

9   See Volker Jacoby, "The Role of the OSCE: An Assessment of International Mediation Efforts", in Laurence Broers (ed.), *The Limits of Leadership, Elites and Societies in the Nagorno Karabakh Peace Process*, London: Conciliation Resources, 2005, pp. 30-3.http://www.c-r.org/our-work/accord/nagorny-karabakh/contents.php.

tain self-determination from Baku. In 1998 the OSCE tried a new approach, developing the idea of a "common state", but Baku rejected this proposal, arguing that such a concept would give Karabakh the status of a recognized state and a subject of international law. Lastly, on various occasions territorial exchanges were discussed, under which Armenia would cede a corridor in its southernmost region of Meghri, enabling Azerbaijan to have a land link with Nakhichevan and through it to Turkey, in return for Karabakh being unified with Armenia.[10] But such ideas were rapidly abandoned.

At the heart of the negotiations is the knotty issue of the final status of Karabakh. The conflict itself started when the Karabakh Armenians demanded that their Autonomous Region be transferred from what was then Soviet Azerbaijan to Soviet Armenia. That was in February 1988. Therefore, at the heart of the conflict is the question, to whom does Karabakh belong? While the initial Armenian demand was reunification, soon this position changed to support Karabakh's self-determination, including its accession to internationally recognized statehood. From Azerbaijan's perspective, the problem is seen through the prism of territorial integrity and Armenian aggression to occupy parts of Azerbaijani land. Azerbaijan also rejects the idea of Karabakh independence, saying that it rejects the creation of a second Armenian state on its own territory. The dilemma for international diplomacy mediating in this conflict has been how to reconcile at the same time two principles of international relations: self-determination as demanded by Karabakh with Armenian support, and territorial integrity on which Azerbaijan insists.

The second major set of problems negotiators faced is, how to address the consequences of the war? These include security arrangements, definition of contested territories and their future control, the refugees and the IDPs, and finally normalization of relations between Armenia and Azerbaijan and opening up of communications.

The Karabakh leadership argues that it is ready to evacuate the Azerbaijani districts it occupies in return for Azerbaijani recognition of its self-determination. Yet the difficulty for Karabakh—which has a post-

10   The first territorial swap project was proposed in 1992 by American political analyst, who at that time worked for Radio Free Europe. The project has since been known as "Goble Plan".

war population of around 150,000—is that it considers those territories as a buffer zone and a security guarantee against a possible Azerbaijani military attack in the future. While the Karabakh Armenians are ready to evacuate five of the seven districts immediately after a peace agreement, they reject the idea that Karabakh should become an enclave once more in the future. The Armenian side argues that the Azerbaijani territories that lie between Karabakh and Armenia proper should have a special status: the district of Kelbajar, lying south of the Mrav mountain chain which currently gives the Armenian troops stationed there the strategic upper hand against any possible Azerbaijani attack from the lowlands. During negotiations, the Armenian side has insisted that this district should be returned only after the final status of Karabakh is agreed upon, and international mechanisms and security guarantees are put in place.

The last remaining Azerbaijani district which is occupied by Armenian forces since 1992 is Lachin. The corridor that connects Karabakh with Armenia passes through Lachin, and the Armenian side has insisted that Lachin should remain under Armenian control, so that Karabakh has direct physical link through Armenia with the rest of the world. In one draft proposal in 1997, the Minsk Group suggested that Azerbaijan should lease the Lachin corridor to the OSCE, which in turn would conclude an agreement with Karabakh authorities giving them control over the corridor.[11]

After being isolated in the OSCE Lisbon conference, Armenia's President Levon Ter-Petrossian reached the conclusion that it was best for Armenia to reach a compromise solution as soon as possible, rather than wait for Azerbaijan to accumulate more political dividends thanks to its "oil diplomacy", strengthen its military capabilities, and be in a stronger position. He argued for this in a lengthy newspaper article in November 1997, saying that "Today Armenia and Karabakh are stronger than ever. But in the event of the non-resolution of the conflict, within a year or two they will be substantially weakened. That which we are rejecting today, we will be asking for tomorrow".[12] He called on the Armenian

11   See "Nagorno-Karabakh: a Plan for Peace", *International Crisis Group*, Brussels, 11 October 2005, p. 22.

12   Levon Ter-Petrossian, "Baderazm te Khaghaghutyun? Lrchanalu Bahe" (Armenian: "War or Peace? Time to Get Serious"), *Hayastani Hanrapetutiun*, Yerevan,

public to get rid of its myths concerning Karabakh, such as the myth that the Armenian side won the war, and seriously consider concessions in order to reach peaceful solution.

However, not many people in Yerevan shared Ter-Petrossian's analysis. And especially not his immediate collaborators, including the Prime Minister Robert Kocharian, the Defence Minister Vazgen Sarkissian, and the head of National Security, Serge Sarkissian. In fact, Ter-Petrossian was making a huge political mistake: after the contested 1996 presidential elections, the opposition had cried foul and launched massive demonstrations. Ter-Perossian succeeded in repressing the opposition thanks to the army, and soon afterwards invited Kocharian to give up his post as President of the unrecognized Mountainous Karabakh Republic and come to Yerevan to head the government. By calling for major concessions on Karabakh, Ter-Petrossian was antagonizing the last forces that supported his rule, the army and the Karabakh elite, at a time when his popularity within the Armenian society was at its lowest. When Kocharian and the two Sarkissians withdrew their support, Ter-Petrossian had no other choice but to present his resignation in February 1998.

Azerbaijan rejects the "land for peace" principle that the Armenian side proposes. For Baku, this would be both recognition of defeat in the war and an act of injustice. In the words of the former Azerbaijani Foreign Minister Tofik Zulfugarov, "the tactic of the Armenian side—an exchange of the occupied territories for status—appears to Azerbaijan as a capitulation, as a forced admission of defeat."[13] Azerbaijan's former President Aliev repeatedly promised to provide Karabakh with "the highest possible autonomy" on condition that it was part of Azerbaijan. But Baku has had difficulties in defining what this autonomy could mean. Moreover, many Azerbaijani politicians even refuse to grant Karabakh Armenians advanced autonomy different from other minorities within Azerbaijan.

---

1 November 1997.

13   Quoted in Artur Terian and Armen Koloyan, "Former leading Azerbaijani officials comment on prospects for Karabakh peace", *Radio Free Europe/Radio Liberty*, Caucasus Report, 2001: http://www.rferl.org/reports/caucasus-report/2001/03/10-090301.asp.

Important international pressure led to the start of face-to-face meetings between presidents Aliev and Kocharian, in the summer of 1999. One sign of the seriousness of the negotiations came when Aliev dismissed his Foreign Minister Zulfugarov in October 1999, replacing him with Vilayet Guliyev, the head of the presidential secretariat, only a short while after the resignation of his foreign policy adviser, Vafa Guluzade. The changes were attributed to Aliev's Karabakh policies, signifying that the Azerbaijani leader was ready for concessions on the matter.[14] The unfortunate "parliament massacre" in Armenia in October 1999, when a group of five desperate and heavily armed men irrupted into the parliament and killed eight prominent politicians, including the Prime Minister Vazgen Sarkissian and the Speaker of the Parliament Karen Demirjian, plunged the country into a period of uncertainty and slowed down the process of negotiations. But after Kocharian succeeded in bringing stability to Armenia and reasserting his authority, the negotiations continued.

During this period of intense negotiations the OSCE did not propose a new approach for conflicts resolution. Instead, the discussions looked at the three previous OSCE proposals ("package deal", "step-by-step", and "common state") and tried to hammer out combinations that could satisfy all sides.

After a series of sixteen such meetings, the high point was reached with the Key West summit brokered by American mediation. Yet, after Florida, the high hopes were shattered. According to international accounts, President Aliev found that the compromise solution he negotiated with his Armenian counterpart did not enjoy any support among his entourage, not to mention the Azerbaijani opposition forces. The ailing Aliev concluded that he was too isolated to risk signing a peace deal with Yerevan, and abandoned the process. The Geneva meeting planned for June 2001, where the last remaining details were to be hammered out and a peace deal concluded, never happened.

---

14   An Azerbaijani paper suggested that the officials resigned because of their opposition to OSCE proposals. See E. Mahmudov, "Capitulatory options proposed to Azerbaijan", *Zerkalo*, 23 February 2001, in English by *BBC World Monitoring*, 23 February 2001.

Structural problems of the Armeno-Azeri negotiations

The major problem of the OSCE-sponsored negotiations has been their limited scope—between the two presidents and their foreign ministers—and their secretive nature. The general public is not informed about the conditions and subject of negotiations, still less given a detailed narrative of its developments. The mediators justify this secrecy as necessary so as to advance in the negotiations without being hijacked by continuous domestic pressure, and go public once the framework of a peace agreement is agreed upon by the two negotiating parties. The side-effect of this approach is that once the two leaders reach an understanding, after going a long mental way through their negotiations, they find themselves alone, without their people, and without even their close collaborators. This is exactly what happened to Levon Ter-Petrossian in early 1998 when he insisted that it was necessary for Armenia to make important concessions, but was opposed by his own ministers and forced to resign; and to Heydar Aliev, the strongman of Azerbaijan who ruled the country for three decades with an iron fist, who after returning from Key West found that his close collaborators were not ready to follow him in concessions, and was forced to abandon the plan. "The conflict should not be solved by two presidents, it should be solved by two nations," announced the Azeri Foreign Minister Guliyev after the Key West talks.[15] Yet even after the failure of Key West, because of the "unpreparedness" of the Azerbaijani elite, the negotiations continued to be limited to the same small group of people: the Armenian and Azerbaijani presidents and foreign ministers, through the mediation of the OSCE Minsk Group troika. The general public remains uninformed and sceptical, even hostile towards the negotiations process. And in spite of two previous failures, the negotiators and the international mediators by and large continue to show no interest in the inclusion and participation of public opinion in a process of reconciliation, without which it is difficult to imagine peace between the two peoples. Since the conflict started in 1988, contact between ordinary Armenians and Azerbaijanis has been rare, and in recent years

---

15   "Karabakh Peace Efforts Face Tough Public Jury", Reuters, Baku, 19 April 2001.

even contacts between activists and journalists has declined, owing to political pressure.

Another problem is the exclusion of Karabakh from the negotiations process. It was not excluded always: Baku and Stepanakert entered intense consultations by late 1993, which led to the Russian-brokered cease-fire agreement in May 1994. It also participated in the negotiations until 1997 as "a party to the conflict". It is difficult to imagine that a peace agreement will be achieved under which the unrecognized yet really existing authorities of Mountainous Karabakh will have to evacuate the Azerbaijani territories they currently occupy, guarantee the safety of the Azerbaijani returnees, etc., if they do not even take part in the negotiations process. The responsibility for excluding Karabakh from the talks lies as much with Yerevan and Baku as with the OSCE.

It is interesting to note that during the negotiations, it is the Armenian side—victorious in the war so far—that is asking for security guarantees. To understand this factor it is important to refer to the "trauma" I discussed earlier, besides the fact that Azerbaijan's oil revenues have increased its capacities for military spending, and Baku continues its threats to solve the conflict militarily. The Azerbaijani threats are creating a reaction and increasing tension on the Armenian side. In the words of a Karabakh-Armenian official, "Azerbaijan is telling us the following: 'We are ready to give you the broadest possible autonomy, but if you do not accept our offer, we will kill you!'".

Georgian-South Osset relations since the cease-fire

The Sochi agreement on South Ossetia between Presidents Eduard Shevardnadze and Boris Yeltsin, signed on 24 June 1992, led to a cease-fire arrangement and a framework for peace negotiations. A perimeter of 15 kilometres around Tskhinvali had to be demilitarized, and a Joint Control Commission (JCC) was set up with a mandate for conflict resolution and the return of IDPs. Moreover, a Joint Peacekeeping Forces (JPKF) of a total of 2,000 men—Russian, North Osset, South Osset, and Georgian troops—under Russian command was set up.

Under Shevardnadze's presidency (1992-2003), there was no major change in the situation in South Ossetia. Georgia was busy elsewhere, for example in the Abkhazia war (August 1992-September 1993) and later negotiations with the Abkhaz on conflict resolution, or in the internal power struggle. The attitude in Tbilisi was that South Ossetia was not viable as an independent entity, and had little geopolitical significance. Therefore, it was better to negotiate directly with Moscow, or reach a settlement of the Abkhazia problem, after which South Ossetia would naturally find its place within the reorganized Georgian statehood. The result of this policy was that not much happened during several dozen JCC meetings, and there was no real progress on Georgian-Osset conflict resolution, to the chagrin of international mediators who, unlike Tbilisi, thought that because South Ossetia was less important geopolitically, it was necessary to concentrate efforts there and bring about a peaceful solution. Such a policy, international mediators argued, would present a positive model for the more difficult case of Abkhazia, and send a strong message to the other restless ethnic minorities of Georgia. On the other hand, the passivity of the Georgians led to the slow normalization of day-to-day relations between Ossets and Georgians. Slowly, Ossets started travelling to Tbilisi, and the element of fear separating the two communities following the war started to disappear. The best symbol of this was the Ergneti market, situated on the edge of a Georgian village three kilometres south of Tskhinvali. Ergneti became a meeting and trading point for not only Ossets and Georgians, but also traders coming from as far as Russia and Armenia.

Following the Rose Revolution in Georgia in November 2003, and the coming to power of Mikheil Saakashvili, the situation changed dramatically in South Ossetia. Although the national-territorial issue was not present during the mobilization for the Rose Revolution, it became important immediately afterwards. Initially, Saakashvili promised that while Georgia's territorial unity was his aim, he would use dialogue and economic incentives to integrate the breakaway regions. He supposed that as Georgia progressed on the path of democracy, and moved away from the corrupt system created under Shevardnadze, it would attract the population of the breakaway regions who would follow him on the path of smaller coloured revolutions. From the perspective of the new rulers of Georgia, influenced by theories of "economies of civil wars", the problem was corruption and incompetence, and once the economic infrastructure of the separatist authorities was destroyed their regime would fall very much like that of Shevardnadze. This view was reinforced after the success Saakashvili had in May 2004 in Ajaria, where pressure from Tbilisi and a mini-Rose-Revolution from inside brought down the rule of the autocrat Aslan Abashidze. Most of Saakashvili's collaborators were young, Western educated people who had not been involved in the political upheavals of the late 1980s, and did not distinguish political problems within Georgian society from identity-related problems between the Georgians on the one hand and other ethnic groups on the other. The new rulers in Georgia viewed South Ossetia very much in the same way as Ajaria, seeing a corrupt and criminal regime that monopolized the political sphere and did not let free political expression.

Pressure on smuggling routes around South Ossetia started days after the Rose Revolution, and by June 2004 the Ergneti market was closed down.[16] As anti-smuggling operations gathered pace, so did the presence of armed Georgian Ministry of Interior troops and sporadic clashes with the Osset militias. The "anti-smuggling" measures taken by the Georgian authorities had an adverse effect: instead of weakening the political elite in South Ossetia—deeply divided in an internal power struggle and on clan lines by then—they increased the popularity of the unrecognized President of South Ossetia, Eduard Kokoity.

It was evident that next to the "anti-smuggling" operation and the "humanitarian offensive" which aimed at wining the "hearts and minds" of the Osset population, the Georgian leadership counted on increasing military pressure. The person behind this policy was Irakli Okruashvili, at the time governor of Shida Kartli region, and a close collaborator of Saakashvili. Okruashvili, who later became Defence Minister of Georgia, was born in Tskhinvali. The increasing deployment of Georgian Interior Ministry troops around Tskhinvali violated the 1992 cease-fire agreement, yet the Georgian Prime Minister Zurab Zhvania answered criticism by saying: "It's nobody's business what military units Georgia will deploy to the Tskhinvali region. This is Georgian territory, and it is up to us to decide whether to bring into the makeup of our

---

16   To counter Georgian accusations of smuggling, South Ossetians argue that they
      live under embargo since 1992 and have no possibility to trade legally because
      of Georgian policies. Other critics see the closing of this market, and the anti-
      corruption drive of the new authorities as a way to redistribute economic assets
      from the control of the Shevardnadze-era *nomenklatura* to a new generation
      which came to power thanks to the Rose Revolution.

peacekeepers…"[17] South Ossetia is a small region, with an area of 3,900 kilometers and a total population of around 70,000.[18] In spite of the conflict, ethnic Osset and Georgian villages remain intermingled, and locals know each other. Yet Georgian police forces sent from outside, who set up new checkpoints, did not know the local population, and tended to treat the Ossets aggressively, causing an increase of the level of violence. In July-August 2004 clashes increased in intensity, mortars and artillery rounds were fired on villages and on Tskhinvali, claiming casualties both among the fighters and the civilians. On 19 August Georgian troops took control of several strategic heights around the South Osset capital, leading to intensified fighting.

However, Tbilisi soon backed down from further escalation as Russian troops were reinforced, the number of casualties increased, and the Georgian forces lacked the capacity to continue a protracted conflict.[19] As the Georgian forces withdrew to their former positions, the fighting marked the first setback to Saakashvili after the Rose Revolution, and ruined a decade of peace-building efforts in South Ossetia. Unfortunately this did not mean an end to sporadic clashes in the region, nor to Georgian threats of more military action: Okruashvili, appointed Minister of Defence in December 2004, promised to celebrate the New Year of 2007 in Tskhinvali, which was interpreted as a barely camouflaged threat to take the town before that date. Saakashvili forced him to resign in November 2006—according to rumour in Tbilisi as a result of American pressure to avoid a major escalation of violence and an open conflict with Russia.[20]

Since then, Tbilisi has taken two initiatives to change the status quo in South Ossetia. The first is to challenge the format of negotiations and

---

17   "Georgia to Deal with Rebellious Autonomy Alone?" *Ria-Novosti*, Moscow, 2 June 2004.

18   Before the conflict, the total population of South Ossetia was 98,000, of which 65,000 were Ossets and 28,000 were ethnic Georgians.

19   For a detailed description on the circumstances leading to the clashes, see *International Crisis Group*, "Georgia: Avoiding War in South Ossetia", Europe Report No. 159, 26 November 2004.

20   Okruashvili has since moved to the camp of the Georgian opposition forces. At a press conference in Tbilisi on 25 September 2007, he made some spectacular statements, for example accusing Saakashvili of corruption and of giving orders to assassinate dissident politicians, and challenging the official version of the "accidental" death of Zurab Zhvania, the former Prime Minister of Georgia.

peacekeeping, which Tbilisi sees as unbalanced. The JCC is composed of Georgia on the one side, and South Ossetia, North Ossetia and Russia on the other, with the OSCE as mediator. "The Georgian side wants to change the format of negotiations, to exclude Russia and strengthen the US position," Marat Jiyoev, the Foreign Minister of the *de facto* authorities of South Ossetia, told me; but, he added, the elimination of the Russian factor "for us means cutting off South Ossetia from North Ossetia."[21] Consequently, changing the current format of negotiations, or the composition of the peacekeeping forces, is unacceptable for the South Osset authorities. Georgia's second step was to support an "alternative" Osset leader who would be at the same time anti-Kokoity, anti-Russian, and pro-Georgian. In November 2006, while the *de facto* government of South Ossetia organized presidential elections re-electing the incumbent Eduard Kokoity, in the territories under Georgian control an "alternative presidential election" was organized and Dmitri Sanakoev was elected "president" of South Ossetia. Sanakoev was a former Defence Minister and Prime Minister of the separatist government, but had left Tskhinvali after Kokoity came to power. Kokoity is seen as heavily dependent on Russia and the security establishment in particular: both Anatoaly Barankevich and Andrei Leptev, two succesive Defence Ministers of the *de facto government*, come from the Russian military. The "alternative *de facto* government" is based in Kurta, a village with an ethnic Georgian population to the north of Tskhinvali. Tbilisi recognized Sanakoev's administration as the legal representative of the Ossets in April 2007, and started urging international delegations to address to Sanakoev for matters related to South Ossetia. This active promotion of Sanakoev by the Georgian authorities led to his losing Osset support which he had enjoyed previously, making him no more than a puppet of Georgian politics.

What remains constant in Georgian policy towards the Ossets since the 1980s is that Georgian leaders do not see the Osset population as a factor in themselves, but as an instrument of Russian ambitions in the South Caucasus. Consequently, Georgia has repeatedly failed to develop a coherent policy towards the Ossets, to offer them something in an effort to integrate them—in spite of much rhetoric in that direction.

---

21   Author's interview with Marat Jiyoev, Tskhinvali, 18 December 2006.

By disregarding the conditions of the Ossets, Tbilisi has lost chances of rapprochement, pushed them to more radical positions, and directly into the Russian lap.[22] Each time its policies take a wrong turn in South Ossetia, Tbilisi explains its difficulties by the Russian factor. This happened once again in 2004, when after closing down the Ergneti market, launching the "humanitarian offensive" that is distributing some help on Osset villagers, and then sending the troops and being faced with hard resistance, Tbilisi once again accused Russia of being the reason behind the difficulties. While it is clear that the Russian peacekeepers within the JPKF did participate in combat operations, and that Russian reinforcements, and mainly Cossack volunteers did join the Osset side in the fighting, this should not hide the fact that Tbilisi lacks a coherent policy of negotiated conflict resolution, and has often overestimated its military capabilities before launching offensive operations.

Deadlock in Abkhazia

In Abkhazia, as in South Ossetia, two processes have been evolving since the cease-fire agreement of late 1993: negotiations on the one side, and military threats and operations on the other. Now, after a decade and a half following the conflict, the gap separating Abkhazia and Georgia seems wider than ever before.

Three themes have dominated Georgian-Abkhaz negotiations since 1993: status, security, and the return of the displaced people. Unlike the talks on Karabakh and South Ossetia, the Georgian-Abkhaz negotiations have taken a multitude of forms with Russia and the UN serving as mediators, sometimes in coordinated efforts, and sometimes in parallel processes. The Georgian leadership insisted on having the UN as the negotiating side in the Abkhazia conflict, rather than the OSCE as in the case of South Ossetia, with the hope that the UN could have more weight and thus bring a more rapid and satisfactory solution to the conflict. But in the 1990s the West was reluctant to engage in the chaos of the Caucasus, for example by commiting peacekeeping troops,

---

22   According to a European diplomat, in the late 1990s high level Osset politicians approached them to ask the Georgian authorities for passports for international travel. As the answer from Tbilisi failed to come, the Osset politicians applied to Russia and received Russian passports—an example among others of "missed opportunities.

and eventually it was left to Russia to stabilize the Caucasus. Although a UN mission was deployed to Georgia (the United Nations Observer Mission in Georgia, or "UNOMIG"),[23] its mission was limited to observing the cease-fire agreement alongside the CIS peacekeeping force, and its military component was around 130 soldiers and around two dozen police officers. The bulk of the peacekeeping effort was left to the Russian military. On 14 May 1994 the Georgian and the Abkhaz side, with Russian mediation, signed an agreement on "Cease-Fire and Separation of Forces" in Moscow, which authorized the deployment of two thousand Russian troops under the banner of the Collective Peace-keeping Forces of the CIS. The operation zone of the Russian troops was on both sides of the Inguri river that separated Abkhazia from the rest of Georgia. Russia continued its mediating efforts with President Yeltsin meeting both Shevardnadze and Ardzinba on several occasions. On 14 August 1997, on the fifth anniversary of the start of hostilities, the Russian Foreign Minister Yevgeni Primakov accompanied Vladislav Ardzinba to Tbilisi to meet the Georgian head of state to bring about an agreement on the status of Abkhazia. Russia faced a dilemma in Abkhazia, best summarized by Oksana Antonenko: "If Russia helps resolve the conflict, it will lose its geopolitical monopoly in Abkhazia. But, if it fails to achieve progress (…) it could well end up marginalized by more dynamic actors willing to fill the void."[24]

As Russian efforts failed to yield an agreement on the territory's status, and as President Yeltsin lost interest in Georgia, the UN intensified its efforts. The Secretary General named a special representative, the first to occupy the post being the Swiss diplomat Eduard Brunner. In 1997 the international body established a "Coordinating Council" with the aim of approaching the positions of the conflicting sides and eventually find a resolution to the conflict, with periodic meetings held in Geneva. Hence the mediating effort is known as the "Geneva Process". In these meetings various proposals were discussed concerning the status prob-

23   UNOMIG was established based on Security Council resolution 858 in August 1993.

24   Oksana Antonenko, "Frozen Uncertainty: Russia and the Conflict over Abkhazia", in Bruno Coppieters and Robert Legvold, *Statehood and Security, Georgia after the Rose Revolution*, MIT Press, 2005, p. 228.

lem, including federation, confederation, and "common state".[25] Yet all these proposals failed to satisfy the conflicting parties, for the simple reason that the aim of Tbilisi was to restore Georgia's territorial integrity, while that of Abkhazia was to emphasize its sovereignty.

In spite of the war Abkhazia did not declare its outright "independence" from Georgia, leaving a margin for negotiations. "We never demanded secession before the war, but Georgia was not ready for compromise," Sergei Shamba, *de facto* Foreign Minister of Abkhazia, told me.[26] For Shamba compromise meant to "create a unified state based on equal subjects". But he was suspicious of any results from negotiations as Tbilisi supported the military activities of guerrilla groups. The activities of the Georgian paramilitary groups, known as the "Forest Brothers" and the "White Legion", continued to intensify. In May 1998, following increased guerrilla activities in the southern Gali region of Abkhazia, the region was ready for a new war. In Tbilisi a number of politicians mobilized, calling for retaking of Abkhazia on 26 May, Georgia's independence day. On 9 May Bezhan Gunava, a parliamentarian of the ruling Citizen's Union of Georgia, accompanied by another parliamentarian, German Patsatsia, and other officials visited the Gali district and raised a Georgian flag. Next, guerrilla attacks killed 17 Abkhaz soldiers in mid-May, after which the Abkhaz army mobilised its forces and launched a major operation, driving away the 30,000 or so ethnic Georgian refugees who had returned to their homes in the Gali district.[27]

The "six day's war" in May 1998 took place at a time of changing geopolitics in the Caucasus, and a change of orientation in Georgia. It was the year of heightened competition over the oil and gas resources of the Caspian region and transport routes including pipelines, as we will see below. In February 1998 Shevardnadze was the target of a second assassination attempt, which he miraculously survived.[28] Immediately,

---

25   For more details on the negotiations on the status of Abkhazia, see "Abkhazia: Ways Forward", *International Crisis Group*, Europe Report No. 179, 18 January 2007, pp. 3-12.

26   Author interview with Sergei Shamba, Sukhumi, 14 May 1997.

27   See Vicken Cheterian, " Ethnic Conflict in Georgia ", *Le Monde diplomatique*, English Edition, December 1998.

28   On 9 February 1998, a group of up to ten assailants opened fire with grenade launchers and automatic weapons on Shevardnadze's car. The Georgian leader

Shevardnadze accused Russia of planning the attack, and in April of the same year he replaced his pro-Russian Defence Minister, Vardiko Nadibaidze, with David Tevsadze, a veteran of the Abkhazian war who had recently returned from military training in the United States. This marked a shift in Tbilisi from seeking Russian military assistance for resolution of its security problems to hoping that an alliance with NATO would yield the expected results.

The assassination attempt against Shevardnadze and the fighting in Gali district cannot be understood without bringing in another dimension, the Mingrelian rebellion. Mingrelians are a Georgian sub-ethnic group living in the Zugdidi region of western Georgia. Most ethnic Georgians who lived in Abkhazia were Mingrelians. They were also supporters of Gamsakhurdia, and following the defeat of pro-Zviadist rebels in western Georgia in 1993 the Georgian authorities tried to integrate the Zviadist militias. This integration was not much of a success, as the Georgian military budget remained less than US$50 million per year, and even that did not reach its destination amid widespread corruption. Did the Georgian authorities start to lose control over the west Georgian militias? Were they behind the assassination attempt against Shevardnadze? At least the chronology of events in 1998 invites such an interpretation: days after the attack on Shevardnadze a militia commando led by Gocha Estebua took four UN military personnel hostage in Zugdidi, demanding the release of those arrested in connection with the attempt on Shevardnadze's life. Some analysts suggested that those who carried out that attack were probably from Mingrelia and trained and supplied by the Georgian secret services for the purpose of carrying out attacks inside Abkhazia, but had for whatever reason turned their weapons against the head of the Georgian state.[29] The trouble in western Georgia did not stop there. A rebellion broke out in Senaki on 19 October, when 200 soldiers rebelled, seized a dozen tanks and advanced on Kutaisi, Georgia's second largest city. The rebellion was led by another ex-Zviadist officer, Lieutenant-Colonel Akakiy Eliava, apparently over

---

was victim of a car bomb earlier, in 1995.

29   See Dodge Billingsley, "Truce means nothing in Western Georgia", *Jane's Intelligence Review*, London, June 1998, and Besik Kurtanidze, "Guerrillas keep on fighting", in *The Army and Society in Georgia*, Tbilisi, June 1998.

delays in pay and the poor conditions of the armed forces. He was sub-sequently killed by the Georgian police in July 2000. Mingrelians re-mained bitter with Shevardnadze until the end, and participated heavily in the Rose Revolution where busloads of Mingrelian activists headed to Tbilisi in support of Mikheil Saakashvili in November 2003.

The May 1998 war was Shevardnadze's second defeat in Abkhazia. The result was not only disastrous for the Mingrelian population which was trying to return to their homes and orchards. It also led to further radicalizing of the Abkhaz position. On 3 October 1999, the Abkhaz authorities organized a referendum to adopt the 1925 constitution, which received 97 per cent of the votes. Few days later, on 12 October, the National Assembly of Abkhazia adopted a declaration of independence.

While the situation in Gali region and across the Abkhazian-Georgian demarcation line remained volatile, in October 2001 a rather curious military operation was launched across the Kodori gorge. The gorge lies within Abkhazia deep in the mountains east of Sukhumi, bordering Svanetia. It is the only region of Abkhazia that lies outside the control of the *de facto* Abkhaz authorities. During the war in 1993 Abkhaz troops advanced towards Kodori but faced fierce resistance by the local Svan inhabitants, estimated to be over four thousand. On 4 October 2001 a multi-ethnic force comprising Chechen fighters and Georgian guerrillas started advancing towards the Abkhaz capital Sukhumi through the Ko-dori gorge. The irony is that the attack was led by the Chechen fighter Ruslan Gelayev who had in 1992 taken part with the Chechen Battal-ion in the battle of Gagra on the Abkhaz side, which marked a turning point in the 1992-93 Georgian-Abkhazian war—yet another example of changing alliances in the Caucasian wars. Gelayev, after resisting Rus-sian troops during the second Chechnya war, had moved to the Pankisi valley in northern Georgia, which is home for around seven thousand ethnic Chechens. It was rumoured that he had reorganized his forces there. There is enough evidence that the several hundred Gelayev-led fighters received orders and support from Tbilisi; otherwise they could not have moved from the Pankisi valley up to Abkhazia across Georgian territory—although it was less clear what the military and political aims behind the operation were. As Abkhaz troops regrouped, the Gelayev-led forces were pushed back.

The Rose Revolution in Georgia brought new challenges. The new authorities in Tbilisi intended to change the status quo, and vowed to unify Georgia. Following the initial success of bringing Ajaria under Tbilisi's control, the new Georgian leadership was euphoric: Saakashvili declared that his time frame to bring Abkhazia under his government's control was "[t]wo years. I am sure with South Ossetia it will be much less than that" and the scenario would be "approximately along the same lines" as in Ajaria.[30]

On the diplomatic front Tbilisi proposed to change the format of negotiations, aiming to exclude Russian mediation. But the Abkhaz side, as well as Moscow, rejected the Georgian proposals. Sergei Bagapsh, the new President of Abkhazia who came to power in 2005, made a new proposal for conflict resolution, in an address to the Abkhaz parliament.[31] He demanded an Georgian official "apology" for "the state policy of assimilation, war, and isolation", abandonment of the current economic blockade and an end to Abkhazia's isolation, and guarantees not to use force in the future.

New events in Kodori led to increased tension between the two sides. In July 2006 relations between Tbilisi and the local strong man of the Kodori gorge, Emzar Kvitsiani, reached a low. Kvitsiani, who headed an armed group known as "Monadire" (or hunters), refused to obey orders coming from Tbilisi and resisted Georgian troops sent to disarm his forces. Although the confrontation was resolved in favour of the government troops in a matter of two days, it created a new crisis with the Abkhaz side. Sukhumi considered the stationing of Georgian government troops a violation of the cease-fire agreement, and called for their withdrawal. But Tbilisi had different plans: Saakashvili ordered the Abkhazian government-in-exile (pro-Georgian) to move from Tbilisi—to Kodori. Even the name of the gorge was changed, rechristened "Upper Abkhazia" by the Georgian government.[32] For Tbilisi, the legitimate authorities of Abkhazia are those based in Kodori, and not in Sukhumi.

---

30 Andrew Jack and Tom Warner, "Georgia's colourful president tells of reunification plans", *Financial Times*, 8 May 2004.

31 The proposal was made in an address to the Abkhaz parliament on 4 May 2006. The text of the Bagapsh proposal titled "Key to the Future":http://www.mfaabkhazia.org/MFADocuments/Bagapsh per cent20Plan per cent20(Key per cent20to per cent20the per cent20Future) per cent20Eng.pdf

32 "Saakashvili gives new name to Kodori Gorge", *Interfax*, 26 September 2006.

In October 2006, Saakashvili called for replacement of the Russian peacekeepers, once again emphasizing his aim to change the status quo in Abkhazia. As a result, the negotiation process is frozen, since the Abkhaz side insists on the withdrawal of Georgian troops from Kodori before they return to negotiations table.

While generally tense, Georgian-Abkhaz relations have also another side: cooperation when interests require it. One monumental example is their cooperation to maintain and run the Inguri hydroelectric power plant. While the dam lies on the Georgian side of the border, the power plant is on the Abkhaz side. The plant is the only source of electricity for Abkhazia, and provides a third of all Georgia's electricity needs. The Inguri power plant did not stop from functioning either during the conflict, or later. For its rehabilitation and maintenance, the Georgian authorities have requested international financial aid, and since 1995 $40 million has been spent on this. During March and July 2006, major repair work was done on the dam, during which the power plant was shut down. During this period Georgia provided electricity to Abkhazia from other sources, free of charge.[33] Unfortunately, such a spirit of cooperation was not expressed elsewhere, for example on the issue of reopening of the Abkhazian railway, which has huge importance not only for Georgia and Abkhazia, but also for Russia and Armenia.

Chechnya and the countdown to the "Second War"

During the Chechen revolution of 1991 there was ambiguity about the real aims of the revolution: was it a Chechen national liberation movement aiming at the independence of Chechnya, or part of a general Caucasian rebellion for the creation of a pan-Caucasian federation? The personification of this ambiguity was Djokhar Dudayev himself, with his contradictory statements and declarations. When the two ideologies came into opposition, the Chechen choice was clearly a secular nationalist one aiming at Chechen self-determination. The first Chechen Constitution, adopted on 12 March 1992, while going to some length to describe "human rights" and the economic rights of its "citizens", paid only limited attention to religion, declaring that "Religious asso-

---

33   Paula Garb, "The Inguri Power Complex", in Jonathan Cohen (ed.) *The Georgia-Abkhazia Peace Process*, op. cit., p. 35; *International Crisis Group*, Abkhazia: Ways Forward, pp. 26-7.

ciations are separate from the State".[34] Although Chechen nationalism was coupled with idealist pan-Caucasian trends, yet this was auxiliary, and it was seen by Dudayev and Chechen national leaders as a means to expand their influence throughout the North Caucasus. To illustrate, the Chechen National Movement completely ignored Ingush sensibilities in 1991, and did not invite the Ingushes to the National Congress of the Chechen People. The Chechen activists, by excluding Ingush grievances (the issue of territorial controversy with the Ossets), and by their head-on clash with the Russian leadership (at this time the Ingush Popular Front was counting on Russian support to receive satisfaction for the Prigorodnyi conflict), led to the inevitable breakdown of the Checheno-Ingush ASSR into its two composing parts. So what counted in the early 1990s were the dreams inspired by Chechen nationalism, and not the preservation and expansion of Caucasian unity.

For a fringe of the most active among Chechen revolutionaries the national project was not the final objective as they embraced the pan-Caucasian cause. The most striking evidence of Chechen support for this is the enlistment of Chechen volunteers in the Abkhazia war, and Chechen support for the Caucasian Peoples Confederation (KNK). While Sukhumi was under the control of the Georgian National Guard (mid-August 1992 to September 1993), Groznyy became the seat of the KNK leadership. In the early 1990s, amid the political uncertainties, Chechen support for this pan-Caucasian movement can also be seen in the light of strategic considerations: Chechnya is a land-locked country, encircled by the Russian Federation to its north and Georgia on the other side of the Caucasian slopes; Chechens, as well as other North Caucasians who were looking for self-rule, absolutely needed seas access to the sea, and Sukhumi was the best situated "window" to the outside world.

The pan-Caucasian dream reached its political end as the Russian forces invaded Chechnya. The solidarity expressed by the North Caucasian peoples towards the Abkhaz was not repeated in the case of the Chechens. The reason here is simple: confronting the Georgian National Guard in Abkhazia, which was by then a foreign country for the

---

34   In Article 4, Paragraph 7 of *The Constitution of Chechen Republic*, Adopted on 12 March 1992, retrieved in January 2006: http://www.oefre.unibe.ch/law/icl/cc01000_html.

North Caucasians, was one thing, while confronting the Russian police and army in the North Caucasus, which remained part of the Russian Federation, was another. Such a confrontation could have led to generalized war in the entire North Caucasus, and the ruling elites stemming from the Soviet era *nomenklatura* from Daghestan to Karachayevo-Cherkessia had no interest in such an adventure.

The war refocused the Chechen political struggle: after losing the illusion of Caucasian solidarity, they were left to fight for their national self-determination. The slogan under which the 1994-96 war was fought from the Chechen side was the establishment of a free statehood as the only future guarantee against continuous Russian threats against Chechen existence. The Russian military withdrawal after the signing of the Khasavyurt agreement (August 1996) represented an unparalleled victory in modern Chechen history: the country was free from Russian military presence for the first time since mid-19th century.

Yet, while the Chechens had a long tradition of anti-Russian resistance, they had no reference of statehood in modern history. Chechen society was basically an alliance of *teips* or clans, which defined geographical identity in a mountainous context characterized by deep internal divisions lacking any overarching centralized structures. This led one Chechen analyst, Khozh Akhmed Nukhaev, to emphasize "the inability of the Chechens to adapt their clan politics to the model of a centralized state as a fundamental problem." But rather than seeking to change Chechen political culture, Nukhaev advocates the rejection of the modern state as a form of organization.[35] Those divisions, the devastating impact of the war on the Chechen social fabric, and the development of armed groups under the leadership of "field commanders" were among the major reasons for the failure of the Maskhadov government to stabilize Chechnya during the inter-war period.

Following his election as President of Chechnya, Aslan Maskhadov tried to build up Chechen state institutions. In this he chose a different policy from the Dudayev period support for a common pan-Caucasian movement in the form of the KNK. The most vivid example of his policy was Maskhadov's visit to Tbilisi in August 1997, in his attempt to

---

35   Michael Reynolds, "Myths and Mystics: A Longitudinal Perspectives on Islam and Conflict in the North Caucasus", *Middle Eastern Studies*, Vol. 41, No. 1, January 2005, p. 48.

normalize Chechnya's relations with neighbouring Georgia. Among his remarks was one regretting Chechen involvement in the Abkhazia war, calling it a "black stain", and another, from Tbilisi, advising the Abkhaz leadership to stop "following dictates from outside [the Caucasus]".[36]

Initially, Islam played no significant role in Chechnya's political mobilization in the late Soviet period. The National Congress of the Chechen People was a secular-nationalist movement belonging to the political family of "national movements" and "popular fronts". This does not mean that there was no public interest in Islam, and indeed new mosques were under construction in every village and neighbourhood, and interest in Arabic language teaching was clearly on the rise. This Islam was part of Chechen (as well as Ingush, Daghestani, etc.) national identity and differed from Middle Eastern *jihadi* Islam, with which it had yet to establish contact. The first elements of political Islam came with the arrival of volunteer fighters mainly from Arab countries, starting from 1995, which coincided with the radicalization of Chechen militants and public opinion due to the bleak situation created by the Russian invasion. The most notorious among the jihadists was a Saudi-born militant known as Ameer Khattab, who was to play a key role in the developments in Chechnya.

The real name of Ameer (commander) Khattab is believed to be Samir Saleh Abdullah al-Suwailem. He was a famous "Arab Afghan" or one of the numerous Arabs who joined anti-Soviet struggle in Afghanistan. Born in 1969 in Arar in northern Saudi Arabia, he joined the jihadist movement and went to Afghanistan in 1988 and he stayed until 1994, and participated in numerous battles, including those of Jalalabad and Khost, and the taking of Kabul. In 1994, as the Afghan Mujahedeen had fallen into bloody infighting, he moved to Tajikistan where he joined the opposition already in its third year of fighting Tajik governmental troops. In 1995 he decided to make a reconnaissance visit to Chechnya, then an unknown country resisting Russian assault, and with twelve other volunteers crossed the Daghestani mountains. The appearance of this "Afghan veteran" made a great impression on the Chechens. There he became the leader of foreign volunteers and a close associate of Shamil Basayev. Khattab was to leave deep marks in Chechen his-

---

36   Quoted in Mikhail Vignansky. *Sevodnya*, September 1, 1997; English translation in *CDPSP*, Vol. XLIX, No. 35, p. 19.

tory, as we will see later, and he played key role in provoking the second Chechnya war.

While the second President of Chechnya, Zelimkhan Yandarbiyev, tried to introduce Islamic laws during the short period of his rule, the election of Aslan Maskhadov by the Chechen voters reflected the choice of the Chechen public for stability, the end of the revolutionary spirit, and a project of state-building based on the administrative structures inherited from the Soviet days. Yet the failure of Maskhadov leadership to create viable state structures, and to provide basic services, led to mass disillusionment with Chechen national independence. His major failure was his incapacity to disarm the former field commanders, which kept Chechnya in a continuous state of war. While the militants lost popular support, and Chechnya became one of the worst examples of a failed state, former fighters turned to more radical ideas such as militant Salafi jihadism. This small but powerful group became so influential that in early 1999 Maskhadov was forced to introduce *shari'a* law.[37] This radicalization of the Chechen fighters, the chaos that dominated Chechnya, and their constant raids across the border in the inter-war period were to provide the necessary pretext for the Kremlin to launch a second military campaign against Chechnya in 1999.

The Chechen revolution of 1991 destroyed the state institutions developed during the Soviet era without succeeding in replacing them. The war of 1994-96 destroyed the social tissue and the last institution respected in Chechen society, that of the clan elders. Advancing Russian troops often negotiated with the village elders to convince the Chechen resistance fighters to abandon their positions within villages and urban areas, in order not to bring their wrath on them with destruction of civilian targets by heavy artillery fire. After the fighters retook these regions in the summer of 1996, they no longer responded to the institution of the elders, because in their eyes those elders who had negotiated with the Russian occupants had lost legitimacy and respect. As a result, the centuries-old customary laws of Chechen *teips*, the *adat*, were shattered. This left Chechen society without the traditional mediator, the judge and the moral reference which since old times had been the institution

37   Julie Wilhelmsen, "Between a Rock and a Hard Place: The Islamisation of the Chechen Separatist Movement", *Europe-Asia Studies*, Volume 57, Number 1, January 2005, p. 38.

to settle daily conflicts. The result was a proliferation of violence and anarchy. To take just one example, while in the whole of the Caucasus a visitor can expect the protection of his host, Chechen bandits made hostage taking of foreigners, even humanitarian workers, journalists, or technicians working in Chechnya, a profitable industry. The Chechen President Maskhadov expressed his indignation towards the field commanders turned warlords: "Judging by all appearances, the opposition [composed by fighters opposing his rule] had minimum support among the people of Chechnya (…) The people were sick of war, terrorism and kidnappings. Unlike field commanders, the Chechen people had never touched guests and never taken hostages, which is [for the commanders] a great disgrace."[38]

On the other hand, the young men who had taken up arms in resistance occupied the high posts in the administration, replacing other professionals and officials. As a result, those administrative services that had managed to survive the Dudayev regime and the Russian onslaught finally collapsed under the weight of the former resistance fighters.

Maskhadov is a figure with dimensions of a character from classical Greek tragedies. He tried and failed to build Chechen statehood. His failure to disarm the major Chechen resistance groups—which were creating an atmosphere in which impunity, criminality, and political radicalism could thrive—is the key reason for the Chechens' failure to achieve normalization in the 1997-99 period. But why did Maskhadov fail to take steps and attempt to disarm the resistance fighters, or bring them into the official Chechen armed forces? The Chechen leader answered this question in an interview, saying that the only reason why he did not concentrate his efforts on bringing order to his land was his fear of the Russians and their intentions. He rightly feared that such an operation from his side would degenerate into a civil war, which would give the Russian generals an opportunity to intervene.[39] But many others criticize Maskhadov for "indecisiveness", such as the President of the neighbouring republic of Ingushetia, Ruslan Aushev.[40]

---

38   See the interview of Maskhadov given to *Kommersant-Daily*, Moscow, 23 October 1998.

39   Anne Nivat, *Chienne de Guerre*, Paris: Fayard, 2000, p. 120.

40   See the interview with Ruslan Aoushev by Paul Quinn-Judge, *Time*, available on the internet: http://www.time.com/time/europe/webonly/chechnya/aushev.html

Another interpretation could be that Maskhadov simply did not have enough strength to face the extremist and criminalized field commanders, and knew that any action from his side would lead to an open civil war in which his chances of winning were not high. In those years, "official" Chechen forces on which Maskhadov could rely on were people of his *teip*, and several field commanders associated with him. This force could not bring much of Groznyy, let alone much of Chechnya, under one rule. In the 1997-99 period, the Chechen President was the target of four assassination attempts. Following the accusation that Salman Raduyev was responsible for the assassination attempt against the Georgian President Eduard Shevardnadze, criminal proceedings were launched against Raduyev, and the prosecutor called for disbanding of his private militia, the "Army of General Dudayev". Shamil Basayev, who was the Deputy Prime Minister at the time, initiated a "Republican Congress of the Chechen Resistance Movement", which brought together something like 10,000 fighters into the Groznyy football stadium on 21 February 1998 to decide the fate of Raduyev. But instead of judging Raduyev, the crowd welcomed him as a hero, chanting slogans and brandishing their sub-machine-guns. Maskhadov, who was to address the crowd, abandoned his plans altogether.[41] The Chechen government itself was composed of former field commanders with more experience of fighting than of running a ministry: they included Vice-President Vakha Arsanov, the Deputy Prime Mnister Shamil Basayev, the Information Minister Movladi Udugov, and others. While these personalities often occupied government posts, they plotted against the Chechen President at every opportunity.

The result was that Chechnya became a failed state, similar to Lebanon in the 1980s and Afghanistan in the 1990s. The basic characteristics of these states are the collapse of any central legitimate authority, the rule of warlords each dominating different parts of the territory, continuous rivalry and clashes among them, the collapse of the economy and basic services, popular discontent against forces previously considered as "freedom fighters", and criminalization of the economy. In Lebanon it was the arms trade, drug production and trade, and hostage taking. In Afghanistan it was (still is) an explosion of heroin production, and in

---

41   "Rebel commander Raduyev feted by Resistance Congress", *ITAR-TASS* news agency (World Service), Moscow, 21 February, 1998.

Chechnya it was illegal siphoning of oil from the pipelines and development of a hostage-taking industry to a level seen hardly anywhere in the 20th century.[42]

The last characteristic of the Chechens' failure to establish legitimate state institutions was that it became a haven to all kinds of radical forces, from the *jihadis* of Khattab who operated a major training camp in the Vedeno region to Nadir Khachilaev, a mafia type Daghestani leader and a former head of the Union of Muslims of Russia, who escaped to Chechnya after a failed coup attempt in Makhachkala.[43] Six of the nineteen suspected hijackers of aeroplanes that attacked the Twin Towers in New York and the Pentagon in Washington were Saudi citizens who had left home, according to reports, to fight in Chechnya.[44] These radical forces created alliances with local warlords, and their ideology, money, and connections further radicalized the hard-core Chechen fighters. Moreover, Chechens fought in several other conflict zones, either for ideological reasons, as in Afghanistan, or simply as mercenaries, as in the involvement of Chechen fighters led by field commander Ruslan Gelayev in attacks organized by Georgian guerrillas against Abkhaz villages east of Sukhumi, in October 2001.[45] In the words of Sergei Arutyunov, radical Islam was attractive to a large segment of a new generation, characterized as "de-tribalized, de-institutionalized, unemployed, and hopeless youth".[46] Cornered between the heavy sacrifices of the decade and the grim memory of a Chechen, this generation could expect nothing from the "really existing independence". They needed a supra-natural interpretation, and the radical form of Islam called Wahhabism could

---

42   Maskhadov accused Russia of having encouraged development of the "slave trade" by paying huge sums to liberate a number of hostages. See "Open letter by President of the Chechen Republic of Ichkeria to all international human rights organizations regarding the appearance of the propagandistic film 'Slave Market'", published in *Turkestan Newsletter*, electronic distribution, 3 August 2000.

43   See Sanobar Shermatova, "The near coup in Daghestan", *Moscow News*, Moscow, 4-10 June 1998, and Vadim Dubnov, "A mass telekinesis séance in Makhachkala", in *New Times*, Moscow, July 1998.

44   Caryle Murphey and David B. Ottaway, "Some light shed on Saudi suspects", *The Washington Post*, 25 September 2001.

45   Liz Fuller, "Who attacked Abkhazia and why?" *RFE/RL, Caucasus Report*, 12 October 2001, Vol. 4, No. 34.

46   Author interview with Sergey Arutyunov, Moscow, 26 January 2000.

provide exactly that.[47] In a word, Salafi jihadism in Chechnya was a way to escape the reality of the failure of the Chechen statehood.

The Russian authorities had two pretexts for starting their latest military campaign in Chechnya in 1999. The first was the invasion of central Daghestan by Chechen militants led by Basayev and Khattab led forces, and the second was terror attacks against civilian buildings in Moscow and other Russian cities. If one sets aside Russian accusations that Chechen groups were behind the bombing campaign that caused the death of 300 people, a claim that is challenged by third party reports accusing the FSB of being behind those bombings, one must still deal with the two attempts to invade Daghestan. Why did Chechen forces provoke the Russian bear?[48]

Islam has only shallow roots in Chechnya. It was introduced to Chechnya relatively late, around the 16th century, and initially recorded only limited success. Chechens accepted Islam as Sufi brotherhoods from Daghestan led the anti-Russian struggle in the 18th and 19th centuries. In fact, Islam spread in the North Caucasus as it served as the ideology which at the same time confronted the Russian Empire and unified the various ethnic and tribal groups of the North Caucasus under one banner. The Ingushes, who are closely related to the Chechens, were only half Muslim in the 19th century, the other half being Christians or animists. The same is true of the Cherkess and the Abkhaz, who adhered partially to Islam, while other tribes were either Christian or followers of older religions. In the case of the Ossets, a minority consisting mainly of the nobility were Muslim, while the majority was Christian. The only exception is Daghestan, the only region in the North Caucasus with a long tradition of Islam. This "country of mountains" came into contact with Islam directly from Arab invasions. By the 9th century Islam had spread in Daghestan, with the historic city of Derbend becoming a cen-

---

47 His traditional Sufism and his antagonism towards field commanders supporting the new Wahhabi Islam, such as Shamil Basayev, influenced the collaboration of the former Mufti of Chechnya, Akhmed Kadyrov, with the Russian authorities. Kadyrov dominated Gudermes, the second major urban centre in Chechnya, which offered no resistance to the Russian troops in 1999.

48 See the interview given by Maskhadov to Deutsche Welle radio station (10 April 2000), in which he considered Shamil Basayev and Movladi Udugov responsible from the Chechen side for the resumption of hostilities.

tre of Islamic schools. Therefore, the movement for an Islamic emirate in Chechnya had to turn its regards towards Daghestan.

The invasion of Daghestan by Chechen fighters and their *jihadist* allies was due to to a combination of ideological choices (replacing Chechen nationalism with Islamic radicalism) and a *fuite en avant* from the failure of Chechen statehood. If the Chechen fighters had not assumed the task of "liberating" Daghestan, they could not have continued much longer before a large-scale civil war exploded in Chechnya itself.

Russia's reassertion of power

Before their Daghestan adventure, Basayev and Khattab may have unwisely thought that Russia was an exhausted power, ready for further collapse. Many developments hinted in that direction: in August 1998 the rouble devaluation reflected how fragile and exposed Russian economy was after years of privatization, contradictory reforms, and mass corruption. The sick President of Russia seemed unable to find a suitable prime minister, and his succession was more than an enigma. Basaev and Khattab thought that the Federal forces would be unable to put up an efficient resistance to their well-trained guerrillas, and the Daghestani administration would be even less able. Their mistake cost them more than their lives.

The Russian victory did not come easily. Russia followed a three-point strategy to subdue Chechnya: first to use massive force; second, to create pro-Moscow Chechen armed groups and recruit into them as many former Chechen fighters as possible; third, to assassinate the leaders of the Chechen resistance, and the more radical political and military leaders.[49] What differed in the second campaign is that the Russian forces were better organized, had a unified leadership and clearer orders, and were ready to go on till the end. In the 1999 invasion Russia concentrated three times more forces in its onslaught than in December 1994, with total number of army and OMON units surpassing 100,000 servicemen. In the first war, the Russian troops called for a

---

[49] This Russian policy is very much like US policies in Afghanistan and Iraq pay-off paying former insurgents to fight on their side, such as the former Sunni insurgents known as *Majales al-Sahwa* (or "Awakening Councils") who changed sides and allied with the US to fight more radical jihadists associated with al-Qaeda.

cease-fire agreement followed by the withdrawal of their forces twenty months after their invasion. In the second campaign, they were ready to go beyond that, in spite of heavy losses.

The Russian military absorbed the lessons of the first war as well. During the second battle of Groznyy (December 1999-February 2000) the Russian forces did not send columns of armour into an urban context before they had encircled Groznyy to cut the resistance form logistic support from outside. The Russian military imposed the blockade on Groznyy in December 1999, started attacking the city in January the next year after several weeks of heavy shelling, and took the city only on 4 February 2000.[50] The Russian army used "vacuum bombs" or fuel-air explosives to drive fighters away from fortified positions, bombs that had a devastating effect on the civilian population trapped inside the city. The Russian troops had better training this time, more equipment, and better coordination. Even so, the Russian side suffered enormous casualties as it attempted to capture the Chechen capital. The Chechen fighters in their turn suffered major losses as they tried to escape the encirclement and to withdraw southward towards the mountains. In January Ruslan Gelayev and his troops, up to a thousand fighters, abandoned their posts in Groznyy. On the first day of February 2000, the remaining fighters with some refugees, two thousand persons in total, tried to escape the city as well, now short of supplies and ammunition. They tried to leave south-westwards but fell into an ambush, and later were forced to cross a minefield, a well prepared Russian trap.[51] Chechen fighters lost six hundred men while breaking out of Groznyy, including Aslambek Ismailov, the Chechen commander for the defence of Groznyy, Khunkarpasha Israpilov, and Lechi Dudayev (former Mayor of Groznyy), while many others were maimed, including Shamil Basayev who stepped on a land mine and lost his right leg.

Probably the major difference between the first and the second Chechen war was the shift in the public opinion in both Russia and Chechnya. Chechen public opinion was already tired of the insecurity

---

50   Sergei Sokut, "Now we need a Victory in the Mountains", (in Russian), *Nezavisimaya Gazeta*, 5 February 2000: http://www.ng.ru/events/2000-02-05/1_victory.html

51   Ilia Maksakov and Dimitrii Chernogorskii, "The Exit of Chechen Fighters from Groznyy was an Operation of Russian Army", (in Russian), *Nezavisimaya Gazeta*, 4 February 2000: http://www.ng.ru/events/2000-02-04/2_exit.html

and misery brought by the rule of the warlords between 1996 and 1999, and opposed the growing Islamization of the fighters and the imposition of Sharia law by Maskhadov in February 1999, while a majority of them opposed the adventurism of the Basayev-Khattab alliance in Daghestan. In 1999 and 2000 the Russian public seemed to give a strong mandate to their new Prime Minister to crush the Chechen rebellion.

The Russian political and military authorities considered that one of their weaknesses in the first war was that they lost the information war. As the second campaign started, the Russian electronic and later print media were brought under the effective control of the Kremlin. Visits of foreign correspondents to the conflict zone were also controlled. The behaviour of certain Chechen fighters in the inter-war period, including hostage taking and killing of foreigners, also drove foreign correspondents away from Chechnya. News networks were saturated with controlled information. As a result, an information blockade was imposed on Chechnya, where only Kremlin-cleared images and messages could reach the public in Russia and abroad.

To form a pro-Russian militia among the Chechens, Yeltsin pardoned Beslan Gantemirov, a former mayor of Groznyy and a long-time rival of the pro-independence leadership, who was in prison for corruption. Gantemirov formed a force of several hundred fighters, who participated in the battle of Groznyy, although the Russian side often distrusted them and hardly supplied them with more than light weapons. To enlarge their power base the Russian authorities removed the uncontrollable Gantemirov and appointed Ahmed Kadyrov as head of the local administration, in July 2001. Kadyrov was a former Mufti of Chechnya (1995-99), who had sided with Dudayev and participated in resisting the Russian troops during the first war. As a supporter of traditional Sufism, he broke with Maskhadov and the more radical commanders who were increasingly turning to Salafi Islam, foreign to Chechen traditions. He played a major role in creating a strong pro-Russian militia which was led by his son Ramazan and known as the Kadyrovtsi, mainly composed of renegade former resistance fighters like the Kadyrovs themselves.

The Federal forces, while more numerous and better equipped this time, were fundamentally the same as those who had entered Groznyy in 1994, suffering from the same ills in spite of the efforts mentioned above. The Russian army remained an under-funded, badly trained military force with ageing equipment. While official statistics remain unavailable, Russian deaths in December 1999 and January 2000, in fighting in the capital and elsewhere, are estimated at 600. By end of 2002 the official count of Russian military casualties was 4,730 dead and over 15,550 wounded.[52] Although by 2004 the number of Chechen fighters had dwindled to no more than 1,600-1,800 fighters, their use of guerrilla tactics was efficient, and they kept inflicting heavy losses on the Federal troops. The Chechen resistance also succeeded in striking hard at the pro-Moscow Chechen administration: the deputy head of that administration, Adam Deniyev, was caught in an explosion as he was being filmed in a television studio in Groznyy in 2001. Three years later, the pro-Russian Chechen President Ahmed Kadyrov was himself killed in a bomb in a stadium in the Chechen capital during Victory Day celebrations. His son, Ramazan Kadyrov, was appointed by Putin as the President of Chechnya on 15 February 2007. The younger Kadyrov has established ruthless rule with killings and torture as routine tools of governance, and increasingly introduced nationalist and Islamist elements to find popular legitimacy. In the 2007 parliamentary elections of the Russian Federation 99 per cent of the population of Chechnya voted, 99 per cent for the pro-Putin United Russia party.[53]

The Russian military losses decreased in 2005, as most of the major Chechen field commanders were killed: Khattab was poisoned by a letter in March 2002; Zelimkhan Yandearbiev, ex-President of Chechnya and close collaborator of Dudayev, was killed in a car bomb in his exile in Qatar on 13 February 2004; Ruslan Gelayev was killed in the Daghestan mountains in March 2004; Aslan Maskhadov, the freely elected President of Chechnya, was killed in an operation by Russian special forces in the village of Tolstoy-Yurt on 8 March 2005 as he prepared to negotiate with Federal troops;[54] and Shamil Basaev was killed on 10

---

52   See Mark Kramer, "Guerrilla Warfare, Counterinsurgency and Terrorism in the North Caucasus: The Military Dimension of t Russian-Chechen Conflict", *Europe-Asia Studies*, Vol. 57, No. 2, March 2005, 209-90.

53   "Nearly hundred per cent Ramazan" (in Russian), *Nezavisimaya Gazeta*, 28 December 2007: http://www.ng.ru/regions/2007-12-28/5_chechnja.html

54   Mariya Pogacheva, "In Tolstoy-Yurt Aslan Maskhadov prepared negotiations with the Federals", (in Russian), *Izvestia*, 19 October 2005: http://www.izvestia.ru/russia/article2902793/

July 2006 in the Ingush mountains when his truck carrying ammunition exploded—a secret operation according to the FSB, an accident according to Chechen rebels.

The two battles of Groznyy have become a classic in military studies of urban warfare. Groznyy was the most important urban fighting since World War II, with a modern industrial army facing a well prepared guerrilla force.[55] It is rare that a guerrilla force facing a regular army decides to sit down and fight a pitched battle. Most military studies stress the weaknesses of the Russian army in planning, training and unit coordination, the low morale of the troops, and the inadequate material used during the battle. This is contrasted with Chechens' resolve, knowledge of the terrain, and adequate use of light weapons in an urban jungle.[56] In spite of the relevance of the military tactics, logistics, and type of weaponry used, it is important to understand the political developments that influenced the military outcome: the Chechen fighters did not perform worse in the second war than in the first. The Russian army did improve its performance quantitatively, and mainly concentrated more forces and for a longer time, yet in the second war the Russian army suffered from the same ills as in the first. The military budget continued to decrease in the second half of the 1990s and the Russian military did not have training in urban warfare (although there was some effort in mountain warfare capabilities), while the army did

---

55   The two battles of Groznyy were more important in scope than the battle of Algiers (1957), the battle of Hué (1968), and the battle of Beirut (1982) where after three months of siege by the Israeli army the PLO leadership agreed to evacuate the city and its southern suburbs. The most recent battle of Falluja (2004) could provide an interesting comparison with the two battles of Groznyy: Falluja had a pre-war population comparable to that of Groznyy, around 400,000 people, and both towns still had around 50,000 civilians trapped inside when the assaults started.

56   See for example: John Arquilla and Theodore Karasik, "Chechnya: A Glimpse of Future Conflict?" *Studies in Conflict and Terrorism*, Vol. 22, No. 3, 1999, pp. 207-29 ; Raymond Finch, "Why the Russian Military Failed in Chechnya, Fort Leavenworth", KS, *FMSO*, 1997; C.W. Blandy, *Chechnya: Two Federal Interventions, An Interim Comparison and Assessment*, Conflict Studies Research Centre, P29, January 2000; Olga Oliker, *Russia's Chechen Wars 1994-2000: Lessons from Urban Combat*, Santa Monica, CA: RAND, 2001; *L'Enfer de Grozny (1994-2000)*, Cahier du Retex, Centre de Doctrine D'Emploi des Forces, Ministère de la Défense, Paris, December 2006: http://www.cdef.terre.defense. gouv.fr/publications/cahiers_drex/cahier_retex/enfer_grozny.pdf

biggest change between ch. 1, 2

not procure major new systems before the second war and basically had the same equipment as in 1994-96.

What really changed between the first and the second Chechnya wars was the support the Chechen fighters enjoyed. Even more critically, the Chechen resistance lacked a political project to fight for. The vaguely articulated jihadist calls inspired only a small number of radicalized youth but repelled the majority of the population, who even accused the likes of Basaev of being responsible for the new calamities. Maskhadov repeatedly declared that he was ready to drop demands for independence and was ready to negotiate with the Russians on the condition that Moscow stopped military operations and withdrew its troops from Chechnya. But Moscow refused to negotiate with Maskhadov, who had failed to control the republic when he was the President in 1997-99. The Chechen fish was left out of water, and the Russian military succeeded in eliminating its leaders and recruiting its soldiers.

The high price of war

As the intensity of fighting receded, normal life slowly started returning to the Chechen capital. Railway services were restarted on June 2004, and on 8 March 2007 a passenger plane left Moscow to land in Groznyy to resume civilian flights interrupted seven years earlier. Yet the scars are there to remain. The war in Chechnya was the most destructive of post-Soviet conflicts. The Russian troops razed Groznyy to the ground for the second time in 1999-2000 to capture it. The exact number of victims is difficult to determine, yet even approximate figures are alarming and reveal the extent of the Chechen tragedy. According to one study, during the war of 1994-96 around 7,500 Russian Federal troops and around 4,000 Chechen fighters perished. The number of civilian victims is put at 35,000. This makes the total number of dead 46,500.[57] In comparison, the Soviet military losses in Afghanistan during ten years of conflict (1979-89) are estimated at around 14,500, the war in Abkhazia caused a total of 9,000 killed, and the Mountainous Karabakh war 35,000.

The resumption of the war in 1999 caused even heavier losses. At the height of the military operations, up to half of the original population of Chechnya were refugees, mainly in neighbouring Ingushetia and Dagh-

---

57   John Dunlop, "How many soldiers and civilians died during the Russo-Chechen war of 1994-1996?" *Central Asian Survey,* 2000, 19 (3/4), p. 338.

estan.[58] The Russian media reported that as a result of over a decade of war in Chechnya, as many as 160,000 people may have been killed, including "30-40 thousand ethnic Chechens", the other victims belonging to "representatives of various peoples".[59] Is the current lull the end of the most recent Chechen rebellion against the Russian power, and can fifty years of stability be expected until the next cycle of violence? Or is it a much shorter period of calm until a new leader, with a new vision or ideology, can lead the Chechens in yet another rebellion?

---

58   According to Human Rights Watch 260,000 people were displaced within Chechnya, while 170,000 others found refuge in neighbouring Ingushetia. See: http://www.hrw.org/campaigns/russia/chechnya/. Various specialists put the number of those currently living in Chechnya between 400,000 and 500,000, although the Russian 2002 census put the number of inhabitants in Chechnya at an incredible 1.1 million: http://www.reliefweb.int/w/rwb.nsf/0/6bea8e036 c71964e85256d80005aec71?OpenDocument

59   "160,000 victims", (in Russian), *Izvestia,* Moscow, 16 August, 2005: http:// www.izvestia.ru/russia/article2515033/

OIL, PIPELINES AND THE NEW GEOPOLITICS

The Caucasus has always been referred to by the rest of the world not just as mountains inhabited by fierce warriors, but also as a land of prosperity and abundance, of oil and caviar. The mysterious fires burning on the Apsheron peninsula enflamed the imagination of foreign travellers and local inhabitants alike, and inspired the Zoroastrian religion. In times of peace and stability, it was one of the land bridges between the Far East, North Africa and Europe, leading to the prosperity of cities such as Ani, Tiflis (Tbilisi) and Derbent. In the early 20th century Baku was known as the world's oil capital: in 1900 the oil wells in and around the city produced one in two oil barrels produced on the globe. The names of great fortunes such as the Nobels, Rothschilds, Mantashevs and Gulbenkians were associated with Baku oil.[1] Later, during World War II, the idea of dominating the Caucasian oilfields was central in Hitler's war plans against the USSR. Following the collapse of the Iron Curtain, it did not take long before the outside world rediscovered its appetite for the Caspian Oil.

The resumption of Western interest in the Caspian oil triggered a new great power competition for the domination of the Caucasus and the Central Asian steppes across the Caspian. In the mid-1990s the Caspian basin was described as the last frontier of unexploited energy. Diplomats, journalists, and oilmen rushed to the shores of the Caspian looking for the new El Dorado. The Western oilmen were the first to articulate American and European interest in these hostile and inhospitable

---

1   On the role of Baku in world energy history, see Daniel Yergin, *The Prize, The Epic Quest for Oil, Money and Power*, New York: Pocket Books, 1993, pp. 57-61.

lands in the early chaotic years following the Soviet collapse, based on commercial interests. Soon, their lobbying efforts to secure state support brought the attention of Washington to the region, which until the mid-1990s it had considered as Moscow's back yard. The interest in Caspian oil and gas resources led to an international competition between American, European, Russian, Turkish, Iranian and Chinese companies and government agencies which the media labelled as the "New Great Game", referring to the 19th-century competition between the British and the Russian empires to dominate and divide Central Asia.[2]

But to bring the Caspian oil to international markets faced a number of challenges: this land-locked sea was not easily accessible; there were some vague estimates about the oil and gas reserves which still needed further study;[3] the ownership of the oil and gas was a matter of serious competition and legal controversy; to bring Caspian oil to international markets new infrastructure, pipelines and terminals would need to be developed, since in the past the region was only linked to the internal Soviet market; and lastly there was a problem of security for the oil infrastructure and transport routes in a conflict region. In a word the Caspian was a riddle and many questions needed an answer: the ownership of the hydrocarbon resources, the means to take the oil out to international markets, and finally who would act as police to guarantee the security of the oilfields and the pipelines in a risky neighbourhood.

In this new strategic competition the Caucasus emerged as a space of global geopolitical significance for the West, and especially for the US leadership which insists on using the Caspian oil as a trump card in order to push Russia and Iran out of the "Game". The South Caucasus was the region of choice through which new pipelines could cross to reach the landlocked Caspian. In this strategy Azerbaijan and Georgia, two countries dismissed in the early 1990s as "failed states", acquired a new significance: the corridor to link the Caspian basin with markets

---

2   R. Hrair Dekmejian and Hovann H. Simonian, *Troubled Waters, The Geopolitics of the Caspian Region*, London: I.B. Tauris, 2003.

3   Until now it is not clear how much gas reserves Turkmenistan has. Turkmen authorities have so far insisted that the country has "unlimited" resources, although neighbouring countries and international companies doubt this. See Bruce Panier, "Turkmenistan: Ashgabat to allow independent survey of its gas resources ", *Radio Free Europe/Radio Liberty*, 25 January 2008.

in the Western Europe and the Mediterranean crossed through them in order to avoid both Russia and Iran.

This "Great Game" that emerged out of the strategic vacuum left behind by the collapse of the USSR still continues. The al-Qaeda attacks in New York and Washington in 2001 accelerated trends which had started in the mid-1990s. The US military intervention in Afghanistan was accompanied by direct stationing of American and other NATO forces in ex-Soviet Central Asia and the Caucasus. The American invasion of Iraq has completed the siege of Iran, encircled by US military bases from all sides. On the other hand, Russia under Putin has regained some of its former self-assurance and insists on having a dominant position over strategic matters in what was once called the "Near Abroad". Russia's self-assurance has much to do with the oil sector: after a decade of falling productivity as a result of change of ownership structures and under-investment in infrastructure, the Russian oil industry started to increase output starting from 1999-2000, well synchronized with the global increase in oil prices. These two events overlapped with the transfer of power from Yeltsin to Putin, giving the second Russian president the material means to have a foreign policy as well as paying salaries back home. The rise in oil prices, the gradual depletion of US and North Sea production, and continuous increase in demand especially from China and India, as well as increasing instability in the Persian Gulf, have kept up the initial attention that the Caspian oil wealth had aroused.

Caspian oil reserves

The geopolitical competition may have had a symbolic start in the "deal of the century", an $8 billion deal between the State Oil Company of the Azerbaijan Republic (SOCAR) and a consortium of mainly Western oil companies, for the development of three offshore fields (the Azeri, Chirag and Guneshli fields). The international oil companies created a consortium named the Azerbaijan International Operating Company (AIOC), initially composed of ten oil companies and led by British Petroleum.[4] This led to a cascade of oil contracts totalling promises of

---

4   Next to BP AIOC currently (2008) includes: Chevron (US), SOCAR (Azerbaijan), Inpex (Japan), Statoil (Norway), ExxonMobil (US), TPAO (Turkey), Devon (US), Itochu (Japan), Amerada Hess (US). The Russian LUKoil had an initial share of 10 per cent in AIOC, which it sold to the Japanese Inpex for

up to US$60 billion in investment in the Azerbaijani oil and gas sector. One question was thus answered: post-Soviet Azerbaijan was looking westwards for investments to regenerate its decomposing oil industry. This was perfectly natural as Baku had no other choice: neither Russia nor, even less, Iran had the financial capacity or the technology to modernize Azerbaijan's oil industry.

Just as oil majors got their contracts and started drilling to see how much oil and gas was waiting under the Caspian, another war of words erupted, about the real amounts of Caspian energy. The *New York Times* quoted a British government official in charge of following Caspian developments, Paul Millar, as saying: "'Estimates range from 20 to 200 billion barrels (...) The true figure is more likely somewhere in between, but it is a brave person that approaches their bank or shareholders for funding on a market estimate that could vary by plus or minus 90 percent."[5] Yet American government officials chose to continuously repeat that the Caspian Sea was home to 200 billion barrels of oil, comparable to the proven reserves of Saudi Arabia.[6] The US position was not based on geological surveys, but on strategic considerations. Numerous US officials declared that the Caspian was now part of American "national security" and that diversification of energy sources would decrease the Western dependence on unstable Middle East. "If Moscow succeeds [in dominating over Caspian energy resources] its victory could prove more significant than the West's success in enlarging NATO" writes a former American Secretary of Defence.[7]

Russian journalists have often made fun of such naivety: "But have you ever thought why Soviet oil workers had to bore into the frostbitten Tyumen soil if there was such happiness on the warm Caspian?" remarks one.[8] Russian sources suspected that the Azerbaijani statistics provided to Western oil companies were much inflated. They also suspected that

---

US$1.25 billion in November 2002. In 2007, the projected AIOC investment was put at $20 billion. HH

5   Stephen Kinzer, "On piping out Caspian oil, U.S. insist the cheaper, shorter way isn't better", *New York Times*, 8 November 1998.

6   Charles Fenyvesi, "U.S. experts say oil reserves are huge", *Radio Free Europe/Radio Liberty*, 5 May 1998.

7   Caspar W. Weinberger and Peter Schweizer, "Caspian access is crucial for the West", *International Herald Tribune*, 10 May 1997.

8   *New Times*, Moscow, August 1996.

the American enthusiasm for the Caspian was not strictly limited to oil and gas and diversifying sources of energy, but was simply about profiting from the historic opportunity of Russian weakness and imposing American influence over the Caucasus and Central Asia. Some strategists in Washington were not only openly advocating reduction in Russian influence over the Caucasus and Central Asia (as well as Ukraine and the Baltic states), but were calling for a weaker Russian state that would be unable to emerge as a Eurasian power: for the influential Brzezinski, the price for Russia to join the Western club of nations is to cast away its past imperial traditions, and even to become a decentralized federation: "A loosely confederate Russia – composed of a European Russia, a Siberian Republic, and a Far Eastern Republic – would also find it easier to cultivate economic relations with Europe…"[9]

Although historically Azerbaijan was the well known oil producing country, decades of extraction had depleted its reserves. The most important Azerbaijani oilfields today are found offshore, where in the past it was difficult if not impossible to extract oil for lack of technological means. Kazakhstan is the leading Caspian oil producer today, and its position was strengthened in 2000 with the discovery of the huge Kashagan offshore field in the northern Caspian, "the world's largest oil find in 30 years" or since the discovery of Prudhoe Bay in Alaska in 1968.[10] Kashagan has extractable reserves estimated between 9 and 16 billion barrels. Kashagan is only fifty kilometres from another major Kazakh oilfield, that of Tengiz, which is located close to the city of Atyrau. Tengiz was discovered in the Soviet era (1979) and has estimated recoverable reserve of up to 9 billion barrels of oil. Kazakhstan has an estimated 30 billion barrels of oil, placing it in the eleventh position among oil-rich countries, with equally important reserves of natural gas.

What is the reality of the Caspian oil reserves? By July 2006, the US Energy Information Administration put the proven oil reserves of the Caspian basin at between 17.2 and 49.7 billion barrels. Oil production reached by 2005 2.1 million barrels a day, and was projected to increase

---

9   Zbigniew Brzezinski, *The Grand Chessboard, American Primacy and its Geostrategic Imperatives,* New York: Basic Books, 1997, p. 202.

10 Guy Chazan, "In the Caspian, Big Oil Fights Ice, Fumes, Kazakhs", *Dow Jones Newswires,* 28 August 2007.

to 3.1 million b/d by 2010.[11] Azerbaijani oil production jumped from 320,000 b/d in 2003 to 860 thousand in 2007 and is expected to reach 1.3 million b/d by 2010.[12] Kazakhstan, the major Caspian oil producer, reached production of 1.3 million b/d in 2005, and is expected to produce 3.5 million by 2015.[13] Now most energy experts would agree that the Caspian region is no match to the Persian Gulf. But it has already emerged as an important player and will become one of the first five regions of oil and gas suppliers to the international market as from the next decade.

Pipeline politics

Once the extent of the Caspian oil and gas reserves was defined, the next issue at stake was who would control the routes through which this oil and gas would flow. The most obvious, fastest and cheapest route was through the existing Russian pipeline network, to pump Caspian oil from Baku through the North Caucasus to the Russian Black Sea terminal at Novorossiysk, from where tankers could take the cargo to any open sea. The existing infrastructure needed some investment (estimated at $50 million) to add new pumping stations and reverse the existing pipeline. This route was Russia's best choice and was dubbed as the "northern route". A second route, with a new pipeline, was proposed to link Caspian oil and gas fields to the Persian Gulf for onward transport to South and East Asia, where most of the energy demand in the next decade would come when the infrastructure to exploit Caspian hydrocarbons would be ready. This route passed through Iran, and was obviously Teheran's preferred solution, as well as a number of oil investors' preferred choice because of its low cost of construction. Here it is important to note that oil prices were much lower in the mid-1990s (around US$20 per barrel or below), Caspian offshore oil already required considerable investment, and its extraction costs were six to seven times higher than those in Saudi Arabia

---

11   "Caspian Sea Region: Survey of Key Oil and Gas Statistics and Forecasts", *Energy Information Administration*, July 2005: http://www.eia.doe.gov/emeu/cabs/Caspian/images/caspian_balances.xls

12   "Azerbaijan, Background", *Energy Information Administration*, December 2007: http://www.eia.doe.gov/emeu/cabs/Azerbaijan/Background.html

13   In comparison, Russia produced 9.2 million b/d in 2006, making it the second global producer after Saudi Arabia.

or Kuwait. This route was known as the "southern route". A third choice was to construct a new pipeline from Baku to the Georgian Black Sea coast, parallel to an old pipeline constructed a century ago,[14] to take Baku oil to the Black Sea and from there to European capitals. This pipeline, which was used in the Soviet period, had fallen into disuse and needed some major repairs. The new project proposed a new pipeline with more capacity, up to a million b/d, from Baku to Tbilisi and later through Erzerum to end at the Turkish terminal of Ceyhan. This route is known as the "western route".[15]

While US strategists would like to construct an underwater pipeline to bring Kazakh oil to Turkish terminals on the Mediterranean, the Russian side was fast enough to set up the Caspian Pipeline Consortium (CPC) in 1992 and start building a pipeline linking Tengiz via Astrakhan to Novorossiysk. The project is a joint venture between Kazakhstan, Transneft (the Russian state pipeline company), Oman and the US oil company Chevron. In the early years, the various participants in the project had major divergences concerning shares and financing, bringing the project to a halt. Chevron refused to invest in the pipeline, dissatisfied with the management structure, while Russia did not give sufficient access for Tengiz oil through its pipeline system. Finally in 1996 an agreement on the project shares was reached and the project took off.[16] The construction of CPC has so far cost $2.6 billion, for the construction of the main pipeline which is 1,510 km long. The current capacity of the CPC is 700,000 b/d, and by 2010 when the next stage of the construction is finalized this will reach 1.3 million b/d.

The next round of the power game was much harsher. After oil majors started negotiating contracts with Almaty and Baku, and especially

---

14   The Baku-Batumi pipeline, laid from 1897 and operational in 1906, was 883 km long.

15   Rosemary Forsythe, *The Politics of Oil in the Caucasus and Central Asia*, Adelphi Paper, No. 30, International Institute for Strategic Studies, May 1996, pp. 44-54; John Roberts, *Caspian Pipelines*, Royal Institute of International Affairs, 1996, pp. 8-12.

16   The agreement reduced Oman's shares in the CPC from 25 to 7 per cent, Russia's holding being 24 per cent, Kazakhstan's 19 per cent, while the remaining 50 per cent went to a group of investors including Chevron, Mobil and Oryx, all US companies, as well as British BG Overseas Holding, Agip (Italy), LUKoil (Russia) and Rosneft (Russia): See Sander Thoenes, "Russia agrees Kazakh oil pipeline", *Financial Times*, 29 April, 1996.

after the 1994 deal with Azerbaijan, Washington became fully engaged in the Caspian game. Until 1994, the US leadership had looked at the Caucasus warily, seeing the region as one of "unnecessary" problems, and thinking that Moscow should be in charge of handling the "little wars" of the Caucasus. When it was obvious that the new Russia was unable to deal with the massive problems in the region, Washington looked at the conflicts of the Caucasus as if they were a struggle between new, pro-democratic forces and old, pro-Communist remnants. For example, in the case of Karabakh the US administration heavily supported Armenia, viewed as "democratic" and therefore Western-like, against Azerbaijan, looked upon as still ruled by remnants of the Communist *nomenklatura*. In the 1992 Freedom Support Act voted by the US Congress to help the newly independent republics, paragraph 907 prohibited any US aid to the Azerbaijani government because of its repression of the Armenian minority and its blockade against Armenia. In the same period, Armenia received $100 million or more as humanitarian and development aid per year, an important boost for a country suffering from a double blockade (from Azerbaijan as well as Turkey) and engaged in an armed conflict with its eastern neighbour. This prohibition remained in power until 2002 when President George Bush granted the first of the annual waivers regularly granted to Azerbaijan since then.

American interest in the Caspian was not limited to the defence of US and Western corporations, or furthering their interests in a new and turbulent region. In fact, Washington strategists had more ambitious plans: to use hydrocarbon interests to underline the "independence" of the newly independent states—that is, independent from Russia, and increasingly dependent on the West.[17] At the same time, Washington did not want to strengthen Iran's position by having Caspian oil cross the Islamic Republic before reaching international markets. Washington's argument was that the Gulf was already the region where a third of global oil was produced, and the Straits of Hormuz the stretch of sea where a fifth of the world's oil supply passed. For the sake of the security of global oil supply, diversification of energy routes was primordial.

---

17   For an excellent article on Russo-American strategic competition, see Gilbert Achcar, "The Strategic Triad: The United States, Russia and China"; *New Left Review*, March-April 1998, pp. 91-126.

For Russia, whose power was in free fall after the retreat from Afghanistan and Eastern Europe and after fourteen former Soviet Republics became independent, it was necessary to develop a certain strategy to maintain some presence and influence over its "Near Abroad". If Russia was to be considered a "great power", it had to reinvent some of its influence over the former Soviet republics of Central Asia, the Caucasus, and Ukraine. For this, Caspian oil and gas were vital: not for supplying them to Russia, which had them, in abundance, but for creating through pipeline routes a new basis for Russian power projection. The appointment of Viktor Chernomyrdin as Prime Minister of the Russian Federation in December 1992, following Yegor Gaidar, the architect of Russian economic reforms, was a clear sign that the Russian elite was counting on modernizing its energy sector as the backbone of its new power. Chernomyrdin was a former apparatchik heading the Soviet Energy Ministry, and he oversaw in the early 1990s the creation of a giant state-owned gas company, Gazprom. The energy industry had survived Gaidar's "shock therapy", and liberated from state-fixed prices that were a fraction of those on the global markets, had become one of the most powerful sectors of the new Russian economy.[18] For the new Russian elite in search of a "*grande idée*", the energy sector had to become the axis around which to build a new "liberal empire". Oleg Lobov, the former head of the Security Council of the Russian Federation, coined a new strategic aim for Russian foreign policy: to become once again a "great energy power".[19] Instead of using its military might, now very much weakened, the new strategists in the Kremlin were counting on Russia's vast energy wealth, and its dominant position between the Caspian and the European market, to regain lost influence.

Once the "early oil" from the Azerbaijani sector of the Caspian started being pumped a rapid solution was needed to bring them to international markets. Although Terry Adam, a BP executive who headed the AIOC, preferred a cheaper solution through Russia, a call from Roman Berger, the boss of the US National Security Council, convinced the

---

18   Russia is the second global producer of energy. Gazprom has the largest natural gas reserves and is the global number one producer. The company supplies a quarter of all gas imports to the EU, and its revenues in 2005 amounted to more than $81 billion.

19   Valeri Kosiuk (ed.), *Le pétrole et le gaz russes*, Centre de Recherche Entreprises et Sociétés et Association de Coopération Internationale, Geneva, 1995, p. 19.

AIOC management that a pipeline westward through Georgia was the answer, free from Russian control. On 2 October 1995, "Mr. Clinton called Mr. Aliyev to lobby for the double-route plan. Fortified by his new tacit alliance with Washington, Mr. Aliyev gave his approval a week later."[20] The existing Baku-Batumi pipeline, which needed much work to become operational, had a capacity of 115,000 b/d. The rest was transported through the existing infrastructure through Russia, or even by rail through Russia or Georgia. It was clear that once the AIOC reached full capacity a new "main export pipeline" would be needed to transport oil from the Caspian area to open seas.

After much arm twisting and intense pressure from Washington and Ankara, on 29 October 1998 five heads of the former Soviet republics of Georgia, Azerbaijan, Kazakhstan, Turkmenistan and Uzbekistan met in Ankara under the patronage of the Turkish President and in the presence of the American Secretary of Energy to announce their choice for the pipeline route: from Baku to Ceyhan, crossing through Georgia.[21] Construction of the 1,730-km pipeline, known as the BTC (Baku-Tbilisi-Ceyhan) pipeline, started in 2002 was completed by 2005 (it took six months to fill it with oil end to end), at a cost of more than $3.6 billion.

The second round of the pipeline game ended with a US victory. Yet the "Game" did not stop there: the great power competition to dominate the inner Asia continues to be as vigorous as ever. This new game is played by such elements as oil and gas fields, pipelines and tankers, yet it is not restricted to access to energy. It is rather about using energy resources and transport routes to carve wider geopolitical influence over the whole of inner Asia. After initial losses, Russia seems to have been catching up with its Western competitors in the contest over oil and gas supply to the European markets in the next decade. European countries already imported 25 per cent of their oil needs from Russia in 2006, while gas imports were even higher: 70 per cent for Austria, 43 per cent for Germany, and 26 per cent for France.[22] Following the January 2006

---

20   Dan Morgan and David B. Ottaway, "Power Play in the Caspian", *International Herald Tribune*, 5 October 1998.

21   Marie Jégo, "Les Etats-Unis et la Turquie privilégient la voie sud pour le transit du pétrole de la Caspienne ", *Le Monde*, Paris, 31 October 1998.

22   "Russia Country Analysis Brief: Natural Gas ", Energy Information Admin-

gas price controversy between Moscow and Kiev Russia cut gas deliveries to Ukraine, raising questions in European capitals as to whether relying heavily on Russian energy imports did not involve high political risks. EU efforts to diversify energy sources and supply routes have been matched with an aggressive Russian counterattack, largely thanks to Moscow's capacity to co-opt individual European companies and states. The EU supports the Nabucco pipeline project, which aims to carry Turkmen gas through Azerbaijan and Georgia, Turkey, Bulgaria, Romania and Hungary to Austria.[23] But realization of the project was put in doubt after Russia reached a deal in 2007 with Turkmenistan and Kazakhstan to transfer natural gas from their Caspian shores to European markets through Russia, through a rival project known as the "Southern Stream".

In early 2008 Moscow scored new successes. It signed deals with Bulgaria and Serbia which advanced its "Southern Stream" project, a step ahead of the Nabucco project that plans to bring Central Asian gas to Europe through Azerbaijan and Turkey. Russia has signed an agreement to build a Burgas-Alexandroupolis oil pipeline which will allow Russian oil exports to bypass the Bosporus. Moreover, Gazprom took over 51 per cent of the Serbian state owned oil and gas monopoly NIS, in what was described by one Russian daily as "Gazprom's Balkan Campaign".[24]

Oil on fire

The coming of massive investment in the oil sector in a region plagued with violent ethno-territorial conflicts was more than alarming. The foreign-led oil projects were possible thanks to cease-fire agreements that were reached in the Abkhazia and Karabakh conflicts (in 1993 and 1994 respectively), which reflected a new balance of power between the antagonistic sides. Yet, in the medium term, the massive investment in the hydrocarbon sector was to lead to a flow of petrodollars which could eventually disturb the existing military as well as political and strategic

---

istration, April 2007: http://www.eia.doe.gov/emeu/cabs/Russia/NaturalGas.html

23   See : www.nabucco-pipeline.com

24   *Kommersant*, 23 January 2008.

balance before conflict resolution was achieved, thus threatening the Caucasus region with a new cycle of violent conflicts.[25]

Initially, the promise of oil investment could have played a positive role. Most probably the Azerbaijani leader Heydar Aliev agreed to reach a cease-fire arrangement with his Armenian antagonists in May 1994 to prepare the ground for the September 1994 "deal of the century". The current Baku-Tbilisi-Ceyhan pipeline passes only 20 km from the front line, and no international consortium was going to invest billions of dollars at a time when the war was still going on, and in a country where governments were overthrown following military defeat on the frontline.

Following the cease-fire, the Azerbaijani leader tried to capitalize on the foreign interest in Azerbaijani oil resources to create positive relations between Baku and the global power centres. During the war (1991-94) Azerbaijan had suffered much from strong pro-Armenian sentiments and policies both in Russia and in Western capitals, and now Baku intended to change all that through its oil policy. Aliev distributed oil deals to American, British, French, Russian, Turkish and Iranian companies to create material interests in those countries to serve as the basis for pro-Azerbaijani politics. Azerbaijan invested its petrodollars to recruit high-profile American lobbyists to advance its cause at the White House, including Lloyd Bentsen, James Baker, John Sununu, Brent Scowcroft, Zbigniew Brzezinski and Richard Armitage, among others.[26]

These efforts did score some success. Azerbaijan stopped being looked upon as a country repressing its minorities and organizing pogroms against them. Now the head of the Azerbaijani state and its diplomatic representatives were welcomed in Western capitals to discuss lucrative deals. Yet this change of image had its limits: it did not create enough political capital to be translated into a strategic asset. While the oil lobby in Washington did work for the interest of Baku, yet its agenda was a more complex one, and when the oil lobbyist talks an official has numerous issues to consider and Baku is not at the top of the list. The oil

---

25   Vicken Cheterian, *Dialectics of the Ethnic Conflicts and Oil Projects in the Caucasus*, PSIS Occasional Paper, No. 1, Geneva, 1997.

26   See Alec Rasizade, "Azerbaijan Descending into the Third World After a Decade of Independence", *Journal of Third World Studies*, Spring 2004, footnote number 46.

lobby was confronted with the ethnic Armenian lobby, which is one of the best organized ethnic lobbies in Washington and has only one topic on its agenda: to support Armenia's interests. The West, Russia, and many others were indeed interested in Caspian oil, yet they were not ready to do more than pay cash for it: Azerbaijani oil was not enough to bring outside help and resolve the Karabakh conflict in favour of Baku. Aliev realized this, probably around 1999, and embarked on a serious negotiations process with his counterpart Robert Kocharian, which culminated in the Key West agreements. This agreement had very few supporters in Baku, and the ageing Azerbaijani leader understood he had no more force to fight this last political battle.

Military build-up

Did Armenia and Azerbaijan lose a golden opportunity to reach an agreement in 2001? Yes, probably. Since the Key West meeting the relations between the two neighbouring countries have continued to deteriorate. Public opinion in the two countries is moving further away from a common understanding of the problem, necessary for bringing reconciliation between them. For the Armenian public, the Karabakh question arose from a historic injustice imposed by Stalin. The issue was raised in 1988 by the Armenians of Karabakh and Armenia, but that led to pogroms and deportations by Azerbaijan. The people of Karabakh took up arms and defended themselves and won the war. For the Armenian public opinion the Karabakh problem "is solved". They forget that for their neighbouring people it is not so. For the Azerbaijani public Karabakh remains an open wound, it is a disgrace that needs to be addressed. For a new generation of Azerbaijanis, Karabakh has become the most powerful source to galvanize their national identity that is going through a period of strong mutation.[27]

Starting from 2003, with the coming of Ilham Aliev to power, the Azerbaijani leadership has chosen an increasing militaristic discourse. The Azerbaijani media are filled on a daily basis with declarations by high level officials saying that Azerbaijan will offer autonomy to Karabakh within Azerbaijan, and that if the Armenian side rejects this Azerbaijan

---

27   See for example Yasemin Kilit Aklar, " Nation and History in Azerbaijani School Textbooks ", *Ab Imperio*, 2/2005, pp. 469-97.

will take back Karabakh and the surrounding territories by force: Ilham Aliev declared on January 2008: "Armenia did not win the war. The war is not over. Only the first stage of the war has been completed", and he even added, "In 1918 the city of Iravan [Yerevan] was given to the Armenians. That was a big mistake. The Iravan Khanate was Azerbaijani land and the Armenians were just guests living there."[28]

The political vision adopted in Azerbaijan is closely linked with the incoming petrodollars. The Azerbaijani military budget rose from US$175 million in 2003 to $300 million in 2004, $600 million in 2006 and $1.3 billion in 2008.[29] Baku has used considerable chunks of this military budget to acquire new weapon systems, including over a hundred T-72 tanks imported from Ukraine and Belarus, various artillery pieces, MiG-29 fighters, and "Smerch" surface-to-surface multiple rocket-systems. Many observers have criticized the increased militarization of Azerbaijan, noting that in spite of the dramatic increase a strategic vision was missing, the military had a long tradition of corruption, and social conditions within the army remained deplorable.[30]

In response, Armenia's military budget is planed to increase 20 per cent in 2008 to $380 million. While Armenia has not officially made major procurements of late—except for ten Soviet-made Sukhoi-25 ground-attack aeroplanes from Slovakia—it profits from its military cooperation with Russia. The Armenian armed forces receive advanced weapon systems, ammunition and intelligence through the Russian bases situated near Yerevan and Gyumri. What should be the biggest reason for the Azerbaijani leadership to think twice before starting a new open-ended military adventure is that their armed forces have already lost a war in Karabakh at a time when they had superior arms and manpower. Moreover, today the Karabakh Armenians have a better strategic position than in the early 1990s: today Karabakh Armenians

---

28   *Trend News Agency*, Baku, 17 January 2008 : http://news.trendaz.com/index.sh tml?show=news&newsid=1113506&lang=EN

29   See *Azer Tag*, Baku, 20 December 2005; "Azerbaijan boosts defence budget, warns Armenia", *Reuters*, 22 October 2007; *International Crisis Group*, "Nagorno-Karabakh: Risking War", 14 November 2007, p. 12-13.

30   Liz Fuller "Azerbaijan: military has cash, but no security doctrine", *Radio Free Europe/Radio Liberty*, 2 February 2006; Rashad Suleimanov, "Azeri Defence Spending Under Fire", Institute for War and Peace Reporting, *Caucasus Reporting Service*, London, No. 421, 29 November 2007.

dominate all the mountains of Karabakh while the Azerbaijani military are in the lowlands.

Politically, the continuous Azerbaijani threats make Karabakh Armenians and their supporters in Yerevan think twice before considering any territorial concessions. The major security guarantee they have is their current geographical position. Two events with symbolic meaning in recent years have revived the "mass trauma" of the Armenians referred earlier. In 2004, within NATO's Partnership for Peace programme, a number of officers from East European countries were following English lesson courses in Budapest, when on the night of 19 February Lieutenant Ramil Safarov of the Azerbaijani Army hacked the Armenian Lieutenant Gurgen Margarian to death with an axe and a knife in his bed. According to the Hungarian police, the crime was committed with "unusual cruelty". While in the days following the event Azerbaijani officials tried to keep some distance from the murder, Azerbaijani media and public organizations not only defended Safarov but also justified his deed, arguing that he was a refugee from the occupied zone, and that the Armenian officers "provoked him".[31] Armenian public opinion was galvanized by this event: the commemoration of the Sumgait massacres few days after the murder of the Armenian officer saw an unusual mobilization, with thousands marching in downtown Yerevan carrying pictures of Sumgait victims as well as that of Gurgen Margarian.

The Jugha (Julfa in Persian) cemetery in Nakhichevan is 1,500 years old, and in the Soviet times still had up to 3,000 *khachkars* or Armenian tombstones. Most of the *khachkars* were from the 16th or the 17th century, although older ones were also found. The cemetery was slowly being destroyed, much like Armenian religious and cultural monuments elsewhere in Nakhichevan. On 10 December 2005, two hundred Azerbaijani soldiers came to the Jugha cemetery, and over four days smashed the remaining *khachkars* with heavy hammers. The debris was thrown into the Arax river. The site of the cemetery has been since converted to a military firing range. The destruction was filmed and photographed from Iran on the other side of the Arax, and caused much distress to the Armenians worldwide. Both the killing of Margarian asleep in his bed

---

31 "Nation stands for Azeri officers' rights", *AssA-Irada*, Baku, 24 February 2004; "Azeri war veterans ask President to stand up for officer", *Zerkalo*, Baku, 4 February 2004.

and the destruction of the Jugha cemetery revived the worst fears among the Armenians, the feeling that neither their physical security nor their culture and identity is safe in the hands of Azerbaijan.[32] Azerbaijani official propaganda concerning Christian churches and tombstones in its territory is still unchanged since Soviet times: they are not Armenian, but "Caucasian Albanian" and therefore Azerbaijani. What is puzzling is that Azerbaijani soldiers pulverize their own historic heritage with heavy hammers.[33]

In 1991-94 Azerbaijan did not just lose territory, but also its national pride. Today, this wounded national pride is increasingly reacting violently, with each act reawakening the Armenian trauma that goes back to the Armenian Genocide, to the Sumgait pogroms, and to the entrenched fear for survival.

Georgia has gone through an impressive rearmament programme since the Rose Revolution of 2003 and the coming of Mikheil Saakashvili to power. In the Shevardnadze era, the yearly defence budget was around US$20-25 million,[34] which practically meant that the country did not have armed forces. By 2007, the military budget of Georgia rose to $567 million, a more than tenfold increase. The Georgian leadership has invested in building two NATO standard military bases, one in Senaki near the border with Abkhazia and the second in Gori, a half-hour drive from the South Osset capital of Tskhinvali. Each base has the capacity to house a brigade, or 3,000 soldiers. The Georgian military has also bought armour such as T-72 tanks and BTRs (troop transport vehicles), mainly from Ukraine, as well as artillery and am-

---

32   For a detailed documentation on Jugha and its destruction, see: Parliamentary Group Switzerland-Armenia (ed.), *The Destruction of Jugha and the Entire Armenian Cultural Heritage in Nakhijevan*, Berne, 2006, 98 pp. See also Stephen Castle, "Azerbaijan 'flattened' sacred Armenian site", *The Independent*, London, 30 May 2006.

33   "Azerbaijan: Famous Medieval Cemetery Vanishes", Institute for War and Peace Reporting, *Caucasus Reporting Service*, London, No. 336, 19 April 2006; "Ganira Pashayeva : 'Ancient Christian Monuments in Azerbaijan are Albanian", *Azerbaijan Today*, 24 January 2008: http://www.today.az/news/politics/42581.html

34   In 2002 the Georgian defence budget was 38.5 million laris, less than $20 million. See Mamuka Komakhia and Jaba Devdariani, "Neglected Forces", *Civil Georgia*, Tbilisi, 2 February 2002 : http://www.civil.ge/eng/article.php?id=1180

munition. Georgia has already enjoyed American military assistance in the form of training and equipment. Already in 2002, and following the September 11 events and the US objective of eliminating Chechen and Arab *jihadi* presence in the Pankisi gorge of northern Georgia, the "train and equip" programme was developed with a budget of $64 million, and US military assistance to Georgia in 2007 was $34 million. As a result of US-Georgian cooperation, some 16,000 Georgian soldiers received American training over the years.

Saakashvili had two aims through his new military policy: the first is to have a credible military force capable of taking part in foreign missions, as in Iraq and Kosovo. The second obvious aim is to have a military force capable of carrying out future operations in the secessionist republics. The fighting in South Ossetia in 2004 revealed the severe limitations of the Georgian armed forces—after two weeks of fighting they were short of ammunition. For many military observers, the choice of the armament purchased and the geographical position chosen for the military bases indicate clearly that the Georgian leadership is seriously preparing its armed forces for future confrontations in South Ossetia and Abkhazia.[35]

What's next?

The conflicts in the Caucasus were the result of an extraordinary historic event: the collapse of the Soviet Union. A state that monopolized politics, economics, and security issues, where political parties and associations independent from the state were not allowed to function freely, started disintegrating and collapsed in a matter of few years. The vacuum left behind was filled either by the party *nomenklatura* now posing as national leaders, as in Central Asia, or by mass mobilization led under the banner of the nation. The conflicts in the Caucasus in the early 1990s were the result of the clashes between those competing national-projects, with contradictory claims to territory, often disregarding the will of the people inhabiting those territories.

As a result of the conflicts a new balance of power was achieved, resulting in the military victory of secessionist minorities. This equilibrium

---

35   Vicken Cheterian, "Georgia's Arms Race", *OpenDemocracy*, 4 July 2007: http://www.opendemocracy.net/conflicts/caucasus_fractures/georgia_military

has been the basis of the cease-fire agreements reached in 1993 for the Georgian-Abkhaz conflict, in 1994 for the Armeno-Azeri conflict, and in 1996 for the Russo-Chechen conflict. The adventure of Chechen fighters in their sortie into Daghestan in 1999 broke the status quo and led to a new and massive Russian military invasion. Russia retook Chechnya and eliminated the Chechen leadership calling for national independence, but paid a heavy price: thousands of soldiers and civilians are dead—160,000 or more—while Russia's rule in Chechnya is based on its alliance with the Kadyrov dynasty and its capacity to recruit former Chechen resistance fighters. Is the current calm is just a lull between two wars, or more lasting peace?

The fate of the South Caucasus is only marginally better. There too geopolitical forces are creating new conditions which will make the cease-fire arrangements of the 1990s untenable: the massive oil and gas investment has profited Azerbaijan, and to a lesser degree Georgia. The arms race that started in the region in 2003-4 is more than worrying. The continuous threats by the Azeri and Georgian leaderships have created public expectations of a resolution of the territorial questions through military means. The conflicts in Karabakh and South Ossetia started as clashes between village defence groups and volunteer brigades; the next war will be different, a clash between heavily armed military forces on each side, with much more damage to human lives and property.

What is the way to peace in the Caucasus? To reframe the question, could there be peaceful resolution of the current conflicts? It is difficult to imagine a solution to the territorial conflicts as long as ethnic nationalism is the primary political reference in the region. Nationalism divides the region, and a more global reference is needed which, often in the past, has come from outside as a result of an imperial project. Throughout history, the Caucasus was the borderland over which various imperial projects clashed: Greeks and Parthians, Romans and Sassanians, Arabs and Byzantines, Ottomans and Safavids, and finally Ottomans and Russians. Soviet rule halted local conflict and great-power competition over the region, and the collapse of the USSR reopened them. Will the renewed interest of great powers and the renewed self-assurance of the Kremlin clash again over the rocky mountains of the Caucasus?

EPILOGUE

As this book was going to press, dramatic events shattered the geopolitical equilibrium of the Caucasus, and profoundly altered East-West relations in a manner not seen since the end of the Cold War. Brewing tension between Georgia on the one side, and the de-facto authorities of Abkhazia and South Ossetia supported by Russia on the other, exploded into violent conflict. When the world's attention was focused on the opening of the Olympic Games in Beijing—the night of 7 August, 2008—Georgian troops launched a major offensive against Tskhinvali, the main town of South Ossetia. For weeks the military situation in South Ossetia had been deteriorating, with Georgian troops and Osset militias exchanging mortar fire between Georgian villages in the south, east and the north of Tskhinvali, and Osset forces defending the town. The situation became all-out war in the early hours of 8 August, when Georgian troops attacked and took eight Osset villages and then entered the Osset capital; they continued to advance northwards but failed to cut off the Java and Roki tunnels, which connect South Ossetia with North Ossetia through the Caucasus Mountains. In a televised speech, Georgian leader Mikheil Saakashvili sounded victorious and declared that his forces controlled "most of South Ossetia", and added: "A large part of Tskhinvali is now liberated and fighting is ongoing in the centre of Tskhinvali".[1]

The Georgian victory celebrations were short-lived as the Russian military responded immediately and devastatingly. According to an official Russian account, advancing Georgian troops overran Russian peacekeeping forces, killing over ten Russian soldiers and wounding others; the Russian military reaction came in a matter of hours. First,

---

1   "'Most of S. Ossetia Under Tbilisi's Control'—Saakashvili", *Civil Georgia*, 8 August, 2008, http://www.civil.ge/eng/article.php?id=18955&search=.

Russian planes attacked Georgian armour in and around Tskhinvali, as well as Georgian military facilities in Vaziani, Marneuli and Senaki. Russian tank columns poured into South Ossetia before the Georgian military could control the strategic tunnels. The Russian 58th Army stationed in Vladikavkaz (North Ossetia) advanced south of the mountains and took control of Tskhinvali, then progressed southwards towards Gori, which is located 20 km. south of the South Osset border. Gori is the birthplace of Joseph Stalin and a strategic Georgian town on a main road linking Tbilisi with west Georgia and its sea ports. Georgian forces abandoned Gori to regroup for the defence of the capital, while the 2000 Georgian troops stationed in Iraq were recalled home.

On 9 August a second front opened up as Abkhaz forces attacked and occupied the Kodori Gorge. The same day Russian navy and Georgian vessels clashed in the Black Sea. Russian forces rapidly advanced and took Zugdidi and Senaki, overrunning an airfield and destroying the newly built military base. Similarly, in Gori another recently constructed Georgian military base, the expression of Georgia's ambitions to join NATO, was occupied by the Russian troops, ransacked, and burnt down. On 14 August, Russian troops entered the port of Poti, a key town on the Black Sea, and eliminated the tiny Georgian navy. In as little as two days of fighting the Georgian army collapsed, leaving few if any military obstacles to impede the Russian tanks on their way to Tbilisi.

Fortunately for the Georgians, the Russians signed a French-brokered cease-fire on 15 August, after which the Russian leadership declared their intention to withdraw troops from Georgia proper in ten days. The six-point agreement is basically a capitulation by Tbilisi that gives full military control of Abkhazia and South Ossetia to Russia, and permits the Russian military to keep forces outside the two secessionist territories while "awaiting international mechanisms". Yet, Russian troops continued to man checkpoints around Gori, as well as Poti, after that date.

The Russian military action deep inside Georgia is an unprecedented event that has profound implications for Caucasus geopolitics and energy competition and marks a radical change in Russian foreign and defence policies. This is the first significant Russian military operation beyond its borders since the collapse of the USSR, or since the withdrawal of Soviet troops from Afghanistan.[2] Although the analysis of these events needs more time and distance, I will offer several preliminary remarks here.

The first question is why did the Georgian leadership take such a gamble? The Georgian side had concentrated some 7,000 troops, supported by up to 100 tanks and armoured vehicles, to face 500 Russian peacekeepers and 2,000-3,000 Osset fighters. The Georgians also used several Sukhoi-25 ground-attack planes during its push to take Tskhinvali; they seem to have planned to take the town in 24 hours and advance north to control strategic tunnels and communication lines in the second day of the war. Moreover, Georgian specialists expected the Russian response to take longer, and Osset resistance to be shorter. Although Georgian forces deployed more modern technology, including Israeli-built drones and US communication and night-vision equipment, the rapid and crushing Russian counter-attack shattered their forces.[3] Georgian deputy defence minister Batu Kutelia admitted that Georgian troops went on an offensive in South Ossetia "despite the fact that its forces did not have enough anti-tank and air defences to protect themselves against the possibility of serious resistance" and did not expect such a strong Russian reaction.[4] This seems very strange since less than three weeks before the outbreak of hostilities, Georgia had closely observed Russia's "Kavkaz-2008" military manoeuvres (which the Russians openly stated were a response to tensions in South Ossetia and Abkhazia) just across its borders and sent protest notes.

This grave miscalculation could cost Georgia dearly. Apart from infrastructure damage and civilian casualties, Georgia once again succumbed to the temptation of using military force to solve ethnic conflicts, just as in 1989-1992. And just like during the collapse of the Soviet empire, Georgia lost its military gamble together with much prized territory.

---

2   One can also note here the deployment of some 200 Russian peacekeeping troops from their bases in Bosnia to Kosovo during the NATO war against Serbia, in June 1999, although the operation did not develop into a significant military action, and failed to change the situation on the ground.

3   Simon Saradzhyan, "Conflict Exposes Obsolete Hardware", *Moscow Times*, 15 August, 2008.

4   See Jan Cienski, "Tbilisi admits it miscalculated Russian reaction", *Financial Times*, 22 August, 2008, http://www.ft.com/cms/s/0/90d1d4c6-6fe0-11dd-986f-0000779fd18c.html?nclick_check=1.

There is evidence that the advancing Russian-Osset troops destroyed ethnic Georgian villages to the north and east of Tskhinvali, driving some 20,000 Georgian civilians from their homes.[5] Similarly, some 1,500 Svan villagers became refugees from Upper Kodori, and it is not clear when or whether the civilian population will be allowed to return after the end of the military phase of the conflict. Georgian IDP's from Abkhazia, apart from the southern region of Gali, are still displaced from their homes following the 1992-93 war. Even if Russia's military response had taken longer to evolve, Tbilisi was wrong to believe that in a two-day "blitzkrieg" it could have "solved" the ethno-territorial conflicts. Its army of 25,000 soldiers is too small to fight a prospective long-term guerrilla war in a mountainous region and its US-trained forces are too young and too inexperienced for prolonged warfare. It would have been wiser to draw a lesson from the recent wars in Iraq and Afghanistan, or even better from its own experience in South Ossetia and Abkhazia wars in the early 1990s. But the Georgian leadership was emboldened by its alliance with the global superpower, and was counting on its support. So, the second question is, what was the role of the US in the war, and why did Washington fail to support Saakashvili?

Some 130 US military advisors were present in Georgia during the conflict, although according to US official sources they did not participate in any of the hostilities. Moreover in July, a month earlier, joint US-Georgian military exercises brought some 1,000 US soldiers to Georgia, for anti-terrorism training. The Georgian army was also supplied with American arms and helicopters. Was Washington indirectly aiding Georgia to re-conquer lost territories, or was this just reparation for Georgian military support in Iraq and to police the Baku-Ceyhan pipeline? At best, Washington sent mixed signals to Saakashvili. According to one account, Condoleezza Rice "privately told Mr Saakashvili not to let Russia provoke him into a fight he could not win. But her public comments, delivered while standing next to Mr. Saakashvili during a news conference, were far stronger and more supportive."[6] Once

---

5   See the report of Tom Parfitt, "Desire for revenge fuels flames as militiamen destroy South Ossetia's 'cleansed' villages", *The Observer*, 24 August, 2008, http://www.guardian.co.uk/world/2008/aug/24/georgia.russia?gusrc=rss&feed=networkfront.

6   Helen Cooper, C.J. Chivers and Clifford J. Levy, "U.S. Watched as a Squabble Turned Into a Showdown", *New York Times*, 18 August, 2008, http://www.

the military operations started, the US was late to react, and its response was limited to vague declarations in support of Georgia. On 25 August, US Navy destroyer *USS McFaul* reached the Georgian port of Batumi to deliver "humanitarian aid", the first sign of possible American military presence near the Caucasian war circle since the start of the latest conflict. Was American support of Georgia stretching the real capacity of American power a step too far? Or is this just the opening of a longer conflict yet to unroll?

Lastly, what was the Russian motivation for intervening so aggressively and hitting Georgia so hard? Has the boomerang-effect of Kosovo, launched by its recognition as an independent state, had a harmful impact on Georgia.[7] The current belligerent Russian stance towards Georgia, although a response to the challenge thrown at the door of the Kremlin by Mikheil Saakashvili, is not designed to address the problems of the Caucasus. It is Russia's answer to what it understands as a Western, and more specifically an American, challenge to its national interests and the status of Moscow as a world power. Since the end of the Second World War, passing through the Helsinki negotiations in the Brezhnev era, including Gorbachev's reforms, Russia's objective has been to achieve Western recognition of its frontiers. The fall of the USSR and the Yugoslav Federation led to international recognition of the union republics, but not the sub-units, such as Kosovo, Chechnya, or Abkhazia. Therefore, the acknowledgement of Kosovo by Washington and a number of important EU capitals was a break with international practice, and a challenge to Moscow. The Russian elite did not understand why after the end of the Cold War NATO had to be preserved, and furthermore, advance to its doorstep to include such post-Soviet states as Estonia, Latvia and Lithuania. The Georgian and Ukrainian ambition to join the Atlantic alliance was for the Kremlin, a "red line" not to be crossed. Lastly, the positioning of an American antimissile shield in Poland and the Czech Republic, supposedly to counter

---

nytimes.com/2008/08/18/washington/18diplo.html.

7   Russian parliamentarians started discussing the recognition of Abkhazia and South Ossetia as independent states as early as 10 August, two days after the start of the hostilities, with clear reference to the Kosovo precedence. See Igor Romanov and Ulyana Makhkamova, "Duma Zagavarili o Kosovo", *Nezavisimaya Gazeta*, 11 August, 2008, http://www.ng.ru/politics/2008-08-11/4_kosovo.html.

Iranian missile threats yet with the capacity to eliminate Russian missile deterrence, was yet another challenge to Russian security. In short, Russia has multiple grievances against the West, and after a decade and a half of weakness and disintegration, today has the means to react.

The military escalation set back diplomatic efforts dating back more than a decade. On 26 August the Russian President Medvedev officially recognized the independence of Abkhazia and South Ossetia, and pledged that Russia would defend their security.[8] Unfortunately, Russian reaction to the West's expansion in its own back-garden complicates its policies in the Caucasus. Since the early 1990s, Moscow had shied away from recognizing Abkhazia and South Ossetia as "independent" for three reasons. The first and simplest is that Russia did not need to recognize the two de facto independent entities in order to extend its influence over those regions. In fact, the Russian intelligence services have been running the government in South Ossetia for a decade, personally nominating ministers and overseeing every action by its government. Its influence over Abkhazia is not comparable, yet consequent. The second reason is that Abkhaz or South Osset formal independence could encourage nationalist and separatist tendencies in Russia proper, from North Caucasus to the Middle Volga. And third, Russia is interested in extending its authority over the entire South Caucasus, and recognising the independence of the two entities would lead to historic Georgian antagonism, and Azerbaijani suspicion. Paradoxically, Russian defiance of Western policies comes at a cost to its internal and Caucasian interests.

Baku, in turn, fears that the Russian recognition of the independence of Abkhazia and South Ossetia, following the acceptance of Kosovo by numerous Western countries, would open the way to international recognition of Karabakh. In Yerevan, pressure is increasing on the authorities to follow suit and recognize the Karabakh as an independent state.

The conflicts of the Caucasus in the early 1990s were the result of mass nationalism set free by the collapse of the Soviet state. The hostilities of today are of a different nature: nationalism is now the result of conscious policies by the ruling elites, the conflicts the outcome of clashes between centrally commanded armies, and not nationalist

---

8 Ekaterina Grigorieva and Alexandr Latishev, "Vne Zavizimosti ot Gruzii", *Izvestia*, 26 August, 2008, http://www.izvestia.ru/politic/article3119878/.

mobs battling in city streets or villages. After the first cycle of combat in the Caucasus there was a chance to bring lasting peace to the region. However the rapid introduction of Western oil projects, offshore Caspian contracts and pipeline policies have sharpened international interest and competition over the region, while keeping the conflicts of the Caucasus in a "frozen" state. As I argued some time ago, Western oil interests could have serious consequences on the power equilibrium behind the cease-fire agreements: "The shift in the fragile balance on the war fronts threatens to break the cease-fires and provoke the resumption of military operations. If in the past the Caucasus went through the violence of ethno-territorial conflicts, this time we could witness 'oil wars'."[9] Fuelled by Caspian oil and ignited by ethnic conflicts, after the dramatic events of 8 August, the Caucasus risks becoming the theatre of a new East-West confrontation.

Geneva, 27 August, 2008

---

9   Vicken Cheterian, *Dialectics of Ethnic Conflicts and Oil Projects in the Caucasus*, Programme for Strategic and International Security Studies, Occasional Paper 1/1997, Geneva, pp. 84-85.

FURTHER READING

Achcar, Gilbert. *La Nouvelle Guerre froide, Le monde après le Kosovo*, Paris: Presses Universitaires de France, 1999

Afanasyan, Serge. *L'Arménie, l'Azerbaïdjan et la Géorgie: de l'indépendance à l'instauration du pouvoir soviétique (1917-1923)*, Paris: L'Harmattan, 1981.

Altstadt, Audrey. *The Azerbaijani Turks, Power and Identity under Russian Rule*, Stanford: Hoover University Press, 1992.

Atabaki, Touraj. *Azerbaijan, Ethnicity and the Struggle for power in Iran*, London: I. B. Tauris, 2000.

Baev, Pavel. *The Russian Army in Times of Trouble*, London: PRIO/SAGE, 1996.

Barkey, Karen and von Hagen Mark (eds.). *After Empire, Multiethnic Societies and Nation-Building*, Boulder: Westview, 1997.

Beissinger, Mark R. *Nationalist Mobilization and the Collapse of the Soviet State*, Cambridge: Cambridge University Press, 2002.

Benningsen Broxup, Marie (ed.). *The North Caucasus Barrier, the Russian Advance Towards the Muslim World*, London: Hurst and Company, 1996.

Bremmer, Ian and Ray Taras (eds.). *Nations and Politics in the Soviet Successor States*, New York: Cambridge University Press, 1993.

Brubaker, Rogers. *Nationalism Reframed: Nationhood and the National Question in the New Europe*. New York: Cambridge University Press, 1996.

Brzezinski, Zbigniew. *The Grand Chessboard*, New York: Basic Books, 1997.

Carrière d'Encausse, Hélène. *L'Empire Eclaté, La Révolte des Nations En U.R.S.S.*, Paris: Flammarion, 1978.

———. *La Gloire des Nations, Ou la Fin de l'Empire Soviétique*, Paris : Fayard, 1990.

Chaliand, Gérard and Yves Ternon. *Le Génocide des Arméniens*, Brussels : Edition Complexe, 1980.

Chernyaev, Anatoly. *My Six Years With Gorbachev*, Pennsylvania: The Pennsylvania State University Press, 2000.

Cheterian, Vicken. *Dialectics of Ethnic Conflict and Oil Projects in the Caucasus*, Programme for Strategic and International Security Studies, Geneva, PSIS Occasional Paper 1, 1997.

Chorbajian, Levon, Patrick Donabedian, and Claude Mutafian. *The Caucasian Knot: the History and Geo-Politics of Nagorno-Karabagh*, London: Zed Books, 1994.

Colton, Timothy and Rober Tucker (eds.). *Patterns in Post-Soviet Leadership*, Boulder: Westview Press, 1995.

Coppieters, Bruno, Ghia Nodia and Yuri Anchabadze (eds.). *Georgians and Abkhazians, The Search for a Peace Settlement*, Koeln: Bundesinstitut fuer ostwissenschaftliche und internationale Studien, 1998.

Coppieters, Bruno and Michel Huysseune (eds.). Secession, *History and the Social Sciences*, Brussels: VUB Press, 2002.

Cornell, Svante. *Small Nations and Great Powers*. London: Curzon, 2001.

Cox, Michael (ed.). *Rethinking the Soviet Collapse: Sovietology, the Death of Communism and the New Russia*. London and New York: Pinter, 1998.

Croissant, Michael. *The Armenian-Azerbaijan Conflict, Causes and Implications*. London: Praeger, 1998

Dadrian, Vahakn. *The History of the Armenian Genocide: Ethnic Conflict from the Balkan to Anatolia to the Caucasus*. Providence: Berghahn, 1995.

Dadrian, Vahakn. *Warrant for Genocide, Key Elements of Turko-Armenian Conflict*. New Brunswick: Transaction Publishers, 1999.

Dawisha, Karen and Bruce Parrott (eds.). *Conflict, Cleavage and Change in Central Asia and the Caucasus*. Cambridge: Cambridge University Press, 1996.

Demoyan, Hayk. *Karabakh Drama: Hidden Acts*, Caucasian Center for Iranian Studies, Yerevan, 2003.

De Tinguy, Anne (ed.). *The Fall of the Soviet Empire*, New York: Columbia University Press, 1997.

De Waal, Thomas. *Black Garden, Armenia and Azerbaijan Through Peace and War*, New York: New York University Press, 2003.

Dekmejian, R. Hrair and Hovann Simonian. *Troubled Waters, The Geopolitics of the Caspian Region*, London: I. B. Tauris, 2003.

Djalili, Mohammad-Reza. (ed.), *Le Caucase Postsovietique: La Transition Dans le Conflit*, Brussels: Bruylant, 1995.

Donabedian, Patrick and Claude Mutafian. *Artsakh, Histoire du Karabakh*, Paris: Sevig Press, 1991.

Ehrenreich, Barbara. *Blood Rites, Origin and History of the Passion of War*, New York: Metropolitan Books, 1997.

Elletson, Harold. *The General Against the Kremlin, Alexander Lebed: Power and Illusion*, London: Warner Books, 1998.

Evangelista, Matthhew. *The Chechen Wars, Will Russia Go the Way of the Soviet Union?* Washington: Brookings Institution Press, 2002.

Gall, Carlotta and Thomas De Waal. *Chechnya, A Small Victorious War*. London: Pan Books, 1997.

Giddens, Anthony. *The Nation-State and Violence*, Los Angeles: University of California Press, 1987.

Goldenberg, Suzanne. *Pride of Small Nations, the Caucasus and Post-Soviet Disorder*, London: Zed Books, 1994.

Goltz, Thomas. *Azerbaijan Diary, A Rogue Reporter's Adventures in an Oil-Rich, War-Torn, Post-Soviet Republic*. Armonk: M. E. Sharp, 1998.

Gorbachev, Mikhail. *Memoirs*, London: Bantam Books, 1995.

Grousset, René. *Histoire de l'Arménie*, Paris: Payot, 1984.

———. *The Empire of the Steppes, a History of Central Asia*, Translated by Naomi Walford. New Jersey: Rutgers, 1999.

Hanf, Theodor. and Ghia Nodia, *Georgia Lurching to Democracy*, Baden-Baden: Nomos Verlagsgesellschaft, 2000.

Hewitt, George (ed.). *The Abkhazians: A Handbook*, New York: St. Martin's Press, 1998.

Hill, Fiona and Pamela Jewett. "Back in the USSR: Russia's Intervention in the Internal Affairs of the Former Soviet Republics and its Implications for the United States Policy towards Russia." Harvard University: J.F. Kennedy School of Government, 1994.

Hill, Fiona,. "'Russia's Tinderbox': Conflict in the North Caucasus and its Implications for the Future of the Russian Federation." Harvard University: J.F. Kennedy School of Government, 1995.

"The Ingush-Ossetian Conflict in the Prigorodnyi Region", *Human Rights Watch/Helsinki*, New York, 1996.

Hovanneisian, Richard G. *The Armenian Genocide in Perspective*, New Brunswick: Transaction Books, 1986.

Hunter, Shireen T. *The Transcaucasus in Transition, Nation-Building in Conflict*, Washington D.C.: The Center for Strategic and International Studies, 1994.

Ignatieff, Michael. *The Warrior's Honour, Ethnic War and the Modern Conscience*, London: Chatto and Windus, 1998.

Jaimoukha, Amjad. *The Circassians, A Handbook*, London: Curzon, 2001.

Jallot, Nicolas, *Chevardnadzé, Le Renard Blanc du Caucase*, Paris : Belfond, 2005.

Jones, Stephen F. *Socialism in Georgian Colors, The European Road to Social Democracy 1883-1917*, Cambridge: Harvard University Press, 2005.

Keegan, Paul. *History of Warfare*, London: Pimlico, 1994.

Kennedy, Paul. *The Rise and Fall of the Great Powers*, New York: Vintage Books, 1989.

King, Charles. *Ending Civil Wars*. London: International Institute for Strategic Studies, Adelphi Paper No. 308, 1997.

Lester, Jeremy. *Modern Tsars and Princes, The Struggle for Hegemony in Russia*, London: Verso, 1995.

Libaridian, Gerard. *The Karabagh File, Documents and Facts on the Question of Mountainous Karabagh 1918-1988*, Cambridge: The Zoryan Institute, 1988.

Libaridian, Gerard. *Armenia at the Crossroads, Democracy and Nationhood in the Post-Soviet Era*, Watertown: Blue Crane Books, 1991.

Lieven, Anatol. *Chechnya, Tombstone of Russian Power*, New Haven: Yale University Press, 1998.

Lordkipanidze, Mariam. *Essays on Georgian History*, Tbilisi: Metsniereba, 1994.

Lukic, Reneo and Allen Lynch. *Europe from the Balkans to the Urals, The Disintegration of Yugoslavia and the Soviet Union* London: SIPRI and Oxford University Press, 1996.

MacFarlane, S. Neil, Larry Minear and Stephen D. Shenfield. *Armed Conflict in Georgia: A Case Study in Humanitarian Action, and Peacekeeping*, Thomas J. Watson Institute For International Studies, Occasional Paper Number 21, Providence, 1996.

MacFarlane, S. Neil and Larry Meaner. *Humanitarian Action and Politics: The Case of Nagorno-Karabakh*. Watson Institute for International Studies, Providence, 1997.

MacFarlane, S. Neil. *Western Engagement in the Caucasus and Central Asia*. London: The Royal Institute of International Studies, 1999.

Medvedev, Roy. *Post-Soviet Russia, a Journey Through the Yeltsin Era*, New York: Columbia University Press, 2000.

Melson, Robert. *Revolution and Genocide, On the Origins of the Armenian Genocide and the Holocaust*, Chicago: University of Chicago Press, 1996.

Migdal, Joel S. *Strong Societies and Weak States, State-Society Relations and State Capabilities in the Third World*, Princeton, New Jersey: Princeton University Press, 1988.

Miller, Donald E. and Lorna Touryan Miller. *Survivors, An Oral History of the Armenian Genocide*. Los Angeles: University of California Press, 1999.

Motyl, Alexander J. (ed.). *Thinking Theoretically About Soviet Nationalities*, New York: Columbia University Press, 1992.

Mouradian, Claire. *l'Arménie, de Staline à Gorbachev*, Paris, Ramsay, 1990.

Nissman, David. *The Soviet Union and Iranian Azerbaijan, The Use of Nationalism for Political Penetration*, Boulder: Westview, 1987.

Nivat, Anne. *Chienne de Guerre*, Paris: Fayard, 2000.

Odom, William. *The Collapse of the Soviet Military*, New Haven and London: Yale University Press, 1998.

Pipes, Richard. *The Formation of the Soviet Union: Communism and Nationalism, 1917-23*, Cambridge: Harvard University Press, 1954.

Radvanyi, Jean. *La Nouvelle Russie, l'Après 1991 : un nouveau «temps des troubles»*, Paris: Masson/Armand Colin, 1991.

Roy, Olivier. *La Nouvelle Asie Centrale, ou la Fabrication des Nations*, Paris: Seuil, 1997.

Pratt, Martin and Janet Allison Brown. *Borderlands Under Stress*, The Hague: Kluwer Law International, 2000.

Rubinstein, Alvin Z. and Smolansky, Oles M. (eds.), *Regional Power Rivalries in the New Eurasia, Russia, Turkey, and Iran*, Armonk: M. E. Sharp, 1995.

Sakharov, Andrei. *Memoirs*, London: Hutchinson, 1990.

Shaffer, Brenda. *Borders and Brethren, Iran and the Challenge of Azerbaijani Identity*, Cambridge: MIT Press, 2002.

Shahmuratyan, Samuel. *The Sumgait Tragedy, Pogroms Against Armenians in Soviet Azerbaijan: Eyewitness Accounts,* Cambridge: The Zoryan Institute, 1990.

Shnirelman, Victor A. *The Value of the Past: Myths, Identity and Politics in Transcaucasia*, Osaka: National Museum of Ethnology, 2001.

Smith, Graham (ed.). *The Nationalities Question on the Post-Soviet States*, New York: Longman, 1996.

Smith, Sebastian. *Allah's Mountains: Politics and War in the Russian Caucasus*, London: I.B. Tauris, 1998.

Smith, Graham, Vivien Law, Andrew Wilson, Annette Bohr and Edward All-worth. *Nation-Building in the Post-Soviet Borderlands, The Politics of National Identities*, Cambridge: Cambridge University Press, 1998.

Strayer, Robert. *Why did the Soviet Union Collapse? Understanding Historical Change*, Armonk: M.E. Sharp, 1998.

Suny, Ronald. *The Baku Commune 1917-1918, Class and Nationality in the Russian Revolution*, New Jersey: Princeton University Press, 1972.

———. *The Revenge of the Past, Nationalism, Revolution, and the Collapse of the Soviet Union*: Stanford University Press, 1993.

———. *Looking Towards Ararat, Armenia in Modern History*, Bloomington: Indiana University Press, 1993.

———. *The Making of the Georgian Nation*. Bloomington: Indiana University Press, 1994.

———. *The Soviet Experiment, Russia, The USSR, and the Successor States*, London: Oxford University Press, 1998.

Suny, Ronald and Kennedy, Michael. (eds.). *Intellectuals and the Articulation of the Nation*, Ann Arbor: The University of Michigan Press, 2001.

Suny, Ronald and Terry Martin (eds.). *A State of Nations, Empire and Nation Making in the Age of Lenin and Stalin*, Oxford: Oxford University Press, 2001.

Swietochowski, Tadeusz. *Russia and Azerbaijan, A Borderland in Transition*. New York: Columbia University Press, 1995.

Ter Minassian, Anahid, *La République d'Arménie*, Brussels: Editions Complexe, 1989.

———. *Histoires Croisées, Diaspora, Arménie, Transcaucasie, 1880-1990*. Paris: Parantheses, 1997.

Tishkov, Valery. *Ethnicity, Nationalism and Conflict in and After the Soviet Union*, London: SAGE, 1997.

———. *Chechnya: Life in a War-Torn Society*, Berkley and Los Angeles: University of California Press, 2004.

Trotsky, Leon. *The Revolution Betrayed, What is the Soviet Union and Where is it Going?* New York: Pathfinder, 2001.

Tsypkin, Mikhail (ed.). *War in Chechnya: Implications for Russian Security Policy*, Monterey, California: Naval Postgraduate School, 1995.

Van Creveld, Martin. *The Rise and Decline of the State*, Cambridge: Cambridge University Press, 2004.

Vasiliev, Sergei. *Ten Years of Russian Economic Reforms – A Collection of Papers*, London: Center for Research into Post-Communist Economies, 1999.

Verdery, Katherine. *What was Socialism, and What Comes Next?* New Jersey: Princeton University Press, 1996.

Walker, Christopher (ed.). *Armenia and Karabagh, The Struggle for Unity*, London: Minority Rights Publications, 1991.

Waltz, Kenneth N. *Man, the State and War*, New York: Columbia University Press, 2001.

White, Stephen. *Communism and its Collapse*, London: Routledge, 2001.

Wilson, Andrew. *Virtual Politics, Faking Democracy in the Post-Soviet World*, New Haven: Yale University Press, 2005.

Wright, John, Suzanne Goldenberg, and Richard Schoefield (eds.). *Transcaucasian Boundaries*, London: UCL Press, 1996.

Zartman, William (ed.). *Collapsed States, The Disintegration and the Restoration of Legitimate Authority*, London: Lynne Rienner Publishers, 1995.

INDEX

INDEX